MEDIEVAL LONDON WIDOWS

1300 – 1500

EDITED BY

CAROLINE M. BARRON AND ANNE F. SUTTON

THE HAMBLEDON PRESS

LONDON AND RIO GRANDE

Published by The Hambledon Press 1994

102 Gloucester Avenue, London NW1 8HX (U.K.)

P.O. Box 162, Rio Grande, Ohio 45674 (U.S.A.)

ISBN 1 85285 085 X

A description of this book is available from
the British Library and from the Library of Congress

Typeset by York House Typographic Ltd
Printed on acid-free paper and bound in
Great Britain by Cambridge University Press

Contents

Preface

This volumes owes its inspiration to Lady Joan Bradbury. It was Lady Joan's benefactions to the Mercers' Company which brought her to the attention of Anne Sutton, and it was Anne's investigations into the life of Lady Joan which led us to realise how much it is possible to discover about women whose lives had seemed to be completely obscured. Encouraged by Anne's success in finding out so much about Lady Joan Bradbury, we decided to ask others working on different aspects of medieval London whether they also had a favourite widow awaiting resurrection. This collection of biographies is the result.

In the course of working on the lives of these women, we have met twice for 'workshops' and have discussed common problems, exchanged possible sources of information and tested out the significance of particular phrases in wills or deeds. On both these occasions we were joined by other scholars who contributed to our discussions but not to this volume: Dr Vanessa Harding, Professor Joel Rosenthal and Professor J.B. Trapp. We are grateful to them for the information and the insights which they shared with us. We are also indebted to the Mercers' Company who generously provided us with lunch at our first workshop: an appropriate gesture since Lady Joan appears to have enjoyed good company and good food.

We are conscious that there are many more medieval women waiting to be called from darkness into light. We hope that this small band of diverse and idiosyncratic women may serve to encourage others to discover and describe the lives of women who lived neither at the summit of their societies, nor at the margins, but who were, like ourselves, of the 'middling sort'.

Caroline M. Barron

Anne F. Sutton

Illustrations

Acknowledgements

We are most grateful for permission to use illustrations from the British Library (Plate 3); Dr Martha Carlin (plan of the Minories), Lambeth Place Library (Fig. 11); the Royal Library, the Hague (Plate 1); and Miss J. Greenham of the Woolf/Greenham Collection (Plate 2). Alex Bayliss, who is preparing a London Ph.D. thesis on medieval bells in England, kindly supplied the information for compiling a map of the distribution of the bells by the Hills and Sturdys (Fig. 5). Assistance has also been received from the Council of the Royal Institution of Cornwall.

Abbreviations

Beaven, *Aldermen*	A.B. Beaven, *The Aldermen of London*, 2 vols (London, 1908, 1913)
BL	British Library
CCR	*Calendar of Close Rolls*
CFR	*Calendar of Fine Rolls*
CIPM	*Calendar of Inquisitions Post Mortem*
CLRO	Corporation of London Records Office
Complete Peerage	*Complete Peerage of England, Scotland, Ireland, Great Britain and the United Kingdom*, ed. G.E. Cokayn; new edition by V. Gibbs, H.A. Doubleday and others, 13 vols (London, 1910–59)
CPMR	*Calendar of Plea and Memoranda Rolls Preserved among the Archives of the Corporation of London, 1323–1482*, 6 vols, ed. A.H. Thomas (vols 1–4) and P.E. Jones (vols 5–6) (Cambridge, 1926–61)
CPR	*Calendar of Patent Rolls*
DNB	*Dictionary of National Biography*
Emden, *BRUC*	A.B. Emden, *A Biographical Register of the University of Cambridge to A.D. 1500*, (Cambridge, 1963)
Emden, *BRUO*	A.B. Emden, *A Biographical Register of the University of Oxford to A.D. 1500*, 3 vols (Oxford, 1957–59)
GL	Guildhall Library
HR	Husting Roll
HW	*Calendar of Wills Proved and Enrolled in the Court of Husting, 1258–1688*, 2 vols, ed. R.R. Sharpe (London, 1889–90)
LBA, LBB, etc.	*Calendar of Letter Books, Preserved among the Archives of the Corporation of the City of London, 1275–1498, Books A–L*, ed. R.R. Sharpe (London, 1899–1912)
L&P HVIII	*Calendar of Letters and Papers, Foreign and Domestic, Henry VIII*, ed. J.S. Brewer and others, 21 vols (London, 1864–1932).
PCC	Prerogative Court of Canterbury

PRO	Public Record Office
RP	*Rotuli Parliamentorum*, ed. J. Strachey and others, 6 vols (London, 1783)
Stow, *Survey*	John Stow, *A Survey of London*, ed. C.L. Kingsford, 2 vols (Oxford, 1908)
Thrupp, *Merchant Class*	S.L. Thrupp, *The Merchant Class of Medieval London* (Chicago, 1948; reprint Ann Arbor, MI, 1962)
VCH	Victoria History of the Counties of England

Introduction: The Widow's World in Later Medieval London

Caroline M. Barron

Of all medieval women, widows are often the most visible for, being without a husband and beyond the responsibility of a father, they were allowed to act independently and were no longer subsumed within the persona of their husbands as 'one flesh' or, to use the phraseology of the medieval lawyers, they were no longer 'femmes couvertes'. In particular, unlike married women, they were free to make testaments and wills, and it is through these documents that they often speak to us most forcibly. In these circumstances it is, perhaps, remarkable that widows have not attracted more attention from historians. Aristocratic widows have, it is true, been studied by Professor Joel Rosenthal, and the lives of peasant widows have benefited from the recent studies of manorial records, most notably by Professor Judith Bennett.[1] But the absence of work on urban widows is surprising since borough custom in medieval England often gave to town widows greater freedom and more extensive opportunities than they enjoyed elsewhere.[2] Aristocratic widows were often the possessors of land and, although they were rarely forced to remarry against their will, their freedom to act independently was circumscribed. London widows, by contrast, were empowered either to continue, or to initiate, a business enterprise on their own, to occupy the family house and work place or shop, and to join in the economic and social life of the fraternities, guilds and companies, although they were excluded from their political activities.[3]

---

[1] Joel T. Rosenthal, 'Aristocratic Widows in Fifteenth-Century England', in Barbara J. Harris and JoAnn K. McNamara, ed., *Women and the Structure of Society* (Durham, NC, 1984), pp. 36–47; idem, 'Other Victims: Peeresses as War Widows, 1450–1500', *History*, 6 (1987), pp. 213–230; Judith M. Bennett, *Women in the Medieval English Countryside: Gender and Household in Brigstock before the Plague* (Oxford, 1987), esp. ch. 6; see also Peter Franklin, 'Widows' "Liberation" and Remarriage before the Black Death', *Economic History Review*, 39 (1986), pp. 186–204, a study of Thornbury in Gloucestershire which found that widows often managed holdings and were active in protest movements, but did not hold public office.

[2] Mary Bateson, *Borough Customs*, Selden Society (London, 1904), ii, pp. c–cxv, 102–129.

[3] Caroline M. Barron, 'The "Golden Age" of Women in Medieval London', in *Women in Southern England* Reading Medieval Studies, 15 (1989), pp. 35–58.

It is clear that the opportunities available to widows varied greatly according to their level of prosperity. We know most about the widows of the urban elite, so we have to be careful not to assume that what was true for the widows of the wealthier citizens was also true of all widows in all towns. The opportunities open to these wealthy women were a far cry from those of poor women for whom widowhood presented, not a range of golden opportunities, but rather another step down the economic ladder. It is also clear that London, and perhaps York, may have offered women greater opportunities for economic and personal independence than could be found elsewhere. In Exeter and Shrewsbury, for example, women were largely confined to working in poorly-paid and marginal occupations, and widowhood presented few welcome opportunities of any kind.[4] So, in so far as the medieval period was a 'golden age' for women, it was a 'golden age' confined to some English towns (perhaps only London and York) and to a brief chronological span, namely the years when demographic decline, due to recurrent plague, allowed women access to work on terms more nearly equal with those of men; that is, the hundred years from about 1370 to 1470.[5] It is notable that the only pre-plague women studied in this volume, namely the tanners' widows, had to struggle to maintain their position within the craft. The male tanners appear to have tried to exclude them from active control of the means of production. In assessing, therefore, the opportunities and choices open to widows (or indeed to women generally), it is important always to ask where and when does she live?

Inevitably, perhaps, the wealthier widows tend to predominate in these essays, but there has been an attempt to redress the balance by including essays about women who came near to the bottom of the economic ladder. The wives of tanners worked in an unsavoury, if important, craft and, as Dr Keene here suggests, their widowhoods were rarely gilded. Obviously, the poorest widows left no testaments or wills and so rarely come within the historian's sights. Even the testaments of 'poor' widows here studied by Robert Wood throw light only on the lives of women who may have been poor, but were certainly not indigent. A third of them had adult children; others had friends among the parish clergy; most had some personal goods. The truly destitute woman left nothing except, perhaps, the record of the coroner's inquest on her death or the meagre payment for her pauper's funeral to be found in a churchwarden's account.[6]

---

[4] M Kowaleski, 'Women's Work in a Medieval Town: Exeter in the Late Fourteenth Century', *Women and Work in Preindustrial Europe*, ed. B.A. Hanawalt (Bloomington, IN 1986), pp. 145–164.

[5] The view that women in medieval London experienced a 'Golden Age' has been challenged by Judith Bennett, 'Medieval Women, Modern Women: Across the Great Divide', *Culture and History 1350–1600: Essays on English Communities, Identities and Writing*, ed. David Aers (London, 1992), pp. 147–75.

[6] E.g. Alditha, wife of William Gryndere, 'pauper and mendicant', who was found drowned in the ditch of the hospital of St Katherine near the Tower, in 1375, R.R. Sharpe ed., *Calendar of Coroners Rolls of the City of London, 1300–1378* (London, 1913), p. 275.

Collections of biographical studies, such as this one, have much to contribute to the new statistical age. Dr Richard Smith, in his recent introduction to a new edition of Eileen Power's *Medieval People*, observes that contemporary historians 'do not so readily use the individual vignette and the individual experience as a means of describing social structure'. At the same time Smith is doubtful whether the currently fashionable 'collective biographies' provide the answer to all our questions. Such biographies do, of course, help the historian to recreate the life-patterns and life-cycles of men and women too low down the social scale to have left more than bare references to themselves in manorial court rolls, coroners' rolls or other legal records.[7] Instead of finding out a great deal about a few people, small amounts of information are discovered about large numbers of people, from which a corporate lifestyle or life-cycle can be constructed. But there is, inevitably, something missing from a composite portrait constructed in this way. As Dr Smith points out, 'the simplifications required to identify uniformities and variations often serve to suppress particularity'.[8] There has in consequence been increased interest in the study of individuals and, as Professor Bennett has shown, biographies can be fashioned not only for aristocratic and merchant women, but also for those in the village elites.

The widows studied in this volume lived over a period of 200 years and differed greatly in their wealth, lifestyle and opportunities, but they were all, to a greater or lesser extent, inhabitants of London and were subject to the customary law of the city. Most were the widows of London citizens (or freemen); among the poor widows, half of those whose husband's craft and status are known described themselves as citizens. At the other end of the scale, Elizabeth de Burgh and Lucia Visconti had been married to members of the aristocracy and not London citizens, but they chose to live in London. It was, however, only in the last decade of her life that Elizabeth de Burgh chose to spend more time in London at her house in the Minories. It was here, also, that Lucia Visconti lived for the sixteen years of her widowhood. These two were Londoners by choice rather than by marriage. Of the other women considered here, most of them, in so far as we can tell, were born in London: Johanna Hill may have come from the Surrey village of Merstham, Joan Gedney from Winchester, Alice Bryce from Wheathampstead, Joan Bradbury from Wellingborough in Northamptonshire and Thomasine Percyvale from the small and distant village of Week St Mary in Cornwall. Whatever their place of origin, all of them[9] found their final resting-place in London, most of them in their parish churches, but a few were buried elsewhere: Elizabeth de

---

[7] Eileen Power, *Medieval People*, ed. Richard Smith (Oxford, 1986), p. xvi.

[8] Ibid., p. xix.

[9] Due to the loss of one of Joan Buckland's testaments, her place of burial is not certain, but it seems likely that she was buried with her parents and husband in the Pardon Churchyard at St Paul's Cathedral, see below pp. 128.

Burgh and Lucia Visconti in the Minoresses' church; Joan Pyel at St Helen's Bishopsgate, and Joan Buckland probably in the Pardon Churchyard of St Paul's Cathedral.

Most of the individual London widows whose biographies are included in this collection left wills or testaments which provide an insight into the character of their widowhood. In this they are not exceptional, for London is well supplied with wills. Strictly speaking, wills related to the disposition of land (or real estate) and testaments related to the distribution of chattels, or movables. In practice, however, testators seem to have used the words will and testament interchangeably and not precisely. In London the city's court of Husting had jurisdiction over the probate of the wills of citizens and their widows. In consequence, some 4,000 wills are entered upon the rolls of the court of Husting between the years 1258 and 1658; the great majority of these wills are earlier than 1500.[10] Testaments fell within the jurisdiction of the church courts and in London these might be proved either in the archdeacon's or the commissary's court.[11] Only one register survives from the archdeacon's court, covering the years 1393 to 1415 and including 1,384 testaments, of which 17 per cent are those of women.[12] The commissary court records are complete from 1374 and thousands of wills are to be found there.[13] These records provide a mine of rich information, but their gaps can still be provoking: testaments which we know existed, like those of Matilda Penne's husband William, or Joan Buckland's second testament, have disappeared. Even when we have wills, they sometimes appear to be incomplete. They were usually drafted by scriveners or clerks who may have influenced the wording and sentiments and even, on occasion, the nature of the bequests. And at best a will may only provide a partial view of the family or household or social network with which the testator was concerned.[14] The wills of women are often more detailed and 'diffuse' (that is, ample and prolix, and dispersing goods widely) than those of men, but they may still fail to mention children or friends for whom provision has already been made or whose remembrance is dependent upon an oral instruction to the executors. Not all women speak as loudly and clearly to us in their wills as, say, Joan Buckland, Thomasine Percyvale and Joan Bradbury. But in spite of the whispered messages of some wills,

[10] Reginald R. Sharpe, *Calendar of Wills Proved and Enrolled in the Court of Husting, London* (2 vols, London, 1889).

[11] In theory it depended upon the parish of the testator whether the will was probated in the court of the archdeacon or the commissary, but, in practice, much appears to have depended upon chance, or convenience.

[12] Marc Fitch, ed., *Testamentary Records in the Archdeaconry Court of London*, British Record Society (1979), i, *1363–1649*. The figures have been supplied by Robert Wood who is using the archdeaconry wills in his London doctoral dissertation, 'London and Bury St Edmunds: A comparison of Urban Piety, *c.* 1400', in progress.

[13] Marc Fitch, ed., *Index to Testamentary Records in the Commissary Court of London* (London, 1969), i, *1374–1488*.

[14] For further discussion of the problems posed by wills, see Derek Keene, below, pp. 13.

when, as in the case of John amd Johanna Sturdy, we have no wills at all, we realise how valuable their evidence can be.

Often the women included in this volume have attracted our attention because the survival of some other particular piece of evidence has further illuminated their lives: the extensive household accounts of Elizabeth de Burgh; the cartulary of John Pyel; the Stonor letters which contain Thomas Betson's frank comments on Margaret Croke; the records of the Mercers' Company which reveal Joan Bradbury's charitable purposes; Richard Carew's whimsical account of Thomasine Percyvale; and the surviving church bells which declare that they were cast in the workshop of Johanna Hill. None of these sources tells us as much as Margaret Paston's letters or Margery Kempe's autobiography, but taken together they allow us to come much closer to the economic and, occasionally, the personal reality of their lives.

The lives of all these women were shaped, to a greater or lesser extent, by the fact that they lived in London. Here, apart from Elizabeth de Burgh and Lucia Visconti who, as it were, were above London custom, and some of the tanners' widows who fell below it, it was London custom which determined the rights and obligations of the widow of a citizen. In London the widow, like widows elsewhere, was entitled to dower, that is to a share of her husband's real estate at his death.[15] This dower consisted of two parts. The first of these was the 'free bench' or share of the house in which she and her husband had been living when he died. In London the widow was allowed to occupy the house until she remarried, or until her own death. In this respect the custom of London was more generous to the widow than the common law of England, which allowed the widow to occupy the 'principal mansion' only for forty days. There were, in fact, good business reasons for allowing the London widow to remain longer than the mere forty days. The second part of the dower was the widow's right to enjoy for her life a third (or half if there were no children) share of the lands and tenements which had belonged to her husband at the time of their marriage. The widow had a life interest in this property and her right to enjoy it was not affected by remarriage. Over and above her right to dower, the London widow was also entitled to a share of her husband's goods and chattels by the custom known as *legitim*. Within a mercantile and manufacturing community, where wealth was held in the form of movable goods, the disposition of a man's chattels was of much more importance than elsewhere (hence the considerable importance of testaments). By the custom of *legitim* the London widow was entitled to a half, or a third, of her husband's movable goods, depending whether there were surviving children or not. The existence of this custom in London secured for the widow a considerable share of her husband's chattels and hence of his wealth. Whereas a widow's dower income was hers only for her life and reverted to her husband's heirs at her death, the wealth secured to a widow by the custom of *legitim* was hers absolutely to

---

[15] Barron, 'Golden Age', pp. 41–43.

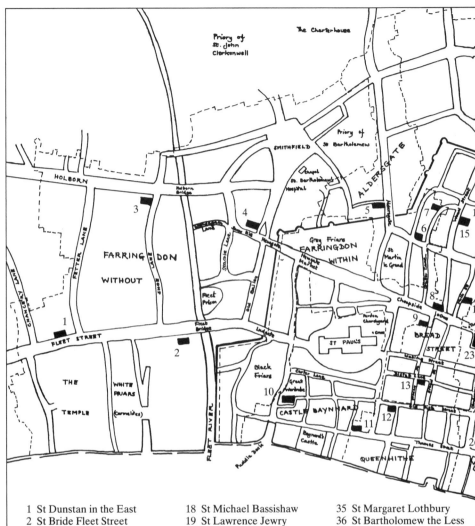

1	St Dunstan in the East	18	St Michael Bassishaw	35	St Margaret Lothbury
2	St Bride Fleet Street	19	St Lawrence Jewry	36	St Bartholomew the Less
3	St Andrew Holborn	20	St Martin Pomary	37	St Christopher le Stocks
4	St Sepulchre	21	St Mary Colechurch	38	St Michael Cornhill
5	St Botolph Aldersgate	22	St Mildred Poultry	39	St Peter Cornhill
6	St John Zachary	23	St Mary le Bow	40	St Edmund Lombard Street
7	St Mary Staining	24	St Mary Aldermary	41	St Magnus
8	St Peter West Cheap	25	St Thomas the Apostle	42	St Botolph Billingsgate
9	St Mathew Friday Street	26	St Martin Vintry	43	St George East Cheap
10	St Andrew by the Wardrobe	27	All Hallows the Great	44	St Mary at Hill
11	St Peter Paul's Wharf	28	All Hallows the Less	45	St Mary Axe
12	St Nicholas Cole Abbey	29	St John Walbrook	46	St Botolph Bishopsgate
13	St Margaret Moses	30	St Swithin	47	St Botolph Aldgate
14	St Mary Magdalen Milk Street	31	St Stephen Walbrook	48	St Andrew Undershaft
15	St Alban Wood Street	32	St Mary Woolchurch	49	St Olave Hart Street
16	St Mary Aldermanbury	33	St Olave Old Jewry	50	St Dunstan in the East
17	St Alphege	34	St Stephen Coleman Street	51	All Hallows Barking

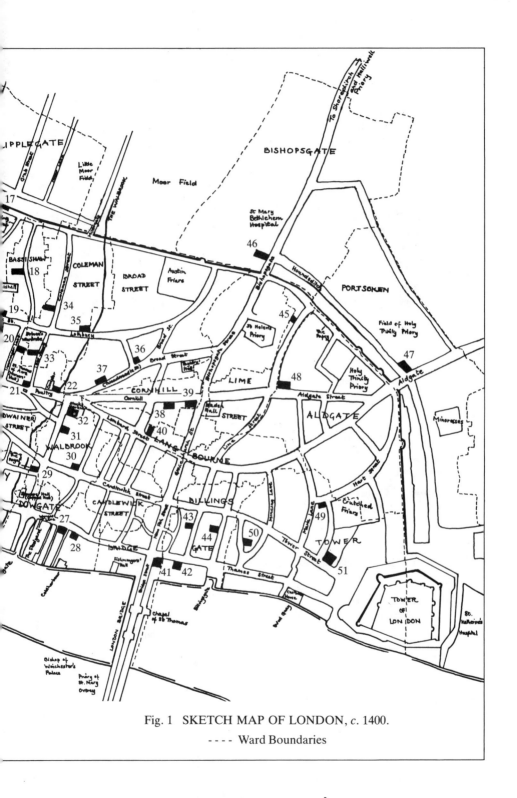

Fig. 1 SKETCH MAP OF LONDON, *c*. 1400.

- - - - Ward Boundaries

London, c. 1400

The Parishes Referred to in this Volume Divided by Ward

Farringdon Without
1 St Dunstan in the East
2 St Bride Fleet Street
3 St Andrew Holborn
4 St Sepulchre

Aldersgate
5 St Botolph Aldersgate
6 St John Zachary
7 St Mary Staining

Farringdon Within
8 St Peter West Cheap
9 St Mathew Friday Street

Castle Baynard
10 St Andrew by the Wardrobe

Queenhithe
11 St Peter Paul's Wharf
12 St Nicholas Cole Abbey

Bread Street
13 St Margaret Moses

Cripplegate
14 St Mary Magdalen Milk Street
15 St Alban Wood Street
16 St Mary Aldermanbury
17 St Alphege

Bassishaw
18 St Michael Bassishaw

Cheap
19 St Lawrence Jewry
20 St Martin Pomary
21 St Mary Colechurch
22 St Mildred Poultry

Cordwainer Street
23 St Mary le Bow
24 St Mary Aldermary

Vintry
25 St Thomas the Apostle
26 St Martin Vintry

Dowgate
27 All Hallows the Great
28 All Hallows the Less

Walbrook
29 St John Walbrook
30 St Swithin
31 St Stephen Walbrook
32 St Mary Woolchurch

Coleman Street
33 St Olave Old Jewry
34 St Stephen Coleman Street
35 St Margaret Lothbury

Broad Street
36 St Bartholomew the Less
37 St Christopher le Stocks

Cornhill
38 St Michael Cornhill
39 St Peter Cornhill

Langbourne
40 St Edmund Lombard Street

Bridge
41 St Magnus

Billingsgate
42 St Botolph Billingsgate
43 St George East Cheap
44 St Mary at Hill

Lime Street
45 St Mary Axe

Bishopsgate
46 St Botolph Bishopsgate

Portsoken
47 St Botolph Aldgate
48 St Andrew Undershaft

Tower
49 St Olave Hart Street
50 St Dunstan in the East
51 All Hallows Barking

dispose of as she liked. The testaments, for example, of Joan Bradbury, Matilda Penne, Johanna Hill, Joan Gedney and Thomasine Percyvale demonstrate this freedom being exercised to the full. A widow might also have at her disposal lands and tenements which she had bought or which she had inherited in her own right, and these she could devise as she chose. It is the ability of London widows to dispose of very considerable amounts of plate, jewels, furnishings and cash, however, which is particularly striking.[16]

It might be suggested that it was one thing for city custom to allocate dower to the widow and another for the widow to gain possession of her dower, whether the house or her share of the income from estates. The rights of the widow might be ignored by heirs and other interested parties. Often ignorance arose from obscurity of kin and the complicated marital relationships which were the product of high mortality and a high rate of remarriage. In these circumstances, widows had to take firm action to uphold their rights, and may well have needed ingenuity, resourcefulness and persistence to achieve this. City custom provided a process, initiated by a writ of dower, whereby a widow might claim dower lands which were withheld.[17] Professor Hanawalt has recently examined a sample of the dower cases brought before the city's court of Husting in the years between 1301 and 1433.[18] In just over half of the cases which were brought to a conclusion, the widow successfully recovered all, or part, of her dower, and in only 13 per cent of the cases did she lose outright.[19] One of Hanawalt's more surprising findings is that in about half of the dower cases brought before the court of Husting, the widow argued her own case and did not use an attorney.[20]

---

[16] For a further example, see the will of Margaret Bate, widow of Ralph Bate, a London citizen and tailor, who died 8 January 1467, calendared in Margaret McGregor, ed., *Bedfordshire Wills Proved in the Prerogative Court of Canterbury, 1383–1548*, Bedfordshire Historical Record Society Transactions, 58 (1979–80), pp. 21–25.

[17] H.T. Riley, *Liber Albus: The White Book of the City of London* (London, 1861), pp. 164–66. If dower was left to the wife in the form of goods and chattels, rather than lands or tenements, it may have been easier for the wife to make good her claim, since the executors would have been able instantly to take possession of the goods of the dead man. The common law of England did not, however, automatically assign dower to the widow; she had to 'earn' dower, see Paul Brand, ' "Deserving" and "Undeserving" Wives': Earning and Forfeiting Dower in Medieval England', paper read at conference on medieval family law, held at Vancouver, November 1992.

[18] Barbara Hanawalt, 'The Widow's Mite: Recovery of Dower in Late Medieval London', *Upon my Husband's Death: Widows in the Literature and History of Medieval Europe*, ed. Louise Mirrer (Ann Arbor, MI, 1992), pp. 21–45, esp. p. 28. There were 299 cases in Hanawalt's sample, and, on average it appears to have taken a year for the case to have been brought to a conclusion.

[19] Hanawalt, 'Widow's Mite', p. 34. In cases where a widow did not lose outright, she might lose by default, or by failing to present the appropriate writ at some point during the case. In only 10 per cent of the cases studied by Hanawalt was the defendant related to the widow, that is, these disputes were rarely between members of the same family.

[20] Ibid., pp. 28–29. This supports the case, argued below pp. xxix, that these London women were reasonably well-educated.

But how many widows were there in London? Indeed, what proportion of the inhabitants of London were women? London was the largest city in medieval England. Recent research has suggested that, with a population estimated at about 80,000 or even more in 1300, it could have stood comparison with Paris or Florence. The impact of the plague of 1348–49 was dramatic and may have reduced the population to about 40,000 by 1400. The signs are that the population did not begin to rise again until the second quarter of the sixteenth century.[21] Of the adult males, perhaps one in three was a citizen (i.e. freeman), although the proportion of freemen in the population appears to have risen during the sixteenth century.[22] What proportion of the inhabitants of London were women? The recent work of Dr Goldberg using the poll tax returns of the 1370s has suggested that in towns women may well have outnumbered men.[23] Many of these women in English provincial towns were servants, some of whom never married, and formed poor 'spinster clusters' in the suburbs. There is no doubt that London had large numbers of female servants and, indeed, girl apprentices, but whether the imbalance between men and women was as great as in some other English towns (e.g. York and Hull) is impossible to tell, for there are no poll tax returns for London. The analysis of the wills enrolled in the archdeaconry court lends some support to Goldberg's suggestions. Whereas 23 per cent of the testaments of laymen were those of men who were either single or not clearly identified as married, the proportion of single women was slightly larger at 30 per cent (see Table 2).

Kowaleski has pointed out that within the urban elite 'women were more likely than men to be widowed because of their younger age at marriage, and the age gap between the spouses'.[24] Of the male testators whose wills were enrolled in the Husting Court of London between 1271 and 1330, 61 per cent left surviving widows.[25] Of the testaments of married laymen in the arch-

---

[21] Derek Keene, 'A New Study of London before the Great Fire', *Urban History Yearbook* (1984), pp. 11–21.

[22] Steve Rappaport, *Worlds within Worlds: Structures of Life in Sixteenth-Century London* (Cambridge, 1989), pp. 47–53.

[23] P.J.P. Goldberg, ' "For Better, for Worse": Marriage and Economic Opportunity for Women in Town and Country', *Woman is a Worthy Wight: Women in English Society, c. 1200–1500*, ed. P.J.P. Goldberg (Stroud 1992), pp. 108–125, esp. p. 109. Cf. Hajnal, 'European Marriage Patterns', *Population in History*, ed. D.V. Glass and D.E.C. Eversley, (1965), pp. 101–43. Not all poll tax returns revealed the same imbalance between the sexes: Worcester appears to have had more men than women, see Caroline M. Barron, 'The Fourteenth-Century Poll Tax Returns for Worcester', *Midland History*, 14 (1989), pp. 1–29.

[24] Maryanne Kowaleski, 'The History of Urban Families in England', *Journal of Medieval History*, 14 (1988), pp. 47–63, esp. p. 55: see also Sylvia Thrupp, *The Merchant Class of Medieval London* (Chicago, 1948; repr. Ann Arbor, MI, 1962), pp. 192–93, 196. Etheldreda Barton married the wealthy London mercer, Richard Gardiner, as her second husband, when he was twenty to twenty-five years older than she was, see Kristine Bradberry, 'The World of Etheldreda Gardiner', *The Ricardian*, 9 (1991), pp. 146–53, esp. p. 147.

[25] Kowaleski, 'Urban Families', p. 55. Kowaleski's calculation here is based on the work of H.A. Miskimin, 'The Legacies of London, 1259–1330', *The Medieval City: Essays in Honour of*
continued

deaconry court, 70 per cent mention surviving wives; a figure which comes very close to the 72 per cent to be found among the tanners' wills.[26] On the evidence of these figures it would seem that a woman in London had a greater chance of dying as a widow than as a wife.

Although there must have been quite large numbers of widows in London at any one time, comparatively few show up in the surviving tax returns. In part this may be explained by the belief that widows should be exempt from taxation. Henry III had expressly relieved 'widow women' from the payment of tallages and other contributions, and the widows of London in 1394 petitioned parliament for exemption of these grounds.[27] But such exemptions did not apply to the widows of wealthy merchants. In 1411 when the king was granted a novel income tax of half a mark (6s. 8d.) on every twenty pounds' worth of rent, 18 per cent of the 1,000 or so Londoners assessed were women, including Joan Pyel and Margaret Philpot.[28] In the tax of 1436 which was paid by those with lands or rents valued at more than £5 per annum, 9 per cent of those assessed were women, but here again, one of our widows appears: Alice Lynne whose lands and rents were valued at £43 per annum.[29] These figures are, however, comparable with those which have been calculated for the *taille* in Paris in 1292 (15.4 per cent) and for the list of heads of households in Florence in 1427 (15.7 per cent).[30] Although a few of the London women who were assessed for tax in this way may have been single women, the majority must have been widows.

Of the fourteen women considered here, eight married only once, one married twice, three married three times and two were married four times. Apart from Johanna Hill, who died less than a year after her husband, the other thirteen widows averaged a widowhood of twenty-six years: Elizabeth de

continued

R.S. Lopez, ed. Miskimin et al. (New Haven, CT, 1977), pp. 209–77. Hanawalt, also using the Husting wills, but over a longer period (1258–1500) found that in a sample of 3,000 men's wills, 1,743, or 53 per cent, mentioned a surviving wife, see Barbara A. Hanawalt, 'Remarriage as an Option for Urban and Rural Widows in Late Medieval England', *Wife and Widow in Medieval England*, ed. Sue Sheridan Walker (Ann Arbor, MI, 1993), p. 146. Kowaleski also calculated that, in Bristol in the years 1382–1405, 82 per cent of male testators predeceased their wives.

[26] See Wood p. 56 and Keene p. 14. Of a sample of the wills of 262 male peers in the fifteenth century, 61 per cent were survived by a wife, Rosenthal, 'Aristocratic Widows', p. 38.

[27] For the charter of 1268, see Rymer, *Foedera*, I, i, p. 475 and *LBC* pp. 36–37; for the petition of 1392, see Caroline M. Barron, 'Richard II's Quarrel with London', *The Reign of Richard II*, ed. C.M. Barron and F.R.H. Du Boulay (London, 1970), pp. 173–201, esp. p. 195.

[28] See J.C.L. Stahlschmidt, 'Lay Subsidy, temp. Henry IV', *Archaeological Journal*, 44 (1897), pp. 56–82.

[29] Thrupp, *Merchant Class*, pp. 378–88.

[30] David Herlihy, *Opera Muliebria: Woman and Work in Medieval Europe* (New York, 1990), p. 128, where Herlihy gives the Florentine percentage as 14.3 per cent, whereas the higher figure of 15.7 per cent is to be found in Herlihy and Christine Klapisch-Zuber, *Tuscans and their Families: A Study of the Florentine Catasto of 1427* (New Haven, CT. 1985), p. 124 n. 66. In Coventry about 12 per cent of households were headed by women, see Charles Phythian-Adams, *Desolation of a City* (Cambridge, 1979), p. 202.

Burgh, after three marriages lasting in all fourteen years, remained a widow for thirty-eight years; Alice Lynne's widowhood lasted fifty-nine years; Margaret Philpot, Alice Bryce, Joan Pyel and Alice Claver were widows for over thirty years.[31] These long and hence 'visible' widowhoods may have contributed to the survival of rather more evidence about these women than about some others who were only briefly widows. But there seems little doubt that widows were ubiquitous in medieval London. What options were open to them?

Remarriage was, obviously, a possibility, but it is interesting that only six of the fourteen individual women considered here chose that path. Here also it is necessary to remember that we are considering widows of aristocrats and merchants: lower down the economic scale there may have been greater pressure to remarry but, equally, poorer widows may not have found it easy to remarry. Wood has found that only two of his forty-nine 'poor' widows appear to have been married more than once.[32] Adamson found, in her study of sixteenth-century urban families, that of the 208 wives of aldermen who became widows, only a third chose to remarry, and Rosenthal found that of 162 aristocratic widows in the fifteenth century, only 45 per cent remarried.[33] The sample of widows considered here, although small, may not be unrepresentative. The widows of aristocrats and of prosperous merchants seem often to have chosen not to remarry (or, perhaps, were not sought as marriage partners, although their considerable wealth makes this rather unlikely). A similar picture emerges from Professor Hanawalt's work on widows' pursuit of dower cases in the London court of Husting. Such dower suits were initiated very soon after the death of the husband and the probate of his will. In the first

[31] In the case of the poor widows by Wood, we know the length of the widowhoods of six of these: apart from Margaret Haveryng who only survived her husband for nineteen days, the remaining five widowhoods lasted from eight and a half years to thirty-eight, and averaged eighteen years.

[32] Below p. 59. Bennett analysed the various economic and demographic factors which might influence whether a widow remarried or not, *Brigstock*, pp. 146–147, and see Hanawalt, 'Remarriage', pp. 147–157.

[33] Adamson, cited in Rappaport, *Worlds within Worlds*, p. 40. Rosenthal, 'Aristocratic Widows', p. 40. Barbara Todd found that, whereas half of the widows in Abingdon in the sixteenth century remarried, by the late seventeenth century this proportion had dropped to a quarter. 'The Remarrying Widow: A Stereotype Reconsidered', *Women in English Society 1500–1800*, ed. Mary Prior (London, 1985), pp. 54–92, esp. p. 65. Vivien Brodsky found in her study of marriage and remarriage by licence in London in the years 1598–1619 that of over 2,000 marriages, 55 per cent were between bachelors and spinsters, 10 per cent between widowers and spinsters, 19 per cent between bachelors and widows, and 16 per cent between widows and widowers. The literary stereotype of the older widow who grabbed a lusty young bachelor apprentice was not, in fact, a widespread phenomenon. In Brodsky's sample, younger widows (age twenty to forty-five) tended to marry single men, usually younger than themselves, and older widows (age forty to sixty) usually chose widowers of their own age or older, V. Brodsky, 'Widows in Late Elizabethan London: Remarriage, Economic Opportunity and Family Orientations', *The World we have Gained*, ed. L. Bonfield, R. Smith and K. Wrightson (Oxford, 1986), pp. 122–154.

half of the fourteenth century only a third of the widows had remarried (and so brought cases jointly with a new husband) by the time the dower case was initiated. Following the Black Death, Professor Hanawalt found that the proportion that remarried rose to a half, but dropped again after 1380 and remained at the lower rate into the fifteenth century.[34] As might be expected, widows left with young children were more likely to remarry than older, childless women. In London the court of aldermen assumed responsibility for the fatherless (hence orphaned) children of citizens. Hanawalt found that, between the years 1309 and 1458, two thirds of these widows with minor children had remarried in the brief interval between the death of their husband and the registration of their orphan children and their goods with the mayor and chamberlain. Among widows whom we know to have had young (i.e. under twenty-one or unmarried) children, remarriage was more common than among widows in general. In part the reason for the rapid remarriage of widows with young children may have been the attractions not only of her dower but also the additional third share of the father's estate which was allocated, by city custom, to the underage children of freemen. The mayor and aldermen assumed responsibility for this inheritance and appointed guardians, usually the mother, or the mother acting jointly with her new husband. Such guardianships could be a source of profit to the guardian.[35]

When widows remarried, whom did they choose? Indeed, did these women really have any choice at all? It is suggested here that Elizabeth de Burgh and Margaret Philpot may well have been organised into second and third marriages: in the first case by the king and in the second by the powerful mayor of London, Nicholas Brembre, who was Margaret's brother-in-law. Likewise, some of the tanners' widows may have been directed into second marriages. But Joan Gedney, who broke her vow of chastity to marry her fourth husband, Joan Bradbury and Thomasine Percyvale all seem to have been acting freely when they remarried. The fact that eight of our widows (of whom only one was a vowess) could remain widows for long periods after only one marriage suggests that only the extremely wealthy, or perhaps the very poor, were subject to the kind of pressures experienced by Margaret Philpot and Elizabeth de Burgh. Most of those who remarried seem to have done so by their own choice.

Thrupp found that merchant widows were inclined to select merchants as their second husbands,[36] and that is certainly true of the widows in this gathering. Apart from Elizabeth de Burgh whose husbands were aristocratic, the remaining five kept within the merchant class, although one of Margaret Philpot's four husbands was an esquire. What seems to have mattered was not

[34] Hanawalt, 'Widow's Mite', p. 36.

[35] Elaine Clarke, 'City Orphans and Custody Laws in Medieval England', *American Journal of Legal History*, 34 (1990), pp. 168–87.

[36] Thrupp, *Merchant Class*, p. 28.

the particular company of the prospective second husband but, rather, his mercantile status as a wholesale trader and importer.[37] Thus these widows who remarried circulated wealth within the elite class.[38] For artisan widows, such as the tanners, it was important to marry a man who could help in the running of the business: the wardship cases brought before the mayor and aldermen suggest that these widows frequently married men of their late husband's craft and, presumably, handed over to him the oversight of the shop.[39] The individual artisan widows examined here, however – Matilda Penne a skinner, Johanna Hill and Johanna Sturdy, bell-founders, and Alice Claver a silkwoman – all chose not to remarry but to run business enterprises themselves.

Another possibility open to a widow was to enter religious life, and there were several suitable nunneries in London or nearby.[40] So far there is little evidence of London widows doing this, although some gentry widows seem to have done so.[41] When the mercer and alderman William Ancroft died in 1390, his widow Alice became a lay sister at the house of the Minoresses at Aldgate and Elizabeth, the widow of John Prudde, a Westminster craftsman and chief glazer to the king from 1440 until his death in 1461, entered the house of Augustinian nuns at Halliwell at Shoreditch and became the prioress in 1472.[42]

Other widows, however, took a vow of chastity and so adopted some, but not all, of the constraints of monastic life. These women continued to live in the world and while embracing chastity they eschewed poverty and obedience. Mary Erler's study reveals the complex motives which led widows to take such a vow: they may have been influenced by the wishes of their dead husbands,[43]

---

[37] Margaret Philpot, 1 mercer, 2 grocer, 3 esquire, 4 goldsmith; Joan Gedney, 1 unknown, 2 fuller, 3 mercer, 4 draper; Alice Bryce, 1 skinner, 2 fuller; Thomasine Percyvale, 1 tailor, 2 tailor, 3 tailor; Joan Bradbury, 1 tailor, 2 mercer.

[38] By the late sixteenth century, widows who remarried had to leave their own company to join that of their new husbands. This could cause problems if the woman wished to continue her own business. In such cases the new husband was required to translate to her company, Rappaport, *Worlds within Worlds*, pp. 40–41.

[39] See, for example, 1376, Katherine, widow of John Mount glasier, within two months had married another glasier, Thomas Ectone; Johanna, the widow of the skinner Nicholas Harpesfeld had remarried John Manytone, another skinner, within five months in 1378; and in the following year, Johanna, widow of John de Flete a goldbeater, remarried Henry Abbot, a goldsmith, see *LBH*, pp. 49, 96, 117. See also Brodsky, 'Widows in Late Elizabethan London', p. 142.

[40] There were houses of Benedictine nuns at Stratford at Bow, Barking and St Helen's Bishopsgate: houses for Augustinian canonesses at Kilburn, Halliwell and Clerkenwell; the Minoresses were established outside the city wall to the east and, from the early fifteenth century; there was a house of Brigettine nuns at Syon in Middlesex.

[41] For example, Sybil de Felton, widow of Sir Thomas Morley, became abbess of Barking abbey, W. Page ed., VCH, *Essex*, ii, (London, 1907), p. 121.

[42] Thrupp, *Merchant Class*, p. 321; A.H. Thomas, ed., *CPMR, 1382–1412* (Cambridge, 1932), p. 177; A.G. Rosser, *Medieval Westminster* (Oxford, 1989), p. 395. I am grateful to Dr Catherine Paxton for providing me with these references; see her unpublished Oxford doctoral dissertation, 'The nunneries of London and its Environs in the Later Middle Ages' (1992).

[43] Hanawalt points out that, in fact, few husbands recorded an objection to the remarriage of their widows, 'Remarriage', p. 148.

or by their own desire to enlist the support of the church in their resistance to remarriage, or by a deeply-felt religious motive. But, as Erler points out, 'the lives of these women do not allow us to glimpse a particular spirituality'. It is, in fact, in the lives and wills of some of the other widows who are studied here that we glimpse that spirituality which we might have expected among the vowesses. Elizabeth de Burgh and Lucia Visconti, although not vowed, chose to live within the precincts of the house of Minoresses and to be buried there, and Rose Gatyn, a poor widow, also died at the Minoresses. Joan Pyel made her home at the nunnery of St Helen's at Bishopsgate; she remembered the nuns in her will and chose to be buried close to their church. These women had found a home, both physical and spiritual, within these female communities. Other widows like Matilda Penne and Johanna Hill also displayed considerable piety in their wills and it is clear that women like Joan Buckland, Joan Bradbury and Thomasine Percyvale came from families where several of their relatives were priests or monks, or had become nuns. There is little sign of novelty, let alone heresy, in their piety, but for all of the women considered here, late medieval Catholicism appears to have offered a satisfactory framework for their lives on earth and a means of easing the journey into and beyond the grave.

Many London widows seem to have chosen neither to remarry, nor to enter a religious house, not to take a vow of chastity but, rather, to live out their lives in London as widows. This choice is not, perhaps, surprising when we consider the opportunities which were available to widows in London in the later fourteenth and fifteenth centuries. Brodsky has noted a 'commonly held view that widowhood afforded unique opportunities for independence, economic self-sufficiency and 'social freedom' absent from the lives of both single and married women', but she goes on to caution enthusiastic feminists against assuming that widowhood was always golden.[44] The caution is justified. Widowhood was unlikely to prove attractive to young women, to those with small children, to those artisan women who needed assistance in order to run a craft workshop, and to poor women who could offer little to a prospective husband except mouths to be fed.

There is no doubt that several of the widows studied here did in fact manage to live successful and independent lives as widows. The death of a husband restored to his widow her separate legal *persona*. It is true that as a married woman, the wife of a London citizen could elect to trade independently as a *femme sole*, to train her own apprentices, both men and women, and to be answerable for her own debts.[45] These opportunities for economic independence were already open to her and it would seem that Matilda Penne and Alice

---

[44] Brodsky, 'Widows in Late Elizabethan London', pp. 123–24.

[45] Barron, 'Golden Age', pp. 39–40. In 1457, Agnes, a silkwoman and the wife of John Gower, was specifically granted the right to trade *sole* in the city, to answer for her debts and to enter into contracts 'according to the custom of the city', CLRO, Journal 6, f. 182v; and see the similar case of Isabelle Sayer, also a silkwoman, ibid., f. 184.

Claver both operated as *femmes soles* during the lifetimes of their husbands. But widowhood augmented a woman's economic opportunities for, as a widow, she was entitled to be a freewoman (sometimes referred to simply as *franche homme*) of the city, provided that she did not remarry. Widows who chose to take up the freedom seem to have had their names inscribed in civic records (although these have not survived) and they may well have paid an entry fee.[46] As a freewoman, a London widow could do business independently in the city as a citizen, could open a shop and trade retail; she could wage her law in city courts and, when she traded outside the city, her goods would be privileged in other towns and markets like those of other London citizens. Finally, she could ensure that her will was enrolled in the court of Husting according to civic custom.[47]

In one respect city custom laid a particular burden upon the widow of a citizen. She was not only allowed, but was indeed *expected* to maintain her husband's household and to continue his business, as can be clearly seen in the cases of Matilda Penne, Johanna Hill and Thomasine Percyvale. It was for this reason, doubtless, that civic custom allowed the widow to continue to occupy the family home for life, rather than for the mere forty days allowed by the common law of England. The London widow was expected to continue the training of her late husband's apprentices and, at the completion of their terms, to present them to the chamberlain for entry to the freedom.[48] If the widow failed to do this the aggrieved apprentice could complain to the Mayor's Court.[49] In those cases where the widow remarried out of her late husband's business, or was uninterested in maintaining his craft or trade, she was expected to assign the apprentice to another, appropriate master, as Joan Bradbury did.

---

[46] Barron, 'Golden Age', pp. 44–45; M.K. Dale cites the case of a vintner's widow who was admitted to the freedom to follow her husband's craft on being publicly presented to the warden and brothers of the craft, CLRO, Recognizance Roll 21, m. 4, and see also Recognizance Roll 19, m. 2d; 'Women in the Textile Industries and Trade of Fifteenth-Century England' (unpublished M.A. dissertation, University of London, 1928), p. 22. In 1389 it was asserted that the widow of a citizen is a citizen, *CPMR, 1381–1413* (Cambridge, 1932), p. 151.

[47] By the sixteenth century it is clear that it was only the widows of freemen who were entitled to the freedom of the city, see Rappaport, *Worlds within Worlds*, pp. 39–40. In 1552 Elizabeth Kyngeston, a poulterer's widow, was 'defranchised from all the liberties and fredome of the said citie for ever' because she had sole poultry above the agreed price, and in 1557 Rose Trott, widow of John, together with her two sons John and Martin, was admitted to the freedom even though the record of her husband's entry to the freedom could not be found, CLRO, Repertory xii, f. 439; xiii, f. 548. I owe these references to the kindness of Professor Mark Benbow.

[48] Barron, 'Golden Age', pp. 45–46. For examples of widows inheriting their husbands' apprentices and failing to 'keep shop' and to train them, see P.E. Jones ed., *CPMR, 1437–1457* (Cambridge, 1954), pp. 31, 46, 69, 96.

[49] See, for example, the case in 1442 when a bowyer's apprentice was released from his indentures because his master had died and the widow 'kept no shop and had failed to instruct or provide for him', P.E. Jones ed., *CPMR, 1437–1457* (Cambridge, 1954), p. 46.

In the almost total absence of medieval freedom registers for London it is difficult to know how many widows continued to train their husband's apprentices and then presented them for the freedom. The two chance surviving sets of freedom registers, however, for 1309–12 and 1551–53 tell much the same story.[50] In the earlier period 253 men were presented for the freedom on completion of their terms as apprentices: sixteen of these, or 6 per cent, were presented by the widows of their late masters.[51] In the two years covered by the mid sixteenth-century freedom registers, 1,000 apprentices were presented, fifty of them by their master's widow, i.e. a very similar percentage to that of the early fourteenth-century period. By the end of the sixteenth century this percentage appears to have dropped to less than 2 per cent: a further indication that women were increasingly being pushed to the margins of the 'official' labour market.[52]

Perhaps half the widows considered here can be seen to have continued 'in business' after their husband's deaths, either, like Matilda Penne, Johanna Hill, Alice Claver or Thomasine Percyvale, running craft workshops;[53] or, like Lucia Visconti, Margaret Croke and Alice Bryce, engaged in wholesale trade either at home or abroad. Even those widows who were not engaged in business seem to have been active in the law courts: Joan Pyel working to establish her dead husband's college; Joan Buckland negotiating to collect in her husband's debts and resisting the claims of other merchants; and Joan Gedney continuing to exploit the economic potential of the manor of Tottenham, as her husband had done before her. The poor widows of the tanners were allowed to run their stalls in the Tanners' Seld and so retain the retail outlets for their goods.

All of the women, except for Margaret Philpot, seem to have acted as their husbands' executors.[54] This seems to have been true also among the poorer widows: in all but two cases the tanners named their widows as principal executors. This was not unusual: Hanawalt noted that 86 per cent of husbands

---

[50] *LBD*, pp. 35–179; C. Welch, ed., *Register of Freemen of the City of London in the Reigns of Henry VIII and Edward VI*, London and Middlesex Archaeological Society (1908).

[51] Beryl R. Nash, 'A Study of the Freemen and Apprenticeship Registers of Letter Book D (1309–1312): The Place Name Evidence' (unpublished M.A. thesis, University of London, 1989), appendix 18.

[52] Brodsky, 'Widows in Late Elizabethan London', pp. 141–42; Rappaport, *Worlds within Worlds*, p. 41, and n. 48. It is clear that widows also had difficulty in exercising the trade of their dead husbands: Ellen Harman, a horner's widow, had to carry her child to the lord mayor, Sir Martin Bowes, to persuade him to allow him to practise her husband's craft, Ian Archer, *The Pursuit of Stability: Social Relations in Elizabethan London* (Cambridge, 1991), p. 55.

[53] For evidence of artisan widows continuing in business after the deaths of their husbands, see Heather Swanson, *Medieval Artisans: An Urban Class in Late Medieval England* (Oxford, 1989), pp. 21, 35, 42–43, 160–61.

[54] The fact that Margaret Philpot never acted as executor for any of her husbands reinforces the suggestion that she was a pawn largely managed by others. We do not know who acted as executors for the husbands of Elizabeth de Burgh or Matilda Penne.

who left a wife made her the executor of their wills.[55] Among the fourteenth-century tanners and the men who left 'poor widows' in the early fifteenth century, c. 90 per cent chose their wives as their executors. Moreover, women at all social levels can be found acting as executors for people outside their immediate families. Wood has found women acting not only as executors, but also as supervisors and witnesses of wills. Alice Lynne was the overseer of John Shirley's will, Joan Buckland was chosen as executor by both her mother and her brother, Joan Bradbury acted as an executor for her brother, as well as for both her husbands, and as overseer of her son's will. Clearly the tasks of an executor, which could be both skilled and laborious, were not considered to be beyond the capabilities of women.

If these women were able to run business enterprises or great households, as Elizabeth de Burgh did, or to tackle the ecclesiastical hierarchy to establish a college, as Joan Pyel did, they must have been literate to some degree. Lucia Visconti's mother tongue was presumably Italian, but she probably learnt some English and spoke French in aristocratic circles. It is likely that the nuns at the Minoresses spoke in French and in that language would have conversed both with Lucia and with Elizabeth de Burgh.[56] Recent work on the education of noblewomen in this period draws attention to their ability to read French and English books, but few of them wrote creatively or commanded Latin grammar.[57] Throughout the medieval period, nunneries offered some kind of education to girls, and not only to those who were destined to become nuns.[58] It is likely that the daughters of London merchants received education and training which had much in common with that of noblewomen. There was no shortage of religious houses in London. In the early fifteenth century William Cresewyk, a grocer, left a bequest of twenty shillings to 'E. Scolemaysteresse' and William Rous, a mercer who died in 1486, instructed his executors to send his daughter to school for four years, like her brothers.[59] Elizabeth Stonor, the

---

[55] Hanawalt, 'Widow's Mite', p. 26. Brodsky found that 80 per cent of married male testators appointed their wives as sole executors of their wills, 'Widows in Late Elizabethan London', p. 145; Todd found that in Abingdon 89 per cent of men appointed their wives as executor, or co-executor, in the sixteenth century, although this figure dropped to 74 per cent in the seventeenth century, 'The Remarrying Widow', p. 68. See also Rowena E. Archer and B.E. Ferme, 'Testamentary Procedure with Special Reference to the Executrix', *Medieval Women in Southern England*, pp. 3–34.

[56] See Eileen Power, *Medieval English Nunneries* (Cambridge, 1922), pp. 237–55.

[57] Nicholas Orme, *From Childhood to Chivalry: The Education of the English Kings and Aristocracy, 1066–1520* (London, 1984), pp. 156–63.

[58] Ibid., pp. 63–65.

[59] The will of Cresewyk, who died in 1408, is remarkably 'feminist' and 'diffuse'. He appointed four executors, two of them women: his wife Alice (if she wished to take up the burden) and Matilda Danyell, a widow, who was left 100s. Thirty-four people were named individually in Cresewyk's will, fourteen men and twenty women who included not only his relatives, but also household servants and neighbours. His wife Alice was to have his copy of the *Legends of Saints* for her life and it was then to go to Holy Trinity, Aldgate, GL, MS 9171/2, f. 88. When William Rous died in 1486 he left nine minor children, four sons and five daughters: the eldest son received

continued

daughter of a London alderman, could read and write in English to her husband, and John Paston III wrote in 1474 to a London woman 'Mistress Annes' (possibly the daughter of the mercer and Alderman John Stokton) declaring his hopes of marriage with her and adding the postscript: 'Mastresse Annes, I am prowd that ye can reed Inglyshe, wherfor I prey yow aqweynt yow wyth thys my lewd hand, for my purpose is that ye shalbe more aqwewnted wyth it or ellys it shalbe ayenst my wyll'.[60] But education was not the exclusive privilege of the daughters of the merchant class. In 1380 the guardian of the daughter of a London corn-dealer listed among his expenses 13s. 4d. spent yearly on 'teaching, shoes and other small necessaries'; and 25s. was spent on school fees for Felicia, the daughter of Roger Reygate, a London chandler.[61] Girls were probably educated at elementary schools, but none of them was likely to have gone on to the formal grammar schools where Latin was taught.

Of the women considered here only Joan Buckland certainly possessed books, for she lists some of these – all liturgical – in her will. But it is clear that several of them, needless to say the wealthiest, were concerned with education. Elizabeth de Burgh founded Clare Hall in Cambridge and Thomasine Percyvale and Joan Bradbury diligently concerned themselves with detailed procedures necessary for founding and securely establishing free schools in the countryside, at Saffron Walden and at Week St Mary in Cornwall. Joan Bradbury's first husband Thomas Bodley came from a 'bookish' family: he and his brother owned books and several of their sons were educated at university and became priests. In the Lynne family, it seems to have been the women who were the bibliophiles. Alice Lynne herself was the friend, and mother-in-law, of the scribe John Shirley. The name of her daughter Margaret, who married John Shirley, together with that of her sister Beatrice, was inscribed in a manuscript containing the poetry of Hoccleve and Lydgate, and Beatrice also inscribed her name in a psalter which she gave to the Minoresses' house at Aldgate. A third daughter, Alice, was the grandmother of John Colet. The ability of women to read and to write probably depended less on gender than on their level of prosperity: the tanners and their widows were unlikely to have been literate; the wealthy tailor Sir John Percyvale and the wealthy mercer Thomas Bradbury, both Mayors of London, must surely have been able to read and write, and their wives likewise.

In drawing up their will, London men looked to their widows to act as their executors and overseers, to see to the distribution of their goods, the maintenance of their businesses, the nurture of their families and the welfare of their

---

continued
£20 and the dwelling-house, the rest each received £22. Rous wished his residual estate to be used to fund 'poor scholars to school in Cambridge', GL, MS 9171/7, f.62.

[60] C.L. Kingsford ed., *The Stonor Letters and Papers* Camden Society, third series, 29, 30 (1919); Norman Davies ed., *Paston Letters and Papers of the Fifteenth Century*, i (Oxford, 1971), p. 591.

[61] H.T. Riley, *Memorials of London and London Life* (London, 1868), p. 447; *LBH* (London, 1907), p. 212.

souls. Often, where we can compare the wills of the husband with that of his widow, the man's will is briefer and much less detailed.[62] This is because a husband who left a widow could talk with her and explain what he would like to be done: for her, for their children, for his household and servants, and for charitable works for the good of his soul. Moreoever, as we have already observed, the real estate and movable goods of the husband were subject to division and dispersal which were beyond his control. He was free to decide *how* to provide for his widow, but not *whether* to do so. The dying man seems often to have left his wife and the other executors to carry out verbal instructions, and the wills of widows bear testimony – for example, in the cases of Joan Pyel, Alice Lynne, Joan Buckland, Johanna Hill and Joan Bradbury – to the faithfulness with which widows attempted to carry out their husbands' intentions and passed on to their own executors the obligations which had been laid on them.[63] By contrast, the widow often had to choose an 'outsider' as her chief executor: it seems to have been more important to her to write all her concerns into her will, perhaps because she was afraid that if her wishes were not written down they would be forgotten or ignored. She had no husband to take care of her interests as she had taken care of his. It is perhaps for this reason that the wills of widows are often much more 'diffuse' than those of their husbands. Apart from his wife and daughter, Richard Hill named seven people in his testament: his widow Johanna named twenty-four. These widows seem more inclined than their dead husbands to recognise the needs of distant kin and to make bequests to named friends, neighbours, servants and godchildren. Matilda Penne, who remembered forty-three people in her will, included her apprentices, servants, friends, neighbours, fellow parishioners, local clergy, her husband's relations, her own family and, intriguingly, even her 'secretary', 'Petronilla scriweyner'.[64] Grandchildren were more often remembered by grandmothers than by grandfathers: Margaret Philipot left silver saucers to her only grandson, John Bamme, and Joan Bradbury remembered her numerous grandchildren with carefully shaded tokens of affection.[65]

[62] This is marked in the cases of Joan Buckland, Johanna Hill and Thomasine Percyvale, but not so marked in the case of Joan Pyel.

[63] Clive Burgess has drawn attention to the activity of widows in carrying out their husbands's charitable purposes, which were often not specified in the husband's will, 'Late Medieval Wills and Pious Conventions', *Piety and the Professions*, ed. Michael Hicks (Gloucester, 1990), pp. 14–33, esp. pp. 20–21.

[64] Joan Buckland also left a bequest to her unnamed scrivener in London.

[65] In a sample of 200 late sixteenth-century wills of London widows, 55 per cent of all legatees were non-relatives, friends, servants, goodwives, neighbours and their children. A high proportion of these unrelated legatees were women, Brodsky, 'Widows in Late Elizabethan London', p. 150; cf. Rosenthal, 'Aristocratic Widows', p. 46. In Bury St Edmunds in 1439–1530, whereas 11 per cent of male wills mentioned godchildren, 19 per cent of women's (i.e. widow's) wills did so, see Robert Dinn, 'Baptism, Spiritual Kinship and Popular Religion in Late Medieval Bury St Edmunds', *Bulletin of the John Rylands University Library of Manchester*, 72 (1990), pp. 93–106, esp. pp. 100–1.

The London widow had great testamentary freedom: she often had considerable wealth in land, and particularly in goods and chattels; she was not *obliged* to provide for her relatives or for her own soul; and she had no husband to act as her executor. For these reasons the wills and testaments of medieval London widows are particularly revealing: verbose, bossy, disorganised, affectionate and anecdotal. Although these wills employ both legal and verbal conventions, they cannot hide the fact that at the point of death, we glimpse these London women when they were, in some senses, at their most impressive and most powerful.

The study of the wills of these women has helped to reveal the networks of female friendships and loyalties which clearly played an important part in stitching together the social fabric of a society largely composed of immigrants. This female bonding occurs within, and across, economic classes. Elizabeth de Burgh was clearly a close friend of Marie de Saint-Pol, widow of the earl of Pembroke, with whom she shared a common interest in the Minoresses and in founding colleges at Cambridge. Two hundred years later, Joan Bradbury acknowledged her friendship with two widows of London mayors, Dame Elizabeth Rich and Dame Christian Colet. Poor widows also gave pots or coverlets or gowns to their female friends, who also acted as their executors and as witnesses to their wills. Almost all these London widows remembered their women servants as friends rather than employees: Lucia Visconti was concerned about her Italian serving women; Margaret Philipot remembered her servants Cecily and Amy, and Agnes Staple, who was comparatively poor, left her bed and her clothes to her servant Alice. In a society where the death rate and mortality were high, older women could be left without any immediate family and servants could become as important as children and of more immediate solace. Joan Buckland left bequests to several servants and directed that all her gowns and kirtles should be 'departed to my wommen servauntes with me at me departyng'.[66] The importance of female networks is shown particularly clearly in the case of Alice Claver, for whom other women were not only friends but business associates. Women who would never have been able to afford the security of a private chantry or a cycle of masses might yet be daily remembered with a grateful prayer from the recipient of a special ring, or a furred gown, or a cooking pot: the informal networks of parish, neighbourhood and household supported those many women who were cut off from their own families and who in their wills acknowledged the friends, 'gossips' and servants who had warmed their lives.

Considering how long some of these women had been widows it is not surprising, perhaps, that about half of them chose not be buried with their late husbands. Both Elizabeth de Burgh and Lucia Visconti chose burial apart from their husbands, in the Minoresses' church, and although this may simply reflect

---

[66] A. Clark, ed., *Lincoln Diocese Documents, 1450–1544*, EETS, original series, 149 (1914), p. 43. I am grateful to Dr Jenny Stratford for providing me with this reference.

aristocratic custom, there is not much indication that these ladies were particularly close to their husbands. Some of the widows of London citizens, like Joan Pyel, Matilda Penne and Margaret Croke, also chose separate burial and only fourteen of Robert Wood's forty-nine poor widows specified burial with their husbands, although they may simply have been too poor to choose. Women like Joan Gedney, Joan Bradbury, Margaret Philpot and Thomasine Percyvale, who had been married more than once, usually chose burial with their last husband. When women specifically chose not to be buried with their husbands they may have been concerned simply with matters of convenience, but they may also have wanted to assert a measure of independence: Matilda Penne wished to be buried not in a tomb with her husband but in her church of St Peter, 'in front of the Cross where I am accustomed to stand': her spot rather than his.

At the end of the fifteenth century the position of women in London, and therefore the position of widows, began to change. These changes were not unique to London.[67] It became increasingly difficult for women themselves to become apprenticed, to take on apprentices or to run their dead husbands' businesses as freewomen of London. The growth of capitalist enterprise and the advent of a new Protestant ethic about the role of women may have both adversely affected the economic independence of women.[68] But demographic change may have been the most important factor. The rise in population converted women's work from a welcome enterprise to a serious threat. All over Europe the opportunities for women to work outside the home closed down as one set of craft regulations after another eroded and curtailed the possibilities. There was, however, another factor at work, not unconnected, perhaps, with demographic change. The distinctions between mercantile and gentle activities were becoming blurred: gentlemen became Merchant Adventurers and traded in cloth abroad, and the daughters and widows of London merchants married into gentle families.[69] As so often, the women were the subtle agents of social change and, as they moved out of London to take over the responsibilities of the lady of the manor, they left behind the opportunities which had been woven into the fabric of London widowhood.

[67] Herlihy, *Opera Muliebria*, pp. 169, 179; Barbara A. Hanawalt, *Women and Work in Preindustrial Europe* (Bloomington, IN, 1986), pt v; Barron, 'Golden Age', pp. 48–49.

[68] See Alison Wall, 'Elizabethan Precept and Feminine Practice', *History*, 75 (1990), pp. 23–38.

[69] See the case of Etheldreda, the widow of the London merchant Richard Gardiner, who married Gilbert Talbot, the brother of the earl of Shrewsbury, Bradberry, 'Etheldreda Gardiner'; Alice, the grand-daughter of Alice Bryce, married, firstly, William Browne who became an alderman of London and, secondly, Sir William Blount, Lord Mountjoy, the patron of Erasmus.

1

Tanners' Widows, 1300–1350

Derek Keene

The historian of London before the Black Death rarely gets the opportunity to make the acquaintance of a craftsman's widow.[1] Richer widows, and later ones, are easier game, as the essays in this volume show. Before 1350, however, the London tanners seem to have been a particularly cohesive group, and that characteristic, in combination with the results of a recent intensive study of the Cheapside district of the city,[2] enables the historian to place them, their families, and to an extent their widows, in a reasonably well-founded social and environmental context. Moreover, in several of the available sources, the wives and widows of the tanners seem more prominent than their counterparts in other London craft groups, a point which emerged in one of the earliest studies of women's work in medieval London.[3] Tanners' widows, then, are an excellent group with which to begin the comparative study of the role and experience of artisan widows in the medieval city.

Very little can be discovered about any individual tanner's widow, so the method of group biography has been adopted. This essay focuses on information concerning about twenty-five tanners' widows who were alive between about 1280 and 1370 (most of them before 1340).[4] The widows are revealed in

[1] The initial research out of which the idea for this essay grew, was undertaken as part of the 'Social and Economic Study of Medieval London', funded by the Economic and Social Research Council. I am especially grateful to Maryanne Kowaleski (Fordham University) for invaluable advice and encouragement, and to Colin Taylor (Museum of London Archaeology Service) for allowing me to consult his material on property holding in the parish of St Sepulchre outside Newgate.

[2] D. Keene and V. Harding, *Historical Gazetteer of London before the Great Fire*, i, *Cheapside* (Cambridge, 1987).

[3] A. Abram, 'Women Traders in Medieval London', *Economic Journal*, 26 (1916), pp. 276–85, esp. p. 283.

[4] These are all the London tanners' widows whom it is possible to identify in the period: in two cases it is likely, but not certain, that their husbands had been tanners. The manuscript material examined includes all the wills of tanners enrolled in the city's court of Husting up to 1370 (not all of the tanners are identified as such in their wills), all the enrolled deeds concerning property holding in that part of the parish of St Sepulchre which lay to the south of Smithfield (collected by Colin Taylor), all evidence concerning Tanner's Seld and the surrounding area of Cheapside up to 1670 (see Keene and Harding, *Cheapside*).

a small number of distinctive situations relating both to work and to family strategies: by exploring these situations we can begin to generalise about the widows' experience. It would be possible to extend the factual base a little, especially concerning the suburban life of the tanners' communities, as portrayed in the details of their property-holding outside the city walls, but it should be recognised at the outset that our information on these widows will always be small. Furthermore, the group biography which can be constructed stands at a great distance from the lives of the widows themselves. In the first place, they are revealed within social structures and processes which were created largely by and for the benefit of men, especially in that world of public events and record from which the surviving documents have emerged. Secondly, while there are some scraps of information on what the tanners'widows actually did, the most valuable sources are the wills of their husbands, which for the most part tell us only what was expected of them. Even these wills are a defective source, since they are known only in the versions in which they were enrolled in the city's court of Husting, a form which during the early part of the period omitted many of the details concerning spiritual, charitable, personal and family matters which would have been contained in the original documents. A more rounded investigation would include a study of the widows as they perceived themselves and the world they lived in. That approach has not often been adopted, even when the evidence is available.[5] Unfortunately, it is virtually impossible for the London tanners' widows before the Black Death.

Nevertheless, tanners' widows in this period of London's history are a rewarding topic for study. A substantial tanning industry was located within the city and its suburbs at this date, and its sites and organisation are reasonably well recorded. Fundamental changes in the location and organisation of the trade took place after the Black Death, with the result that the later city tanners form a much less coherent and identifiable group for investigation. The comparative study of the family and work strategies of different craft and other social groups in medieval London has hardly begun. The tanners are a good point at which to start. In what follows an attempt has been made to indicate what may have been distinctive about their behaviour and preferences, especially with regard to widows, and what may have represented more widespread practice.

In the records of medieval and early modern towns in northern Europe women are revealed as working independently on their own account in almost as wide a range of crafts as those pursued by men, although not in such large numbers. Most such women were single, many of them were probably widows. A widow commonly continued the business that had previously been identified as her husband's, a fact which suggests that she may often have been an active

---

[5] See B. Potash, ed., *Widows in African Societies: Choices and Constraints* (Stanford, CA., 1986), which contains several notable examples of the widow-centred approach.

participant in the trade during his lifetime. Widows are to be found working as blacksmiths, and even as tanners, as well as in more delicate trades. The broad profile of the women's craft occupations which are recorded, however, differ significantly from that for men. A higher proportion of single women ran businesses associated with the textile trades, especially those which handled silk and linen, than was the case with men, and a lower proportion was associated with the leather trades.[6] This appears to have been the case both in northern Europe and in Tuscany. In part it reflects the distinctive independent manufacturing and commercial activity of women in the silk trades, even when they were married to husbands who pursued an entirely different line of business.[7] In Paris around 1220 there was a clear expectation that shopkeepers who dealt in linens and other light goods would be women rather than men, in contrast to the dealers in other commodities.[8]

There were thus differences between crafts in the degree to which women participated in the trade, and over the extent of their independence when they did so. By comparison with some other crafts, it seems that in the leather trades women were less prominent as independent traders, which may mean that wives were correspondingly less active in assisting their husbands in the practice of the craft. Nevertheless, it is clear that in fourteenth-century London wives and daughters did assist husbands and fathers in the leather trades, and that it was possible for other women formally to learn the craft

[6] Abram, 'Women Traders'; E. Dixon, 'Craftswomen in the *Livre des Métiers*', *Economic Journal*, 5 (1895), pp. 209–28; C. Phythian-Adams, *Desolation of a City: Coventry and the Urban Crisis of the Late Middle Ages* (Cambridge, 1979), p. 91; J.C. Brown and J. Goodman, 'Women and Industry in Florence', *Journal of Economic History*, 40 (1980), pp. 73–80; G. Jacobsen, 'Women's Work and Women's Role: Ideology and Reality in Danish Urban Society, 1300–1550', *Scandinavian Economic History Review*, 31 (1983), pp. 1–20; D. Hutton, 'Women in Fourteenth-century Shrewsbury' in *Women and Work in Pre-Industrial England*, ed. L. Charles and L. Duffin (London, 1985), pp. 83–99, esp. p. 93; M. Kowaleski, 'Women's Work in a Market Town: Exeter in the Late Fourteenth Century', in *Women and Work in Preindustrial Europe*, ed. B.A. Hanawalt (Bloomington, IN, 1986), pp. 145–64; P.J.P. Goldberg, 'Womens' Work, Womens' Role in the Late Medieval North' in *Profit, Piety and the Professions in later Medieval England*, ed. M. Hicks (Gloucester, 1990), pp. 34–50, esp. p. 46; D. Herlihy, *Opera Muliebra: Women and Work in Medieval Europe* (Philadelphia, 1990), 142–48, 159; I.K. Ben-Amos, 'Women Apprentices in the Trades and Crafts of early Modern Bristol', *Continuity and Change*, 6 (1991), pp. 227–52; J.M. Bennett, 'Medieval Women, Modern Women: Across the Great Divide' in *Culture and History 1350–1600: Essays on English Communities, Identities and Writing*, ed. D. Aers, (London, 1992), pp. 147–75, esp. p. 156; P.J.P. Goldberg, *Women, Work, and Life Cycle in a Medieval Economy: Women in York and Yorkshire, c. 1300–1520* (Oxford, 1992), pp. 87–92, 127–30.

[7] M.K. Dale, 'The London Silkwomen of the Fifteenth Century', *Economic History Review* 1st series, 4 (1933), pp. 324–35, reprinted in *Sisters and Workers in the Middle Ages*, ed. J.M. Bennett, E.A. Clark, J.F. O'Barr, B.A. Vilen, and S. Westphal-Wihl (Chicago and London, 1989), pp. 26–38; K.E. Lacey, 'Women and Work in Fourteenth- and Fifteenth-Century London' in *Women and Work*, ed. Charles and Duffin, pp. 24–82; B.B. Rubin, *The Dictionarius of John de Garlande* (Lawrence, KS, 1981), pp. 70–2.

[8] Rubin, *Dictionarius*, pp. 40–41.

through apprenticeship.[9] There are some indications that among the tanners it was as daughters that women were most likely to have learned skills associated with the craft, and that may have contributed to the dense network of family relationships which seems to have characterised the London trade. In several other English towns in the later fourteenth century households active in the leather crafts, including tanning, constituted one of the groups which were distinctive for containing grown-up but unmarried daughters, who presumably assisted in the trade. This probably reflects the relative poverty of the leather workers, daughters being retained instead of paid servants: indeed, female servants seem to have been relatively uncommon in those households.[10] Female apprenticeship was not common in medieval London, if the picture for the early modern period holds goods for earlier times too, although in the fourteenth and fifteenth centuries the silkwomen were a significant exception to that general rule.[11] It is possible that with women apprenticeship served more as a means of retaining cheap and relatively unskilled labour than as a way of passing on skill, as was certainly the case elsewhere with extended apprenticeships for domestic servants.[12] In later thirteenth-century Paris the only women whom the tanners could take as apprentices were their own daughters, and those daughters were in turn forbidden to take apprentices unless they were themselves married to practising tanners.[13] Conditions were a little different in fourteenth-century London, where it appears to have been permissible for a wife not following the same trade as her husband to take an apprentice in practice, although the apprentice was formally bound to the husband.[14] Restrictions of one sort and another on the freedom of women to pursue a skilled trade were long established. It has been argued that at various times during the middle ages, perhaps especially towards 1500, these restrictions become more extensive and more formalised.[15]

---

[9] H.T. Riley, ed., *Memorials of London and London Life* (London, 1868), p. 546.

[10] Goldberg, *Women*, pp. 101, 193.

[11] V. Brodsky, 'Widows in Late Elizabethan London: Remarriage, Economic Opportunity and Family Orientation' in *The World We have Gained: Histories of Population and Social Structure*, ed. L. Bonfield, R.M. Smith and K. Wrightson (Oxford, 1986), pp. 122–54; S. Rappaport, *Worlds within Worlds: Structures of Life in Sixteenth-Century London* (Cambridge, 1989), pp. 36–42 (citing the work of N. Adamson); M. Kowaleski and J.M. Bennett, 'Crafts, Gilds, and Women in the Middle Ages: Fifty years after Marian K. Dale', in Bennett et al., *Sisters and Workers*, pp. 11–25, esp. pp. 17–20.

[12] S.A. Epstein, *Wage Labor and Guilds in Medieval Europe* (Chapel Hill, NC, and London, 1991), p. 114.

[13] Epstein, *Wage Labor*, p. 115.

[14] *LBK*, p. 291.

[15] Herlihy, *Opera Muliebra*, pp. 176–9; Jacobsen, 'Women's Work'; Epstein, *Wage Labor*, pp. 209–13; Goldberg, *Women*, p. 200. M.C. Howell, *Women, Production, and Patriarchy in Late Medieval Cities* (Chicago and London, 1986), esp. pp. 27–46, 174–83, and in 'Women, the Family Economy, and the Structures of Market Production in Cities of Northern Europe during the Late Middle Ages', in Hanawalt, *Women and Work*, pp. 198–222, associates the change, too categorically in my view, with the growth of the market and supposed new forms of production. For a different perspective, see Bennet, 'Medieval Women, Modern Women'. See also above, p. xiv.

Much of the work undertaken by women was conducted outside the formal structures, including apprenticeship, provided by the guild or other regulatory body. Most women would have acquired and practised their craft skills as wives or daughters in the private, domestic sphere.[16] Much of that work, which made a fundamental contribution to the urban economy, was no less skilled than that undertaken by craftsmen, but it lacked the public recognition, with connotations of quality for the product and status for the practitioner, which was accorded to the work of men. Within the home women prepared and distributed food and drink and made and managed clothing for their families, or they worked as servants performing similar tasks. These domestic activities could be extended into the commercial world beyond the threshold so as to generate a money income, most conspicuously in the case of brewing and selling ale. This process of extension is evident in many of the often informal or part-time commercial enterprises undertaken by women: spinning, dress-making, washing clothes, the retailing of foodstuffs and other small items, and prostitution.[17]

In the commercialised environment which prevailed in London and other great cities, women acquired a special role in managing retail trade, where they could supply skills in the handling of goods, money and people which resembled those used in running a household.[18] In London, by the end of the thirteenth century, women had a distinctive position in the shops and bazaars of the city's busiest commercial districts, especially in selling high-value textiles, clothing, and personal accoutrements. Such work was undertaken by single women, including widows, by wives in partnership with husbands, and by wives independently. For much of the time it involved sitting, watching and waiting: perhaps one of the most characteristic public settings for the woman in business was in the shop window, or with a tray of goods by the door or in the street. It is part of the shopkeeper's job to attract business by display or other means, and there is little doubt that women's physical charms made an important contribution to their effectiveness in distributive trade.[19] In an uneasy fashion the commercial relationship parallels that of sexual inter-course, and so conspicuous success by a single woman or widow in retailing, brewing, or the cloth trade might be a cause of anxiety and suspicion among

---

[16] See esp. Jacobsen, 'Women's Work'.

[17] For a recent, but partial, survey see Goldberg, *Women*, pp. 104–57.

[18] Jacobsen, 'Women's Work'; D. Keene, *Survey of Medieval Winchester*, Winchester Studies, 2 (Oxford, 1985), pp. 389–96; Kowaleski, 'Women's Work'; M.M. Wood, 'Paltry Pedlars or Essential Merchant? Women in the Distributive Trades in Early Modern Nuremberg', *Sixteenth-Century Journal*, 12 (1981), pp. 3–16.

[19] Personal-names, place-names and iconographic representations of shops and associated activities provide a strong case for arguing that the charms of the woman shopkeeper were as important for attracting trade in thirteenth-century London as they were in the seventeenth-century and later city: D. Keene, 'Shops and Shopping in Medieval London' in *Medieval Art, Architecture and Archaeology in London*, ed. L. Grant, British Archaeological Association Conference Transactions, 10 (1990), pp. 28–46, esp. p. 41.

men, occasioning responses such as the biased and authoritarian application of bye-laws, aggressive ribaldry, or physical assault.[20] Such tensions probably informed the whole structure of social relations within which spinsters, married women and widows performed their work.

London widows enjoyed customary and legal rights similar to those in other English medieval towns.[21] These included a share in the late husband's real property during the widow's lifetime and a share in his chattels in perpetuity (dower), with the intent that she should be provided with, among other things, lodging and the means of continuing to prepare food. In their wills husbands sometimes reinforced and added to these provisions. Moreover, after about 1350, the practice developed of husbands and wives establishing a joint title to properties which belonged to the husband, with the wife's right being limited to her lifetime.[22] This might clarify and increase the widow's entitlement to the estate, but at the same time it effectively curtailed some of the longer-term, if accidental, effects of her right of dower, such as a claim by her heirs or a subsequent husband that the property she had held was in fact her inheritance. This and other aspects of the practice are among several indications that women were progressively disadvantaged during the slow shift from customary to more formalised or contractual social arrangements, and perhaps also that demographic change was accompanied by attempts to contain the property rights of women.[23] Widows might also have property in their own right, especially as heiresses. It seems likely that as old age or retirement approached some men or couples, in London and elsewhere, switched their resources to investment in rents and houses rather than trade so as to provide a steady income. Some widows were therefore very well endowed, a state which provided them with the opportunity of leading an independent life, or which made them attractive as partners to new husbands. Income from real estate may have been less significant for the widows of craftsmen that for those in wealthier circumstances, but it could play a part in their strategies. For a craftsman's widow the right to household and other chattels may have been even more important, since it could enable the widow to carry on her husband's business or to trade in some other way. There was a deeply entrenched notion, however, that the widow should only continue to use her husband's craft resources in the trade that he had pursued.[24]

[20] Kowaleski, 'Women's Work', pp. 148–49; Howell, *Women, Production, and Patriarchy*, 182–83, D.S. Ellis, 'The Merchant's Wife's Tale: Language, Sex and Commerce in Margery Kempe and Chaucer', *Exemplaria*, 2 (1990), pp. 595–626.

[21] See above, p. xvii.

[22] Keene, *Medieval Winchester*, p. 190. The practice became widespread in London at the same time: Keene and Harding, *Cheapside*, passim.

[23] S. Payling, 'Social Mobility, Demographic Change, and Landed Society in Late Medieval England', *Economic History Review*, 45 (1992), pp. 51–73, has some important implications for the study of urban society on this point.

[24] H.T. Riley, ed., *Liber Custumarum* in *Munimenta Gildhallae Londoniensis: Liber Albus, Liber Custumarum et Liber Horn, in archivis Gildhallae asservati*, vol. 2 (in 2 parts), (Rolls Series, London, 1860), p. 125; Kowaleski and Bennett, 'Crafts and Gilds', p. 16.

While the widow's rights were firmly established and widely recognised, it was not uncommon, in many different periods and types of society, for those rights to be ignored by heirs and other interested parties. Often, perhaps, that ignorance arose from the obscurity or uncertain status of many kin and marital relationships, itself the product of high population mobility and a rate of remarriage which in a city like London was almost certainly very high by modern standards. Widows may often have found it necessary to take direct action so as to uphold their entitlement. In medieval London, as elsewhere, the ingenuity, resourcefulness and persistence of the widow were probably at least as important as her customary rights if she was to hold her own.[25]

To judge from contemporary rural and from later urban practice, in London and other towns, remarriage by bereaved partners was common in the city around 1300.[26] It was probably much more common among men than women. In the last resort this presumably reflected the relative fertility of men and women, as expressed in their sexuality and emotional needs, but it also arose from differentials in mortality and in age at marriage. Post-menopausal women perhaps rarely remarried. They, in particular, may have taken the opportunity of independence presented by widowhood to fashion new identities for themselves, which they reinforced through work and through associations with other widows and single women.[27] This option was in theory open to the younger widow with dependent children, whose role was to maintain household and family rather than to manage their dissolution, but the pressures to remarry, both internal and external, were probably greater in her case. Both younger and older widows may have found the prospect of affection and companionship sufficient inducement to remarry, but younger widows, who in general would have had less experience of independent activity than of life as a daughter, servant and then wife under a male head of household, may have been less inclined to strike out on their own.

The perceived value of the resources with which the widow was endowed was probably a major influence on her role in the serially monogamous life-cycle characteristic of many of those male Londoners who could afford to

[25] See above, p. xxi and n. 18; I. Chabot, 'Widowhood and Poverty in Late Medieval Florence', *Continuity and Change*, 3 (1988), pp. 291–311; I. Archer, *The Pursuit of Stability: Social Relations in Elizabethan London* (Cambridge, 1991), pp. 55, 184. Several of the papers in Potash, ed., *Widows in African Societies*, esp. C. Obbo, 'Some East African Widows', pp. 84–106, contain vivid discussions of this point. See also Keene, *Medieval Winchester*, p. 190.

[26] Goldberg, *Women*, p. 267.

[27] Phythian-Adams, *Coventry*, pp. 92, 155; B.A. Hanawalt, *The Ties that Bind: Peasant Families in Medieval England* (New York and Oxford, 1986), pp. 220–26; J.M. Bennett, *Women in the Medieval English Countryside* (New York and Oxford, 1987), 142–76; P.J.P. Goldberg, 'Women in Fifteenth-Century Town Life' in *Towns and Townspeople in the Fifteenth Century*, ed. J.A.F. Thomson (Gloucester, 1988), pp. 106–28; Goldberg, *Women*, pp. 318–21; Keene, *Medieval Winchester*, pp. 388–89; Potash, *Widows in African Societies*, p. 125.

establish families.[28] In the artisan community, during the relatively hard times which prevailed at the beginning of the fourteenth century, the craftsman's widow would have been an especially attractive match, despite the low value of her goods on an absolute scale, just as she seems to have been at a time of similar economic conditions in the late sixteenth century.[29] On the other hand, the period around 1300 was one of great expansion in London's retail trade, especially in luxury items, and that may have provided special opportunities for widows to earn a living on their own. Even among artisans and shop-keepers, the balance of opportunities open to widows probably differed according to the trade with which they were associated. There is no way, however, of estimating the rate of remarriage among London widows at that time, least of all among those of craftsmen. Scarcely less obscure are the social pressures to remarry which bore upon artisan widows. They presumably involved the woman's potential as a provider for a man and as a generator of heirs, both for the husband and for the kin- or craft-group as a whole. For the kin, the remarriage of a widow might constitute one means of continuing and strengthening the family and business networks which had focused on her late husband. Remarriage to a close associate of the husband or to a permitted relative was one way of accomplishing this, while remarriage to a stranger was a way of assimilating new resources and new energy into the clan. Such pressure from the kin, well attested since biblical times, may have been especially strong within a closely-knit craft community.[30]

What is virtually certain, despite the lack of direct evidence from London in this period, is that widows greatly outnumbered widowers. While some women in the citizen class enjoyed positions of wealth and independence as widows, many widows were poor. Their independence as householders was generally achieved at the cost of a very simple, even harsh, daily existence, remote from the city's main theatres of work and profit, in which most women could only participate as the attachments of men. Widows thus gravitated towards, or congregated in, cheap accommodation, often in marginal localities. As such, in many periods and societies, they constituted a distinct urban group, widely recognised as deserving charity from their kin and from the world at large.[31] In thirteenth-century London a royal charter affirmed the rights of widows to

---

[28] For discussion of this in the rural context, see J. Ravensdale, 'Population Changes and the Transfer of Customary Land on a Cambridgeshire Manor in the Fourteenth Century', in *Land, Kinship and Life-Cycle*, ed. R.M. Smith (Cambridge, 1984), pp. 197–225; Bennett, *Women*, pp. 142–76.

[29] V. Brodsky, 'Widows in Late Elizabethan London'; cf. Goldberg, *Women*, pp. 271, 273.

[30] For the importance of such expectations, see Potash, *Widows in African Societies*, esp. pp. 96, 110; and Genesis 38:8–10 (the story of Onan and the obligation of the levirate). D. O'Hara, 'Ruled by my Friends: Aspects of Marriage in the Diocese of Canterbury, c. 1540–1570', *Continuity and Change*, 6 (1991), pp. 9–41, explores some of these issues.

[31] Chabot, 'Widowhood'; Goldberg, *Women*, pp. 313–18; Archer, *Pursuit*, pp. 190, 192, 260; Phythian-Adams, *Coventry*, pp. 155, 243; cf. M. Mollat, *The Poor in the Middle Ages: An Essay in Social History* (New Haven and London, 1986), 28–29; see below, pp. 23–25.

exemption from certain taxes, although it must be admitted that some of the women involved were substantial traders.[32]

The manufacture of leather from raw hides, a process in which tanners played a fundamental part, was a major industry in medieval England. In the earlier middle ages tanning was often distinctively associated with towns, and with particular neighbourhoods within them. The process itself was a messy one, using foul materials and large quantities of water: the stink of the tannery, and doubtless of the tanner himself, would have been obvious to neighbours. Within society at large, association with a tanner was a mark of low status, as the story of William the Conqueror's parentage shows.[33] Nevertheless, the trade required significant capital investment in raw materials and plant, including land upon which to site the tanneries, and resources which would enable the tanner to wait the many months which it took for leather to be processed.[34] Already in the twelfth century, the London tanners formed a distinctive craft community and had their guildhall in Broad Street, on part of the site later occupied by Austin Friars.[35] That was an appropriate location, close to the marshy area around the upper Walbrook stream within the walls, where presumably the tanners had their pits and troughs.[36] In the thirteenth and early fourteenth centuries, following the expansion of the city, the tanners' dwellings and yards were commonly to be found outside the walls, especially outside Newgate, Cripplegate and Bishopsgate.[37] Outside Newgate, in the parish of St. Sepulchre, a number of them lived in Seacoal Lane, Wendagain Lane and other lanes near the Holborn or Fleet stream, next to which they presumably had their workplaces. Both there and outside Cripplegate, in the parish of St Giles, they had ready access to the market in raw hides which was

[32] *LBC*, pp. 36–7; W. Illingworth and J. Caley, ed., *Rotuli Hundredorum* i (London, 1812), p. 403.

[33] D.C. Douglas, *William the Conqueror: The Norman Impact upon England* (London, 1964), pp. 379–80.

[34] For the tanner's trade in medieval towns, see F. Barlow, M. Biddle, O. von Feilitzen and D.J. Keene in *Winchester in the Early Middle Ages: An Edition and Discussion of the Winton Domesday*, ed. M. Biddle, Winchester Studies, 1 (Oxford, 1972), pp. 427, 434; Keene, *Medieval Winchester*, pp. 287–89; D. Keene, 'Tanning' in *Object and Economy in Medieval Winchester*, ed. M. Biddle, Winchester Studies 7.ii (Oxford, 1990), pp. 243–45; M. Kowaleski, 'Town and Country in Late Medieval England: The Hide and Leather Trade' in *Work in Towns, 850–1850*, ed. P. Corfield and D. Keene (Leicester, 1990), pp. 57–93.

[35] P.L. Hull, ed., *The Cartulary of Launceston Priory (Lambeth Palace MS 719): A Calendar*, Devon and Cornwall Record Society, new series, 30 (1987), nos 247, 250.

[36] For the physical characteristics of this locality in London, see C. Maloney and D. de Moulins, *The Upper Walbrook in the Roman Period*, Council for British Archaeology Research Report, 69, (London, 1990).

[37] E. Ekwall, ed., *Two Early London Subsidy Rolls* (Lund, 1951), pp. 158, 160, 179, 189, 230, 283–87, 312–13. The groups of tanners outside Cripplegate and outside Newgate were about the same size, with the former being perhaps the larger. The group outside Bishopsgate seems to have been much smaller.

associated with the livestock trade in Smithfield and with the butchers inside Newgate. Tanners outside Cripplegate occupied sites adjoining the well-watered area known as 'the Moor', especially in Moor Street, and those outside Bishopsgate, in the parish of St Botolph, probably occupied a similar position in relation to the Moor.

The tanners of this period were characterised by a dense network of family and apprenticeship relationships. This seems both to have arisen from, and is reflected in, the physical proximity of their households in the suburbs, their interdependence in the practice of their craft, a distinctive pattern of migration between certain country districts and the city, and perhaps, as we have seen, the retention of daughters within the trade. A limited number of place-names, most notably those of a group of villages on the borders of Essex and Hertfordshire within about seven miles of Bishop's Stortford,[38] tend to recur among the tanners' bynames. In this case, rural resources and rural patterns of association contributed to the formation of a craft community within the city. In the absence of firm information on family structures, of comparable studies cf other crafts and of an agreed methodology for assessing the social density and cohesion of an artisan group, it is difficult to say how distinctive these characteristics were. Nevertheless, the links indicated by recurrent place-names and personal names over a long period, by the relative social and occupational homogeneity of the suburban neighbourhoods where the tanners worked, and by their unique corporate control of the trading outlet at the heart of the city known as Tanners' Seld, do seem to indicate at least a different degree of social density than is to be found, for example, among bakers, shoemakers, weavers or hosiers in the thirteenth and early fourteenth centuries. These issues remain to be explored, and one purpose of this essay is to encourage that process. It remains likely, however, that the noxious character of the tanners' trade occasioned a segregation from the main mass of Londoners which had social as well as physical manifestations and promoted an especially strong cohesion within the craft.

By the early fourteenth century membership of the tanners' guild, as with that of other craft associations, had come to be one of the means by which individuals could obtain the citizenship of London. Little is known of the structure of the guild other than the fact of its existence, which may have been continuous since the twelfth century. While in about 1300 the tanners had an acknowledged, and probably recently-acquired, place in the city's political structure, they were far from prominent within it. In terms of taxed wealth they ranked well below the mercantile elite, although the richest tanners were among the wealthiest of the artisan groups. Geoffrey of Houndsditch, for example, was the wealthiest taxpayer in Bishopsgate ward in 1292, and fifteen

---

[38] Henham, Stansted and Ugley (Essex), and Braughing, Hadham, Hormead and Standon (Hertfordshire).

years later his son still had his gold ring, as well as other valuable possessions.[39] Geoffrey seems to have been exceptional, however, and the valuation of his goods for subsidy was higher than that known for any other tanner. In this period no tanner became an alderman, and most tanners were to be found among the lowest ranks of those assessed for subsidies, along with many other small dealers and craftsmen. Even so, those of them who were so assessed probably fell within the richest 10 to 20 per cent of the city's householders, and so were far from poverty-stricken. Around 1300 there appear to have been between twenty and twenty-five tanners who were wealthy enough to be assessed for subsidies, and similar numbers of them are recorded as committing trade offences or dealing at the seld. These men were presumably the elite of a craft in which there would also have been lesser artisans and journeymen. The size of the elite suggests that overall the tanners were a little more numerous than the kissers (a leather-dealing or -working craft), but much less so than the cordwainers (who made and sold shoes), the fishmongers, and the cornmongers.[40]

The most remarkable feature of the London tanners' community before the later fourteenth century was the establishment known as Tanners' Seld, which was in Cheapside almost opposite the church of St Mary le Bow. Cheapside was the city's principal commercial street. It contained a lively street market, mostly in foodstuffs, with both sedentary and ambulatory traders. It was also the main retail trading district, especially for luxury goods. This trade was conducted from several hundred small shops facing on to the street, and from many more stations within the private bazaars known as selds which stood behind the rows of shops. Near Tanners' Seld were shops and selds occupied by saddlers, girdlers and cofferers, all of whom would have used the leather supplied by the tanners. Next to St Mary le Bow was Cordwainer Street (now Bow Lane) where shoemakers once had their shops, although by 1300 they were giving way to hosiers and drapers. Tawyers, who processed and dealt in skins and leather,[41] had shops near Tanners' Seld which was evidently the focus within Cheapside for the leather market.

So far as it is possible to tell, Tanners' Seld was the principal, if not the sole, trading outlet within the walls for the hides supplied by the city's tanners. Out of town or unenfranchised tanners, who by the fourteenth century had a

[39] CLRO, HR 35 (72): will of William of Houndsditch. Wills enrolled in the court of Husting are identified hereafter by reference to the manuscript. Calendared versions, often omitting important information, are readily identifiable in *HW*

[40] Ekwall, *Subsidy Rolls*, pp. 102, 109 (see also n. 37, above); A.H. Thomas, ed., *Calendar of Early Mayor's Court Rolls Preserved among the Archives of the Corporation of the City of London at Guildhall, A.D. 1298–1307* (Cambridge, 1924), hereafter referred to as *Early Mayor's Court Rolls*. pp. 60–4.

[41] For the craft of the tawyer (*allutarius* or *megucer*), see E.M. Veale, *The English Fur Trade in the Later Middle Ages* (Oxford, 1966), pp. 25–6; Keene, *Medieval Winchester*, pp. 286–9; and Rubin, *Dictionarius*, s. n.

defined status as non-citizens, were at this time supposed to sell their hides from a much less advantageous location near Cheapside in Friday Street.[42] While saddles could command fabulous prices, most leather goods were not among the highest value commodities traded in Cheapside. Dealers in those high value goods, including woollen cloth, mercery (linen, silks, etc.), gold and jewellery, and spices, all competed for trading space within the immediate neighbourhood of Tanners' Seld, driving up the site values of shops and selds to extraordinary levels.[43] This seems to have compelled the city tanners who had come to be established there to take special measures to preserve for themselves a retail outlet in what was some of the most expensive dealing space in the city. By 1300 it was almost certainly anomalous for a group of relatively humble extra-mural craftsmen to have access in this way to space in the heart of the city's business district for the sale of processed hides.

Tanners' Seld presented a striking contrast to the other selds.[44] Like them, it occupied a long, narrow site measuring about 100 feet in length by 25 feet next to Cheapside, but it lacked the intervening row of shops and opened directly on to the street. Inside, rather than the lockable chests and cupboards to be found in the other selds, there were rows of tables, boards, or stalls (all these terms are used), on which the tanners presumably displayed their hides for sale.[45] While the land and the building which stood on it were charged with substantial quit rents to private landlords, the tanners communally managed to control the property, probably from at least as early as 1246 when the name Tanners' Seld is first recorded. The association of the property with the trade in hides is mentioned even earlier in the thirteenth century, and more than any other seld in Cheapside this one was closely linked with a particular craft. Each plot of land with a table on it inside the seld seems to have been in the possession of an individual tanner, but the imperative to preserve the seld as a corporate outlet was so strong that the plots were passed on, often by testamentary disposition, only to practitioners of the craft. This was in sharp contrast to the practice among the owners of plots in other selds in the neighbourhood. In a couple of cases tanners provided for a plot to revert to the 'society' or 'fraternity' of tanners, should there be a failure of heirs in the craft. The tanners seem communally to have maintained the building which sheltered the stalls and which several times was described as a house. They apparently paid the quit rents due from the whole property, perhaps by means of a levy on each plot. Thus, in 1351 a group of tanners, 'with the assent of the

---

[42] *LBG*, p. 260.

[43] For this characterisation of the neighbourhood, see Keene and Harding, *Cheapside*, passim; D. Keene, *Cheapside before the Great Fire* (London, 1985); H.T. Riley, ed., *Munimenta Gildhallae Londoniensis: Liber Albus, Liber Custumarum et Liber Horn, in archivis Gildhallae asservati*, iii (Rolls Series, London, 1862), pp. 441–2.

[44] The following account of the seld is derived from Keene and Harding, *Cheapside*, no. 103/42 (in the parish of St Mary le Bow), and the sources there cited.

[45] There are many references to the tables and boards in the seld, but only one to a chest.

brothers and sisters of the house of Tanners' Seld', leased to another tanner a plot of land there where he could sell his merchandise, in return for a rent which was to be paid to the wardens of the fraternity, and the grantors being responsible for the services due to the lords of the fee.[46]

The lease of 1351, with its implication of corporate possession by the guild of tanners, was exceptional, and perhaps reflects the lack of heirs to those many tanners who had died during the Black Death. Most parts of the seld remained in the seisin of individuals. In 1313 at least eighteen tanners held plots there but, with the city's decline in population, and probably also with changes in the organisation of the trade, the number fell, to about eight by 1358 and to four or five by 1400. The common interest of the tanners declined in the later fourteenth century, when parts of the seld descended or were sold to people outside the craft. A royal claim in 1405 that the seld had been granted to the craft of tanners without licence could not be substantiated, but at about that time, perhaps as a defensive response to this royal intervention, the craft lost its explicit association with Tanners' Seld, and seems soon afterwards to have list its identity as a guild. The trade in leather nevertheless continued in this part of Cheapside, probably with a more mercantile and less communal character than before. The house itself came to be known as 'The Cowface', presumably in reference to a sign which denoted its present or former links with the trade. With changes in the organisation and relative scale of the leather industry during the later middle ages, it seems that citizen tanners, making leather on sites just outside the city walls, had a much smaller role in London's leather trade than formerly, and that out-of-town producers came to the fore. Consequently, in the fifteenth century, the city authorities made more careful provision of places away from Cheapside where the outsiders could trade, and the leather-dealing area in Cheapside itself came to be associated with 'leather-sellers' rather than tanners and tawyers, and with the higher-value, more finished goods.[47]

The direct evidence concerning the tanners' expectations of their wives and widows is to be found almost entirely in their wills. Testamentary provisions rarely, if ever, convey a full picture of the arrangements made for passing on property to widows and children. Apart from the widow's customary rights in her husband's property, it is possible that she held property in her own right or for her lifetime as a joint freeholder or tenant with her husband, who might have no need, therefore, to make explicit provision for her in his will. Likewise, grown up children might have benefited from the gifts made when their father was alive. The provisions of a will, therefore, might be a specific response to one of a wide range of possible circumstances, the details of which, for Londoners before the Black Death, are usually unknown. Nevertheless, tanners' wills do reveal some crucial preferences which affected their widows.

[46] Merchant Taylors' Company, Miscellaneous Documents B3 (at the hall).
[47] Keene and Harding, *Cheapside*, no. 104/42.

Many of those preferences were probably common to most married male testators in London at this time, or to most craftsmen, but a few seem to have been characteristic of tanners alone. The wills and related evidence throw light on a range of issues: the widow's role in maintaining the household and family; her role in the transmission of property and other resources to a future generation; the specific provision made for her livelihood as a widow, according to the circumstances of the family; the wife's role as a direct participant in the work of the tannery or on the distributive side of the trade; her role as a generator of income from domestic activities; the circumstances in which she might continue such activities as widow, or in which she might be compelled to cede control of the business to adult children or to a new husband; and her experience of remarriage. The evidence concerning these questions is often indirect and its context uncertain; it rarely has statistical significance. For those reasons the interpretation initially focuses on the form of the bequests themselves.

Above all, the tanner, like most testators, identified his widow as the person who after his death would ensure the continuity of his household and look after his children. It was much less likely that she would immediately be presiding over the dissolution of the household. Only one tanner mentioned neither wife nor children in his will, and that was during the Black Death.[48] All but three of the thirty-two tanners' wills identified between 1282 and 1370 refer to surviving children. In only one of those twenty-nine cases does it appear that the only surviving child had come of age,[49] although eight other tanners appear to have had adult children in addition to those who were minors. Twenty-three (72 per cent) of the wills mention a living wife, about the same proportion as for London wills overall.[50] All but two of the twenty-three women were named as the principal executor of their husband's will, a clear sign of the widow's responsible role.

Many of the provisions concerning property which the tanners made for their widows were probably common among London citizens of the time, especially among artisans. Twenty-one of the tanners' wives were left a life-interest in a house or other real property in the city. Since in no case was it stated that the legacy was in lieu of dower, it seems at first sight that these legacies were intended to supplement the resources from the tanner's estate to which the widow and children were entitled by custom. Some of the legacies, however, concern interests which closely resemble those associated with dower, and so in some instances they may have served as an unambiguous means, backed up by a written record, of providing the widow with her

---

[48] HR 76(156), dated 1 April 1349: John of Shenfield, the only tanner to mention the fraternity to which he belonged.

[49] HR 28(34): Geoffrey of Houndsditch in 1299; but since the wills of that date are enrolled in an abridged form it is impossible to be certain that he had no other surviving children.

[50] See above, pp. xxii.

customary entitlement. After the widow's death, according to the provisions of the wills, these properties were to remain, in order of preference, to one of the testator's sons and his heirs, to his daughter or daughters and their heirs, or to the testator's nearest heirs. In a case where the wife had a predecessor, and there were no surviving sons of the previous marriage, it was specified that the tenement should remain to the legitimate heirs of the testator and his wife,[51] and in another case legitimate daughters were preferred to an illegitimate son,[52] but it is overwhelmingly clear that, while tanners might leave rents or houses to their daughters as well as to their sons, they hoped that one of their sons would succeed to the property with which they had provided their widow. While a husband certainly took care that his widow was provided for during her lifetime, it is also clear that an important motive for doing so was to enable her to maintain his children, and that one of the roles in which a man cast his widow was as the agent for transmitting property to a male heir.

If some of these wills were in practice defining those parts of the tanner's estate (or some of them) which were to pass to the widow as dower, the arrangement offered several advantages to the husband. He could control the allocation of the properties to his children after his widow's death. Moreover, property entailed in this way was presumably not at risk from a claim by any subsequent husband who became a widower that it was his wife's inheritance, and that consequently he was, by curtesy, entitled to it during his lifetime. In this way the benefit the children gained from the properties would be increased, but at the cost of devaluing the widow for any future husband.

It is not easy to assess the value of the endowment received by tanners' widows in this way. William of Hadham, a widower and not a prominent tanner, left to his under-age daughter a modest estate for which a valuation, made in 1308, survives.[53] The goods, including domestic utensils, furnishings, two dickers of hides,[54] and four tanners' troughs, were worth £9 0s. 2d. Of this total, a silver cup and eleven silver spoons accounted for £1 1s. 0d., the troughs for 13s. 4d., and the hides for £4. His dwelling with two shops next to it in Seacoal Lane had an annual rental value of £1 12s., less 12s. 2d. in rent charges. The capital value of the whole estate was thus about £18 11s. 10d., at least a quarter of which was represented by the stock in trade. Some tanners' widows would have acquired control of estates four or five times that size.

Two tanners did not appoint their widows as executors, probably for good reason. These stand out as special cases. Thomas de la More, by his will proved in 1282, left two houses in East Smithfield to his widow for life, but left the capital messuage where he lived in Houndsditch to another woman on the same terms. His other properties were to be sold on his death. The strong

---

[51] HR 67(20).

[52] HR 76(224)

[53] HR 36(97).

[54] The dicker, containing ten items, was the standard unit of quantity for hides.

implication is that he was living with (or being cared for by) the other woman, but he may have been senile and confused, since at probate the other woman stated that he had not been of sound memory for two years.[55] Adam Baudry, a member of an extensive clan of tanners outside Cripplegate, whose will was enrolled in 1318, was, however, quite clear in his intention to reduce the role of his widow in the affairs of his family to the minimum possible. He left houses to each of his three children who were minors, including the tenement where he lived to his daughter Amy. His wife Agnes's only legacy was to be a third of the money obtained from selling another tenement. The stock and furnishings in his houses, except for his trade goods and cash (*mercimonia mea et denarii*), were to be divided between his children, who included a grown-up son William. Guardianship of his three younger children was entrusted to his executors, who were to use all the resources of the Guildhall (that is, they were to use the city courts if necessary) to secure their custody. It seems likely that the tanning business was passed on to William.[56] Adam's son John was still a minor in 1331, when his guardianship was granted to the tanner Thomas Kent, a former servant of another Agnes, the widow of John Baudry, tanner.[57] The reason for the breakdown, if such it was, in Adam's marital relationship is not known. The only other tanner who made no specific bequest of real property in favour of his wife (whom he did name as executor, however) was Alexander Baudry, who died in 1335–36 and was a neighbour and landlord of Thomas Kent.[58] At least two of Alexander's three sons were of age, so he may have envisaged that his widow did not require resources with which to maintain children, and possibly that she was too old to be worthy of an endowment which might attract another husband.

Sometimes the widow was left a life interest in what had been the entire marital home, thus augmenting her customary right of dower. Geoffrey of Houndsditch, for example, in a will enrolled in 1299 left his capital messuage in the parish of St Botolph outside Bishopsgate to his wife Cecily, with remainder to his son William. By his will, enrolled in 1307, William in turn left his father's former tenement, in which he himself lived, lying in the same parish, to his wife Elisia on similar terms.[59] Probably seven tanners out of the sample made bequests of this sort to their wives.[60] A further two left to their wives houses

---

[55] HR 13(76).

[56] HR 46(79): early clauses in the will which may have benefited William are omitted from the enrolled version.

[57] *LBE*, p. 260: HR 55(33).

[58] HR 63(138). For other members of the Baudry family in the trade, see HR 78(234); *LBD*, p. 99; *LBE*, p. 117; Ekwall, *Subsidy Rolls*, pp. 158, 283, 287; *Early Mayor's Court Rolls*, p. 60.

[59] HR 28(34), 35 (72). The capital messuage or tenement was generally the one inhabited by its owner: Richard Ussher referred to the tenement where he lived in that way (HR 67(58)); see also Keene, *Medieval Winchester*, pp. 235–36.

[60] The other wills are: HR 38(108), 43(18), 67(58), 75(69), with HR 37(65) being an uncertain case. There may be other cases where the widow acquired the entire dwelling which is simply not so identified among the tenements bequeathed.

next door to the one in which they themselves lived,[61] indicating that the establishment was to be rearranged so that the widow could keep house on a smaller scale than before. Some widows were assigned a part of the house. In 1331 John of Ashridge, another associate of Thomas Kent, left his wife her whole chamber with furniture and furnishings, including most of his clothes.[62] Walter of Shenfield, by providing his widow Joan with her chamber, along with the vessels and utensils for the hall, spence and kitchen, and a third of all his chattels, was giving explicit testamentary expression to her rights under dower. He may have thought that necessary because of the complexity of their marital relationships: Joan had apparently had a previous husband, by whom she had a daughter Alice, to whom Walter left a sum of money. Walter, who had also been married before, appointed Joan the guardian of their two daughters, Alice and Immana, who were eventually to receive his tenements and houses. In addition, Walter had a grown-up illegitimate son (by Alice of Hadham, who was still alive), whom he appears to have intended to take over his tanner's business.[63] In another case, William *dictus* Godalle, who was probably a tanner, specified a long list of domestic furnishings which were to pass to his wife Rose, whom he seems to have expected would have a residence by right of dower in his tenement near Austin Friars.[64] Such careful listing of chattels, which in any case were probably due to the widow by her right of dower, suggests that in practice the widow may often have found it difficult to establish her right to these items against other members of her family who occupied the house.[65]

Many of the properties which the tanners' widows acquired by their husbands' bequest were intended to provide a rental income for them and their children. It is noteworthy how often such legacies included shops, a term which often denoted small houses built in rows for letting rather than purely commercial premises. Richard Ussher, for example, 1339 left the tenement and shops in which he dwelled in the parish of St Sepulchre to his wife Sarah for the term of her life, along with another house and eleven other shops in the same parish.[66] When John le Ussher left a brewhouse and a shop in Holborn, both occupied by tenants, to his wife Immana, he stated that it was in aid of his children, probably those by a previous marriage. On Immana's death those properties, along with others he had left her in Seacole Lane, were to revert to

[61] HR 54(85), 78(234).

[62] HR 60(83).

[63] HR 76(224).

[64] Leathersellers' Company Archive (at the hall), box 10, no. 21. Godalle was not described as a tanner, but owned a chest in Tanners' Seld; tanners were still active close to Austin Friars in the fourteenth century (*Early Mayor's Court Rolls*, p. 161).

[65] It is possible that these lists denoted items which were invested by the testator or the legatee with a special value as gifts, but that explanation seems less likely than the one suggested here since the items are not identified individually in the way that legacies of clothing or jewellery often were.

[66] HR 67(58).

the heirs of his body.[67] Any claims to his real estate which might descend from Immana were thus strictly barred.

Strategies which may have been characteristic of the artisan class, and even of the tanners within that group, are perhaps more apparent in the testamentary provisions which seem to concern the widow's ability to make a living by trade. Sometimes, when an estate was to be divided between the tanner's widow and his children, she was provided with the property which might enable her most readily to make money on her own account. Most often this was a brewhouse. Brewing, customarily a female activity, may have been a critical resource for the tanner's widow with children to support. In this context it is probably significant that Richard Ussher, who was a grandfather, left his two brewhouses and their equipment to his adult son John, who was a working tanner, and only a dwelling and a portfolio of lettable properties to his wife Sarah, whom he presumably perceived as not in need of the extra income that brewing could bring.[68] In contrast, William Twomere left to his wife Idonea a life interest in a brewery, a house, and shops in Moor Street outside Cripplegate, while he left the capital tenement in the same street, where they had presumably lived and which may have contained his tannery, to his son William. Within three years of the will being enrolled Idonea had apparently died and the son was still a minor.[69] Simon of Braughing appears to have had a similar intention when he left his capital brewhouse (which presumably served as his residence too) opposite the church of St Giles outside Cripplegate to his wife Alice for life, and another tenement in the same parish to his son Thomas.[70] William Forester left to his wife Isabel the money he had handed over to her with which to trade and to brew (*ad mercandizandum et braciandum*).[71] She may thus have been intended to carry on the tanning business, since William seems to have left no sons, although it seems more likely that William's male apprentice was designated for that role. William of Houndsditch left his wife Elisia the implements for brewing and tanning, but while she was also left a life interest in the family house outside Bishopsgate, where the tannery was probably situated, her rights to the tools of the two trades were restricted to the time during which she remained unmarried or chaste. When that came to an end, the implements were to pass to William's son Thomas, a minor who was evidently cast as the true successor to the family business. Young Thomas was also designated as the immediate recipient of his grandfather's silver cup, brooch and ring, and of his father's best mazer and best dicker of hides.[72]

---

[67] HR 68(53). For other legacies of shops, apparently with the same purpose, see HR 38(112), 56(101), 75(69); Leathersellers' Company, box 10. no. 21.

[68] HR 67(58).

[69] HR 64(111); *LBE*, p. 42.

[70] HR 38(108). For Simon as a tanner, see *LBD*, 169.

[71] HR 79(121).

[72] HR 35(72).

Several of these cases suggest that there was a preference for distancing the widow from the family tanning business whenever a suitable male successor (not necessarily a legitimate son) could be identified. This strategy may have been common among artisans. Richard le Longe expressed the preference clearly when he directed that his capital tenement (that is, his dwelling) be sold, and that his widow be provided with a house next door, which specifically excluded his house known as *le Betynghous*. The latter was probably the part of his tannery where the foul process of bating (dehairing the hides in dung) was conducted.[73] Despite what may have been a common preference, however, some tanners certainly envisaged that their widows would take over the business. Thomas Swift in 1347 left his wife Avice the ramaining term of his apprentice Ellis, if she wished it, plus his whole establishment opposite the Fleet Prison.[74] William King, who drew up his will in 1348 after all his children had died, left his tenements in Seacoal Lane to his wife Agnes for life along with two leaden tanning troughs and the six remaining years of service of his apprentice John, who was to have one of the troughs when Agnes died.[75] Agnes, widow of John Baudry, tanner, seems to have run a tannery through the agency of her servant Thomas Kent, whom she designated in her will, enrolled in 1327, as the preferred purchaser of lands in Moor Street when the life-term she left to her brother came to an end. Kent was later a tanner in his own right and did purchase the property.[76] Widows who maintained a tanning business on their own, at least for a time, could play an important part in the continuity of the trade, as we shall see in the case of those who remarried.

The notion that the trade was to be passed on to the children, and that the widow had no more than a temporary guardianship role,[77] is especially evident in the tanners' bequests of the tools of their craft. This was a common policy among artisans, but the tanners appear to have had a special concern to secure the descent of craft resources to their heirs, a feeling which may have been widespread among all poorer craftsmen. Geoffrey of Chelsea left a leaden trough each to three of his four under-age children, and a trough not made of lead (it was presumably made of wood) to the child then in his wife's womb. He appears to have had an adult son Geoffrey, who may have been active in the trade, but his widow was to have a life interest in the tenement where he lived in St Sepulchre's parish and, since she was specifically designated as guardian of two of the children with troughs, was probably intended to run at least a part of the family tanning business until they came of age.[78] John le Ussher left three troughs of lead, three of wood, other vessels of wood, and unspecified instruments of the tanner's trade to his wife Immana, specifically for the

---

[73] HR 54(85).

[74] HR 75(69).

[75] HR 79(74).

[76] HR 55(33), 64 (90).

[77] For a similar attitude at a later date, see Phythian-Adams, *Coventry*, p. 91.

[78] HR 43(18).

maintenance of his children.[79] Roger of Chipstead left 10 marks and his third-best leaden trough to his daughter Maud, who was to remain in the custody of his widow until she was of age. He had two sons, one of whom was of age and probably already established as a tanner, so that Maud's trough may have been seen as her due share of the family business.[80] The bequests of troughs may in some sense have been symbolic. They suggest that wives, widows and daughters actively participated in work in the stinking and sloppy surroundings of the tannery. They may represent that share of the income from a tannery run by a widow which was to be designated for the support of an individual child, and which could not be alienated on, for example, the widow's remarriage. When a child came of age they provided a means by which a son could set up in business on his own, or a dowry with which a daughter could attract a tanner husband. Always, they were for the benefit of children who were minors, not for the direct benefit of the widows themselves, and not for that of children already established in business.

Four of the tanners' widows were left tables, stalls, or plots of land in Tanners' Seld. Widows in other crafts associated with Cheapside selds were not marked out by their husbands for bequests of trading sites of this type. Given the general prominence of women and widows in distributive trade, it might seem that the tanners' widows, by possession of one of these outlets in Cheapside, enjoyed an opportunity to make an independent income which was greater than that enjoyed by widows in other trades, and that this paralleled their experience as wives.[81] On close examination, however, it appears that the bequests were concerned with the widow's role, as perceived by her husband, to conserve and transmit a scarce resource for the benefit of male members of the craft, rather than primarily to secure to the wife a means of continuing her independent activity in trade. The conditions placed upon the legacies of parts of the seld were more restrictive than those concerning brewhouses and rents, and show how highly the tanners valued the outlets as a part of their businesses. To leave one to a widow was something of a last resort. Moreover, among London-based tanners, the association between women and the distributive side of the trade may have been less strong than in some other crafts, on account of the distance (a walk of at least fifteen minutes duration) between Tanners' Seld and the extra-mural dwellings where the women would have been based. The opportunity to 'mind the shop' and look after a household at the same time, which would have been open to many of the women in Cheapside who kept shop while their families lived behind, was not available to the tanners' wives. The apparently standard conditions which the tanners placed upon these bequests show that it was evidently the custom for the widow to retain the table in the seld only so long as she remained a widow, or if

---

[79] HR 68(53).
[80] HR 64(79).
[81] Cf. Abram, 'Women Traders'.

she married another tanner. Tanners placed a premium on retaining this resource within the craft, and on the widow's particular role as a means of recruiting and assimilating new manpower and resources to the family and craft group.[82]

All four tanners who bequeathed tables on these terms seem to have had children who were minors.[83] They directed that once the widow remarried outside the craft, the tables were to remain to a son, to a nephew or to a male apprentice. The wills do not explicitly state that the remainders came into effect on the death of the widow. Possibly, if the widow married another tanner and then died before him, the table was that tanner's to dispose. For the tanners there seems to have been no special association between women and distributive trade at the seld. Walter of Shenfield, who died in 1348–49 leaving a widow and two daughters under age, bequeathed his table in the seld not to them but to his illegitimate son, John of Hadham.[84] William Forester, who left no children and who provided his widow with money for her to trade and to brew, hoped that his table would pass to an heir in the tanner's trade, but if that was not possible to his apprentice John.[85] Five other tanners, of whom three had wives when they composed their wills, left tables or other interests in the seld to their sons, and in one case to an apprentice if the son did not wish to follow the trade.[86] The stalls in Tanners' Seld were evidently thought of as inseparable from the production side of the tanner's business, which wherever possible was in the hands of men: the restricted market in these stalls stands in sharp contrast to the much freer one in the plots and other trading stations within all other Cheapside selds and shops. This is not to say that tanners' wives played no part in managing stalls at the seld which were held in their husbands' names, indeed the reference to the 'brothers and sisters of Tanners' Seld' suggests (but does not prove) that some of them assumed that role. Even so, women seem to have been less prominent as stall-holders in Tanners' Seld than they were in other shops and selds nearby, especially in those associated with the sale of textiles and clothing where some of the women were certainly working away from home.[87] Among the tanners in the early fourteenth century, the widow was only allowed to control a table at the seld when there were children to be maintained. In general, it seems that the distributive trade in tanned hides did not offer to women the same opportunities for making an independent living as that in textiles and some other goods. This was in part a

---

[82] For this common role of the widow, cf. Potash, *Widows in African Societies*, p. 110.

[83] HR 64(53, 79), 68(53), 98(55).

[84] HR 76(224).

[85] HR 79(121).

[86] HR 28(34), 67(58), 77(244), 89(60); Leathersellers' Company Box 10, no. 21.

[87] Keene, 'Shops and Shopping', p. 41. This comparison is not without problems since it is difficult to determine whether the prevalence of women as shopkeepers in the textile and clothing trades was a distinctively late fourteenth-century phenomenon or whether it was equally characteristic of the thirteenth century. On balance the latter seems more likely.

reflection of the distinctive structure of the tanners' business in the city and of the relatively low value of the product, but it also arose from a policy of restriction imposed by male tanners with a view to conserving a commercial resource for the craft.

Despite their limited, though essential, role in strategies concerning family and craft succession constructed by their husbands, some tanners' widows evidently managed to pursue an independent life supported by an income from rents, from brewing, perhaps from small-scale money-lending,[88] or even from the tanner's trade. How such women fended for themselves, how they were regarded by others, and the degree of solicitude and affection for them as individuals which may have informed their husbands' bequests remain largely unknown. Nevertheless, those who remained *sole* for any length of time while active in the tanning trade seem to have been few in number. Presumably the pressure to remarry, especially to another tanner, was strong, on account of the resources vested in them and the relative poverty of the craft. The phrase, 'brothers and sisters of the house of Tanners' Seld' appears to have denoted a conventional association between husbands and wives in the guild,[89] and perhaps the part that some women played in managing stalls on behalf of their husbands, but not any distinctive role enjoyed by the women at the seld as independent, unmarried traders. Thus among the forty-three tanners who are named as committing trade offences or as occupying the seld in lists compiled in 1300, 1313 and 1358, there is only one woman, Joan Michel. Nothing is known of her family or marital status, and it is far from certain that she was a widow. She achieved some prominence and was independently active at the seld over at least nine years, appearing first in 1351, when in conjunction with four tanners and the two wardens of the craft she leased a plot of land in the seld to William Baldwin, tanner.[90]

Most tanners' widows are identifiable as individuals only in their husbands' wills. Moreover, confusion over the names and identities of the tanners and their wives seems to have been common, perhaps a reflection of an exceptional complexity and informality in their family relationships, as well as of a more widespread fluidity in naming-practice.[91] Only two of the widows in this period who left wills, Agnes widow of John Baudry and Agnes of Henham, are known

---

[88] No certain case of money-lending by a tanner's widow has been identified, although in 1371 Margery widow of John Styrap lent £15 to a tanner, taking his property in Wendagain Lane and his stall in Tanners' Seld as security: HR 99(14, 15).

[89] Cf. Kowaleski and Bennett, 'Crafts and Gilds', pp. 14–15.

[90] *Early Mayor's Court Rolls*, p. 60; *London Assize of Nuisance, 1301–1431*, ed. H.M. Chew and W. Kellaway, London Record Society, 10 (1973), nos. 187, 501; Merchant Taylors' Company (at the hall), Miscellaneous Documents, B3. CLRO, Husting Pleas of Land, 80, m. 9; Husting Common Pleas, 84, m. 16d.

[91] Christiana, the daughter of William of Houndsditch, was once described as the daughter of William's father, and her mother's name is recorded both as Elisia and as Elena: HR 35(72); *LBD*, pp. 181. 187.

certainly to have been the widows of tanners, although two others probably were.[92] Not one of the four wills is particularly informative, so it is difficult to generalise concerning the tanners' wives' experience of widowhood or remarriage. Nevertheless, the marital careers of several of them can be reconstructed, indicating some experiences which may have been common. Richard de la More, a tanner whose will was enrolled in 1285, left his capital house and appurtenances in Seacoal Lane to his daughter Hawise. Her unusual name provides clues as to her later career. She was probably the Hawise, widow of John of Hadham, who in 1309 with her co-executor Richard Ussher (a tanner who had several connections with people from Hadham) testified that Walter of Hadham had been her late husband's apprentice as a tanner, and who did same for Henry of Stansted in 1310.[93] She seems later to have been known as Hawise of Mimms, probably by virtue of a marriage to William of Mimms, a tanner who was active in 1292 and 1313. As Hawise of Mimms, widow, in 1314 she granted a tenement in Seacoal Lane which she had acquired from another tanner, to Richard Ussher, tanner, who subsequently made his home in the property. By her will enrolled in 1316, in which she revealed that her father's name had been Richard, she directed her executors (Richard Ussher, Richard of Hadham and Lawrence of Hadham) to sell her tenements, houses and shops in Seacoal Lane.[94] As the daughter and then twice as a widow, Hawise seems to have provided a key element of continuity in a tanning business conducted on the same site over more than thirty years. If she had any distinctive success as a widow in business, that may have been due ultimately to her position as her widowed father's heir.

A similar chain of associations can be traced with a branch of the Henham family. In or before 1282 Walter of Henham, tanner, and his wife Cecily granted land and houses outside Newgate next to the Holborn stream to Robert of Henham and his wife Agnes, who was probably their daughter. By 1292 Cecily had been widowed and had married Richard Berynger of Standon, a tanner. Agnes of Henham was then widowed and took a tawyer (*allutarius*) as her second or subsequent husband, whom she outlived by at least five years. By her will, proved in July 1311 with two tanners as witnesses, she left a tenement in Wendagain Lane to Walter of Chipstead, tanner, and his wife Cecily, who was Agnes's daughter, and their heirs, with remainder to Cecily's son by an earlier partner. Walter gained the freedom of the city of London in April 1311.[95] Here the associations of the leather trade, of the neighbourhood outside Newgate, and of villages near Bishop's Stortford, seem to have combined with the remarriages of widows and with a legacy, or the

---

[92] HR 11(22), 35(48), 40(21), 45(11).
[93] *LBD*, pp. 100, 117, 138. On the latter occasion she was identified as the widow of Richard of Hadham (although a tanner of that name was still alive at the time).
[94] HR 21(44), 45(11), 75(73); *Assize of Nuisance*, no. 187.
[95] HR 13(51), 20(51), 21(63), 35(48), 40(21); *LBD*, p. 68.

immediate prospect of one, to enable a tanner to make a decisive step in his career: significantly, the interests of the son whom Cecily brought to the marriage with Walter were put second to those of the offspring of the new partnership. Nevertheless, descent via widows seems to have been a key aspect of the transmission of the resource.

The fourth widow whose will is known was Cecily, widow of Robert Harding, who by her testament enrolled in 1280 left separate parts of her inherited property in Seacoal Lane to her sons William and John. The boys were to pass into the guardianship of their uncle William of Hadham, who is separately recorded as a tanner. It seems possible that Robert Harding and William of Hadham were also known as Robert of Hadham and William Harding respectively.[96] John may well have been the John of Hadham, tanner, who, as we have seen, married Hawise daughter of Richard de la More, indicating the close network of marital connections within the group of tanners

Two tanners' widows were upwardly mobile. Christiana married John Neweman, a tanner outside Cripplegate who was admitted to the freedom of London in 1312. Her brother, John Graunt, was apprenticed as a tanner in the same year. Neweman died in or before 1322, apparently with only modest wealth and leaving four children under age. Christiana then married a furbisher in Ironmonger Lane (not far from Tanners' Seld), who died in 1327–28. From her first husband Christiana acquired a life interest in a tenement outside Cripplegate, which on her second widowhood she augmented by similar interests in houses and rents in Ironmonger Lane, near St Benet Gracechurch, and in Eastcheap. This estate stood her in good stead for a third marriage to a William of Pontefract, who was probably the alderman of that name.[97] This possibly fortuitous career after marriage to a tanner surpassed even that of Elisia (or Elena), left a widow by William of Houndsditch in or before 1307. She had at least one child under age and possessed the family home outside Bishopsgate which had probably once been the headquarters of Geoffrey of Houndsditch, apparently the most successful London tanner of the age. By 1310, she had married William of Pontefract, a skinner who was probably not identical with the later alderman of that name, although he may have been related to him. The skinner seems to have moved to the house outside Bishopsgate, where in 1319 he was a prominent local resident. While Elena was entitled to the house for the term of her life, by her remarriage she forfeited her right to her former husband's tanning and brewing equipment, which passed to their son.[98]

---

[96] HR 6(7), 9(19), 11(22).

[97] HR 50(82), 56(22), LBE, p. 162; Ekwall, *Subsidy Rolls*, pp. 230, 283; Keene and Harding, *Cheapside*, no. 95/3–5; Beaven, *Aldermen*, i (London, 1908), p. 385 confuses him with the skinner of the same name.

[98] HR 35(72), *LBD*, pp. 181, 187, 223, 230; Ekwall, *Subsidy Rolls*, p. 230.

These women stand in sharp contrast to most tanners' widows who immediately disappear from the historian's view. Nevertheless, circumstantial evidence allows some speculation as to their fate. It seems likely, for example, that many widows who had young children to maintain soon chose remarriage,[99] very often to another tanner in the neighbourhood. Many of the widows without dependent children, or who had passed child-bearing age, probably did not remarry. Widows with adult children tended to be excluded from practising the trade of tanning, the resources for which would have passed to a son (legitimate or not), to a son-in-law, or to the husband's apprentice. Perhaps it was the older widows who lacked children (either their own or their husband's), or those who had young children but had not remarried, who had the best chance of continuing work in the tanner's craft on their own account for an extended period of time. There were probably not many of them.

It is only possible to guess at the conditions in which most of the tanners' widows lived on their own, and at the survival strategies and support networks which they may have developed among themselves. Like single women and widows generally, they presumably tended to group together in poor, marginal locations outside the city walls. In their case, these were also the neighbourhoods in which they had lived and worked as wives, but they may well have drifted to the less desirable and less expensive locations. Even the wealthier tanners' widows were to be found in houses which were intermingled with the tanning yards and other installations. To judge from the assumptions implicit in the tanners' wills, which were powerful instruments for constructing their widows' lack of entitlement as well as for providing them with support, the widow who continued independently with any success in the trade was likely to have been an exception. It seems possible too that one who was conspicuously successful in commerce would have been regarded with some suspicion or unease. But whether Hawise of Mimms or Joan Michel was ever the nightmare of the male imagination, which, it has been argued, found expression in the character of the Wife of Bath, is more than it is possible to know.[100]

This examination of the widows in a single craft group in early fourteenth-century London shows that the tanner's widows shared a number of characteristics with widows in other artisan groups and with widows in general. Husbands often made special provision for the maintenance of their widows, to reinforce or augment what was due to them as dower, especially when there were children to be supported. These provisions, and the itemisation of the chattels due to the widow, betray an awareness that she might be cheated out of what was rightfully hers. A widow could carry on her husband's business, if

[99] See above, p. 8.
[100] Cf. Ellis, 'Merchant's Wife's Tale'. See also the subtle account in J. Pitt-Rivers, 'Honour and Social Status', in J.G. Peristiany, ed., *Honour and Shame: the Values of Mediterranean Society* (London, 1965), pp. 19–78, esp. pp. 70–71.

only for a short time, on her own. The pressure on her to remarry was strong, especially within the craft, and this seems to have been a particular feature of groups whose resources were scarce. Older widows seem to have been less likely to remarry than younger ones, or than widowers of the same age, although the case of the tanners throws no particular light on this issue. Some widows, by accident or design, came to be exceptionally well-endowed, which enabled them to remarry with conspicuous success.

Other characteristics appear to be distinctively associated with the tanners' widows, although given the difficulties of the sources and the absence of comparable studies for other craft groups certainty is impossible. Most conspicuous, perhaps, is the degree to which tanners' widows were cast by their husbands in the role of vessels for the transmission of resources from one generation of male practitioners of the craft to the next. Within marriage they may frequently have participated in the production and distributive sides of the tanner's trade, but as widows their freedom of action independently to follow even the distributive side seems to have been more circumscribed than that of widows in some other trades. Their relative prominence in testaments concerning Tanners' Seld reflects the need that their husbands felt to set limits to their activities rather than their special role as independent traders.

Several reasons can be suggested for this apparently distinctive position. The tanners were among the poorer of the artisan groups. Their trade had foul associations and was pursued on the margins of the city. By an historical accident, however, they enjoyed a commercial outlet in one of the city's most expensive neighbourhoods. All this promoted the tanners' cohesion as a professional group, and caused them to develop a distinctive strategy for retaining among themselves the valuable manufacturing and commercial equipment and buildings which they needed in order to survive. In almost all crafts full-time, professional activity had come to be seen as the distinctive preserve of men. Widows were potentially a channel for the leakage of craft resources to other groups. Nowhere did this pose a greater threat than with Tanners' Seld in Cheapside. Ultimately, in the later fourteenth century, the loss of shares in the seld by the marriage of daughters and widows outside the craft was one of the factors which brought to an end the tanners' remarkable and long-lasting communal control of the property. The tanners' response was exactly comparable to the male pressure on widows to remarry which is commonly to be found in other contexts, in both town and country, when incomes and possessions were difficult to come by. This pressure to conserve the resource by setting limits to the widow's freedom of action may have disappeared after the Black Death, when living standards rose and the opportunity to profit from small-scale manufactures and trading increased, and when in any case there were major changes in the leather trade. Before then, many of the tanners' widows may eventually have escaped those restrictions by remarriage out of the craft, or by survival into an independent, but perhaps often impoverished, old age. A few may have found that widowhood provided an opportunity for independent prosperity. We should not conclude that the daily lives of the tanners' widows were necessarily as restricted as seems to be indicated by those male transactions which provide virtually the only evidence for them. Yet any pleasures or sorrows that the widows may have found in their release remain beyond our knowledge.

1. The disconsolate widow, her book of devotions in her hand. Behind her is the bereft marriage bed and the corpse of her husband is being prepared for burial. By Jan de Tavernier, 1454. The Hours of Philip the Good, Koninklijke Bibliotheek, MS 76.F.2, f. 169 (*By permission of the Royal Library, The Hague*)

2

Elizabeth de Burgh, Lady of Clare (d. 1360)

Jennifer C. Ward

Elizabeth de Burgh, as the cousin of Edward III and coheiress to one-third of the inheritance of the Clare earls of Gloucester, ranked among the higher English nobility, and although her connections with London were significant her landed responsibilities and social contacts gave her a much wider import-ance in the kingdom of England. It was only in the 1350s that she had her London house and spent part of the year there; before that, London was simply a source of supply of luxury and imported items for her household. Why London became of greater importance to her in her old age is a question to be addressed later.

Elizabeth was the youngest daughter of Gilbert de Clare, earl of Gloucester and Hertford and of Joan of Acre, daughter of Edward I. She was born in September 1295, three months before the death of her father; her mother died in 1307. The following year Elizabeth was married to John de Burgh, the eldest son of the earl of Ulster, in a double ceremony in which her brother Earl Gilbert married the earl of Ulster's daughter.[1] The name by which Elizabeth was known by her contemporaries came about as a result of this first marriage. Her household accounts gave her the title of Elizabeth de Burgh, lady of Clare, and royal documents sometimes also describe her as the king's kinswoman.[2] John died in 1313 leaving Elizabeth with one son, William, the last de Burgh earl of Ulster, who was killed in Belfast in 1333.[3]

Widowhood in theory gave a woman independence; she counted as a *femme sole* and held property in her own right. As John de Burgh's widow Elizabeth enjoyed her jointure, the lands which had been settled on her and John jointly at the time of their marriage, for the rest of her life. However the independ-ence of the widow can be exaggerated and this is apparent in Elizabeth's case. The death of her brother Earl Gilbert, childless, at the battle of Bannockburn in 1314, leaving his three sisters as coheiresses to the Clare inheritance, meant that Elizabeth came under considerable pressure from fortune hunters and

---

[1] Details of Elizabeth's marriages are given in *Complete Peerage*, iii, p. 245; iv, pp. 43–45; xii, part 2, pp. 177–78, 251.

[2] E.g. *CPR, 1327–30*, p. 32.

[3] *Complete Peerage*, xii, pt 2, pp. 178–79.

from the king. The Clare lands comprised the wealthiest non-royal baronial inheritance, being worth about £6,000 a year,[4] and the problems of dividing such an inheritance at a time of political instability were such that it was not carried out until 1317.[5] Elizabeth's attraction as an heiress may well be the explanation for her runaway marriage in 1316 with Theobald de Verdun who was alleged to have abducted her from Bristol Castle.[6] Widowed again within a few months, she came under pressure from the king to marry Roger Damory in the spring of 1317, and it was shortly after her third marriage that the estates were partitioned.[7] Five years later Damory died in rebellion against the king and Elizabeth found that, in spite of protests, she could not prevent Hugh le Despenser the younger from taking over her lands in Gwent. It is small wonder that she backed Queen Isabella's invasion of 1326 and Edwards III's accession.[8] Once she enjoyed royal favour, as she did from 1327 until her death, she could really take advantage of her independent status as a widow.

There is little indication of Elizabeth's relations with her husbands. Theobald de Verdun maintained that he and Elizabeth had been betrothed in Ireland and that he did not abduct her from Bristol Castle but that she came out to meet him; it would not however be safe to assume too much from this statement.[9] All three husbands' anniversaries were commemorated in her chapel, and a special distribution was made to the poor on the day of the death of Roger Damory, St Gregory's day, 12 March. Those commemorated in the requiem masses in Elizabeth's will included her husbands.[10] Unlike many noblewomen, Elizabeth did not choose to be buried beside any of her husbands, but in the abbey church of the Minoresses outside Aldgate. Again too much should not be read into this; Marie de Saint-Pol, the widow of Aymer de Valence, earl of Pembroke, referred in her will to Aymer as her very dear lord over fifty years after his death, but chose to be buried in the Minoresses' church at Denny rather than next to her husband at Westminster.[11]

Elizabeth never remarried after 1322. For the rest of her life she herself was responsible for her household and estates, and she was one of the longest-lived as well as one of the richest dowagers of the fourteenth century. She enjoyed

[4] M. Altschul, *A Baronial Family in Medieval England: The Clares, 1217–1314* (Baltimore, 1965), p. 297.

[5] Ibid., pp. 165–75.

[6] *RP*, (London 1783), i, pp. 352b–53a.

[7] PRO, SC 1/63/150; C 47/9/25, 26; SC 11/808.

[8] G.A. Holmes, 'A Protest against the Despensers, 1326', *Speculum*, 30 (1955), pp. 207–12; Jennifer C. Ward, *English Noblewomen in the Later Middle Ages* (London, 1992), pp. 47-48, 169.

[9] *RP*, i, pp. 352b–53a.

[10] PRO, E 101/91/25, m. 15; E 101/93/12, mm. 3, 3d; J. Nichols, *A Collection of all the Wills of the Kings and Queens of England* (London, 1780), p. 29.

[11] H. Jenkinson, 'Mary de Sancto Paulo, Foundress of Pembroke College, Cambridge,' *Archaeologia*, 86 (1915), p. 433.

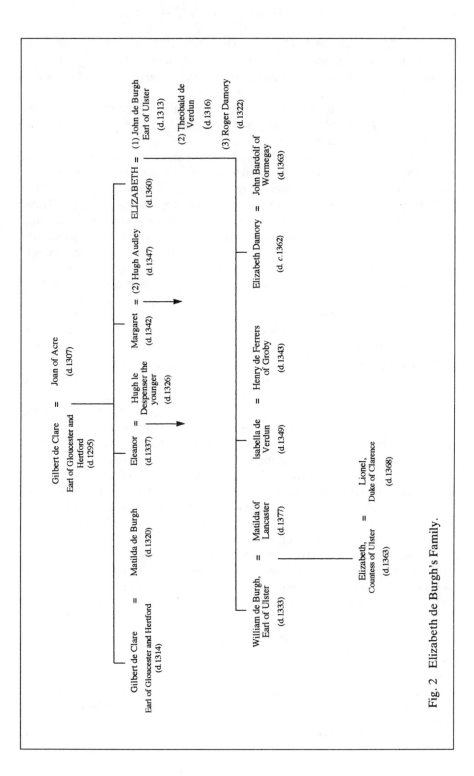

Fig. 2 Elizabeth de Burgh's Family.

an income of approximately £2,500–£3,000 a year.[12] Her principal estates were those of her Clare inheritance, which comprised much of the honour of Clare in eastern England, lands in Dorset centred on Cranborne, and the lordship of Usk in Gwent. She had a one-third share of the Clare lands in Ireland, together with her jointure there. Her dower from Theobald de Verdun also included Irish lands together with manors in the Midlands, and she also had a few estates which had been held jointly with Roger Damory.[13]

The period of her widowhood is well documented. There are references to her in the royal and papal records and valors, accounts and court rolls provide considerable detail on her estates. From the point of view of her connection with London, her household accounts are the most valuable source. These survive from the end of Edward II's reign to within a year of her death and comprise several types of document, all dealing with some aspect of household expenditure for the financial year which ran from Michaelmas (29 September) to Michaelmas. Elizabeth's main financial department was the chamber for which a few accounts survive. From 1350–51 the chamber account was combined with that of the wardrobe and household which gave details of purchases of food, drink, cloth, furs and miscellaneous expenses for the year. There are a few subsidiary accounts of household departments, and the accounts of Elizabeth's own chamber listing her private expenditure are particularly informative. The daily accounts which give expenditure day by day and list visitors are especially valuable in throwing light on standards of living and social relationships, and they show that Elizabeth lived in considerable style and entertained a wide circle of friends. Counter-rolls combined the wardrobe and the daily account. The livery rolls sometimes only list the purchases of cloth for robes, but in 1343 the roll named the retainers and described the livery each received; among the retainers were some of Elizabeth's tradesmen. The information in the household accounts is corroborated and extended by Elizabeth's will which was drawn up in 1355, five years before her death.

Until the early 1350s, Elizabeth divided her time between her residences at Clare in Suffolk, Anglesey in Cambridgeshire, Great Bardfield in Essex, and Usk in Gwent.[14] London was therefore primarily of importance for supplying the household, and it is particularly fortunate that the wardrobe and household accounts from the later 1330s often specify the place of origin of the supplies and the merchants and tradesmen involved. The basic foodstuffs required by the household were supplied from Elizabeth's demesne manors and from

---

[12] Ward, *English Noblewomen*, p. 126.

[13] All the English and Welsh estates are covered in her valors of 1329–30 and 1338–39; PRO, SC 11/799, 801. Summaries are printed in G.A. Holmes, *The Estates of the Higher Nobility in Fourteenth-Century England* (Cambridge, 1957), pp. 143–47.

[14] Anglesey was particularly favoured in the early years of her third widowhood, while Great Bardfield was increasingly used as she grew older. There is no record of her visiting Usk after 1350.

markets, fairs and individual tradesmen in the area round her residences; this applies to all types of grain and meat, and to much of the fish, although Yarmouth was always vital for the supply of herrings. Occasionally parchment and Spanish iron were obtained in London,[15] but the principal London purchases comprised certain types of fish, wine, spices, cloth and furs.

In most years some purchases of fish were made in London, usually of salmon, sturgeon and lampreys. Amounts varied, presumably depending on where Elizabeth was living and on the needs of the household. Thus 206 salmon were bought in London in 1338–39, but two years later only twenty salmon were purchased there together with twenty-eight 'lampreys of Nauntes', probably the large sea-lamprey.[16] The sellers of fish in London were not named in the accounts until 1355–56 when sixty salmon were bought from Thomas Maister and twenty-four from Thomas Cousyn, and Thomas Cousyn supplied 281 salmon between March and August 1359 and half a barrel of sturgeon in March.[17]

Wine was essential to the household, and had to be purchased as English cultivation of vines had largely ceased.[18] Most of the wine bought was Gascon with a small quantity of Rhenish wine, and in 1336 one pipe of Greek wine was obtained in London.[19] Elizabeth usually purchased about twenty-five tons of wine a year, and never bought all her wine from a single source. There was sometimes a need to search out supplies, as in the autumn of 1344 when a groom was sent to Colchester, Ipswich and Orwell to find out about the arrival of the wine ships.[20]

Prices were comparable as between London and the provincial ports, and the decision where to buy wine depended largely on where the lady was living, as costs of carriage had to be taken into consideration. If Elizabeth was living at Clare or Bardfield it cost less to bring wine from Colchester or Ipswich than from London; in 1344–45 the costs of carting and the expenses of the official making the purchases amounted to £2 14s.1d. for five tons bought in London, and 17s. 3d. for three tons bought in Colchester. She was often at Anglesey until the mid 1340s so wine purchased at Lynn could be transported by water, and the purchasing at Bristol was the obvious choice when she was at Usk. When she had her house in London, she bought more wine in the city than she had done on most occasions in the 1340s.

---

[15] PRO, E 101/92/11, m. 7; E 101/92/27, m. 6.

[16] PRO, E 101/92/9, m. 5; E 101/92/13, m. 6.

[17] PRO, E 101/93/19, m. 6; E 101/94/2, m. 5.

[18] Wine was occasionally received as a gift. Elizabeth's son-in-law, Henry de Ferrers of Groby, gave her one pipe of white wine in 1336, and one ton of Rhenish wine in 1339–40; PRO, E 101/92/3, m. 4; E 101/92/11, m. 4. Two pipes comprised one ton; the statutory capacity of the ton in England was 252 gallons.

[19] PRO, E 101/92/3, m. 4.

[20] PRO, E 101/92/27, m. 4.

Table 1

Wine Supplied to the Household of Elizabeth de Burgh

Date[1]	Residences	Ipswich	Colchester	Lynn	Bristol	London
1339–40	Anglesey Bardfield Clare	5		2		17
1340–41[2]	Eastern England Dorset Usk	16			18	2
1344–45	Anglesey Bardfield Clare	$21\frac{1}{2}$	8	4		7
1349–50	Usk Clare Bardfield		13[3]		9	$2\frac{1}{2}$
1350–51[4]	Clare and region	5	7			$3\frac{1}{2}$
1355–56	Bardfield Clare London		14			$9\frac{1}{2}$
1358–59[5]	Bardfield Clare London		8			15

1 The figures are taken from PRO, E 101/92/11, m. 4; E 101/92/13, m. 4; E 101/92/27, m. 4; E 101/93/6, m. 4; E 101/93/8, m. 5; E 101/93/19, m. 5; E 101/94/2, m. 4. All figures are in tons.
2 In addition three tons were purchased at Wareham, half a ton at Weymouth, and one and a half at Caerleon.
3 The account does not differentiate between the purchases at Ipswich and Colchester.
4 In addition 154 gallons were purchased at Clare to mix with vinegar.
5 These were the probable places of residence during the year.

The purchase of seventeen tons of wine in London in 1339–40 shows however that transport costs were not the only determinant of the place of purchase. The presence of a trusted wine merchant was also important. This may well have been the case in 1339–40 when eight tons were bought from John Fynch and five from John Stuteye, and it may also be significant that Elizabeth was able to store at least some of the London wine temporarily in the cellar of Robert de Eynesham, the skinner whom she patronised, until it was transported to her residence; some of her purchases of spices were also taken to Robert's house.[21] For all her purchases, both in London and outside, she

[21] PRO, E 101/92/11, mm. 4, 5, 11.

often used the same merchant over a number of years; the Londoner John Michel supplied wine in 1355–56 and 1358–59.[22]

The majority of the spices needed by the household were purchased in London, although at the end of the 1330s substantial purchases were made at the great fairs.[23] The amounts bought from tradesmen in the provinces were small; for instance Nigel Tebaud of Sudbury was paid £9 16s. 5$\frac{1}{4}$d. in 1339–40.[24] The term spices covered in addition to the spices themselves dried fruit, nuts, oil, rice and sugar; wax and canvas were purchased from the same merchants, and also confections which comprised sweetmeats and medicines. Expenditure on spices varied from year to year, but on average £86 was spent on spices, wax and canvas, and £8 10s. 0d. on confections. Expenditure ranged from £56 12s. 3$\frac{3}{4}$d. in 1340–41 to £119 11s. 4$\frac{1}{2}$d. in 1349–50.[25] Of the grocers who supplied Elizabeth, Bartholomew Thomasin was outstanding, providing spices from 1336 until 1352. His importance can best be gauged from the roll of 1349–50 when the lady was at Usk until April but relied on Bartholomew for most of her spices; during the year he probably supplied goods worth £87 12s. 5d. while purchases in Bristol only totalled £5 13s. 10d. In 1350–51 he probably supplied everything the lady needed apart from a small quantity of wax and canvas.[26] Other London suppliers were John Hamond in 1344–45, and William de Eynesham in 1358–59.

The cloths for the lady and her family, for gifts, and principally for liveries, were almost all bought at the great fairs and in London, and it is likely that increasing reliance was placed on London for the supply of good quality cloth in the last twenty years of Elizabeth's life. In 1336 purchases of cloths worth £115 13s. 4d. were made at St Ives fair in Huntingdonshire, compared with purchases of £8 in London.[27] In 1340–41 however, out of a total expenditure on cloth of £195 15s. 6d. purchases in London totalled £117 11s. 10d, compared

---

[22] At Ipswich Richard de Leyham supplied her in 1336 and 1339–40, and Thomas Coteler in 1338–41 and 1344–45. The switch from Ipswich to Colchester was probably at least partly due to her reliance on John atte Forde of Colchester in 1350–51, 1355–56 and 1358–59. PRO, E 101/92/3, m. 4; E 101/92/9, m. 4; E 101/92/11, m. 4; E 101/92/13, m. 4; E 101/92/27, m. 4; E 101/93/8, m. 5; E 101/93/19, m. 5; E 101/94/2, m. 4.

[23] In 1336 £17 18s. 9d. was spent at St. Ives fair on spices, confections and wax; £29 9s. 4d. on spices, wax and canvas at Stourbridge fair in 1338–39; and £39 14s. 6d. on the same at Boston fair in 1339–40; PRO, E 101/92/3, mm. 5–6; E 101/92/9, m. 6; E 101/92/11, m. 5.

[24] PRO, E 101/92/11, m.5.

[25] The averages are worked out from the totals of eight wardrobe and household accounts of 1338–39, 1339–40, 1340–41, 1344–45, 1349–50, 1350–51, 1355–56, 1358–59; PRO, E 101/92/9, m. 6; E 101/92/11, mm. 5–6; E 101/92/13, m. 6; E 101/92/27, m. 5; E 101/93/6, m. 7; E 101/93/8, m. 7; E 101/93/19, m. 7; E 101/94/2, mm. 5–6.

[26] PRO, E 101/92/3, mm. 5–6; E 101/93/6, m. 6; E 101/93/8, m. 7; E 101/93/12, m. 3. The 1349–50 account does not specify the seller of every item, but it is very likely that purchases from Bartholomew amounted to this total. Bartholomew probably continued to supply Elizabeth until his death.

[27] The entries for cloth and furs on PRO, E101/92/3, m. 5 have been crossed through because they were entered the following year on E 101/92/4, m. 11.

with £32 at St Ives fair, and £28 10s. 6d. at Boston fair in Lincolnshire.[28] The purchase of cloths from the Londoners John de Bures and Stephen de Cavendisshe in 1344–45 and 1358–59, and the arrangements for the carriage of these and other cloths from London in those years and in 1350–51 indicate that London remained the main centre of supply.[29]

London skinners supplied furs for the household liveries, and the accounts differentiate between the purchase of furs, budge and lamb. According to Elizabeth's roll of liveries of 1343, the furs comprised Baltic squirrel skins of various types: popel, the early summer skins; strandling, autumn skins; minever pured, the white belly skins with the grey trimmed off; minever gross, the belly skin with the grey still on.[30] In 1344–45 it was stated that almost all the fur, all the budge and over half the lambskins were bought at Boston fair.[31] Otherwise it was usual to name the London merchant from whom the purchase was made. Thus in 1339–40 when £97 8s. 6d. was spent on furs, the principal suppliers were Robert de Eynesham and Adam Aspal, and Adam supplied most of the budge and lambskins.[32] Robert de Eynesham was the only supplier named in 1340–41 and provided all the budge, totalling £11 9s. 0d., lambskins worth £11 8s. 0d., and furs amounting to at least £77 2s. 0d. out of a total for the year of £117 2s. 8d.[33] Walter Forester of London supplied budge and lambskins in 1350–51 and 1358–59; unfortunately in these years no merchants' names were given for the furs.[34]

The fact that Elizabeth gave several of her suppliers her livery testifies to their importance to her. Among her esquires in the livery roll of 1343 were Roger Turtle of Bristol, Robert de Eynesham, Bartholomew Thomasin, Thomas Coteler of Ipswich and Nigel Tebaud of Sudbury.[35] Each received $6\frac{1}{4}$ or $6\frac{1}{2}$ ells of cloth, one fur of lambskins, and Roger and Bartholomew also received a hood of budge.[36] What the livery list fails to show is the prominence many of Elizabeth's London suppliers enjoyed in their trades and in city politics. Of these merchants Bartholomew Thomasin probably enjoyed the

[28] PRO, E 101/92/13, m. 8.

[29] PRO, E 101/92/27, m. 7; E 101/93/8, m. 9; E 101/94/2, m. 8.

[30] PRO, E 101/92/23, m. 1. E.M. Veale, *The English Fur Trade in the Later Middle Ages* (Oxford, 1966), pp. 228–29. Budge was imported lambskins; ibid., pp. 216–17.

[31] PRO, E 101/92/27, m. 7.

[32] PRO, E 101/92/11, m. 11. The sellers of a few items were not noted, but Robert supplied furs worth £42 18s. 2d, and Adam furs worth £46 13s. 4d. £7 5s. 8d. was spent on budge of which Adam supplied goods worth £7 0s. 8d; £6 14s. 6d. was spent on lambskins of which Adam was paid £6. Robert's shop in Walbrook ward is referred to in *CPMR, 1323–64*, ed. A.H. Thomas (Cambridge, 1926), p. 122.

[33] PRO, E 101/92/13, m. 8. Lambskins worth £10 10s. 0d. were bought at Stamford. With the furs, the seller was not always named.

[34] PRO, E 101/93/8, m. 8; E 101/94/2, m. 9.

[35] PRO, E 101/92/23, m. 2. Roger Turtle supplied wine and spices in 1340–41; E 101/92/13, mm. 4,6.

[36] The fur constituted the lining to the robe.

longest connection with her, from 1336 to 1352. He was a native of Lucca but, according to a royal grant of 1351, he settled in London as a young man and made it his permanent home with his wife and children; he had citizenship in London before 1346 and the grant of 1351 gave him the right to enjoy all rights of citizenship for life.[37] He supplied the royal household with wax and spices and also made loans to the crown;[38] the 1351 grant referred to his good service to the king, Queen Philippa, and the Queen Mother Isabella. Elizabeth was clearly obtaining her spices from one of the best London merchants.

Other of her suppliers achieved prominence in the city. Adam Aspal acted as a searcher for the Skinners in 1344, and John de Bures and Stephen Cavendisshe represented the Drapers on the common council in 1351–52. John Not, who sold Elizabeth canvas in 1350–51 and spices in 1358–59, was one of the masters of the Grocers' Company in 1357–58.[39] Both the drapers and John Not served as sheriffs of the city, as did John Hamond and Walter Forester. John Hamond was mayor in 1343–45, at the same time that he was supplying Elizabeth with spices. Stephen Cavendisshe acted as mayor in 1362–63, and John Not the following year. William Eynesham grocer, probably the son of the skinner Robert de Eynesham, reached aldermanic rank under Richard II.[40]

For the greater part of her widowhood London's significance for Elizabeth consisted in being an important source of supplies for her household. She only made occasional stays in the city. Preparations were made for her to stay at Stepney in May 1340 when supplies of wheat and ale were purchased, but these were subsequently sold because the lady did not come. The reason for her remaining at Clare may well have been the visit of Edward III for the weekend of 27–29 May. Elizabeth subsequently spent one night at Stepney on her way to Canterbury in early June.[41] She is known to have stayed in London in April 1341 on her way to Cranborne and Usk, and probably leased the house of the bishop of Lincoln; two tons of red wine were bought from Robert de Eynesham in preparation for her arrival and were taken to the house of the bishop of Lincoln.[42]

What made Elizabeth decide in the 1350s to have her own house in London in the outer precinct of the abbey of the Minories outside Aldgate can only be

---

[37] *LBF*, p. 139. *CPR, 1350–54*, p. 22. S.L. Thrupp, *The Merchant Class of Medieval London* (Chicago, 1948), p. 220n.

[38] E.g., PRO, E 403/336, 31 October 1345, Bartholomew was paid £264 6s. 4d. for wax, napery and spices supplied to the king's wardrobe. I would like to thank Dr Helen Bradley for drawing my attention to Bartholomew's Italian and royal connections.

[39] *CPMR, 1323–64*, ed. A.H. Thomas (Cambridge, 1926), p. 209. A.H. Johnson, *The History of the Worshipful Company of the Drapers of London*, i (Oxford, 1914), p. 93. *List of the Wardens of the Grocers' Company from 1345 to 1907* (London, 1907), p. 6.

[40] *LBF*, pp. 284–85. Thrupp, *Merchant Class*, pp. 329, 339, 348, 358. *HW*, ii, pt 1 (London, 1890), pp. 313–14.

[41] PRO, E 101/92/10; E 101/92/11, mm. 2, 13; E 101/92/12, mm. 7–9.

[42] PRO, E 101/92/13, mm. 4, 11–12; E 101/92/14, m. 7.

surmised, but it is likely that she was influenced by a mixture of social and religious considerations. There is no doubt that Elizabeth enjoyed the company of her friends and relations among the nobility and, although she frequently entertained them when she was at Clare, Bardfield and Usk, London must have been seen as an increasingly convenient meeting-place. In contrast to the early fourteenth century when the Scottish wars dictated the moves of court and government to York, the court in the 1340s and 1350s was usually to be found in or near London. For a member of the higher nobility having a house in London was a good way of seeing family and friends and of carrying out business.

There were probably also religious reasons behind Elizabeth's decision. She was pious and concerned with her own salvation and that of her husbands, kinsmen and dependants; her generosity to religious foundations is reflected in grants made during her lifetime and in her will.[43] Elizabeth was familiar with the Order of the Minoresses, the Franciscan nuns who followed the rule established by Isabella, sister of Louis IX of France, long before she built her London house. Her greatest friend was Marie de Saint-Pol, widow of Aymer de Valence earl of Pembroke, who founded the house of Minoresses at Denny in Cambridgeshire in 1342.[44] There are strong parallels between the religious benefactions of the two noblewomen, not only seen in their attitude towards the Minoresses but in their foundations of Clare and Pembroke Colleges at Cambridge.

Elizabeth's desire to have close contact with the Minoresses is seen in the papal indulgences she asked for and obtained in the 1340s and 1350s. In 1343 she was allowed to enter the enclosures of Minoresses with three ladies, an indulgence extended twelve years later to four or five honest women and three honest and mature men; this indulgence also allowed her to stay the night accompanied by two women. Her confessor was permitted in 1346 to allow the religious to eat meat at her table.[45] Elizabeth had taken a vow of chastity before she was granted the indulgence of 1343. Taking the evidence of the indulgences and the London house together, it appears that Elizabeth wanted to participate in some way in the religious life of the Minoresses while at the same time enjoying a full social life.[46]

The land in the outer precinct on which Elizabeth built her house was rented from the abbey for £3 6s. 8d. a quarter, the first payment being made in January 1352 when the plan for the house was drawn up (see *Fig. 3*). The work was under way during the spring and summer. Master Richard de Felstede,

---

[43] Ward, *English Noblewomen*, pp. 148–49, 153–59.

[44] A.F.C. Bourdillon, *The Order of Minoresses in England* (Manchester, 1926), pp. 18–22.

[45] *Calender of Entries in the Papal Registers relating to Great Britain and Ireland: Petitions, 1342–1419*, pp. 102, 300. Ibid., *Papal Letters, 1342–62*, pp. 113, 190, 561, 586.

[46] M. Hicks, 'The English Minoresses and their Early Benefactors, 1281–1367', *Monastic Studies*, i (1990), pp. 164–65.

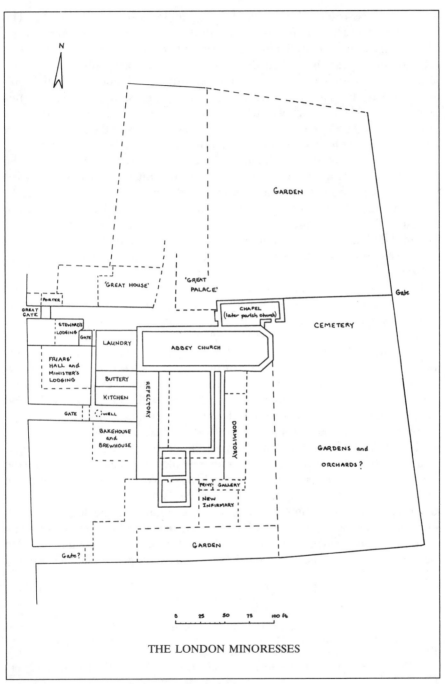

N

GARDEN

'GREAT HOUSE'

'GREAT PALACE'

Gate

PORTER

GREAT GATE

CHAPEL (later parish church)

CEMETERY

STEWARD'S LODGING

GATE

LAUNDRY

ABBEY CHURCH

FRIARS' HALL and MINISTER'S LODGING

BUTTERY

REFECTORY

KITCHEN

GATE   WELL

BAKEHOUSE and BREWHOUSE

DORMITORY

GARDENS and

ORCHARDS?

'PRIVY' GALLERY

NEW INFIRMARY

Gate?

GARDEN

0   25   50   75   100 Ft

THE LONDON MINORESSES

Fig. 3   The London Minoresses in the later middle ages. A reconstruction by Martha Carlin, showing the 'great house' built and occupied by Elizabeth de Burgh and later by Lucia Visconti, countess of Kent (and other rich widows).

carpenter, was responsible for the building and was paid £171. 14s. 5d. The house was probably situated to the north of the building which later became the parish church of Holy Trinity Minories, and it had its own private garden.[47] The amount spent shows that the house must have been substantial, and a useful comparison can be drawn with Richard de Felstede's work at Kenilworth Castle for Henry of Grosmont earl of Lancaster. According to this contract of 1347, Richard was to be paid £166. 13s. 4d. for roofing the hall, measuring eighty-nine feet by forty-six feet, together with the pantry, buttery and kitchen, and he was to supply the doors, shutters and screens for the hall. All the timber was to be supplied by the earl, while Richard was to find the workers he needed, together with scaffolding and other equipment. He was to begin work as soon as the masonry was ready and was to receive the earl's livery for the duration of the work.[48] The fact that Earl Henry was a close friend of Elizabeth's may have influenced her in her choice of architect. Richard de Felstede was a London citizen who in addition to work in the city and at Kenilworth is known to have worked for the king and the younger Despenser in the early 1320s.[49]

In her last years Elizabeth divided her time between Clare, Bardfield and London, and it was usual for her to spend the summer months in her house outside Aldgate. In 1355 she was in London from 9 July until 16 October, with a short trip to Greenwich on 28 and 29 August; in 1358 she arrived in London on 12 May and left for Clare on 10 September.[50] When moving from one residence to another many of her furnishings travelled with her, and packhorses and carts were assigned to particular departments of the household. Some of these furnishings were described in her will, drawn up in 1355, and may well have been used in the London house. Silver and silver-gilt plate was abundant, and the hangings were brightly coloured like the worsted ones with blue cockerels and parrots on a tawny ground bequeathed to her younger daughter, Elizabeth Bardolf. Her chamber would have been dominated by the green velvet bed, striped with red, which was also left to her daughter. The chapel had vessels of precious metal, vestments for all seasons in expensive and embroidered materials, service books and volumes on theology and canon law. Other furnishings were mentioned among the lady's bequests to the abbey of the Minories, including a bed of black tartarin, eighteen fine woollen hangings from two of her other black beds, and twelve green hangings with the

---

[47] PRO, E 101/93/12. M. Carlin, 'Holy Trinity Minories: Abbey of St Clare, 1293/4–1539' (Centre for Metropolitan History, London, 1987), pp. 37–40. I would like to thank the Centre's Director, Dr Derek Keene, for allowing me to see this report.

[48] The contract is printed in LF Salzman, *Building in England down to 1540* (Oxford, 1967), pp. 436–37.

[49] Ibid., pp. 433–34. J. Harvey, *English Medieval Architects. A Biographical Dictionary down to 1550* (Gloucester, 1984), p. 107.

[50] PRO, E 101/93/17, mm. 1d–4d; E 101/93/18, mm. 1–2; E 101/93/20, mm. 7d–21d.

border powdered with owls. Other bequests mentioned one bed of sendal and two of tawny with furred coverings.[51]

Elizabeth's dresses and jewels presumably matched the splendour of the furnishings. Her will contained some bequests of jewels, but gave little description of dress. Her robes were graded from best to sixth best and left to her ladies; there are also references to her black robe, two robes of tiretaine, and the russet robe which was left to the Minoresses.[52] These robes were outfits and consisted of at least three garments (tunic, over-tunic, and cloak and hood) which were often fur-lined.

Elizabeth's exercise of hospitality while she was in London throws light on her social relationships. She was never a recluse, even at the end of her life. Visitors were numerous and were well entertained. Most were kinsmen and members of the higher nobility, but she also entertained religious communities and business contacts. In the first two weeks of October 1355, she entertained the duke of Lancaster, the Minoresses, and Joan countess of Kent.[53] The following summer she received visits from the earls of Stafford and Northampton, Sir Thomas de Rokeby, the Minoresses, her grand-daughter Elizabeth, countess of Ulster, and the bishop of London.[54] During her summer visit in 1358 she entertained, sometimes more than once, the Black Prince and his brother Lionel, Joan of Bar, countess of Warenne, the earl and countess of Warwick, the earl of Northampton, the mayor and sheriffs of London, the king's justices, the 'bishops of Armenia', and the Minoresses.[55]

Certain of the figures who might have been expected at the London house are missing. Elizabeth never kept up with her husbands' kinsmen, apart from Nicholas Damory, probably a relation of her third husband Roger Damory, who was a member of her council. She had one child by each of her three marriages, and by the time she was coming to London two of her children were dead, William de Burgh, earl of Ulster, in 1333, and Isabella de Ferrers in 1349. Her relations with both appear to have been close, as was the case with her youngest daughter, Elizabeth Bardolf, who outlived her.[56] Although Elizabeth Bardolf often visited her mother at Clare and Bardfield, there is no surviving evidence that she visited her in London. Elizabeth de Burgh also seems to have enjoyed a close relationship with her grand-daughter and eventual heiress, Elizabeth, countess of Ulster, who married Edward III's second surviving son Lionel of Antwerp, created duke of Clarence in 1362.

---

[51] John Nichols, *Wills of the Kings and Queens of England* (London, 1780), pp. 24–27, 30–32, 34–37. Elizabeth Bardolf was also known as Isabella. Tartarin was a type of silk or brocade; sendal was a fine silk material.

[52] Ibid, pp. 24–25, 30. Russet was a poorer woollen material and tiretaine was a light woollen fabric.

[53] PRO, E 101/93/18, m. 2. Henry of Grosmont was created duke of Lancaster in 1351.

[54] PRO, E 101/93/18, mm. 5d–12d.

[55] PRO, E 101/93/20, mm. 8d–21d.

[56] Ward, *English Noblewomen*, pp. 99–100.

Both visited Elizabeth at her other residences and paid several visits when she was in London; the countess was with her in 1356 on 26 August and 15 and 16 September, and Lionel in 1358 on 12, 24 and 25 July, and 21 August.[57] It was usual among the nobility for husband and wife to make separate visits.

Elizabeth was on good terms with several members of the nobility related to her on her mother's side, and they visited her at her other residences as well as in London. These included Joan, countess of Kent, and Henry of Grosmont; there was a further tie here, as Henry's sister had married William de Burgh. Her cousin William de Bohun, earl of Northampton, appears to have been a close friend, although considerably younger than Elizabeth, and a frequent visitor; he was entertained by her in London on 17 and 18 July 1356, and on 30 June, 29 July and 29 August 1358.[58] Even younger, and yet again close to Elizabeth, was the Black Prince who visited her four times in London in the summer of 1358, and who was remembered in her will.[59] Some of her other noble visitors were connected to her by marriage. Ralph, earl of Stafford, had run off with her niece Margaret Audley and always remained in close touch with Elizabeth.[60] The eldest son of the earl and countess of Warwick had married Philippa de Ferrers, Elizabeth's grand-daughter. There is no reference to a visit from Elizabeth's closest friend, Marie de Saint-Pol, but she went to France in 1352 and remained there for the next five years.[61]

In addition to friends and kin, Elizabeth kept in touch with officials who could be of assistance in running her estates. Since she held lands in Ireland by way of jointure, dower and inheritance, it was probably useful to be able to entertain Sir Thomas de Rokeby on 27 July 1356, three days after he had been reappointed justiciar of Ireland.[62] Her entertainment of the king's justices on 24 June 1358 is a reminder of landowners' desire to be on good terms with them.[63] This extended in Elizabeth's case to the desire for good relations with the city authorities and she entertained the mayor and sheriffs three weeks before the justices.[64]

Elizabeth's entertaining of church figures similarly covered a wide field. It was usual to combine hospitality to them with the entertainment of a member of the nobility, as when the bishop of London, Michael Northburgh, was entertained with the countess of Ulster on 15 September 1356, and the 'bishops

[57] PRO, E 101/93/18, mm. 5d, 7d; E 101/93/20, mm. 9d, 12d, 14d.

[58] PRO, E 101/93/18, mm. 11d–12d; E 101/93/20, mm. 8d, 11d, 15d.

[59] PRO, E 101/93/20, mm. 10d, 11d, 13d, 21d. Nichols, *Wills of the Kings and Queens of England*, p. 37.

[60] *CPR, 1334–38*, p. 298. Ralph visited her on 16 July 1356; PRO, E 101/93/18, m. 12d.

[61] Jenkinson, 'Mary de Sancto Paulo', p. 410. *CPR, 1350–54*, pp. 362–63, 506; ibid., *1354–58*, pp. 48, 51, 170, 203, 409, 460–61. She had returned to England by the summer of 1358; ibid., *1358–61*, p. 85.

[62] PRO, E 101/93/18, m. 11d.

[63] PRO, E 101/93/20, m. 16d.

[64] PRO, E 101/93/20, m. 19d.

of Armenia' with Lionel of Antwerp on 12 July 1358; these men may have been the monks Stephen and James of Greater Armenia who had arrived in England in the spring.[65] The nuns of the abbey of the Minories were entertained once or twice during Elizabeth's visits to London, sometimes with another member of the nobility; Henry of Grosmont, the grandson of the abbey's founder, was also a visitor on Saturday 10 October 1355, and the Black Prince on Wednesday 15 August 1358.[66]. On one occasion, Tuesday 16 August 1356, meat was served; the other days of their visits were fast days when a variety of fish was set on the lady's table.

Elizabeth was lavish in dispensing hospitality, although there was a great range in her daily expenditure when visitors were present. To take two extremes in the summer of 1358, £3 3s. $9\frac{1}{2}$d. was spent when Lionel of Antwerp was with her on 21 August, while £12 4s. $10\frac{3}{4}$d. was spent at the feast of the Assumption of the Virgin Mary the week before when the Black Prince and the Minoresses were present.[67] The reason for the large total was the number of types of fish purchased by the kitchen, including herring, salmon, conger-eel, plaice, pike, crabs, dace, mullet, eels, whiting, bream, roach and shrimp; the most expensive item was a porpoise which cost £1 19s. 0d. Stockfish and saltfish were supplied from the household stores. This is not an isolated instance of generous hospitality. When the mayor and sheriffs were entertained in June, beef, bacon, venison, pork, mutton, lamb and veal were served, together with rabbit, capon and goose, and one heron, two swans and four bittern; the sum total for the day amounted to £5 19s. 5d.[68]

Elizabeth did not only show concern for people of her own rank and those who were of service to her. She took almsgiving seriously, and, in addition to casual gifts and the distribution of leftovers, was in the last few years of her life dispensing money to a set number of poor people at certain of her demesne manors and at her residence. In the summers of 1356, 1358 and 1359 there were regular monthly entries in the accounts of £2 12s. 0d. given to 540 poor people in London and eighty-four at Standon at the rate of one penny each.[69] As the accounting month comprised four weeks, Elizabeth was giving alms to 135 poor people in London a week, or nineteen or twenty a day.

Elizabeth died on 4 November 1360. The importance of the abbey of the Minories to her is seen in the fact that she chose to be buried there rather than beside one of her husbands. This was specified in her will.[70] Her funeral, like her life, was to be lavish. Two hundred pounds of wax were to provide the

[65] PRO, E 101/93/18, m. 5d; E 101/93/20, m. 14d. Carlin, *Holy Trinity Minories*, p. 38.

[66] The Minoresses also visited on their own on Friday 12 August and Tuesday 16 August 1356. PRO, E 101/93/18, mm. 2, 8d, 9d; E 101/93/20, m. 10d.

[67] PRO, E 101/93/20, mm. 9d. 10d.

[68] PRO, E 101/93/20, m. 19d.

[69] E.g., PRO, E 101/93/18, m. 8d; E 101/93/20, m. 18d. Standon in Hertfordshire was one of Elizabeth's demesne manors.

[70] Nichols, *Wills of the Kings and Queens of England*, p. 23.

lights round the body on the eve and day of her burial, any surplus being divided among the poor churches round Aldgate. £200 was allowed for the expenses on the eve and day of the burial, and this included the money to be distributed to the poor on the day of the funeral. These provisions were typical of Elizabeth's contemporaries among the higher nobility, who regarded the funeral as their last opportunity for display and who wanted the prayers of the poor to ease the passage of their souls through purgatory. Elizabeth's will gave no details of her tomb, but it is likely to have been impressive. John Hastings, earl of Pembroke (d.1375), wanted his tomb to be made as like as possible to the tomb of Elizabeth de Burgh and left £140 for its construction.[71] Originally Elizabeth's tomb was in the abbey church, since the arrangements for the chantry established by her executors provided for daily mass at an altar near the tomb or elsewhere in the church; however by the sixteenth century the tomb had been moved out, probably to the cloister.[72]

The chantry at the Minories supplemented the provisions made by Elizabeth in her will for masses and good works.[73] She left £140 for masses to be sung in the year after her death in the most convenient places her executors should decide on. These masses were to be sung for the benefit of her own soul, the souls of her three husbands, and the souls of all her good and loyal servants who had died or would die in her service. One hundred marks were to be devoted to finding five men-at-arms for the Holy Land, and this money, to be spent in the service of God and for the destruction of his enemies for the benefit of her own soul and the souls of her husbands, was to be handed over within seven years of her death; if no crusade took place within that time, the money was to be given to other charitable works, such as the relief of religious houses which had fallen into poverty, for the profit of her and her husbands' souls and the souls of her benefactors and all Christians.

The bequests to religious houses were extensive including abbeys and priories in England and Wales associated with the Clare family, and most of the houses of friars in the eastern counties. Two beneficiaries however stand out: the abbey of the Minories outside Aldgate and Clare Hall in Cambridge. Apart from the Minoresses, the only London bequests were £8 to the four orders of friars, and a new vestment of white camaca for St Paul's Cathedral.[74] She bequeathed to the Minoresses her russet robe, and the beds and hangings which have already been mentioned. The abbey was to receive £20 in money, five cloths of gold, a crystal reliquary, a large silver-gilt chalice, two cruets, a vestment of white cloth of gold and one of black cloth of gold. The abbess, Katherine de Ingham, was left £20, and each sister was to receive one mark on

[71] *Testamenta vetusta*, ed. N.H. Nicolas (London, 1826), i, p. 87.

[72] Carlin, *Holy Trinity Minories*, p. 39.

[73] Nichols, *Wills of the Kings and Queens of England*, p. 29.

[74] Ibid., pp. 31, 33. £2 per community was Elizabeth's usual bequest to the friars. Camaca was a thick silk fabric.

the day of Elizabeth's burial when each of the four brothers were to receive half a mark.[75].

For Elizabeth de Burgh, even in the last years of her life, London was only one among many centres of interest. With her extensive estates and her residences elsewhere, her work and responsibilities were comparable to those of the higher nobility and could never be restricted to a single city. Throughout her widowhood she played an active role in managing her property, supporting her family and friends, and making her grants to the church.[76] The documents from her estates point to constant supervision and occasional intervention by the lady. Her hospitality enabled her to take her part in noble society, keep up with kinsmen and friends, hear the latest news and gossip, and learn what was going on in the world of war, politics and the church. The fact that many noblemen and women visited her constantly over the years shows that they enjoyed her company as well as the entertainment she provided. Her talents of management are best revealed in her benefactions, notably to Clare Hall in Cambridge where she insisted on securing full rights as patron before she made her principal grants. As a pious noblewoman she was concerned with securing the prayers of her foundations, but she also showed a practical turn of mind and a concern for the welfare of the inmates. The impression which comes over from all her activities is of an able and generous woman who participated fully in noble society and could hold her own in what was very much a male world. She enjoyed life, and looked forward in hope towards salvation.

Her noble status and great estates mean that Elizabeth stands in strong contrast to most of the women discussed in this volume who were involved in their husbands' businesses, in parish gilds, and in city mercantile society. Yet there are parallels between Elizabeth and the wealthy widows of the urban elite. Some women were heiresses and derived their wealth from inheritance; all had the wealth which came from the jointure and dower provided by their husbands. Love of display, whether in life or death, was another common factor, even though Elizabeth's consumption was far greater than that of a merchant household. All had concern for the well-being of family and friends, as well as for salvation and the easing of the soul's passage through purgatory. Above all, noble and mercantile widows showed that once faced with the necessity of running their estates, business and family they could rise to the occasion with efficiency and success.

[75] Ibid., p. 30. One mark amounted to 13s. 4d.
[76] These topics are taken further in Ward, *English Noblewomen*, pp. 99-101, 104–107, 111, 148–49, 153–59.

3

Matilda Penne, Skinner (d. 1392–3)

Elspeth Veale

William Penne, citizen and skinner of London, died in 1379/80.[1] Without a copy of his will we can only speculate on the position in which he left his widow, Matilda, and on the relations between them. No children were mentioned in Matilda's will and she must, according to London custom as noted above, have had as dower a half share of any income from tenements William had on their marriage. On her death this would have reverted to his heirs. According to the custom of *legitim* she must also have inherited at least a half share in his movables. She could dispose freely in her will of what goods and chattels she had inherited as well as what she had acquired, and this included the tenancy of the house and shop. On William's death Matilda had every right to stay in their home, enjoy whatever income he had left her and run the business of preparing and selling furs. This is what she did: she did not remarry, handled the business herself and at the time of her death held the house and shop and bequeathed the lease and part or all of the contents in her testament, dated 4 November 1392, enrolled on 3 February 1393.[2]

Matilda's main beneficiary and one of her executors was Peter Herlawe, her nephew, son of her brother John, who lived with her. Yet no other reference at all to Peter Herlawe has been traced. One Peter Penne, however, citizen and skinner of London, was active in the years following Matilda's death and was linked indirectly with her: William Irby, citizen and haberdasher, was with Peter Herlawe one of Matilda's executors, and when in 1409 he came to prepare his own will he chose Peter Penne as one his own executors.[3] There may indeed have been two Peters, but it seems most probable that Peter Herlawe was heir to both William and Matilda Penne, that he took over the business and its goodwill and changed his surname to theirs.

Whatever the family relationships, William remains a shadowy figure. Apart from stating that she was his widow Matilda made no reference at all to him in

---

[1] William Penne's will is listed, with the year of his death, in the original list of contents, p. 12, to GL, 9051/1, the register of wills proved in the Archdeaconry Court of London, 1393–1415, but the will itself is missing.

[2] Ibid., ff. 5v–6.

[3] GL, register of wills proved in the Commissary Court of London, 9171/2, f. 163v.

her will and did not ask to be buried near him. He may have been the William appointed as collector for a levy for the ward of Cripplegate Within in 1369, and the one who granted a lease of a bakehouse in Bread Street in 1370.[4] But apart from his membership of the Skinners' fraternity he can with certainty be traced only when fined 60d. for selling an improperly-made fur of *bys* in 1365, i.e. a fur lining which did not consist of the required number of squirrel backs of the same quality. He was one of thirty-six men fined following a drive by merchant skinners on those who failed to maintain the recently defined standards.[5] We know however that he and Matilda lived in some style and that, at a time when furs were so generally worn, their preparation and sale was a profitable business.

The Pennes' shop was in Wood Street, in the parish of St Peter West Cheap, which lay at the junction of Wood Street and Cheapside.[6] Matilda was to stay there and carry on her husband's business for over twelve years after his death. It was rare but not unknown for skinners to bequeath their businesses and the terms of their apprentices to their wives. For instance, Walter Thame in his will of 1403 assumed that his widow would be able to practise the craft but arranged that if she did not do so, and did not marry another skinner, the terms of his apprentice should be sold.[7] But the craft was almost entirely dominated and exercised by men. Only three references to women skinners have been traced despite the many London skinners named in the records. Alice Brod, wife of a skinner, was in 1392 described as trading *sole* as a skinner, and in 1523 Thomas Myrfyn left a bequest to a female apprentice and to 'six poor women fre of the craft of skinners in London yf any suche be founde'.[8]

The most interesting woman skinner about whom information survives was Matilda Penne. She may have developed the relevant skills while helping her husband or have been formally apprenticed, but she was certainly able to execute the more specialised work in the trade: the inspection and purchase of good-quality skins, supervision of their preparation and the selection of skins matched for quality and colour to make an elegant fur lining. That her work was not always up to the highest standards is revealed by the confiscation from her and subsequent sale of a fur of trimmed *menuvair* of 240 skins, valued at 18s. when in April 1388 the skinners' surveyors seized furs from four skinners.[9] However her reputation was such that another skinner left one of his apprentices to her in his will of 1386, to be trained in her art.[10] The apprentice, Robert Broun, later worked in London as a skinner although he seems to have had a

---

[4] *LBG*, p. 253; *CPMR, 1364–81*, p. 116.

[5] CLRO, Letter Book G, f. clxix: see E.M. Veale, *The English Fur Trade in the Later Middle Ages* (Oxford, 1966), pp. 117–23, 224.

[6] *HW*, ii, p. 257: will of Blase de Bury.

[7] GL, Archdeaconry Court Wills, 9051/1, f. 105v.

[8] CLRO, Mayor's Court, Original Bills, ii, m. 131; PCC, 13 Bodfelde (1523).

[9] *LBH*, p. 324, i.e. a fur lining made of white squirrel belly skins.

[10] *HW*, ii, p. 257.

financially precarious career.[11] Matilda bequeathed the terms of her own apprentices – their number is unfortunately not stated – to Peter Herlawe/ Penne, as well as leaving them all 6s. 8d. each. Even in November 1392, shortly before her death, she was still training youngsters and no doubt found their labour essential.

Matilda's casual reference to her apprentices' *ventures* suggests that some may have been serving as factors for her as well. As she must have had frequent dealings both with suppliers of skins, often Hanseatic merchants, and customers for her furs, she seems to have been a shrewd enough business-woman to ensure that debts were well secured. She also had then in her service as well as her domestic staff a *serviens*, Thomas Spencer, who almost certainly helped in the shop, probably as a trained man. Although he was not given anything, his debts to her were pardoned which suggests that he was also involved in some trading on his own account, possibly buying skins through her. She may also have had outworkers, as was a frequent practice in the fur trade, among the others whose debts to her were to be either fully or partly pardoned at the discretion of her executors.[12] It is tempting to suppose that Petronilla *Scriweyner* to whom Matilda gave a small piece of silver and a mazer, was responsible for some of the clerical work she would have required. Unfortunately, although Matilda referred to her goods and merchandise and bequeathed the chests and utensils in both shop and house to Peter Herlawe/ Penne, she provided no details of them in her will.

Matilda lived some distance from the parish of St John Walbrook where many skinners were established and the church with which their fraternity was associated. But her name was listed with that of other wives in the roll of the fraternity of Corpus Christi, as was her husband's, and she bequeathed 20s. to the fraternity in her will.[13] She would have taken full advantage of the opportunities, particularly social ones, which this brought her. Similarly Peter Penne, citizen and skinner, presumably trained by William and Matilda, joined the yeomanry fraternity in 1400, took office as one of its wardens in 1409 and at some date joined the masters' fraternity.[14] Robert Broun, however, does not appear to have joined either. Perhaps this is a reminder that a trained man, although active as a skinner, might not always have achieved the freedom of the city nor troubled to join the fraternities. It is worth noting that in her will Matilda added the customary description of 'citizen' to her husband's name but not to those of Thomas Carleton, William Wadsworth and William Irby, all of whom we know from other sources were acknowledged citizens. Did the

[11] *CPMR, 1381–1412*, pp. 249, 284.

[12] Veale, *English Fur Trade*, pp. 88–89, 116.

[13] Ibid., pp. 44–46; the Worshipful Company of Skinners of London, Roll of the Fraternity of Corpus Christi, ff. 22, 26.

[14] Skinners' Company, Roll of the Fraternity of our Lady's Assumption, ff. 24, 28; Roll of the Fraternity of Corpus Christi, f. 24.

distinction between citizens and others seem less important to a woman whose status as a freewoman was usually only achieved through marriage?[15]

Matilda was at the heart of two interlocking networks, both centred on Wood Street. A few hints of her business relationships are suggested by her will. One of her executors was William Irby, citizen and haberdasher, who also had a shop, with cellar and solar, in Wood Street, and other property in Gutter Lane in the same parish.[16] His first wife, Isabella, later to be buried in the church of St Peter West Cheap, was also one of Matilda's friends, and she left him 40s. and his wife a gold ring. Of William's work we know little, although mercantile contacts and a debt from Stow-on-the-Wold, Gloucestershire, due jointly to him and Mabel Eton, possibly the wife of John Eton, mercer, indicate that he had a country trade.[17] When William himself prepared his will in November 1409, of which probate was granted on 6 January 1409/10, he made Peter Penne, citizen and skinner, one of his executors, and also asked to be buried in the church of St Peter West Cheap.

Joanna Carleton, widow of Thomas Carleton, alderman 1382–88, citizen and broderer, was also left by Matilda a goblet of mazer with a boss (*booz*)[18] and cover, usually objects of considerable value. Joanna had received from her husband, who died in March 1388/9, among other tenements a tenement called 'le lyon on the hope' with shops in Wood Street, and he left bequests to the churches of St Peter West Cheap and the neighbouring parish of St Alban Wood Street.[19] It seems possible that the Carletons had also had a shop in Wood Street. Another possible contact is suggested by Matilda's gift of a gold ring to Beatrice Swanton, who may have been the wife of John Swanton, a leatherseller in Cheap, knowledgeable about furs.[20] Can we see a little group of related businesses there – a haberdasher, broderer and skinner catering for the clothing trades so important in Cheapside?[21]

William Wadsworth, whom Matilda asked to supervise the execution of her will, does not appear to have been associated with this group. He was a common councillor and a prominent grocer, chosen several times to be one of the grocers' representatives, and it may be that through his support of the church of St John Walbrook he was well known to skinners.[22]. Matilda left him

---

[15] C.M. Barron, 'The "Golden Age" of Women in Medieval London', *Reading Medieval Studies*, 15, (1989), pp. 44–45.

[16] GL, Commissary Court Wills, 9171/2, f. 163v.

[17] *CCR, 1402–5*, p. 221 (1403); *CPR, 1405–8* p. 253 (1406); *CPMR, 1413–37*, p. 48.

[18] A medallion in the centre of the bowl: *The Age of Chivalry*, Royal Academy Exhibition Catalogue (1987), no. 155.

[19] *HW*, ii, p. 272.

[20] *LBG*, p. 293; *LBH*, p. 42; *CPMR, 1381–1412*, p. 102.

[21] D. Keene and V. Harding, *Historical Gazetteer of London before the Great Fire*, i, *Cheapside* (Microfiche, Cambridge, 1987), introduction, pp. liv et seq. There was also a draper with shops in Wood Street, *HW*, ii, p. 271 (1388/9).

[22] *HW*, ii, p. 355; *CPMR, 1381–1412*, pp. 86, 127; *LBH*, pp. 38, 42, 281, 357.

a ring worked with a sapphire, a 'great' mazer and her best brass pot to his wife, and 20s. to his daughter towards her dowry.

The church of St Peter Wood Street was the centre around which much of the life at the south end of Wood Street revolved. Although the parish was a small one, the church itself, on the west side of Wood Street at its junction with Cheapside, was well-supported and had a sizable establishment in 1379: a rector, seven chaplains and a clerk.[23] Matilda arranged that she should be buried there and asked the rector, Master John Ledbury, to be one of her executors, leaving him 20s. for offerings. One chaplain, Laurence, received 6s. 8d., the others, with the master- and sub-clerk, 12d. each to say prayers for her soul. Twenty shillings was left for the repair of the fabric of the church. A chaplain there was to sing masses and celebrate on the anniversary of her death.

Matilda is revealed as a deeply religious woman with a strong personal attachment to her local church. She specified exactly where she was to be buried: 'in a coffin within the church in front of the Cross where I am accustomed to stand'. The gifts bequeathed to the rector were ones she obviously valued and suggest that he was her friend as well as her pastor. He was to receive a goblet of mazer, a piece of her best silver and a girdle garnished with silver and gold. She also left a bequest to Master John Whyn who had once been her chaplain, presumably while he was a chaplain at St Peter Wood Street as he had been in 1379. She still had the cope of cloth of gold and the silver chalice and paten once proudly provided for him for her private devotions. She bequeathed the chalice and paten to him, and asked that the cope be used in the church in perpetual memory of her.[24]

Matilda, as was usual, remembered other institutions in her will but her bequests were no formality: she named individual monks from Westminster Abbey whom she must have known personally. John Wrottyng and John Stowe were both monks at the abbey in 1381 and they may have long been her friends.[25] They were to receive 6s. 8d. each and John Stowe was also to receive a basin with ewer. Hugh Stafford may have been a younger man – he was left 3s. 4d. Similarly Matilda left 6s. 8d. to Elene atte Vorde, a sister at Elsing Spital, and 6d. to the other sisters. Small sums of money, totalling perhaps as much as £3, were left, some to support repairs at St Paul's, requesting prayers for her soul from each order of friars, the poor in the hospitals of St Mary without Bishopsgate, St Bartholomew and St Thomas of Southwark, the two leper hospitals of Hackney and St Giles Holborn, and each enclosed anchorite

[23] *The Church in London, 1375–92*, ed. A.K. McHardy, London Record Society, 13 (London, 1977) no. 103. The church was burnt in the Great Fire and not rebuilt; the big plane tree which still stands in the churchyard is supposed to mark its site.

[24] McHardy, ed., *The Church in London*, no. 103. The churchwardens' accounts of St Peter West Cheap (GL, 645/1) begin effectively with a list of benefactors and an inventory of 1431. Matilda's name in not included (f. 166), not can her cope be distinguished from the many rich vestments then belonging to the church (f. 174).

[25] Ibid., no. 390.

in both city and suburbs. Torches for services were to be set up in the churches of St Peter West Cheap, the Charterhouse, St Martin le Grand and the chapel 'de la Barnet'.[26]

Matilda's personal bequests provide a vivid picture of a comfortably prosperous household. Concentration on the retail trade in furs rarely brought vast profits but there were many shops of London skinners in the late fourteenth century which flourished, and the Penne business seems to have been one of them. Matilda, for instance, thought soon before her death that she was in a position to dispose of sums which must have amounted to between £60 and £70, a very considerable sum.

We have many more details about the career of William Horscroft, citizen and skinner, common councillor and surveyor for the skinners, with the mercantile interests which contributed to his downfall and the production in 1400 of the full inventory of his possessions which survives. He was more active in public affairs than the Pennes, friendly with the less prominent merchants of the day. His goods were valued at just over £100, nearly £70 of which comprised the stock in skins and furs in his shop.[27] The household possessions of Horscroft and Penne reflect, so far as we can tell, a very similar life style. Penne had more plate and jewels than Horscroft but he may have had to dispose of such items to meet his debts. But neither of them lived in the relative luxury enjoyed by Richard Toky, citizen and grocer, of whose goods a detailed inventory of 1391 survives.[28]

The Penne property was not small: it included at least a shop, a hall and parlour and two, probably more, chambers.[29] In 1392 the hall and parlour were well furnished with hangings and cushions, the chambers with beds, one Matilda's best feather bed, with coverlets, testers and curtains, sheets and blankets. Five pieces of silver could be displayed as well as the silver chalice and paten. Among household equipment were four goblets of mazer, the cups made of turned maple, one of which with a boss and cover was probably a valuable item, and a 'great' and small mazer, brass pots, basins with ewers and a variety of brass and tin wares. Matilda herself wore a gold signet and had three other valuable rings, two of gold and one worked with a sapphire, one pair of paternosters of silver and coral and another of jet (*geet*). She owned furred gowns and even her everyday gown was furred, valuable enough for her

---

[26] Presumably the chapel of St John and St Mary in the vill of Barnet to which John Botiller also left a bequest in 1361: *HW*, ii, p. 43. John Ledbury was a vicar at St Martin le Grand in 1379 and this may help to explain this bequest, McHardy, *Church in London*, no. 16.

[27] Veale, *Fur Trade*, pp. 84–87; the inventory and that of Thomas Betele, a much humbler skinner whose stock was valued at only £1 2s. 6d., are transcribed in full in E.M. Veale, "The London Fur Trade in the Later Middle Ages, with Particular Reference to the Skinners' Company' (unpublished Ph.D. thesis, University of London, 1953), pp. 486–92.

[28] *CPMR, 1381–1412*, pp. 209–13; cf. pp. 127, 167–68, 205–6.

[29] Cf. the contract for the erection of three shops and houses in Friday Street in 1410, A.R. Myers, ed., *English Historical Documents, 1327–1485* (London, 1969), pp. 1081-83.

to bequeath it to a friend, as was a girdle garnished with silver and gold.[30] At least two women servants worked for her: Margery received 40s., a tunic and a pot, and Emma her maid servant, a tunic and kirtle. Nor did she forget those who had once worked for her. Servants also received her remaining clothes.

These cherished possessions were listed with great care in Matilda's will and she obviously gave much thought to their disposal. She remembered some members of her husband's family: £3 6s. 8d. went to three women, two daughters and a grand-daughter of Elene Penne who lived in Oxford. It seems possible that William himself had come from Oxford and was buried there.[31] But her chief concern was for her own family, the Herlawes.[32] To her nephew Peter she left £20 and her gold signet, to Lucie his wife £20 from her goods and merchandise and her second furred gown. To them both she left the remaining two years' lease in the property and most of the contents: two pieces of silver, two mazers, two basins with ewers, two second-best pots of brass and all other vessels of brass and tin as well as two sets of bedding with testers and curtains, hangings and cushions in the hall and parlour and utensils used in the house and shop. Peter was also made an executor of the will, responsible for collecting money owed to her, and he received the remaining terms of her apprentices. Presumably, as already suggested, he carried on the business he inherited, changing his name from Herlawe to Penne.[33] His father, Matilda's brother John, and his brothers, John and William, received £4 6s. 8d. between them. Leticia, his daughter, was eventually to receive £6 13s. 4d. towards her dowry.[34]

Altogether Matilda named forty-three people in her will, twenty men and twenty-three women, among whom she divided her money, clothes and household goods. Among them were men and women who received a string of small bequests, presumably personal friends, of whom no other record has been traced. On the other hand the most interesting and best-known recipient of Matilda's largesse was Dame Margery Twyford. She was the widow of Sir Nicholas Twyford, citizen and goldsmith, alderman 1375–90 and mayor 1388–

---

[30] Compare with C. Dyer, *Standards of Living in the Later Middle Ages, 1200–1500* (Cambridge, 1989), pp. 205–7; M. Campbell, 'Gold, Silver and Precious Stones', J. Blair and N. Ramsay, ed., *English Medieval Industries* (London, 1991), pp. 151, 154–57.

[31] There was another William Penne, skinner, whose will was registered in 1426: GL, Commissary Court Wills, 9171/3, f.177, but no link has been traced. It seems unlikely that there was any connection between William and Matilda's family and John Penne, citizen and skinner, alderman 1408–22. He was an eminent skinner, one of the group who held leases for the Company's hall (Skinners' Company, Calendar of Records, typescript, 1965, deeds 130, 134), who traded with the great wardrobe (e.g. PRO, Exchequer, Accounts Various, E 101/405/14, ff. 5v, 6), and was active on city business.

[32] This was not a common surname in London at the time but Matilda provided no clue to a possible origin in Harlow, Essex.

[33] Little information survives of Peter's activities: *CCR, 1405–9*, p. 468; *CPMR, 1413–37*, p. 9; *LBI*, p. 87.

[34] Added in a codicil, to be paid at the discretion of the executors.

89, who died in 1390. He was a wealthy man with lands in Suffolk and Middlesex, knighted by Richard II for his services to the king in 1381. Dame Margery was presumably living in 1392 in the newly-built house in the parish of St John Zachary, between Staining Lane and the church, to which Nicholas referred in his will. Why did Matilda leave her her best feather-bed? Staining Lane was near Wood Street and we can only suppose either that Dame Margery was a treasured customer or a friend and neighbour. That Matilda set some store by this contact is suggested not only by the value of the gift but by the place in her will given to this bequest and that to Joanna Carleton, widow of an alderman. Both women, socially prestigious, were named immediately after members of Matilda's own family. Dame Margery was soon to marry Drew Barentyn, one of the wealthiest and most influential goldsmiths of the day, and it is unlikely that she and Matilda moved in the same social circles.[35]

Matilda Penne comes to life through her will. We can almost hear her, elderly and perhaps ill, checking over the people she wished to remember and the gifts she had to bestow. She emerges as a generous woman with many friends, proud of her social contacts. She was above all a devout woman with a genuine feeling for her faith. She enjoyed the independence and status which widowhood brought her and still had a firm grip on her household. She was also that rare figure, a woman skinner, a shopkeeper and craftswoman in her own right. She proved well able, with her nephew's help, to carry on a successful business in the preparation and sale of furs for the twelve or thirteen years following her husband's death. Her reputation was high among her fellows and she still had apprentices in her service a few weeks before her death. It is a tribute to her skill and shrewd business sense that she was able to keep the enterprise afloat for so long, and although we do not know if it were more or less successful than in her husband's day it survived and prospered in the precarious world of late fourteenth-century London.

---

[35] Full details of the careers of Twyford and Barentyn are given in T. Reddaway and E.M. Walker, *The Early History of the Goldsmiths' Company, 1327–1509* (London, 1975), pp. 279–82, 311–12.

4

Poor Widows, *c.* 1393–1415

Robert A. Wood

Chaucer's describes a poor widow in the Nun's Priest's Tale. But she is not a town-dweller; she lives in the country. She has a small cottage with a small yard attached. In this yard she keeps a few animals which provide fresh milk and meat for herself and her two daughters. Life is simple, hard but not entirely bereft of cheer:

> A povre wydwe, somdeel stape in age
> Was whillom dwellyng in a narwe cotage,
> Biside a grove, stondynge in a dale.
> This wydwe, of which I telle yow my tale,
> Syn thilke day that she was last a wyf,
> In pacience ladde a ful sumple lyf,
> For litel was hir catel and hir rente.[1]

But what of the modest urban widow living in the town or city? Very little is known about how she fared in the late fourteenth early fifteenth centuries. There appears to be very little in the literature of the time to tell us of her way of life or the conditions in which she lived. We must look for other contemporary material in an attempt to build up a picture of the poor urban widow and her lot. A possible source of information for our period is to be found in the testamentary records of the church courts. This study is based on an examination of wills enrolled in the Archdeacon's court of London.[2]

Although the index to the enrolled wills begins in 1363, it is not until 1393 that any of the copy wills survive. Between 1393 and 1415, when the wills again cease until the beginning of the sixteenth century, this register contains 1,374 copy wills. Table 2 gives the results of the analysis of these wills.

The 703 married men constitute 51 per cent of the total wills registered. Of these 618 or 88 per cent named their wives as executors. Of the seventy-one women recorded without marital status, some refer to children in their wills but it is unclear if these women were widowed, or whether the children

---

[1] *The Complete Works of Geoffrey Chaucer*, ed. F.N. Robinson (Oxford, 1966), 'The Nun's Priest's Tale', lines 1–7.

[2] Archdeacon of London's Register of Copy Wills, i, 1363–1649. This volume is now in the Guildhall Library catalogue reference 9051/1 (hereinafter referred to as GL, MS). I am grateful to Caroline M. Barron for the many helpful comments on earlier drafts of this essay.

Table 2

Total of Wills proved in the Archdeacon's Court of London,
3 November 1393 to 10 September 1415

		Numbers		Percentage
Clergy:	Rectors/vicars	26 ⎫		
	Chaplains	86 ⎬ 139		10
	Clerks	27 ⎭		
Laity:	*A. Males*			
Denizens	Married	686 ⎫		
	Widowers	61 ⎬ 947		69
	Single/unknown	202 ⎭		
Foreigners	Married	17 ⎫		
	Widowers	2 ⎬ 52		4
	Single/unknown	33 ⎭		
	B. Females			
Denizens	Married	7 ⎫		
	Widows	157 ⎬ 234		17
	Single/unknown	70 ⎭		
Foreigners	Married	0 ⎫		
	Widows	1 ⎬ 2		0
	Single/unknown	1 ⎭		
TOTALS		1,374		100

referred to were illegitimate. The common law of England, on which the custom of the city of London was based, had long established that married women had to obtain the consent of their husbands before drawing up their wills. Of the seven married women in this sample only one states that her will was made with the consent of her husband.[3] All except one of these married women named their husbands as executor of their wills and the exception appointed her husband as supervisor of the executors.[4]

In attempting to arrive at a representative sample of widows who come close to Chaucer's poor widow, I have further analysed the wills of all 158 recorded widows. I have devised the categories by analysing the donations made in lieu

---

[3] Alice Benyngton made her will with the consent of her husband William on 24 January 1395, proved on 3 October 1403. GL, MS 9051/1, f. 8v. The other married women were Agnes Twykford and Isabell atte Melle, who, like Alice, do not appear to have been married before; their wills are to be found in GL, MS 9051/1, f. 16 for 1393 and f. 2 for 1410 respectively. Johanna Seles, Isabell Coleman, Alice Bastewyk and Emma Kelke, who had been widows, remarried. Their wills are GL, MS 9051/1, f. 14 for 1396; f. 7 for 1403; ff. 1v–2 for 1407; f. 6 for 1406 respectively.

[4] Alice Bastewyk appointed her husband Robert Bastewyk, citizen and vintner, to supervise her executors. She made her will on 5 January 1406, proved 4 April 1407. See note 3 above.

of forgotten tithes or monetary gifts to the high altar. The figures shown in brackets in the totals column (Table 3) have been derived from other monetary bequests contained within the wills of widows who made no specific bequests to the high altar. In producing Table 3 I have drawn on a similar methodology used by Dr Robert Dinn in his recent work on Bury St Edmunds.[5]

Table 3

Donations to the Church in London by widows 1393–1415

Category	Donations	Totals			Percentages
Very Poor	Nothing	6	(4)	10	8⎫ 32
Poor	Up to 3s. 4d.	33	(6)	39	24⎭
Modest	3s. 4d. to 6s. 8d.	40	(11)	51	32
Wealthy	Above 6s. 8d.	45	(13)	58	36
TOTALS		124	(34)	158	100

From this analysis it will be seen that ten widows may be termed 'very poor' and thirty-nine widows 'poor'. It is the forty-nine women in these two categories who will be studied in this essay.

In the disposition of their souls all of these widows expressed the common form of sentiments current at this time. This usually took the form of dedicating their souls to God Almighty the Creator, the Blessed Virgin Mary His mother and All Saints. Almost certainly these dedications were those commonly used by the clerks and scriveners who drew up these wills in the first place rather than reflections of the widows own particular beliefs. None of the wills contains any reference either to local or particular saints and there is no suggestion of unorthodox beliefs or sentiments. Isabell Daventre, who died in 1407, stated that her funeral was to be without pomp although she did not possess sufficient personal wealth to pay for such a funeral.[6]

Burial was usually either in the parish church or churchyard although not universally so. For example Matilda Kyrkeby was a parishoner of St Bride's Fleet Street, but she requested burial in St Stephen's chapel in the church of St Sepulchre. A further nine widows requested burial in St Paul's Churchyard, which was always a popular burial place for Londoners in the middle ages.[7]

---

[5]   R. Dinn, 'Baptism, Spiritual Kinship, and Popular Religion in Late Medieval Bury St Edmunds', *Bulletin of the John Rylands University of Manchester Library*, 72 (1990), pp. 93–106, esp. p. 99.

[6]   GL, MS 9051/1, f. 6v for 1407. For full details of all the widows in this study and to avoid continual repetition of manuscript references, see Appendix A.

[7]   In the 'very poor' category, Johanna Pygeant and Juliana Deux were buried there. Neither gave the parish where they lived. In the 'poor' category, Margaret Lyncoln from St Michael le Quern, Elizabeth Tyllworth of St Mararet Moses, Agnes Martyne from St Augustine Paul's Gate, Joan Drewe of St Mary Axe and Alice Edred were to be buried there. Denise Benet makes no reference to her parish in her will.

Some widows were very precise as to where they were to be buried in their churches. Matilda atte Wyne, who died in February 1408, directed her executors to bury her before the altar of St John the Baptist in the church of St Edmund King and Martyr, Lombard Street.[8] Fen Swan comes nearest to expressing true affection for her late husband. She wished to be buried in All Hallows the Great 'next to my friend Henry Creye my late husband'. It is interesting however, to note the different surnames.[9] In all fourteen widows from this sample of forty-nine wished to be interred with their late husbands.

Four widows did not specify their resting-place. Julianna atte Melle, Cecilia Michell and Agnes Regnald simply requested a church burial. Rose Gatyn, the widow of John Gatyn, lived in the parish of St George Eastcheap. She was however being cared for by the Minoresses in their house, where she drew up her will on 1 March 1405/6. Her will gives John's craft as fishmonger but does not mention where he was buried nor where she was to be buried. In all probability Rose was close to death as probate was granted to her daughter Alice two days later. John Gatyn's will drawn up fifteen days earlier also survives. He described himself as citizen and fishmonger. He requested a church burial (unspecified), and left all his fixed and movable goods to his executors, Thomas Oswekyrke, rector of St George Eastcheap and Hugh Ryebred, fishmonger. Rose, who is not mentioned, may have already been very ill and was being cared for by the Minoresses before John died. In the event Rose only lived for another fifteen days after her husband.[10]

Very occasionally we get a glimpse of the testator's state of health when drawing up her will. Alice Claryngton stated that she was 'sick in body and near to death which is certain but the hour of death is uncertain'. For Alice the uncertainty did not last very long. Only two days elapsed between the drawing up of her will and the granting of probate to her sole executor Thomas Bernes, a son from a previous marriage, whom his mother described as 'living in the house of good master Sir Roger Bechete'.

---

[8] See Table 4. Margaret Stodeley directed that she was to be buried in a shroud in the middle of her parish churchyard of St Michael, Bassishaw. This may suggest that she was too poor to have a coffin. Isabell Daventre requested burial in her parish church of St Magnus on the south side before the Cross. Felicity Ramseye was to buried in the chapel of St Mary, next to her late husband John Ramseye, in St Botolph's Aldgate.

[9] It is possible that she reverted to her maiden name following Henry's death. Unfortunately, Henry's will does not survive, but there is a record of probate being granted in 1407 in the registers of the commissary court of London; this in spite of the fact that the archdeacon had jurisdiction in the parish of All Hallows the Great where he lived. Alternatively, his will may have been referred to the commissary court for clarification over jurisdiction or for some other cause. For details of the various church courts in London and their jurisdiction, see A.J. Camp, *Wills and their Whereabouts* (London, 1974), pp. 85–87.

[10] John's will is GL, MS 9051/1, f. 19v for 1405, made 13 February 1405/6; proved 15 February 1405/6. His will was witnessed by the fishmongers Edmund Redhed and John Rybred, probably Hugh's brother or son.

Only two of the widows had been married more than once but both chose to keep their most recent husbands' surname in preference to that of their former husbands. Amelia Fullerer was the widow of John Fullerer by whom she had two sons Henry and Thomas. Her previous marriage to John(?) Powderman had also produced two sons; John senior and John junior. Each son received goods specified in her will but her eldest son from her second marriage, Henry, was made her sole executor.[11] Matilda atte Wyche's first husband was Thomas(?) Watford by whom she had had a son, Thomas. On the death of her first husband she subsequently married Walter Fulhard citizen and glover. It would seem that on Walter's death she reverted to her maiden name. Fen Swan also appears to have reverted to her maiden name on the death of her husband Henry Creye – yet she described him as her friend. A third widow, Alice Skarlet, also reverted to her maiden name on the death of her husband Robert Andrew.[12]

The crafts of former husbands are recorded in ten cases. From the cloth industry we have a wool bearer, a clothier and a haberdasher. There is also a girdler and a glover. The building industry is represented by a lockyer (locksmith) and there are three examples of specialist crafts: a bowyer, a wire-drawer and a goldsmith. Lastly there is a victualler, or fishmonger.[13]

The wills of six of the widows' husbands have survived so that it is possible to obtain some information about the length of widowhood and the relative prosperity revealed by their testaments. Helen Wayte was a widow for no less than thirty-eight years. Her husband William died in 1372/3 but, as the archdeacon's register has many gaps throughout this period, his is one of those whose will is only known from the index to the register. Thomas Trayle, citizen and draper, died in 1394. His wife Helen was a widow for nineteen years. Thomas gave a basin covered with a russet cloth by way of a burial fee to the church of St Christopher and two candles for his funeral service. He left 4d. to each chaplain in the church for prayers and the chief clerk and sub clerk also received 4d. each. The residue of all his chattels went to Helen after probate had been granted and she was named his executor along with John Stoke citizen and mercer. Helen seems to have improved her position as she was able to leave 3s. 4d. to the high altar for prayers and a further 3s. 4d. for the nave fabric of St Christopher's church and 2s. 0d. to the fabric of St Michael's Cornhill. She also left 8d. to the chief clerk and 6d. to the sub clerk.[14]

---

[11] Unfortunately, we do not know what craft John Powderman practised.

[12] For Henry Creye, see n. 9 above.

[13] In the 'very poor' category, Sibil Spencer's husband Richard was a citizen and haberdasher; Rose Gatyn's husband John was a fishmonger; Johanna Pygeant's husband Roger was a citizen and goldsmith. In the 'poor' category, John Frer was a wire-drawer, Elias Wyllyngham was a wool-bearer, Geoffrey Couper a bowyer, Thomas Trayle a draper, Walter Fulhard a citizen and glover, Walter Salman a citizen and girdler and John Lorkyn was a citizen and lockyer.

[14] Thomas Trayle's will is to be found in the commissary court register, GL, MS 9171/1, f. 326, made 28 November 1394; proved 9 December 1394.

Rose Frer was widow for fifteen years. Her husband John Frer, citizen and wiredrawer, had left her comparitively well off. He had property in the parish of St Martin Pomeroy which he left to Rose. He was a member of St Katherine's fraternity in St Martin's church to which he left money for the purchase of two tin candelabras. Rose herself makes no reference to the properties left by John in her will but she was able to donate 3s. 4d. to the lamp of St Katherine in St Martin's church where she was to be buried with her late husband. She also donated 12d. to the high altar and left instructions that there were to be two torches at her funeral service. Each stipendiary chaplain in the church was to have 12d. and the parish clerk was left the same sum. Could it be that Rose may have suffered some decline in her personal fortunes during her widowhood?[15]

In the eleven years that Johanna Lorkyn was a widow she seems marginally to have improved her position since her husband's death. John Lorkyn died in early November 1403. He gave 12d. to the fabric of his parish church of St Sepulchre Newgate and 2d. each to two poor men for prayers for his soul. After two further bequests of 4d. each, to Helen Skeldergate and Alice Burne, he directed that the residue of his goods were to go to Johanna to pay all of his debts and as his executrix to be disposed of as she thought best and most pleasing to God.[16] When Johanna made her will, on 1 July 1413, she was able to leave 12d. to the high altar and 20d. for the maintenance of the fabric of St Sepulchre Newgate and 12d. to the vicar. Three chaplains, William Kybwortham, John Pycon and John Redman were left 4d. each and the clerks received 2d. each. Her son Robert Lorkyn was to dispose of all remaining goods and the residue, after the bequests and outstanding debts had been paid, was to be equally divided between Robert and his sister Agnes, the wife of John Chaddisle spurrier who with Robert were named Johanna's executors. Thomas Asshehurst, woodmonger, was their supervisor.

There was little difference in the relative wealth of two other widows whose husbands' wills have survived. Although Johanna Wyllyngham's widowhood lasted eight and a half years she made identical bequests to those that her late husband Elias, citizen and wool-bearer had made in 1396. Indeed she also appointed William Deware, wool-bearer, to be one of her executors as had her late husband. Margaret Haveryng's widowhood lasted for just nineteen days. Her husband John had made his will on 2 September 1409 and it was proved three days later. John desired to be buried in St Leonard's churchyard, Shoreditch. He made just four specific bequests: 2s. to the high altar for forgotten tithes; 12d. to St Mary's light; 12d. to the parish clerk; and 12d. to his sister. Margaret was named as his sole executrix and he appointed John Toller

---

[15] See *HW*, ii, p. 271.

[16] John Lorkyn made his will on 31 October 1403; proved 12 November 1403. GL, MS 9051/1, f. 10v.

and William Clerk, of his parish, supervisors of his will. Margaret in turn made her will on 20 September just three weeks after her husband's had been made. She wished to be buried next to John and made six specific bequests: 6d. to the lamp before the cross; 12d. to the vicar; 12d. to Peter the clerk; 12d. for the roads; 6d. for the king's road; and 12d. to her married sister. John Toller and William Clerk were to be her executors. Rose Gatyn's widowhood was the shortest at only fifteen days.[17]

In their bequests to the church and to the secular clergy the widows seem to have followed common practice. In all 50 per cent of the widows in this study made donations to their parish churches. For some it was a straight gift, but for others it was a settling of account for forgotten tithes and obligations. The sums varied according to individual means. Excluding those widows who left nothing to the church, the smallest donation was 4d., left by Matilda atte Wyche; the largest was 3s. 4d., left by Helen Trayle. The most favoured sum was 12d., which no fewer then eleven of the thirty-nine widows donated. Sometimes it was the incumbent who received these donations such as the 2s. 6d. that Agnes Martyne left to the rector of St Augustine by St Paul's Gate or the 20d. which Alice Claryngton gave to the rector of St Margaret Patyns for forgotten tithes. However, she left instructions to her executors that she was to be buried in the churchyard of Holy Trinity Priory, Aldgate, before the gate.[18]

Personal beliefs are more intangible but we occasionally get glimpses of devotion to a particular saint or saints. Alice Skarlet left 12d. to the light of St Bartholemew's church, whilst Katherine Depham left 6d. to St Katherine's lamp in St John Zachary. Margaret Haveryng's and Rose Frer's donations have already been noted. It is interesting that where particular saints are mentioned they are all female saints.[19]

Some of these widows gave gifts to their parish churches: Idomena Braytoft left her best towel and boardcloth to the high altar of St Alphege's, Cripplegate and another towel and boardcloth to the altar dedicated to the Virgin; Fen Swan gave a gown of Munster cloth to All Hallows the Great; and Alice Coket alias Clerk left her best cloth to her parish church of St Andrew, Baynard's Castle, where she desire to be buried in the choir.

The parish clergy seemed to have played an important part in most of the widows' lives judging from the number of bequests to parish chaplains and

---

[17] Elias Wyllyngham's will is GL, MS 9051/1, f. 13, made 1 August 1394; proved 16 December 1396. John's will of 1409 is to be found in GL, MS 9051/1, f. 5. Both testators named their wives as executors of their respective wills.

[18] The eleven widows who left 12d. to the high altar were Agnes Smith, Rose Frer, Joan Drewe, Margaret Yonge, Margaret Sporier, Johanna Wyllyngham, Matilda Kyrkeby, Katherine Depham, Matilda atte Wyne, Agnes Furneys, Agnes Sewale and Johanna Lorkyn.

[19] See Eamon Duffy, 'Holy Maydens, Holy Wyfes: The Cult of Women Saints in the Fifteenth and Sixteenth Centuries', W.J. Sheils and Diana Wood, ed., *Women in the Church*, Studies in Church History, 27 (Oxford, 1990), pp. 175–196, especially pp. 180, 184–87.

clerks. These bequests usually took the form of monetary gifts, varying between 4d. to 12d. each, but occasionally they took other forms. Margaret Sporier left a fur coat and three cushions to William Upton, a chaplain in St Nicholas Olave church, in return for prayers for her soul and the souls of all the faithful departed.[20]

For some of these widows the parish clergy also acted as witnesses and on occasion executors of their wills. Agnes Adam named John Owdeby, chaplain, as her executor. Idomena Braytoft chose William Palmere, rector of St Alphege's church as one of the two executors in her will of 11 March 1398. Thomas Greneowe, rector of St Edmund King and Martyr, Lombard Street was to act as supervisor to the will of Matilda atte Wyne.[21]

Only four widows remembered the orders of mendicant friars in London. Agnes Smith left 5s. to the Friars Minor for two trental masses and 2s. 6d. each to the Preaching Friars and Carmelite order for one trental mass. Katherine Depham requested that the Carmelite order say one trental mass for the benefit of her soul and that of her late husband John, but no sum was specified in her will. Alice Coket donated 2s. 6d. each to the Carmelite Friars, the Preaching Friars and the Friars Minor. Her will is interesting in that she named brother John Banstede of the Preaching Friars as one of her executors. Banstede sought and obtained the consent of his prior to act as an executor as Alice's will states that the licence to Banstede from his prior was issued on 30 July 1411, just four days before Alice's will was proved. Finally, Flora Cornewaile left 40d. to the Austin Friars; she also requested to be buried in their church.

Parish fraternities have recently been receiving considerable attention. Of this group of poor London widows only one, Margaret Yonge remembered her parish fraternity in her will. This should come as no great surprise, given that we are dealing with some of the poorer members of London society: and Margaret seems to have had difficulty in paying her subscriptions. Although living in Shoreditch, she was a member of the fraternity of St John in the church of St Lawrence, Jewry. She was in arrears in paying her subscriptions, as she directed that the 3s. 4d. she owed was to be paid by Walter Adam and William Turner. We do not know who these two individuals were; perhaps they were members of the fraternity as well and that somehow they were indebted to Margaret and this was her way of clearing the debt. They were not her

---

[20] In all twenty-three widows in this study, or just under 50 per cent gave donations to the secular clergy.

[21] William Palmere had been rector of St Alphege's since 1397 and remained there until his death in 1400. He was a remarkable man owning books on medicine and physic as well as a copy of the *Piers Plowman* manuscript, see R.A. Wood, 'A Fourteenth-Century London Owner of *Piers Plowman*', *Medium Aevum*, 53 (1984), pp. 83–90. For Thomas Greneowe, rector of St Edmund King and Martyr, see G. Hennessy, *Novum repertorium ecclesiasticum parochiale Londinense* (London, 1898), p. 142.

executors, as she directed that her son Richard and daughter Margery were to undertake that task.[22]

That children appear to have had an important part in the lives of these women is hardly surprising. In all 35 per cent of the wills refer to children. Eleven wills refer to sons only, ten to daughters and one only to a son and a daughter. Children were often the main beneficiaries of their mother's wills and were often named as executors, either sole or with others. Joan Drewe left her son Thomas Drewe (chaplain?) six silver spoons, a mazer, a worsted bed (cover), two pairs of sheets, three pots, three pottels, two furs (skins), a board cloth, a new towel and two other towels. Margaret Yonge left her daughter, Margery, her best red cap and tunic and her best fur coat.[23]

Some of these widows' wills contain references to other family members. Margaret Haveryng left her married sister 12d., whilst Agnes Sewale left her sister Johanna Streteman a bowl called 'Notte', her best bed with two pairs of sheets, six silver spoons, a veil called 'Crewell' and her best pair of amber paternoster beads. Matilda atte Wyche left the tester on her bed to her grandson, Robert Watford, and a pair of sheets. Isabel Daventre left her cousin Agnes a blue tapestry bed with red borders and a lion in the middle, a pair of sheets and a pair of blankets, a mattress, her best cloth and another cloth with a towel, a great pot and a great water pot.[24]

Outside the family it was the close friends, often other women friends and very occasionally, men friends, who were the main beneficiaries. Fifteen of the widows in this survey left bequests to other women friends. Items of clothing such as gowns, fur-edged cloaks, kirtles and coats would be distributed along with items of bedding and cooking utensils. Sometimes the degree of friendship can be gauged by the quality of the article given: 'my best gown', 'my better quality bed' and so forth. Especial friends would be given choice items of jewelry such as the silver beads and best cloak left by Matilda Kyrkeby to the

---

[22] See for example Caroline M. Barron 'The Parish Fraternities of Medieval London, *The Church in Pre-Reformation Society*, ed. C.M. Barron and Christopher Harper-Bill (Woodbridge, 1985), pp. 13–37; idem 'The "Golden Age" of Women in Medieval London', *Medieval Women in Southern England*, Reading Medieval Studies, 15 (1989), pp. 35–58, especially pp. 48–49. For the activities of women in York fraternities including widows, see P.J.P. Goldberg, 'Women in Fifteenth-Century Town Life', *Towns and Townspeople in the Fifteenth Century*, ed. John A.F. Thomson (Gloucester, 1988), pp. 107–28, especially pp. 110–111.

[23] In the 'very poor' group of widows, Alice Skarlet, Johanna Rede, Julliana atte Melle left all their goods to their sons who were all named as their sole executors. In the same group, Rose Gatyn left all her goods to her daughter and executor. In the 'poor' group, Amelia Fullerer, Isabell Daventre, Alice Claryngton, Denise Benet, Felicity Ramseye, Margaret Lyncoln and Johanna Lorkyn remembered their sons, although not all the sons were named as executors. Daughters were remembered by Margery Bene, Agnes Yonge, Rose Frer, Margaret Yonge, Margaret Sporier, Matilda Kyrkeby, Felicity Ramseye and Alice Edred. Half of these widows named their daughters as their executors; they were Margery Bene, Agnes Yonge, Margaret Yonge, Alice Edred and Agnes Spicer.

[24] Rose Frer named her son-in-law John Pedyngton, skinner, as the supervisor of her will and Matilda Kyrkeby remembered her sister-in-law and her brother.

wife of John Maryng. John was named as Matilda's executor. Four of these widows' wills contain bequests to laymen. One widow made a cash bequest, another made bequests of cash and bedding, a third widow made bequests of clothing and bedding and the fourth left an item of furniture.[25]

Some of these widows had servants who were also remembered in their employers' wills. Often the bequests reflect a very close attachment to one another, particularly when there were no surviving children or other family members. Agnes Staple, who does not mention children, left instructions to her executors that her servant Alice was to have her coverlet decorated with fleur-de-lys, a pair of sheets, a bolster and a pillow, a blue gown and a green cap and a ruby kirtle.[26]

The choice of executors was very important. Each testator wanted to be reasonably confident that her wishes would be carried out without undue delay, particularly in the provision of masses for her soul. For some the choice was easy; they had children in whom they could feel reasonably confident. For others without surviving offspring, the parish clergy provided a good alternative. In a few cases women took an important and active role. Three of the widows in this study named women to act as executors to their wills. Joan Drewe named Helen Boston along with William Lanerok, clerk, as her executors. Johanna Wyllyngham appointed William Deware and Isobell Horold executors of her will dated 3 March 1399 but not proved until six years later. Agnes Reynold's nuncupative will named her sister Katherine and Johanna Brewer as her executors.

Medieval canon law expressly forbade women to act as witnesses to wills. The fact remains that in London, and to a lesser extent in other parts of England, women are to be found witnessing wills. The will of Johanna Teele was witnessed by two women, Johanna Sydyngborne and Johanna Colynge. She also appointed Margaret Sydyngborne and Margaret More to act as the supervisors of her executors John Alby and Thomas Hunt, clerk.[27]

---

[25] Agnes Martyne left a white bed to John Bernard and two pieces of kerchief to Walter Wheler, living near Bishopsgate. Andrew Tailor's son Hugh, of Phelippes Lane, and John Skynnere's son Hugh, of Golden Lane, both received 8d. under the will of Idomena Braytoft. Margaret Sporier left Richard Watkings 6s. 8d. and Thomas Walsh a coverlet and tester, two blankets, a pair of sheets and a new cover, should they agree to act as her executors. Their acceptance is confirmed by probate being granted to them four days after her will was drawn up on 31 December 1406, possibly by Richard Watkins himself, who is described in Margaret's will as citizen and scrivener. Gilbert Page was to receive a cupboard and his wife a cloak under the will of Matilda Kyrkeby. See Table 4 for will references.

[26] Elizabeth Tyllworth's servant Cristene was left a pair of linen sheets, a pair of blankets, one covered bed and all Elizabeth's clothes for her use during her lifetime. Idomena Braytoft left her house servant, John Payne, a tin vessel of two quarts' capacity and six better quality tin vessels. Possibly Idomena had had dealings as a water-carrier although her will makes no reference to this trade. See Table 4 for details of these widows' wills.

[27] I have two other examples of widows having their wills witnessed by women. These are both from the 'moderately wealthy' group. Matilda atte Mone's will was witnessed by three women: Johanna Miller, Alice Coltille and Lucy Davy. Her will was drawn up on 15 March 1411/12; proved

continued

Other widows chose either close friends or neighbours or the former business associates of their late husbands. Johanna Pygeant's late husband, Roger, was a citizen and goldsmith and she appointed John Bette junior, citizen and goldsmith, as her executor. Rose Gatyn was the widow of John Gatyn, fishmonger. Although she appointed her daughter Alice as her executor under the supervision of Martin Seman, clerk, two of the witnesses to the will, Thomas Lyncolne and John Southous, were bakers.

Perhaps the most interesting example of continuing association with a late husband's craft is provided by the cases of Agnes Salman and Agnes Sewale. Agnes Salman's late husband, Walter, was a citizen and girdler. His widow appointed two other girdlers as her executors, William Batescroft and Ralph Ans. Agnes Sewale was named as supervisor. Agnes Sewale's husband is not mentioned in her will, but she too appointed William Batescroft and Ralph Ans, citizens and girdlers, as her executors. It is almost certain therefore that Agnes Sewale's late husband was also a girdler. These two widows lived in adjacent parishes; Agnes Salman in St Lawrence Jewry and Agnes Sewale in St Mary Aldermanbury. They died within four months of each other.

For the remainder of our widows their executors appear to have been their friends and fellow parishoners. John Haveryng's will was made on the 2 September: he appointed John Toller and William Clerk whom he described as 'my fellow parishioners' to act as supervisors to his widow Margaret. She in turn drew up her will fifteen days after probate was granted to her for her husband's will. She also named John and William to be her executors, although they were not described as 'my fellow parishioners' in her will. She died four days later on the 24 September 1409.

There are no discernable patterns concerning parishes in which these widows lived in either the 'very poor' or the 'poor' groupings. Virtually all the parishes subject to the jurisdiction of the archdeacon's court are covered in this study. None of the widows in the 'very poor' group lived in the extra-mural parishes. In the 'poor' group three widows lived in the poor parish of St Sepulchre, Newgate, three in St Leonard, Shoreditch and one in St Botolph, Aldersgate. The remaining widows in this study lived in parishes within the walls.[28]

For most of the widows there was little residue left for any charitable or pious works after the personal bequests had been taken care of. Indeed Alice

---

continued

2 April 1411/12. GL, MS 9051/1, f. 2v. Johanna Berkyng had her will witnessed by Johanna Suel on 4 March 1413. See GL, MS 9051/1, f. 4v.

For an important study of the role of medieval women as executors and witnesses see Rowena E. Archer and B.E. Ferme, 'Testamentary Procedure with Special Reference to the Executrix', *Medieval Women in Southern England*, Reading Medieval Studies, 15 (1989), pp. 3–34, especially p. 10 and notes 41–43.

[28] Five of these parishes, St Mary Aldermanbury, St Stephen Colman Street in the 'very poor' group and All Hallows the Great, St Magnus and St Lawrence Jewry in the 'poor' group have two widows residing there, whilst the remaining parishes have one each.

Reynold made no personal bequests at all. She instructed her executors to pay all her debts first and the remainder of her goods were to be used to provide masses, works of charity and other pious purposes for the benefit of her soul and that of her late husband John and for all the faithful departed. Rose Frer's executors were instructed to use the residue of her goods and chattels to pay any debts and then to make donations for masses and other charitable works for the benefit of her soul and her benefactors' souls at their discretion. Fen Swan wanted her executors Reginald Holt, armourer, and Everard Pepir, tailor, to distribute the remainder of her goods after paying debts and distributing her personal bequests, for the benefit of her soul, her late husband Henry Creye and all the faithful departed. Katherine Depham left instructions that the residue of her estate was to be spent on the provision of masses in her parish church, for the benefit of her soul and those of Nicholas Knyght, her late husband John Depham and her benefactors, by her executors as the rector directed them.

None of these widows makes any reference to places outside London. If there were any family ties with other places the ties had perhaps been broken long ago, relations had died or had been long forgotten. The fact that most widows had little in the way of property or disposable income with which to remember distant relations or birthplaces, is another indication of their poverty.

Several themes can be seen running through all these widows' wills which have been detected in other studies of medieval piety for other parts of the country.[29] First there is the uniform commendation of souls to God and the Virgin and All Saints. All wished to remind the Almighty of their impending death and to be looked upon in a favourable light for the next world. Secondly, having made their peace with God, the widows turned to the arrangements for their burial. Most wished to be buried with their late husbands in their parish church or churchyard. Presumably they felt safe in the knowledge that they would still be remembered by their friends and relations and would be in familiar surroundings. Thirdly, they wished to make their peace with their parish church by settling outstanding tithes. Fourthly, the parish clergy seem to have figured largely in their widowhood; the frequent bequests to clergy and

---

[29] See for example J.T. Rosenthal, *The Purchase of Paradise: Gift-Giving and the Aristocracy, 1307–1458* (London, 1972); M.G.A. Vale, *Piety, Charity and Literacy amongst the Yorkshire Gentry, 1370–1480*, Borthwick Papers, 50 (York, 1976); P. Heath, 'Urban Piety in the Later Middle Ages: The Evidence of Hull Wills, *Church, Politics and Patronage in England and France in the Fifteenth Century*, ed. R.B. Dobson (Gloucester, 1984), pp. 209–34; P.W. Fleming, 'Charity, Faith and the Gentry of Kent 1422–1529', *Property and Politics: Essays in the Later Medieval English History*, ed. A.J. Pollard (Gloucester, 1984), pp. 36–58; M.A. Hicks, 'Piety and Lineage in the Wars of the Roses: The Hungerford Experience', *Kings and Nobles in the Later Middle Ages: A Tribute to Charles Ross*, ed. R.A. Griffiths and James Sherborne (Gloucester, 1986), pp. 90–108; Norman P. Tanner, *The Church in Late Medieval Norwich, 1370–1532* (Toronto, 1984), especially chapter 3; Goldberg, 'Women in Fifteenth Century Town Life' n. 22 above.

the direct use made of them as executors, witnesses and supervisors suggests the important role which they played.

The family and other close relations were important to women throughout this period and in some of the wills we find references to grandchildren, cousins, and sisters as well as sons and daughters. One of the widows used her mother to supervise her will.[30] That there are no references to godchildren in any of the wills is yet another indication of poverty. Usually the best pieces of jewelry or clothes and household effects would be reserved for close relatives before distributing the remaining possessions to friends and more distant relations. There was also the desire to make some provision in their will for the performance of good works and for the saying of masses for the benefit of their souls and for their late husbands' souls.

Finally, they all seem to have been unconcerned with events outside their own world, which was based on their family, their friends and fellow paris-honers. They seem to have played little or no role in London life and were concerned only with their own households. Just occasionally we can catch a glimpse of their world from other sources. Flora Cornewaile's will, made on 20 July 1407, was witnessed by one John Broun, scrivener. In 1404 John had come to the attention of the city authorities when he had been found guilty of adultery with Johanna Benyngtone, and unmarried woman living in Bread Street ward. John was described as a married man.[31] More respectably, Richard Elyot, citizen and bladesmith, had been an executor of Alice Coket's will in 1411. He had served as one of the two masters of his craft in 1417. In 1419 his house was broken into and his goods stolen by Thomas Broun of London 'breueresman' in the parish of St Sepulchre, Newgate.[32]

Although these widows were not amongst the extremely poor of London, who had nothing at all to leave, the fact that they did make testaments which have survived is important. It enables us to see a little into their lives, hopes, aspirations and priorities as death approached.

---

[30] This was Elizabeth Tyllworth who described herself as the widow of Thomas Tyllworth and the heiress of her mother Johanna. See Table 4.

[31] *LBI.*, p. 274.

[32] Ibid., pp. 173 and 230.

Table 4

The Wills of Poor Widows proved in the Archdeacon's Court of London,
1393–1415

Index to widows in both categories in Table 3 of the text and their will references,
Guildhall Library, MS. 9051/1. All wills are written in Latin except those denoted thus
(*), which are in English.

Very Poor

Name	Year	Folio	Date Made	Date Proved
Alice Skarlet	1393	f. 17v	5 August 1393	5 February 1393/4
Sibil Spencer	1399	f. 21	2 October 1399	2 January 1399/1400
Rose Gatyn	1405	f. 19v	1 January 1405/6	3 March 1405/6
Alice Reynold	1406	f. 2	13 July 1405	3 March 1406
Johanna Rede	1408	f. 1	25 May 1408	26 May 1408
Juliana atte Melle	1411	f. 1v	6 March 1410/11	1 April 1411
Agnes Arderne	1411	f. 14	26 April 1411	31 January 1411/12
Johanna Pygeant	1412	f. 13v	17 October 1412	19 October 1412
Juliana Deux	1412	f. 14v	20 August 1412	17 October 1412
Cecilia Michell	1413	f. 9	26 June 1413	1 July 1413

Poor

Name	Year	Folio	Date Made	Date Proved
Margery Bene	1395	ff. 4v–5	13 October 1394	29 November 1394
Elizabeth Tyllworth	1395	f. 9	25 January 1394/5	30 January 1394/5
Agnes Smith	1395	f. 12	8 April 1395	18 April 1395
Agnes Martyne	1396	f. 4	31 August 1396	15 September 1396
Idomena Braytoft	1398	f. 23r–v	11 March 1400	26 March 1400
Agnes Yonge	1403	f. 12	8 October 1399	11 December 1403
Margaret Stodeley	1404	f. 2v	14 February 1403	11 May 1404
Rose Frer	1404	f. 12	4 November 1404	13 December 1404
Johanna Wyllyngham	1405	f. 5v	3 March 1399	25 April 1405
Amelia Fullerer	1405	f. 9v	19 August 1405	24 August 1405
Joan Drewe	1406	f. 8v	1 July 1406	18 September 1406
Margaret Yonge	1406	f. 9	14 September 1406	28 September 1406
Margaret Sporier	1406	f. 13v	31 December 1406	4 January 1406/7
Isabell Daventre	1407	f. 6v	14 June 1407	21 June 1407
Fen Swan	1407	f. 11	4 August 1407	14 August 1407
Matilda Kyrkeby	1407	f. 20v	14 October 1407	18 October 1407
Flora Cornewaile	1407	f. 23	20 July 1407	31 October 1407
Katherine Depham	1407	f. 31v	1 February 1407/8	15 February 1407/8
Matilda atte Wyne	1407	f. 32	7 February 1407/8	16 February 1407/8
Alice Claryngton	1408	f. 7v	20 July 1408	22 July 1408
Denise Benet*	1409	f. 1	Not given	1 April 1409
Felicity Ramseye	1409	f. 5	8 August 1408	7 September 1409
Margaret Haveryng	1409	f. 7	20 September 1409	24 September 1409
Alice Edred	1409	f. 10r–v	21 July 1403	13 November 1409
Johanna Teele	1410	f. 4v	31 August 1410	2 September 1410
Agnes Spicer*	1410	f. 12v	15 September 1410	12 December 1410
Agnes Furneys	1410	f. 14v	20 June 1410	1 February 1410/11
Helen Wayte	1411	f. 2	10 April 1411	29 April 1411
Alice Coket alias Clerk	1411	ff. 5v–6	16 July 1411	3 August 1411
Matilda atte Wyche	1411	f. 14	27 November 1411	30 January 1411/12

Alice Graveneye	1413	f. 1	13 March 1412/12	4 April 1413
Helen Trayle	1413	f. 1v	29 March 1413	10 April 1413
Agnes Adam	1413	f. 7	4 June 1413	15 June 1413
Agnes Salman	1413	f. 8v	1 April 1413	15 January 1413/14
Margaret Lyncoln	1413	f. 9v	6 November 1413	22 February 1413/14
Agnes Staple	1413	f. 15	26 August 1413	1 September 1413
Agnes Sewale	1414	f. 6r–v	15 May 1414	19 May 1414
Johanna Lorkyn	1414	f. 13v	1 July 1413	9 December 1414
Agnes Regnald	1415	f. 7	8 September 1415	Not given

5

Joan Pyel (d. 1412)

Stephen O'Connor

Joan Pyel was the wife of John Pyel, a London mercer, active in the city from the 1340s, who became an alderman in 1369 and was elected mayor in 1372.[1] Only the barest outline of Joan's life can be reconstructed with any certainty. She was probably born between 1330 and 1335 and was married by February 1349.[2] Although her husband came from Irthlingborough in Northamptonshire, it is likely that Joan married him only after his arrival in London, and she herself may well have been a native Londoner. Certainly she retained a London bias and does not seem to have shared her husband's enthusiasm for his Northamptonshire homeland. Later in their married life she became involved, at least nominally, in Pyel's property dealings, mostly in London. From 1373 to 1377 she was named jointly with her husband in several land acquisitions in the city, although she also appears as a joint recipient of some lands and rents in Irthlingborough and Cranford in Northamptonshire.[3] She was also appointed executor of both Pyel's wills, the first of which, made in 1377, concerned his real estate in London and the suburbs, while the second, drawn up in 1379, focused on his Northamptonshire assets.[4] She died in 1412, having survived her husband by thirty years, and was buried at the convent of St Helen's Bishopsgate.[5]

Of Joan's life before her husband's death virtually nothing is known. For all that we can tell she lived out the years in obscure domesticity. Only two references to her seem to have survived: in February 1349 she and John Pyel received a plenary indulgence in February and in July 1355 Joan in her own right was granted a papal indult to choose a confessor at the time of her death.[6] Her relationship with her husband, and something of her personality, can,

[1] For the biography of John Pyel see Stephen O'Connor ed., *A Calendar of the Cartularies of Adam Fraunceys and John Pyel*, Camden Society, 5th series, ii (1993).

[2] See below, n. 6.

[3] Cartulary of John Pyel, London, College of Arms, MS Vincent 64.

[4] CLRO, HR 110 (117); Episcopal Register of John Buckingham, bishop of Lincoln, Lincoln Archive Office, Episcopal Register, xii, ff. 244r–245v.

[5] Joan Pyel's will: Lambeth Palace, Episcopal Register of Thomas Arundel, ii, f. 161v.

[6] *Calendar of Papal Petitions* (London, 1896,), i, p. 152; *Calendar of Papal Letters* (London, 1893), iii, p. 559.

however, be gleaned from the small scraps of evidence that remain from her years as a widow, and particularly from her remarkable achievement in completing the most cherished project of her husband's later life, the foundation of a college of priests in Irthlingborough.

Joan Pyel's association with London is reflected in the division of John Pyel's bequests between his two wills. The first, drawn up in June 1377 and enrolled in the court of Hustings, left all his landholdings in London and the suburbs to his wife, and thereafter to Irthlingborough College. The executors were to be Joan herself and John's brother Henry, archdeacon of Northampton. At the end of February 1379 Pyel drew up a more detailed will which dealt more specifically with Northamptonshire, not only in terms of his property there but also with regard to beneficiaries living in the county. Henry was replaced as executor in this second will, doubtless because he was by now in failing health (he died about six weeks later), and Joan was joined by a further four executors and two supervisors. In the document proper she is referred to only once, as co-beneficiary with her two sons of the residue of Pyel's movable property, but in a codicil added to the will on 25 June 1379 she was granted 50 marks p.a. for life from her husband's lands in Northamptonshire, with the proviso that this should take effect seven years after his death.[7] This, John made clear, was to replace her rights of dower, and he added, somewhat coolly, that if Joan did not agree to this provision, she would receive nothing at all from the bequest.[8] John may have felt that Joan was already well catered for by receipt of his London holdings, but the somewhat grudging tone in which the grant was made appears in contrast to the general tenor of the codicil, which displays generosity towards friends and retainers and their wives in the county, as well as to a number of religious houses. In fact, immediately before Joan's allotment, a certain Margaret Joye, perhaps a local widow, received a series of personal items, including a bed, goblet, tablecloth, towel, basin and ewer and £10 in cash, as well as all lands, tenements and rents in what appears to be Finedon, Northamptonshire. Joan, it is true, may have received some personal effects by verbal instruction, but it is interesting to compare the personal quality of the legacy to Margaret, whoever she may have been, with the stiff formality of his duty towards his wife.

That consciousness of formal duty was reciprocated by Joan when she went to great lengths to establish Irthlingborough College after her husband's death. John Pyel had started the process in 1373, when Pope Gregory XI, at Pyel's own request, authorised the bishop of Lincoln, John Buckingham, to take the steps necessary to erect the parish church of St Peter's Irthlingborough

---

[7] In the event she received this legacy on 26 August 1386, a few years earlier than was stipulated (*CCR, 1385–89*, p. 143).

[8] 'et si la dit Johane ne soye agree de ceo qe ieo ly ay ordeigne par ycestes ove touz les profitz de mes terres et en mon testament en lieu de sa dower ieo violle qele neyt riens de mon devys'.

into a collegiate church.[9] Royal letters patent were granted in February 1375 and in November 1375 the abbot and convent of Peterborough, who were patrons of St Peter's wrote to Bishop Buckingham asking him to proceed with the pope's commission. Buckingham was unwilling to comply and seems to have taken advantage of a technical flaw in the papal bull to postpone its implementation. Edward III's death in 1377 and the outbreak of schism in 1378 further delayed matters. By the time that Pyel's will was written in 1379 there was an explicit recognition that he might not live to see the foundation completed.[10] The frequent references to the staffing and equipment of the college, and the monetary provisions made for the necessary building works, indicate the great importance which Pyel attached to the project; his executors would have been in no doubt that, should he die before its completion, they were to do all in their power to effect a speedy conclusion.

John Pyel died in May 1382 and Joan, the first-named executor of the second will, set about reviving the project with the help of two of her husband's other executors. In November 1383 and December 1386 she obtained releases of two of the blocks of London property which were to provide the endowment of the college. She also secured confirmation from Urban VI on 10 June 1386 of Gregory XI's original bull.[11] Joan evidently foresaw the possibility of renewed obstruction by the bishop of Lincoln and so contrived to circumvent his authority. The document of papal confirmation was therefore directed not to John Buckingham but to Thomas Baketon, archdeacon of London, on the pretext that John Pyel had been a citizen of London. Joan also sought and obtained new letters patent from the crown on 12 March 1388, at a cost of 20 marks.[12] Baketon convened a court of enquiry in January 1387, in which the relevant documents were examined and witnesses summoned, including the bishop of Lincoln and the archdeacon of Northampton. Again Buckingham dragged his feet, refusing to attend the enquiry, until in May 1388 the whole procedure had to be repeated, with the documents re-examined and witnesses recalled. Whether the bishop of Lincoln deigned to appear on this second occasion is doubtful, but Baketon was satisfied that the correct procedures had been taken and that sufficient provision had been made to support the college and he confirmed the endowment accordingly. It was settled that the college would be instituted on the death or resignation of the present rector of the parish, Roger Aswardby, who resigned as rector in February 1393.[13] Thus

---

[9] For what follows see A. Hamilton Thompson, 'The Early History of the College of Irthlingborough', *Reports and Papers of the Norhtampton and Oakham Architectural Society*, 35 (1920), pp. 267–88.

[10] 'en cas qu ieo deuie devant qe le dit college soit fait et qe le dit college ne poet estre accompliz . . . '

[11] Thompson, 'Irthlingborough College', p. 271.

[12] Dugdale's *Monasticon anglicanum*, ed. J. Caley, H. Ellis and B. Bandinel, 6 vols (London 1815–30), vi, *1384–85*.

[13] Thompson, 'Irthlingborough College', p. 273.

almost eleven years after the founder's death, Irthlingborough College was finally established, a tribute to the shrewdness, energy and sheer tenacity of his widow.[14]

Her duty complete, Joan seems to have withdrawn from her former life and from her family, possibly retiring to a convent. Apart from her support of St Bartholomew's priory in London and a convent of nuns in Cheshunt, Hertfordshire, both recorded in 1392, we hear nothing more of Joan until January 1412, when, as a woman approaching eighty years or more and close to death, she had her own will drawn up. The severance of ties with her family seems by now to have been complete. Joan refers to herself as lately the wife of John Pyell, citizen, while he lived, of London, but that is the only mention she makes of her husband, her sons or her grandchildren. She left instructions that she should be buried outside the south door of the convent church of St Helen's Bishopsgate, and it seems fairly clear that she had never left London, preferring to remain, at least initially, in her husband's house in Broad Street in the parish of St Bartholomew the Less, to which church she left two of the candles which were to be burned at her funeral, perhaps later moving to the precinct of St Helen's, possibly as a vowess or a corrodian. She clearly had a close association with St Helen's, leaving in her will sums of money for the high altar, to the subprioress, to one named nun, Isabel Lucas, and lesser sums to each of the other sisters and to the chaplains and clerks who officiated in the convent. Almost all her other bequests were to religious houses in London, or to individual religious. Among the exceptions were her servant, Joan Lucas, perhaps a relative of the nun Isabel, and her former servant John Sharp. She also made a gift of 20s. to the 'fraternity of the tailors' (*fraternitati cissorum*), of which she was probably a member, a sum the Merchant Taylors' Company duly recorded in their accounts for 1412–13.[15] The residue of her goods was to be distributed for the sake of her soul and the souls of those to whom she was obligated, though she did not specify who these might be. Her executors were Robert Brown, chaplain, John Smart, possibly a parishioner of St Mary le Strand, and Ralph Stoke, a London grocer. At the end of her days it seems that Joan Pyel was still a woman of means. Apart from the evidence of her various legacies, she was also assessed as being worth £23 9s. 4d. p.a. in rents in the 1411 subsidy return for London.[16] Her years of widowhood, however she may have spent them, were apparently passed in some comfort.

For the most part Joan Pyel lived in the historical shadow of her husband, one of the most prominent London citizens of his day, yet despite the pitiful dearth

---

[14] The church of St Peter houses the effigies of a merchant and his lady, their faces badly mutilated, but no doubt meant to represent John and Joan Pyel. Pevsner thinks that they may date from the fifteenth century, in which case they demonstrate the continuing esteem in which the effective co-founders of the college were held by later generations.

[15] Merchant Taylor's Company Accounts, i, 1397–1445, f. 68v (Guildhall Library Microfilm 297). I am grateful to Matthew Davis for this reference.

[16] J.C.L. Stahlschmidt 'Original Documents', *Archaeological Journal*, 44 (1887), p. 63.

of evidence relating to her life, we can still manage to put some colour into her otherwise pale features. She was evidently a competent and intelligent woman, quite capable of running Pyel's London household and probably looking after some of his other affairs in the city during his frequent absences. Since Pyel spent much of his time away from London, at least until 1369, the inference is that they lived apart for a good deal of their married life, which may account for some of the apparent coolness in their relationship. Certainly Joan showed little inclination to follow her husband to Irthlingborough when he retired from the city in the late 1370s, and it would seem she also cut herself off from her sons as well. She was to be given no part in their upbringing and education, which Pyel entrusted, after his death, to Nicholas Brembre, grocer and future mayor of London. Both boys settled in Northamptonshire but she probably seldom saw them or her grandchildren. It is perhaps no great surprise that this apparent estrangement led her to seek solace in religion. She certainly seems to have been a woman of great piety; all that we know of her is connected in some way with religious observance. The grant of plenary indulgence, the indult to choose a confessor, the completion of the college at Irthlingborough at a great personal cost, support of the nuns at Cheshunt, and finally her will, which seems almost to be a catalogue of the religious houses of London, mark her out as woman of fervent faith. She died on or about 1 February 1412, having outlived her sons, John and Nicholas, and her grandson, John. She was survived by her granddaughter, Elizabeth.[17]

[17] For the Pyel descendants see O'Connor, *Cartularies of Adam Fraunceys and John Pyel*.

6

Lucia Visconti, Countess of Kent (d. 1424)

Helen Bradley

Lucia was the daughter of Bernabò lord of Milan and Beatrice della Scala of Verona, one of ten legitimate sisters whose marriages served the purpose of extending Visconti influence throughout Europe. Although the girls were mostly targeted at the continental powers, the family did have some contact with England. Lucia's cousin Violante had married the duke of Clarence, her sister Caterina was in negotiation with Richard II in the late 1370s, and another sister Donnina had married Giovanni Achud – more recognisable to us as John Hawkwood – who was in the family's service for some time. In 1385 Lucia's father's rule was cut short when he was taken prisoner and poisoned by her cousin, Gian Galeazzo. Known to his enemies as the 'maladetto tirano' ('damned tyrant'), the new lord of Milan's main domestic problem was how to deal with the considerable array of his uncle's disinherited offspring. Two legitimate sons, Mastino and Carlo, prudently adjourned to England in 1388 for an indefinite stay, spending some of their time in London. Gian Galeazzo arranged suitable matches for their remaining unmarried sisters.[1]

During 1382–84 Lucia's father had actively promoted her marriage to the future Louis II of Anjou, with the objective of having her installed as queen of Sicily, but this stratagem collapsed with his death. In 1399 her cousin Gian

[1] D.M. Bueno de Mesquita, *Giangaleazzo Visconti, Duke of Milan, (1351–1402)* (Cambridge, 1941), table II; see also, C. Santoro, *La politica finanziaria dei Visconti*, 3 vols (Varese, 1976–83); T. Rymer, ed., *Foedera, conventiones, literae, et cujus cunque generis acta publica, inter reges Angliae, et alios, quosvis imperatores, reges, pontifices, principes, vel communitates*, 10 vols (The Hague, 1735–45), iii, pt 3, p. 84, 18 March 1379; H.T. Riley, ed., *Thomae Walsingham quandam monachi S. Albani Historia anglicana*, Rolls Series, 2 vols (London 1863–64), ii, p. 46; PRO, E 101/400/8 (1378); Santoro, *Politica finanziaria*, ii pp. 2–3, no. 5, 27 June 1385; A.B. Hinds, ed., *Calendar of State Papers and Manuscripts Existing in the Archives and Collections of Milan, 1385– 1618*, (London, 1912), i, p. 1, no. 1, 1 July 1385; Archivio di Stato di Firenze a Prato, MS 664/ 308922, 20 September 1402 and similarly MS 777/313049, 5 March 1398 'il terano che Christo lo distrugha . . . ' ('the tyrant may Christ destroy him'); Rymer, *Foedera*, iii, pt 4, p. 31, 23 August 1388; PRO, E 403/524, 16 July and 23 August 1389; E 403/527, 15 December 1389, 25 January and 7 February 1390. The Archivio di Stato di Firenze a Prato contains a vast collection of business letters addressed to Francesco di Marco Datini – Iris Origo's *The Merchant of Prato* (London, 1957; revised edn, New York, 1963, repr. 1979) – many of which were written by Italians in London.

Galeazzo considered a number of suitors for her, the most outstanding of whom was Henry, duke of Lancaster; at least, Lucia obviously thought so. He had been in Milan in 1393 when she had been thirteen years old, and he had made an impact upon her imagination. In 1399 she told her sister Caterina that if she could be sure of having Henry, she would wait for him 'to the very end of her life, even if she knew that she would die three days after the marriage . . . ' Political security came regrettably low on her check-list of desirable qualities in a husband, but Gian Galeazzo insisted that Henry must be back in favour first, and Lucia realised that she could not be certain that the marriage would ever take place. Negotiations then went ahead with Frederick of Thuringia, later elector of Saxony; but after Gian Galeazzo died in 1402, Lucia obtained an annulment on the grounds of duress and was back on the market again.[2]

In May 1406 a marriage contract was drawn up on her behalf with Edmund Holland, earl of Kent. He was to collect her from a Channel port in the latter half of November that year and marry her in return for a dowry of 70,000 florins: 12,000 down on consummation, and 8,285 per year thereafter until the entire sum was paid off. The rate of exchange was pegged according to a sliding scale of sterling, and the deal was guaranteed by the commune of Milan in a separate instrument.[3] Lucia and Edmund were married at St Mary Overy, Southwark on 24 January 1407; Henry – now Henry IV of England – gave her away. Her feelings at the celebration feast afterwards, held at the bishop of Winchester's palace, may well have been mixed.

Although her heart had been set on Henry, Edmund was not such a bad bargain and Henry himself had been instrumental in making the match. In 1403 Edmund had fought for him at Shrewsbury; a 'sory bataill . . . ' according to English accounts; 'la quala fu aspra & dura' ('which was bitter and hard'), according to the Florentines living in London. Conditions had been so bad on the field that two captains from the opposing side came forward to suggest that less butchery might be in order: 'diciendono non si facie si micidio nella battaglia altrimenti era maciello' ('saying not to behave so murderously on the battlefield otherwise there would be slaughter'). More elegantly, Edmund took part in jousting at Smithfield in 1405 to favourable reviews from the chroniclers: 'ye erle of Kent bare hym so valyauntly, that to hym was gyven ye

---

[2] G. Romano, 'Il primo matrimonio di Lucia Visconti e la rovina di Bernabò', *Archivio storico lombardo*, 10 (1893) pp. 585–611; L. Toulmin Smith, ed., *Expeditions to Prussia and the Holy Land made by Henry Earl of Derby (afterwards King Henry IV) in the Years 1390–1 and 1392–3 being the Accounts kept by his Treasurer during Two Years*, Camden Society, new series, 52 (1894; repr. 1965), pp. lxviii, 241–42; Hinds, ed., *Calendar*, pp. 1–2, no. 2, 11 May 1399; G. Romano, 'Gian Galeazzo Visconti e gli eredi di Bernabò', *Archivio storico lombardo*, 8 (1891), pp. 5–59, 291–341, 302; see also, J. Tait's review of K. Wenck, *Eine mailändisch-thüringische Heiratsgeschichte aus der Zeit König Wenzels*, (Dresden, 1895), *English Historical Review*, 10 (1895), p. 791; and K. Wenck, 'Lucia Visconti, König Heinrich IV von England und Edmund von Kent', *Mittheilungen des Instituts für Oesterreichische Geschichtsforschung*, 18 (1897), pp. 69–128.

[3] BL, MS Add. 30662, ff. 17v–24 (May 1406); see also Hinds, ed., *Calendar*, pp. 275–76, no. 431, (1490).

pryce of yt iourney to his great honour . . . ' 'And the Erle of Kent had the felde, and gate hym there grete worship'. That same year, on an expedition to Normandy and Flanders, an encounter with three Genoese carracks threatened the safety of Henry's son: 'the fight verie cruell, till the earle of Kent came to the rescue . . . ' The carracks 'furono prese dal'armata di chostoro che futa chativa nuova per gli merchanti . . . ' ('were taken by their armed shipping which was bad news for the merchants') according to the Florentines. After more jousting in London in 1406, Edmund 'was in such favour with king Henrie, that he not onelie advanced him to high offices and great honors, but also to his great costs and charges obteined for him the ladie Lucie . . . '[4] Edmund was everything that Lucia could have wanted; his only drawback was his financial situation. There were three dowager countesses, and the military support expected of him by Henry was by no means cheap. On the other hand, at the time of their marriage, Lucia was twenty-seven and Edmund just twenty-five; he was a great hero, with every prospect of a distinguished political and military career, and he would collect a dowry which would go some way towards solving his problems.[5]

Nothing definite is known of the relationship between them; their silverware reveals little except a penchant for the combined arms of Kent and Milan, which perhaps acknowledges some sense of equality in their respective pedigrees.[6] But if there was any question of marital disharmony, Lucia had plenty of ammunition. Firstly, the man she should have married was now king of England. Secondly, Edmund had a daughter from a prenuptial liaison with Constance, daughter of Edmund of Langley, duke of York, and wife of Thomas Lord Despenser. Constance had attended their wedding but had not spoken up. According to Edmund's sisters, the marriage 'continued withouten ony interruption of the saide Custance, or eny oyer, duryng the lyf of the saide Edmond . . . ' In fact, he had been careless in his choice, as it was a politically dangerous connection. Lady Despenser and her brother, Edward, duke of York, were accused of treason concerning the March children in 1405, 'for they seyden that the eldere chyld was trewe kyng . . . '[7] Lucia was settling into her new life, and in May 1408 she obtained denization, but her marriage was only

---

[4] Sir N.H. Nicolas and E. Tyrrell, ed., *A Chronicle of London, 1089–1483*, (London, 1827), p. 88; Archivio di Stato di Firenze a Prato, MS 664/308929, 9 August 1403; R. Fabyan, *The New Chronicles of England and France*, (London, 1811), p. 572; J.R. Lumby, ed., *Polychronicon Ranulphi Higden monachi Cestrensis*, Rolls Series, 9 vols (London, 1865–86), viii, p. 543; R. Holinshed, *Chronicles of England, Scotland and Ireland*, 6 vols (London, 1807–8), iii, pp. 35–36; see also H.T. Riley, ed., *Johannis de Trokelowe, et Henrici de Blaneforde, monachorum S. Albani, necnon quorundam anonymorum, chronica et annales*, Rolls Series (London, 1866), p. 401; Archivio di Stato di Firenze a Prato, MS 664/509889, 10 May 1405; *Holinshed's Chronicles*, p. 41.

[5] I am grateful to Dr M.M.N. Stansfield, whose thesis, 'The Hollands, Dukes of Exeter, Earls of Kent and Huntingdon, 1352–1475' (unpublished D. Phil thesis, University of Oxford, 1987), entailed some research on Lucia, for his help, particularly with the Kent background.

[6] *CPR, 1408–13*, p. 147, 8 November 1409.

[7] *RP*, iv, pp. 375–76 (1430–31); Nicolas and Tyrrell, *Chronicle of London*, p. 90.

to last another four months. In September that year, Edmund was killed in Brittany by a head injury from a crossbow bolt, 'sclayn, thorough his own folye, at Bryak in Bretayne, for he rood withoughte basnet, and was marked with a quarell . . . '[8] Ironically, in view of later developments, he had been attempting to enforce payment of the queen's dowry.

Lucia had been married for barely a year and a half, and she had no children. Sudden widowhood must have left her at a loss; still relatively new to England, she had no reason to expect a rousing welcome on return to Milan. Yet if she were to secure her future in England, Lucia could not afford to be slow about her business. The Kent inheritance was not in tail male. Edmund had four living sisters and a nephew – the earl of March – and he had been over 4,000 marks in debt. Her sister, Donnina Hawkwood, had complained to the king about her situation after her husband had died intestate; Lucia followed the same course.[9] No doubt she had the advantage of Henry's personal sympathy too. A few months after Edmund's death, she was granted the keeping of his lands with one third of the income; the remaining two-thirds was devoted to the payment of Edmund's debts. Her dower lands were specified, and two long-serving Holland officials acted as her attorneys. She also had wardship of the earl of March's one-fifth share. A year later, she obtained a royal pardon covering all debts and a grant of the silverware which Edmund had pawned in Southampton just before his departure for Brittany.[10] Nor did this exhaust her efforts to stabilise her situation. The duchy of Milan had not yet paid her dowry and in 1414, determined to mobilise her own resources, she pressed for economic sanctions. Backed by her English male relatives, she petitioned parliament for letters of marque against the Milanese to compel payment not only of her dowry but of £5,000 in expenses. The petition carefully pointed out that other English creditors of Milanese merchants would also be able to collect their money more quickly 'saunz ceo q'ils vorroient tielment estre mokez come ils nous mokent en cest p‹a›rtie . . . '[11]

While the non-payment of her dowry may indeed have made Lucia and her in-laws a laughing-stock, circumstances in Milan were far from promising. After the death of Gian Galeazzo in 1402, the duchy was in considerable

---

[8] *CPR, 1405–8*, p. 462, 4 May 1408, and Rymer, *Foedera*, iv, pt 1, p. 131, 4 May 1408; Nicolas and Tyrrell, *Chronicle of London*, p. 91.

[9] *CPMR, 1381–1412*, pp. 257–58, 24 February 1398, pp. 308–10, 15 June 1411; PRO, SC 8/24/1161 (2 May 1421) and *RP*, iv, pp. 143–45 (1421). Gian Galeazzo had provided for the return of his female cousins in the event of widowhood (or marital poverty) in 1397, Romano, 'Gian Galeazzo', pp. 299–300, but the option was either unattractive or uncertain after his death.

[10] *CPR, 1408–13*, pp. 35–36, 9 and 18 November 1408; *CCR, 1405–9*, pp. 422–23, 1 December 1408; Rymer, *Foedera*, iv, pt 1, p. 144, 1 December 1408; *CPR, 1408–13*, p. 147, 8 November 1409. She also obtained advowsons for Bourne Abbey and Beaulieu Abbey, *CPR, 1408–13*, p. 387, 28 April 1412, p. 80, 1 June 1409, and had a life grant of four tuns of Gascon wine in the port of London each year, p. 68, 28 March 1409.

[11] *RP*, iv, p. 29 (1414).

physical and financial disarray. In 1423 Milan reclaimed the dowry paid with Lucia's sister Valentina, whose marriage to Peter, king of Jerusalem and Cyprus, had been childless.[12] The dowry, like any modern stud fee, was refundable in cases of disappointment. This did not augur well for Lucia, who was similarly placed. Meanwhile, in May 1421, Lucia petitioned parliament again, this time for relief from Edmund's creditors. She cited the huge expenses he had incurred before they had been married, fighting for Henry at Shrewsbury and overseas with Clarence, and also in the jousts at Smithfield, and said that he had been so much in debt that he had been unable to find an executor. She complained of harassment both in the king's council and at common law, 'verisemblablement a sa destruccion' and she picked out the most persistent creditors – all citizens of London – by name. To settle the matter, she officially gave up title to 6,000 marks of her dowry to several English lords in July 1421, but even after her death Edmund's creditors still pressed their claims. For example, the widow of the London brewer John Stawnton sued in Chancery for supplies sold to his household.[13] Nevertheless, the dowry battle raged on for some years, to the great inconvenience of Milanese merchants trading in Europe. By 1471 Lucia's letters of marque had stopped Anglo-Milanese trade and, although these were lifted by 1490, further letters of marque issued by the emperor were in force and Milanese goods were detained on the Rhine. The duke of Milan declared Lucia's will to be a forgery and claimed to be her next heir. Adding insult to injury Richard Heron, appointed to act on behalf of one of the men who inherited her claim, was described as 'a man of ill condition and worse report'.[14]

During her widowhood, Lucia stayed for many years at the Minories (see *Fig. 3*). She had papal permission to visit nuns of any enclosed order in September 1411, and this may mark the beginning of her residence; she was most certainly living there by July 1421.[15] Lucia probably lived in the town house which Elizabeth de Burgh had built in the precinct in 1352. Other tenants had included Thomas of Woodstock, duke of Gloucester, in the 1370s, who placed his wife's sister Mary with the Minoresses in the hope of acquiring the whole of the de Bohun inheritance. No doubt to Thomas' irritation Mary married Henry, earl of Derby, and Thomas's daughter Isabel became a nun at the Minories. In fact, Isabel was abbess in 1421 when Lucia was living there. The house in the precinct acquired a reputation as the home of well-born wives

[12] Santoro, *Politica finanziaria*, iii, pp. 115–17, no. 105, 23 June 1423.

[13] PRO, SC 8/24/1161 (2 May 1421) and *RP*, iv, pp. 143–45 (1421); *CPR, 1416–22*, p. 379, 12 July 1421 refers to her petition in parliament at Westminster on 2 May last; PRO, C 1/8/15.

[14] Hinds, ed., *Calendar*, pp. 146–47, no. 202, 5 January 1471 and passim; p. 278, no. 438, 11 February 1491; pp. 268–69, no. 422, 21 November 1490; p. 276, no. 434 (undated).

[15] Her will at London, Lambeth Palace Library, MS Chichele 1, f. 371v, 11 April 1424, mentions her long stay at the Minories; J.A. Twemlow et al. ed., *Calendar of Entries in the Papal Registers Relating to Great Britain and Ireland*, 14 vols (London, 1893–1960), vi, p. 293, 3 September 1411; *RP*, iv, p. 145 (1421).

and widows of men who had suffered a temporary or permanent political reversal. Nor was the order overlooked by London merchants. Alice Marchex-ano, widow of a London-based Genoese merchant, had papal permission to visit the Minoresses as often as she liked in return for her financial help with repairs and the nuns' keep. John de Pulteneye, John Pountfret and John Shadworth left legacies to the London foundation, and John Philipot's daughter was a nun at the Cambridge house of Denny in 1381. Despite the earlier rule that only noblewomen could be professed sisters, by the later fourteenth century the upwardly mobile daughters of City merchants were also accepted at the Minories.[16] Lucia seems to have lived there comfortably enough. She ran a household staff headed by five ladies-in-waiting and three esquires or pages; many of these were Italian and had probably accompanied her to England when she married. She had her own steward, receiver, chaplain, butler, cook, physician, and at least seventeen other servants including a fool. She slept under a set of green silk bed hangings embroidered with bears, complete with matching curtains and cushions, and her jewellery collection included 160 large pearls and several gold brooches set with precious stones.

Socially, Lucia kept company with the more important Italian merchants living in London, including the Venetians Giovanni Marconovo, Prancratio Giustiniano and Matteo Conrade, and these may have been her household suppliers. Marconovo was the principal behind a well-known business in Langbourn ward; he was a liveryman of the Grocers' Company and a frequent trader on the London galleys, especially in the 1420s and 1430s. Giustiniano and Conrade were, like Marconovo, very active in the galley trade. Lucia herself was listed as an exporter in the London customs particulars for 1423, when she had goods aboard the same galley as Marconovo, Giustiniano and Conrade.[17] The Milanese merchant Bernardo Dalzate was also acquainted

---

[16] M. Carlin, 'Holy Trinity Minories: Abbey of St Clare, 1293/4–1539' (Centre for Metropolitan History, London, 1987), pp. 37–38, 40–41. The house was north of the building which became the parish church of Holy Trinity, Minories, p. 39. The church, at 9 St Clare Street, was previously the nuns' chapel, R. Ellis, 'Excavations at 9 St Clare Street', *London Archaeologist*, 5 (1985), p. 116; E.M. Tomlinson, *A History of the Minories, London*, (2nd edn, London, 1922), pp. 43, 45, 67–69, 71; W.E. Hampton, 'The Ladies of the Minories', *The Ricardian*, 4 (1978), pp. 17–19; Twemlow, *Papal Registers*, x, p. 46 (10 December 1448); see also H. Fly 'Some Account of an Abbey of Nuns Formerly Situated in the Street now called the Minories in the County of Middlesex, and Liberty of the Tower of London', *Archaeologia* 15 (1806), pp. 92–113; A.F.C Bourdillon, *The Order of Minoresses in England* (Manchester, 1926); P. Jones, 'Anne Mowbray', *The Ricardian*, 4 (1978), pp. 17–20; R. Warwick, 'Anne Mowbray: Skeletal Remains of a Medieval Child', *London Archaeologist*, 5 (1986), pp. 176–79.

[17] London, Lambeth Palace Library, MS Chichele 1, f. 371v, 11 April 1424; PRO, E 122/161/1, f. 27. For Marconovo, see E 122/72/17, ff. 2, 2v, 3v, 6v, 13, 13v; E 122/76/3, f. 3v; E 122/161/1, ff. 7v, 25v, 29, 32v; E 122/76/14, ff. 2, 2v; E 122/74/11, ff. 16, 30v; E 122/76/25, f. 2v; E 122/77/1, ff. 1v, 2, 3v, 4, 5; E 122/76/31, f. 1v; E 122/73/6, ff. 29, 29v; E 122/203/1, f. 24; E 122/73/5, f. 7; E 122/76/34, ff. 3v, 4, 11v; E 122/77/3, f. 15; and J.A. Kingdon, ed., *Facsimile of First Volume of Manuscript Archives of the Worshipful Company of Grocers of the City of London, AD 1345–1463*, 2 vols (London 1886), pt 2, pp. 176, 180, 181, 186, 193, 196, 218, 225, 229, 230, 234, 238, 400. For

continued

with her, as was Antonio Francisci of Volterra, another prominent galley trader of the 1420s. Lucia issued an acquittance to Antonio's firm about six weeks before she made her will. Marconovo, Giustiniano and Conrade, together with the London grocer Edward Gisors, acted as her executors. Like many of the Italian merchant community, Lucia also knew Simone de Teramo, the papal nuncio and collector in England, who was held in great regard, particularly by the Florentines who conducted his financial business.[18]

When she died in 1424 Lucia left a magnificent string of cash bequests and showed a great concern for the welfare of Edmund's soul. She bequeathed 6,000 marks of her dowry to the English lords to whom she had passed her title, 'ex elemosina et ad exonerand‹um› animam mei dicti nuper mariti'. The remaining 8,000 marks were to be distributed for religious purposes. These included gifts to St Mary Overy where she had been married, Bourne Abbey where Edmund was buried, and of course the Minoresses at Aldgate. All these gifts were conditional upon the operation of perpetual chantries to pray for Henry IV, Henry V, Edmund, herself and their relatives. There were special observances for Edmund and herself: the psalm *De profundis* every day; a sung placebo and dirige every month, with a sung requiem mass on the day following, and a trental of Gregorian masses every year. This accounted for half of her portion of the dowry. The other half she left to religious houses in Milan where she set up chantries 'in forma predicta prout in predictis domi-b‹us› in Anglia'.

There were also some very personal touches contained within her will. Her steward was reminded of his promise to go on pilgrimage to Jerusalem and Compostella for the sake of her soul and Edmund's, and her executors were to make sure that her fool was kept for the rest of his life. She was unable to provide for one of her ladies, Antonia de Arengo, as well as she had hoped and her executors were specially charged to pay Antonia in full. They were to do the same for one of Antonia's colleagues, Magdalena de Boisio, and the

continued

Giustiniano, see PRO, E 122/72/17, ff. 13, 13v; E 122/161/1, ff. 25, 28, 29, 31v, 32v; E 122/76/3, f. 3v. For Conrade, see E 122/72/17, f. 13v; E 122/76/3, f. 3v; E 122/161/1, ff. 25, 29, 32v; E 122/74/11, f. 25. For Dalzate see E 122/76/33, f. 5v; E 122/73/9, ff. 3v, 4, 4v; E 122/73/11, ff. 2v, 3; E 101/128/33; E 179/144/45; E 179/144/56; E 179/144/47, f. 3; E 179/144/52, f. 7; E 179/144/53, f. 24; E 179/144/50, f. 16; E 179/144/54, f. 23; E 179/144/42, ff. 23, 27. For Francisci, see E 122/72/17, ff. 3v, 4, 5v, 6, 7, 8, 9, 9v, 10, 12, 13, 13v, 14; E 122/76/3, f. 3v; E 122/76/14, ff. 2, 2v; E 122/161/1, ff. 3, 6, 18, 30, 33v; in partnership with Alessandro and Galeazzo Borromei, E 122/73/10, ff. 3, 3v, 16, and licence for exchange E 101/128/27, no. 46; *CPMR, 1413–37*, p. 171 (9 March 1424).
[18] London, Lambeth Palace Library, MS Chichele 1, f. 371v, 11 April 1424; *RP*, iv, p. 145 (1421). Earlier correspondence of Florentine merchants in London contains references to a previous papal collector: 'ill collectore al papa ch'era là e morto che grandanno viene segue dela sua morte perch'era nostro padre e nostro signore Iddio gl'abbia l'anima' ('the papal collector who was there is dead, so great damage will follow his death because he was our father and our lord, God rest his soul'), Archivio di Stato di Firenze a Prato, MS 777/313052, 16 November 1398; see also Archivio di Stato di Firenze a Prato, MSS 664/10037, 15 November 1406, and 664/10038, 19 March 1407.

steward Nicholas de Aliardis. These three must have been particularly close to her; she had made a gift of her goods and chattels to Antonia, Magdalena and Nicholas just over a month before she made her will. Lucia left a special bequest for the Minoresses: red velvet altar hangings with matching chaplain's vestments, and a set of silver altar vessels. She also bequeathed to them her velvet kirtle, which was to be made into a chasuble, and instructed Antonia to find some cloth of gold to be sewn onto it in the sign of the cross. Her gift was conditional upon the Minoresses claiming nothing else from her estate. The residue was to provide two chaplains serving perpetual chantries for herself and Edmund, one where she was buried and the other at the Minoresses' chapel.[19]

As a widow, Lucia was known in England as the countess of Kent, late the wife of Edmund, or the king's kinswoman, but for the purposes of communication with the papacy she was Lucy de vicecomitibus of Milan, countess of Kent. She used whichever of her titles was more likely to produce results, but her epitaph is interesting evidence of the way in which she was perceived as a widow. She did not give specific instructions for her funeral and was buried in the middle of the choir at Austin Friars, rather than at Bourne Abbey with Edmund. Austin Friars was fashionable enough among the English nobility; it was also by far the most popular burial-ground for fifteenth-century Italian testators in London. The choice served to pass over Lucia's English marriage and underline her Milanese origins. Her epitaph shows a clear reversion to her premarital connections: it dwelt upon the splendid marriages made by her sisters and the status achieved by her niece and great-niece (respectively queens of France and England), concluding with reference to Lucia's own virtues, charm of character and beauty.[20] It contains not one single mention of Edmund.

---

[19] London, Lambeth Palace Library, MS Chichele 1, f. 371v, 11 April 1424; *CPMR, 1413–37*, p. 171, 9 March 1424.

[20] BL, MS Harley 6033, ff. 31–32.

> Magnifice nata Bernabonis ecce Lucia
> Mediolanensis domini clarissima proles
> Domine Cipri fuere sibi Reginae sorores
> Bavariae Irinae Ducisse sic austriee quarta
> Quintagessima Ducatum mediolani possidet alumnum
> Et Wertinbergis Comitissa Mantue quoque
> Domina prodigna neptis fuit illa Regina
> Francorum proneptis erat Regina proclamare
> Anglie sic mundo toto sua fama volebat
> Virtutibus venustate morum ac forma intenti
> Quid ne tantus honor mundane deliciae quid nunc
> Prosunt ei cum nec veleaule Defendere tantum

This late sixteenth-century version of the epitaph gives a corrupt text, the last quarter of which cannot be sensibly translated; the manuscript contains a series of notes on burial places and funerals.

7

Margaret Stodeye, Lady Philipot (d. 1431)

Carole Rawcliffe

It is a commonplace among historians of late medieval urban elites that the quickest and easiest way for a go-ahead young man to reach the top was through marriage to either a daughter or the widow of an established member of the ruling hierarchy. Those with real ambition aimed, as it were, to hit the jackpot by winning the hand of a woman who was both an heiress *and* a widow, thus securing for themselves a double portion of political influence, commercial contacts and city property. But attractive matches were hard to come by, since such desirable women were jealously guarded by brothers-in-law, uncles, step-sons, trustees and other interested parties, who were no less anxious to line their own pockets by playing the marriage market for all it was worth.[1] The wealthy aldermen of late fourteenth-century London adopted the same approach to matrimony as their contemporaries among the gentry and baronage: the only difference between them being that whereas the latter were primarily concerned to accumulate estates, the former had their eyes on capital for investment in trading ventures or the possibility of acquiring a profitable business.

The strategic deployment of marriage by members of the knightly class as a means of cementing alliances with like-minded local families, and even sometimes of winning over or appeasing erstwhile enemies, was also a popular tactic with the rulers of London, especially during the fraught early years of Richard II's reign, when factionalism in the city inevitably fostered something of a siege mentality among the merchant capitalists, who came repeatedly under threat.[2] With the exception of those who elected (or were obliged) to take the veil, almost all the close female relatives of these men found themselves in a position akin to pawns in a chess game; and none more so than Margaret Stodeye, the woman whose career as a widow forms the subject of this essay. Indeed, as she moved from one husband to another, changing one set of weeds for the next, she may truly be said to have progressed from being a

---

[1] C. Rawcliffe, 'The Politics of Marriage in Late Medieval England: William, Lord Botreaux, and the Hungerfords', *Huntingdon Library Quarterly*, 51 (1988), pp. 161–75.

[2] See R. Bird, *The Turbulent London of Richard II* (London, 1949), passim, for the political background to this essay.

mere pawn to dominating the board as queen: not least because the legacies of her father and of her four spouses combined to make her outstandingly rich.

Whatever disappointment he may have felt at failing to produce any sons, the prosperous vintner John Stodeye (d. 1376) could at least congratulate himself on finding suitable husbands for three of his four daughters. Idonia, who seems to have been the eldest, married Nicholas Brembre at some point before 1369, thus becoming the wife of one of the most powerful and controversial figures of the period. A man of spectacular wealth and ambition, Brembre may, like his father-in-law, have become involved in government finance at a comparatively early date; and although most of the evidence about his speculative ventures occurs much later, there can be little doubt that he already commanded an important position in civic life. A grocer or pepperer by trade, he made most of his great fortune through investment in wool, establishing himself as a property owner of some consequence while Stodeye was still alive.[3] His brother-in-law, Henry Vanner, on the other hand, owed his eligibility as a husband more to family and inherited commercial connections, since he was the son and heir of one of Stodeye's senior colleagues in the Vintners' Company who had died in 1354 leaving a substantial estate in Kent, Middlesex and London. Henry's mother had married another affluent vintner, Thomas Cornwallis, as her second husband, so there was no shortage of expertise to help Vanner in taking over his father-in-law's flourishing business as one of the city's major importers of wine. Although he was never as eminent as Brembre – a fact which must have offered some temporary consolation when the latter was hanged by the Lords Appellant in 1388 – Vanner went on to play a notable role in the government of London as an alderman, M.P. and sheriff, predeceasing his wife, Margery, to whom he owed so much, in the spring of 1395.[4]

Perhaps in the hope of diversifying his family's economic interests, Stodeye arranged for Margery's elder sister, Margaret, to marry a mercer named John Berlingham. The match had almost certainly taken place by December 1370, when Berlingham joined with Brembre and his new father-in-law in property transactions concerning two manors in Middlesex.[5] Along with many other leading citizens, Berlingham helped to raise a corporate loan for the crown at this time, although his offering of £30 was exactly one-tenth of that made by Brembre and about a sixth of Stodeye's contribution. It is interesting to note how closely he and Brembre were involved in the affairs of the Stodeye family,

---

[3] Ibid., pp. 2–7.

[4] Vanner's career is discussed in detail in *The History of Parliament, The Commons, 1386–1421*, ed. J.S. Roskell, L.S. Clark and C. Rawcliffe, 4 vols (Stroud, 1993), iv, pp. 706–8. For his close connection with Brembre, which he shared with other members of the Stodeye circle, see *CCR, 1377–81*, p. 494; *1381–85*, p. 387; *CFR, 1373–91*, p. 29; CLRO, HR 115(169), 116(57); *CPMR, 1381–1412*, pp. 103, 134; *Cal. Inquisitions Miscellaneous*, v, nos 149, 192; Bird, *Turbulent London*, pp. 3–5.

[5] *LBG*, p. 273.

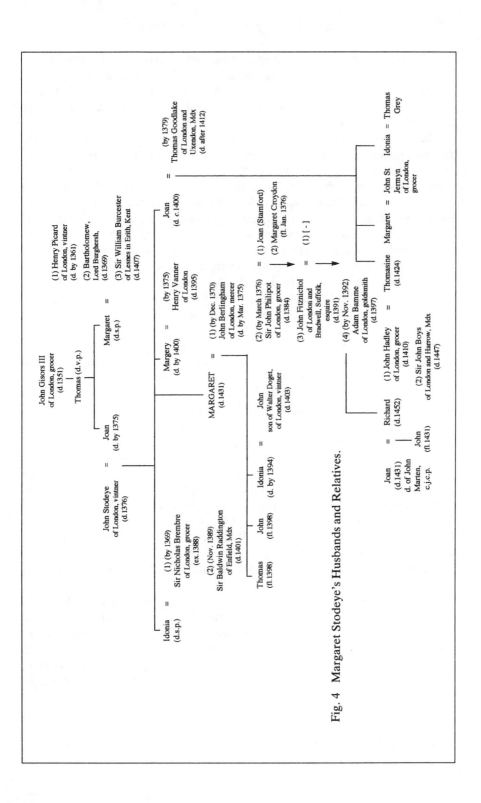

Fig. 4 Margaret Stodeye's Husbands and Relatives.

standing surety in 1371, for example, when the elderly vintner was granted a valuable wardship by the civic authorities. That Berlingham seemed destined to pursue a distinguished career in city politics is evident from his return to parliament in October 1373, but his early demise a couple of years later dashed any hopes in this quarter.[6]

Margaret was then pregnant with her third child, but the question of her remarriage was far too important to wait until after her confinement. We know that her late husband's business had been conducted on a fairly impressive scale: in October 1375, for instance, his executors delivered 200 marks to the attorneys of two Italian merchants from whom he had presumably purchased luxury goods; and as well as the customary third of his estate Margaret also received 'divers sums of money' to hold in trust until her young children came of age. Since her only daughter, Idonia Berlingham, was eventually assigned £100 as a marriage portion from her patrimony the total amount at stake may well have been considerable.[7] John Stodeye was, moreover, growing old, a consideration which further enhanced Margaret's prospects of making a far more impressive marriage than the first, as undoubtedly did Brembre's rapid rise in the civic hierarchy and his determination to exploit his family connections to consolidate his own power base in the city. In 1372 he had served as sheriff along with the fishmonger, John Philipot, an outstandingly rich and powerful individual with whom he was naturally anxious to forge a lasting alliance. Philipot's second wife had conveniently died at about the same time as Berlingham, and there was thus no obstacle to a marriage between him and the young widow. This had been solemnised by March 1376, when Stodeye drew up a will dividing his valuable store of property and plate into four parts, one for each daughter. His three sons-in-law were named as executors, but custody of the youngest girl, Joan, who received an additional £200 for her marriage, went, significantly, to Brembre alone.[8]

As the possessor of a vast personal fortune, not to mention numerous shops, tenements and other holdings in at least six city parishes, together with land in Stepney and Hoxton in Middlesex, all of which he may well have settled as a jointure upon his new wife at the time of their marriage, Philipot was hardly dependent for survival upon the profits of her inheritance, although the properties allocated to her were worth a great deal. Even allowing for his remarkable business acumen, there can be no question that Stodeye had derived enormous advantages by marrying Joan, the grand-daughter and coheir of John Gisors III (d. 1351), who was himself a grandson of the great Sir John Gisors, vintner, financier and, above all, intimate of King Henry III. Between them, Stodeye and his brother-in-law, another eminent merchant capitalist, Henry Picard, had shared all Gisors' possessions in London on his

[6] Ibid., pp. 275, 286, 313.

[7] *CPMR, 1364–81*, p. 205; *1381–1412*, p. 103; *LBH*, p. 49.

[8] *HW*, ii, pp. 191–92; CLRO, HR 108(62).

death in 1351. Picard did particularly well out of the division of spoils, but since he and his wife left no issue the Stodeyes eventually acquired the *entire* estate, comprising two impressive town houses and other premises centred upon Vintry Ward.[9] Yet it was politics as much as money which led Philipot to formalise his association with Brembre and Stodeye: after all, the three men were heavily involved in royal finance (just as Picard and Gisors had been before them); and following Stodeye's death and the accession of Richard II the two brothers-in-law dominated the government of London, occupying between them seven mayoralties over the eventful decade ending in October 1387.[10]

Unlike most of the other rather grubby and self-seeking figures who briefly occupied the limelight during these years of factional struggle in the City, when the wealthy oligarchs faced a serious challenge from the radical party of John of Northampton, as well as a series of fraught confrontations with the king's uncle, John of Gaunt, and other members of the royal council, Philipot stands out as a genuinely attractive and popular person. His financial skills and evident probity won him, for example, the respect of Richard earl of Arundel (d. 1376), one of the major royal creditors of Edward III's last troubled years, who employed him as an agent and commercial adviser.[11] Not for nothing, either, did the people of London enlist Philipot as their spokesman during times of crisis or conflict with the government, when he could be relied upon to behave tactfully but with unusual firmness. He was, of course, fortunate in commanding the services of a personal propagandist in the monastic chronicler, Thomas Walsingham, who made no secret of his admiration for anyone brave enough to confront the discredited court party and its disastrous handling of foreign policy. 'There was, as a consequence, among the people universal acclaim, praise and esteem from all quarters, but only John Philipot enjoyed this adulation', he wrote, casting his hero in the role of a lone and loyal patriot surrounded by a snarling pack of resentful noblemen and courtiers.[12]

Margaret Stodeye's personal feelings towards her second husband remain open to conjecture, but his personal courage in attacking corruption at court and almost single-handedly assuming financial liability for two important naval and military offensives against the French (at least according to Walsingham) won him enthusiastic support in the city, where the knighthood bestowed upon him by Richard II at the time of the Peasants' Revolt, in 1381, was seen as being richly deserved. Philipot's readiness to endow Margaret with a life estate in almost all his London and Middlesex properties (except those set aside for pious or charitable uses) at the expense of his grown-up sons and daughters,

[9] For a discussion of Stodeye's great wealth, see Bird, *Turbulent London*, pp. 2–3; and A. Crawford, *A History of the Vintners' Company* (London, 1977), pp. 46–47.

[10] Beaven, *Aldermen*, i, p. 390, gives a comprehensive note of their offices.

[11] G. Holmes, *The Good Parliament* (Oxford, 1975), pp. 72–73, 75–77, 152–53.

[12] T. Walsingham, *Historia anglicana*, ed. H.T. Riley, Rolls Series, 2 vols (London, 1863–64), i, pp. 370–71.

who had to content themselves with the reversionary interest, suggests that he regarded her with genuine affection; and he certainly rated her abilities highly enough to entrust her with the task of implementing some of the religious bequests set out in his will, even if he did not name her among the executors. She, in turn, was evidently quite prepared to sacrifice the prospects of her two sons by Berlingham in order to further Philipot's long-term dynastic ambitions: although initially confirmed, in 1381, as heirs to her share of the Stodeye fortune, the boys were disinherited at the stroke of a pen once it became necessary to provide Sir John's elder daughter with a suitably impressive marriage portion. Some alternative provision may have been made for them out of his movable goods, however, for he was generous to their sister, to whom he gave £100 in cash towards the purchase of a jointure.[13]

The death, in the summer of 1384, of the incomparable 'Lord John Philipot, knight and citizen of London, the noblest of men, who worked above all others for the king and kingdom, and so many times helped to raise the finances and morale of both' may thus have been a real cause of grief to Margaret,[14] and it certainly proved a bitter blow to Brembre. He also had been knighted in 1381, but unlike Philipot he could not rely on such a groundswell of affection on the part of his fellow Londoners. He had, to be sure, successfully (and some argued brutally) put down the last desperate demonstration of opposition on the part of Northampton and his democratically minded followers, in February 1384, but he still had many enemies among the citizenry, and some even more powerful ones in the clique of disgruntled noblemen who were becoming increasingly dissatisfied with King Richard's style of government. The role of royal creditor and favourite was more thankless than might at first appear, and Brembre was already aware of the need to tread warily, safeguarding himself in the event of any political upheavals. One day a systematic attempt will be made to disentangle his convoluted business activities, although it is most unlikely, even then, that we will really get to the bottom of all the conveyances and recognizances to which he was a party. Suffice it to say that by the time of Philipot's death Brembre had placed most of his assets in the hands of trustees, prominent among whom were his three brothers-in-law.[15] It is, indeed, worth noting that Thomas Goodlake, who married the fourth and youngest of Stodeye's daughters shortly before November 1379, had long been involved in Brembre's affairs as a feoffee-to-uses, and was quite probably given the girl's hand as a means of drawing him more closely into the charmed circle and keeping him under his patron's eye. His appointment as an esquire of the body to Richard II in 1385 was undoubtedly contrived by Sir Nicholas to reward past

---

[13] CLRO, HR 118(30); *CPMR, 1381–1412*, p. 103. In 1395, when Henry Vanner drew up his own will, Margaret's two sons by Berlingham were recognised as heirs to their aunt Margery's share of the Stodeye estates (HR 126(76)).

[14] Walsingham, *Historia anglicana*, ii, p. 115.

[15] See above, note 4.

services and ensure future loyalty, as was a subsequent grant of the keepership of the royal warrens and parks at Isleworth in Middlesex, although this did not prevent him from exploiting the circumstances of Brembre's fall to feather his rapidly expanding nest.[16]

Being now the widow of one of the most celebrated Londoners of the age, with overflowing coffers to match, Lady Philipot might reasonably have been expected either to marry one of the more outstanding members of the civic elite, or else to have found herself a third husband from the ranks of the minor baronage. After all, her aunt, Margaret Picard, had risen to become the wife of Lord Burghersh; and a few decades later Joan, the well-connected but only moderately prosperous widow of the mercer, William Parker (d. 1403), was to be betrothed to Richard, Lord St Maur.[17] But Margaret's fate was inextricably bound to Brembre's; and, instead of contracting a suitably prestigious or financially rewarding alliance, she married a bureaucrat who had, like her brother-in-law, been drawn into the uncertain and sometimes dubious world of government finance. John Fitznichol's chief claim to fame lay in his long association with Edward III's sometime son-in-law, John Montfort, earl of Richmond and duke of Brittany. The earliest evidence of their connection dates from 1369, when Fitznichol was employed by the duke as his envoy in negotiations with the royal council at Westminster, being perhaps already in receipt of an annuity of £80 charged upon his employer's Breton estates. It is unlikely that he saw much of this fee, however, as the duchy was embroiled in civil war, and Montfort had to rely heavily upon English support in his struggle against a rival claimant backed by the French. An enormous loan of £9,000 advanced to him by the government in 1373 was actually underwritten by Fitznichol, whose involvement in such a potentially risky venture brought him into contact with Brembre and other speculative financiers.[18] The two men soon became firm friends: before long Fitznichol had assumed the trusteeship of Sir Nicholas's country estates; and the royal stay of execution issued in 1386 (after the forfeiture of the earldom of Richmond) excusing him from any liability for the duke's massive debts may well have been secured with Brembre's help.[19]

By the time of Montfort's desertion to the French and subsequent disgrace, in 1384, Fitznichol had become one of his most trusted employees, having long served not only as his attorney general in England, but also in the far more demanding posts of receiver-general and steward of all his property there. In return for these 'bons et agreables servises' he had successfully petitioned for his annuity to be reassigned from war-torn Brittany to the more peaceful

---

[16] *The Commons, 1386–1421*, iii, pp. 208–9.

[17] Ibid., iv, sub William Parker, pp. 14–16; *Complete Peerage*, ii, p. 427.

[18] *CCR, 1381–85*, p. 100; *Recueil des actes de Jean IV, duc de Bretagne*, ed. M. Jones, 2 vols (Paris, 1980–83), i, nos 141, 223, 234–35.

[19] *CPR, 1385–89*, p. 205; *1388–92*, p. 218; *Cal. Inquisitions Miscellaneous*, v, nos 149, 192.

manor of Cheshunt in Hertfordshire, and in 1377 the duke granted him a further sum of 100 marks a year from the revenues of Wassingborough in Lincolnshire. Unfortunately, this (the larger of his two pensions) ceased abruptly when the earldom was confiscated, leaving him, a loyal subject of King Richard, in a less than enviable position.[20] On the face of things, a man, however able, who had recently lost his patron, a substantial part of his income and, even worse, a great deal of personal influence seems an implausible candidate for the hand of one of London's richest widows, but, as always, Brembre's motives in arranging the match were dictated by his customary blend of shrewdness and opportunism rather than an uncharacteristic access of sentiment. His ready acceptance of Fitznichol into the family fold may either have been the outcome of a calculated bid to retain some measure of control over Margaret's great fortune or else have been determined by Richard II's desire to do well by one of his kinsman's erstwhile servants. Quite possibly both factors came into play, since they gave Brembre the chance to please his royal master while at the same time strengthening his own position. It is worth noting that the duke of Brittany had married Richard's half sister, Joan (d. 1384), as his second wife, and that Fitznichol, who must have known her well, was currently busy raising money to settle her debts: a thankless exercise which clearly called for some reward (albeit preferably not at the crown's expense).[21]

Yet if, as seems likely, the king himself had a hand in arranging Margaret's third marriage, Brembre can only have welcomed his choice of husband. Not surprisingly, he and his brother-in-law, Vanner, who almost always acted with him in personal matters, had acquired the trusteeship of *all* Margaret's inheritance while she was still a widow. They also made plans in 1385 for her daughter, Idonia Berlingham, to marry the son of one of Vanner's associates in the Vintners' Company: the very idea of relinquishing their hold over such a profitable asset to anyone but a trusted friend must have caused them grave anxiety.[22] Fitznichol owned a modest amount of property in London and the manor of Bardwell in Suffolk, as well as continuing to draw his old annuity from the above-mentioned manor of Cheshunt (which he now farmed at the exchequer, jointly with the earl of Northumberland); but, comparatively speaking, he could still hardly match the income of any reasonably affluent Londoner. The key to his advancement lay in his association with King Richard and Sir Nicholas, patrons to whom he was now deeply, albeit as matters turned out temporarily, obligated. The marriage seems to have taken place during the last months of Brembre's life, perhaps just after a confirmation made by Margaret ('in her pure widowhood'), on 10 June 1387, of his fiduciary interest in her estates. Significantly, on that very same day Fitznichol joined with Sir Nicholas in acquiring a rent worth £8 p.a. in London, and by

---

[20] *Recueil des actes de Jean IV*, i, nos 249, 235, 299, 399, 486; ii, no 958.
[21] *CPR, 1381–85*, p. 540.
[22] CLRO, HR 115(164), 116(111); *CPMR, 1381–1412*, p. 103.

September he had assumed, jointly with Vanner, the position of his principal trustee and therefore, implicitly, of his brother-in-law. Whatever the precise circumstances of Margaret's third marriage, they seem to have fostered a closer connection between her family and the royal court. At the end of the decade her sister, Idonia, became the wife of Sir Baldwin Raddington, a leading member of Richard II's household. Sir Baldwin, who already had strong personal ties with the merchant capitalists, actually assumed the keepership of London during the city's celebrated quarrel with the king in 1392, and he, too, may have been one of Fitznichol's patrons.[23]

It has been conjectured that, had he lived, Sir John Philipot would have succeeded in raising London for Richard II in December 1387, and would thus have prevented the triumph of the Lords Appellant and the judicial murder of Sir Nicholas Brembre and other royal favourites.[24] Certainly, none of Brembre's other relatives, however much they may have made out of him while he lived, were able or willing to take a stand on his behalf when the Merciless parliament of 1388 condemned him to forfeiture and death; a last-ditch attempt on his behalf to settle all his movables on a new set of politically acceptable trustees proved futile against the wrath of his enemies. Vanner and Fitznichol fought hard to regain control of his property, most notably three manors and extensive farmland in Kent, but the struggle was still in progress when Fitznichol died in late February or early March 1391.[25] Once again, now for the third time, Margaret found herself widowed, her already substantial collection of dower properties and jointures being augmented by a life interest in the manor of Bardwell and all the Fitznichol holdings in London, as well as a generous share of her late husband's effects.[26]

It might be supposed that Brembre's death and the ensuing shift in city politics from a mood of confrontation to one of consensus made the question of Margaret's next marriage less urgent, but she was too valuable an asset to be left peacefully to enjoy a few years of reflective widowhood. On the contrary, her great wealth and social status could now, through a complete *volte-face* on the part of the ruling elite, be used to win over, pay off or otherwise placate the last remnants of opposition from the ranks of the radical party; and within a matter of nine months or less she was again offered up as a commodity on the marriage market. The last of her matrimonial ventures was in fact the most politically expedient, and illustrates vividly the hard-nosed and unsentimental pragmatism which determined the lives of so many women of her class. Her new husband, the goldsmith, Adam Bamme, had previously been one of the

---

[23] *CFR, 1383–91*, pp. 25, 60; PRO, PCC Rous 7; CLRO, HR 115(164, 169), 116(57); T.F. Tout, *Chapters in the Administrative History of Medieval England*, 6 vols (Manchester, 1920–33), iv, p. 197.

[24] Bird, *Turbulent London*, pp. 3–4, 17.

[25] PRO, SC 8/250/12480; CLRO, HR 115(169); *CPR, 1388–92*, p. 218; *CPMR, 1381–1412*, p. 134.

[26] PRO, PCC Rous 7.

chief supporters of the reforming mayor, John of Northampton, in his vendetta against Brembre and the other merchant capitalists; and had, indeed, as sheriff, in 1382, played a leading part in the indictment for treason of five of Brembre's associates among the London aldermen. Even so, being as calculating as he was ambitious, he had with considerable foresight abandoned his leader just before the latter fell from power two years later, and thereby narrowly escaped the reprisals which followed Brembre's triumphant (but short-lived) return to office.[27]

Some echoes of the old animosity between the great victualling companies (as represented by Brembre) and the craft guilds had, however, lingered on, as the contested mayoral election of 1389 between Bamme and the grocer, William Venour, reveals. But Bamme was by now too old a hand at the dangerous business of civic in-fighting to launch a full-scale attack on such powerful adversaries, preferring instead to win over his enemies with a statesmanlike show of magnaminity. His readiness to step down in favour of Venour not only ensured his success at the next election, but also won him the long awaited prize of full acceptance into the ranks of the senior oligarchs.[28] Together, Lady Philipot's hand and fortune represented an offer which Bamme could simply not refuse, especially as his first wife, Eleanor (herself the widow of a prosperous London goldsmith and provider of welcome funds for investment), had recently died.[29] On the other hand, as a particularly skilled and successful practitioner of the goldsmith's craft, whose customers included John of Gaunt and his acolytes at the royal court, he ought arguably to be regarded, in terms of wealth at least, as a far more appropriate choice of husband than his late predecessor, Fitznichol.[29] Nor did he lag far behind Sir John Philipot when civic pride and concern for the community were at stake. During an extremely severe famine, which coincided with his first mayoralty in 1391, for example, he personally underwrote a loan of £400 made from the corporation's funds to purchase additional supplies of wheat, as well as arranging for 'corne from partes beyond the seas to be brought . . . on suche abundance, as sufficed to serue the Citie, and the Countries adioyning'.[30]

It was specifically in recognition of Bamme's past 'services' as mayor that Margaret, her step-son, John Fitznichol the younger, and the executors of her

---

[27] Thomas Usk, who appealed Northampton, Bamme and the other leading radicals before the court of the coroner of London in 1384, claimed that they had planned to overthrow Brembre with the help of the common people and 'to haue had the town in thair gouernale, and haue rulid it be thair avys and haue holden vnder, or elles de-voyded owt of towne, all the persones that had by myghty to haue with-sayde hem . . . ', *A Book of London English, 1384–1425*, ed. R.W. Chambers and M. Daunt (Oxford, 1931), pp. 24–25.

[28] See *The Commons, 1386–1421*, ii, pp. 109–12, for a full account of Bamme's civic career.

[29] CLRO, Husting Pleas of Land, 97, Monday before the feast of St Margaret, 49 Edward III; Husting Common Pleas, 100, Monday before the feast of St Margaret, 50 Edward III. Bamme's first wife, Elene or Eleanor, was still alive in 1381, HR, 110(181).

[30] J. Stow, *A Survey of London*, ed. C.L. Kingsford, 2 vols (Oxford, i repr. 1971), ii, p. 108.

third husband's will, were formally excused by Richard II, in December 1391, from having to pay off the above-mentioned debt of £9,000, so Margaret herself derived some immediate benefit from the marriage. Allegations made two years later by the duke of Brittany that Fitznichol senior, whom he had regarded in his lifetime as a model employee, had in fact failed to render any proper accounts for the property under his surveillance and had, even worse, pocketed large sums of money advanced as loans at the exchequer, are hard to credit. As late as 1383, Montfort had released his receiver-general from all personal legal actions, evidently as a mark of confidence in his financial probity, but now that he was seeking compensation from the crown for its excessive severity at the time of the confiscation of the earldom of Richmond his 'bien ame esquier' suddenly presented a useful (and conveniently dead) scapegoat. The duke's petition suggests that the deceased's effects had, in fact, already been seized and his executors ordered to submit appropriate accounts, but Margaret herself escaped unscathed, no doubt thanks to Bamme's efforts on her behalf.[31] He also assisted her in trying to recover at least £600 due to the estate of the late Sir John Philipot, the collection of such large sums being clearly a matter of some self-interest, since the money would, effectively, be his to employ as he saw fit.[32]

As might be expected, Bamme exploited his new connection for all that it was worth. In 1392, for instance, he gained possession of the Kentish manors recently confiscated from Brembre's trustees. The irony of a situation which made him the lessee (retrospectively from 1381) of estates accumulated by the most inveterate of his enemies in return for the cancellation of a debt of 200 marks due to him from the king can hardly have been lost upon his Stodeye kinsfolk, although they were too inured to the harsh realities of political life to utter any protest, and may well have been relieved to see the property back in the family at any price.[33] If the relationship between Henry Vanner and his new brother-in-law is any guide, we may assume that they were happy enough to enjoy the protection of such a powerful and evidently well-disposed individual. At all events, Vanner lost no time in conveying most of his estates to Bamme as a trustee, and also chose him to supervise the implementation of his will.[34]

[31] *CPR, 1391–96*, p. 4; *Recueil des actes de Jean IV*, ii, no 958.

[32] CLRO, Husting Pleas of Land, 120, Monday before the feast of St Margaret, 20 Richard II. It is interesting to note that in July 1398, a year after Bamme's death, two of the three creditors, from each of whom Margaret *still* claimed to be owed £200, were granted royal pardons. They had previously been outlawed for failing to appear in court to answer her charges but, as came to light in the course of a separate suit brought by them in chancery, had in fact settled their accounts long before. Margaret's assertions to the contrary look suspiciously like fraud: years of association with the likes of Brembre had evidently begun to take their toll (*CPR, 1396–99*, p. 376).

[33] PRO, E 210/2378; *CCR, 1392–96*, p. 178.

[34] CLRO, HR 122(62), 123(8, 9), 126(76). Of course, Margaret was herself heiress to much of this property, which belonged to the Stodeye estate, so some of these enfeoffments served to confirm her reversionary title, in which Bamme enjoyed a life interest; T. Milburn, *The Vintners' Company* (London, 1888), p. 43.

Perhaps because he did not produce a son and heir until the very end of his life, Bamme had previously preferred to acquire land by leasehold rather than outright purchase, so when he died suddenly, on 6 June 1397, during the course of his second mayoralty, most of the premises left by him were held for a limited period of years only. He had, nonetheless, negotiated these tenancies on advantageous terms, and decades were still left to run on his leases of shops, inns and tenements in the parishes of St Peter West Cheap and St Margaret Moses.[35] His own holdings comprised a hostel known as 'Le Contour' with various appurtenances and a brewery in the parish of St Mildred Poultry, along with other shops and rents around West Cheap.[36] All these freehold and leasehold properties ought, in theory, to have remained in Margaret's hands until the infant Richard Bamme came of age and took seisin of his rightful share but, since Adam had died owing the crown almost £500 from his time as a collector of the wool custom in the port of London, the government stepped in and confiscated most of the revenues, pending a full settlement of his account.[37]

We need not feel too sorry for Margaret, whose fourth and final widowhood was marked by two further important acquisitions of property, and who was, most important of all, finally permitted to retire from the world of matrimonial politics to enjoy thirty-four years as London's wealthiest and most celebrated dowager. Since she was now well into her forties, if not actually past child-bearing age, and at least one of her sons showed every sign of surviving to healthy adulthood, some of her attractions as a bride had waned. Moreover, now that both Brembre and Vanner were dead, she enjoyed far greater liberty to manage her own affairs without constant interference, so there can have been few objections to her decision to remove herself permanently from the marriage market by taking a formal vow of chastity. This she did, some seven weeks after Bamme's death, before Bishop Braybrook of London, in the vestry of St Paul's Cathedral.[38] How far she was acting in accordance with her last husband's wishes or out of respect for his memory remains a matter of conjecture: a desire to stay single would in itself provide a sufficient motive, especially as there are no signs that she was otherwise unduly interested in spiritual or religious affairs.

Ironically, in view of their grandiose dynastic ambitions, neither Brembre nor Vanner had left any surviving issue, with the result than when their wives both died, soon afterwards, Margaret and the children of her youngest sister,

---

[35] *CFR, 1399–1405*, pp. 46, 63, 87, 150; CLRO, HR 134(90), 144(67, 75). Bamme also enjoyed a life tenancy (which was to extend for one year after his death) of the manor of 'Wylby' in Tottenham, Middlesex, of the grant of John, Lord Beaumont (*CPR, 1399–1401*, pp. 172–73; *CFR, 1391–99*, p. 220).

[36] CLRO, HR 140(37, 38), 149(51).

[37] *CPR, 1408–13*, p. 220; *CFR, 1399–1405*, pp. 42, 63, 150.

[38] GL, MS 9531/3, f. 346v (I am most grateful to Dr Caroline Barron for drawing my attention to this reference, and to Professor Mary Erler for providing a transcription).

Joan Goodlake (d. 1400), divided the other half of the Stodeye inheritance between them in two equal shares.[39] Margaret opted to sell a substantial part of her holdings in Vintry ward in 1405 for a cash payment of 200 marks and a pipe of wine, perhaps with the intention of clearing some of the late Adam Bamme's debts, although a final quittance had still to be obtained from the exchequer five years later.[40] Yet this still left her with an annual income of over £116 from her remaining possessions in the city. The death of her kinswoman, Joan Gisors, the widow of the wealthy grocer, Hugh Fastolf, and heiress of the grocer, Simon Dolsley, brought further additions of rents and tenements in at least four city parishes, which had reverted to her by 1423.[41]

In electing to style herself as Lady Philipot throughout her last widowhood, Margaret was almost certainly motivated as much by snobbery as by sentiment, since she asked to be buried next to Adam Bamme in the church of St George, Bucklersbury, rather than beside the late Sir John, who lay in the Greyfriars' church. It is worth noting, however, that in her will of 24 March 1431, drawn up less than a month before her death, she described herself as the widow of both men, discreetly omitting altogether any mention of her first and third husbands or her three children by Berlingham, at least one of whom seems to have predeceased her by some years.[42] No doubt exists as to her affection for her surviving son, Richard Bamme, whose name appears along with hers in conveyances of Bamme family property from 1407 onwards (when he was about eleven), and upon whom she settled all her holdings in London.[43] Not surprisingly, Richard was named as an executor of her will, in which she left him some plate and a bed complete with hangings, as well as taking care to arrange that a debt of £43 which she still owed him would be promptly repaid. His duties were to be shared with just one other executor, a 'servant' called John Cockermouth, who probably helped with the running of Margaret's household, and to whom she promised 20s. as compensation for the work involved. Whether or not her gift of a silver-gilt cup engraved with 'popyn-geayes' (birds notorious for their vanity) to Richard's wife, the daughter of chief justice Marten, carried with it a less than subtle message we can only guess, but the generosity shown by her to her two old waiting-women, Cecily and Amy, 'for their labour and diligence' suggests that she was not without kindness. So too does an individual bequest of four silver saucers to her young grandson, John Bamme, who may well have been a source of comfort to her

[39] CLRO, HR 130(77), 144(14); J.C.L. Stahlschmidt, 'Lay Subsidy temp. Henry IV', *Archaeological Journal*, 44 (1887), p. 69.

[40] Milburn, *Vintner's Company*, p. 43.

[41] Stahlschmidt, 'Lay Subsidy', p. 63; CLRO, HR 151(39), 157(59, 60).

[42] GL, MS 9171/3, f. 275. Idonia Berlingham was certainly dead by 1394, but her husband, John, son of Walter Doget, remarried and survived until 1403 (*CPMR, 1381–1412*, p. 103; *HW*, ii, p. 354). Her brothers, John and Thomas, were still alive in 1398, when they took formal seisin of their paternal inheritance, but are not mentioned thereafter (*LBH*, p. 49).

[43] CLRO, HR 134(90), 140(37, 38), 144(14), 157(59, 60).

during her long retirement. For in marked contrast to the dramatic events of her early life, Margaret's last years passed without incident, and she chose to live quietly out of the public eye as befitted a vowess, clad in the black gown trimmed with miniver which passed to her god-daughter, Margery Wake.[44]

Despite her great wealth and important social position, which set her apart from most of the widows considered in this volume, Margaret remains an elusive figure, overshadowed by her politically active and ambitious menfolk. She may possibly have engaged in some form of commercial activity during her first marriage, but from then onwards she occupied too exalted a place in the civic hierarchy to do business over the counter or help with the family accounts. Perhaps she lacked the intellectual capacity or training to become involved in the demanding world of the merchant capitalist; there is certainly no evidence to suggest that she had much of an education or ever became at all interested in books, although she could certainly sign her own name. Significantly, neither Sir John Philipot nor John Fitznichol, both of whom left wills, chose her to be an executrix, although the complexity of their financial affairs (compounded in Fitznichol's case by the prospect of interminable litigation over the duke of Brittany's debts) would have made such a task unusually demanding, even for an expert, and we cannot necessarily assume a lack of confidence or trust on their part. Sir John, at least, felt her capable of exercising some control over the way his pious bequests were carried out, so he cannot have formed too low an opinion of her abilities. Margaret's own attitude to religion seems to have been entirely conventional, her desire for chaste seclusion in later life being quite probably more a reaction against the experiences of her youth (or even evidence of her attachment to her last husband) than a search for spiritual fulfilment. It may be anachronistic to suggest that she was finally free to follow her own inclinations after years of deferring to the wishes of powerful male relatives, but one hopes that her modest household and affectionate family brought her a degree of contentment.

---

[44] GL, MS 9171/3, f. 275.

8

Johanna Hill (d. 1441) and Johanna Sturdy (d. *c.* 1460), Bell-Founders

Caroline M. Barron

The two women who provide the focus for this essay ran bell-founding workshops in the extramural parish of St Botolph Aldgate in the middle years of the fifteenth century. St Botolph's parish, which pocketed the suburban cluster outside the city walls to the east of the city at Aldgate, had been associated with bell-making since the mid thirteenth century.[1] In the mid fourteenth century there emerged a prosperous bell-founder, William Burford, whose principal tenement, the Three Nuns (and presumably his foundry) lay immediately to the east of the church of St Botolph.[2] He described himself as a 'bell-maker' and acted as common councilman for Portsoken ward.[3] When he died in 1390 he left a widow, Johanna, and a son Robert who acted as his executor and took over his father's business:[4] he was to have the Three Nuns tenement in Aldgate 'et omnia instrumenta mea ad artem meam pertinent' (and all the equipment of my craft). Johanna his widow, on the other hand, was to have 'alia bona sive iocalia ad meum houshold pertinent' (all the goods and jewels pertaining to my household), together with silver dishes and cooking utensils. In fact Johanna may have been acting independently as a brewer, for she appears to have been left brewing utensils in her husband's will, and the Three Nuns was certainly a brewery by 1418.[5]

---

[1] See J.C.L. Stahlschmidt, *Surrey Bells and London Bell-Founders* (London, 1884), p.13 *et seq.*

[2] For details of William Burford's career, and the careers of other medieval inhabitants of the parish of St Botolph Aldgate, I am indebted to the extensive archive of the Centre for the Study of Metropolitan History (Director, Dr Derek Keene). Burford was a collector of the fifteenth in Portsoken ward in 1369, *LBG*, p. 252; in 1372 he was granted a tenement by Alice Perrers, CLRO, HR 100 (12); he witnessed deeds in 1373 and 1382, HR 100 (128), HR 111 (131), PRO, LR 14/347. For one of his tenements, the Crown, Burford paid a quit-rent to Holy Trinity Priory, PRO, Rental, E 164/18. Bell mould has been found in excavations at two sites which may well have been the sites of the foundry of Burford and his successors, Museum of London site code AL 74 (62–64 Aldgate High Street) and ER 991 (St Botolph's Churchyard).

[3] 1384–86, *CPMR, 1381–1412*, pp. 88, 122; *LBH*, pp. 240, 271, 281.

[4] For Burford's will, see calendar in *HW*, ii, p. 301, and for a transcript, *Surrey Bells*, pp. 38–41. Johanna and Robert were to act as joint executors. William had first been married to Elene for whom he provided prayers in his will.

[5] Ibid., p. 40; CLRO, HR 146(32). Johanna's will was drawn up in October 1397, GL, MS 9171/ 1, f. 411v.

Bell-founding at this period was a profitable business, as enthusiastic parishioners rebuilt the belfries of their parish churches and installed rings of bells. The will of Robert Burford, who died in 1418, is rich in bequests. Like his father he wished to be buried in the chapel dedicated to the Virgin in St Botolph's church: appropriately, he left the considerable sum of £40 towards the cost of building a new 'campanil' (bell tower) at the church.[6] Robert apparently had no children; his widow Margaret was to have £100 and the tenement in St Botolph's parish for life.[7] She was not made one of his executors, which may be significant since widows in London were frequently appointed to act for their husbands.

It is not clear what happened to the Burford bell-founding business on Robert's death. Margaret remarried, to a man named John Dommer who is usually referred to in civic documents as a mercer.[8] He was a substantial inhabitant of Portsoken ward and served as a common councilman.[9] It is difficult to know whether Dommer and his new wife carried on with the bell-founding business; it seems unlikely, although John Dommer is, occasionally, referred to as a bell-maker or bell-founder.[10] What seems probable is that Dommer and Margaret leased the tenement next to St Botolph church which had been left to Margaret for life by her first husband, Robert Burford. John Dommer may therefore have been nominally a founder, but really a mercer living in part off foundry rents.

The foundry may have been leased to, or managed by, Richard Hill. This is suggested by the fact that Richard Hill witnessed a deed in which Dommer and his wife were beneficiaries.[11] He and Dommer also acted together as witnesses and executors of the will of Alexander Sprott, vintner, a St Botolph parishioner who had earlier been an executor of Robert Burford.[12] On this occasion, Dommer and Richard Hill were both described as founders. When Dommer died in 1439, there is no suggestion that either his widow or his son was expected to follow the bell-maker's craft.[13]

[6] Robert Burford's will is enrolled in the Commissary Court of London and is transcribed in Stahlschmidt, *Surrey Bells*, pp. 42–45.

[7] At her death the tenement was used to support a chantry for Robert in St Botolph's church, ibid. p. 44.

[8] E.g. in 1420, *CPMR, 1413–37*, p. 86; 1428, BL, Cotton MS App. XIX, f. 4v.; 1437, CLRO, HR 165 (41).

[9] In 1421 and again in 1435–36, *CPMR, 1413–37* pp. 119, 121; *LBK*, p. 197.

[10] John Dommer 'founder' in 1439, CLRO, HR 167 (15). In 1456, nearly twenty years after his death, he was described as 'belle maker' in a property abuttment, CLRO, HR 185 (11).

[11] 1 June 1437, CLRO, HR 165 (41).

[12] Sprott's will, dated 21 June 1438, is calendared in *HW*, ii. p. 485.

[13] Margaret Dommer (ex. Burford) was dead by 1439, see BL, MS Cotton, App. XIX, ff. 10v–11v. Dommer had re-married Margery before 1439. Dommer's will was proved in the Prerogative Court of Canterbury, PRO, 26 Luffenham, Probate 11/3. By October 1441 Margery was remarried to Robert Eldrebek. Dommer left £20 to his son who was, in due course (1455) apprenticed to a draper, Richard Brid, *LBK*, pp. 251–52, 367.

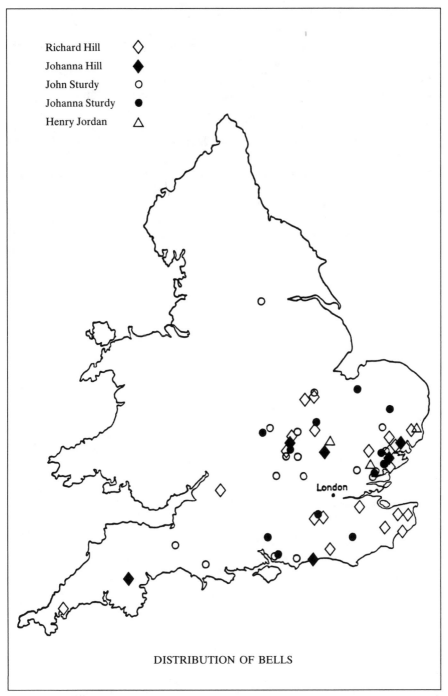

Richard Hill ◇
Johanna Hill ◆
John Sturdy ○
Johanna Sturdy ●
Henry Jordan △

DISTRIBUTION OF BELLS

Fig. 5 The distribution of the surviving bells of Richard and Johanna Hill, John and
Johanna Sturdy and Henry Jordan.

Richard Hill may well have taken over Robert Burford's business, but he was already a substantial bell-maker in his own right by the time of Burford's death in 1418; two years earlier he had served as a master of the founders craft.[14] His first workshop was possibly in one of the intramural parishes of St Mary Axe or St Olave Jewry, for he later remembered both those parishes in his will,[15] but when he died he was clearly a parishioner of St Botolph Aldgate.

Richard Hill is a comparatively obscure figure as far as London documentation goes. He acted as master of the Founders' Company (1416), as a trustee and executor; he was involved in establishing a chantry in St Botolph church for William and Robert Burford and their wives, inter alios, in 1439, and he was a common councilman, presumably for Portsoken ward.[16] Yet if Richard Hill is not a very prominent London figure, he was certainly a prolific bell-founder. Twenty-three of his bells survive in counties stretching from Cornwall to Rutland, displaying his distinctive mark of a cross and ring in a shield (see figs. 5 and 6).[17] Moreover, one of the three sets of capitals used by Hill on his bells had earlier been used by William and Robert Burford. He also marked his bells with a cross which had been used by the Burfords.[18] Obviously, sets of letters can move comparatively easily from foundry to foundry, but the fact that Richard Hill used some of the Burfords' foundry equipment lends credence to the suggestion that on Robert Burford's death in 1418, Richard Hill, already an established founder, moved from his smaller foundry in St Mary Axe into the Burford's substantial and well-equipped foundry in the parish of St Botolph.

[14] 1416, *LBI*, p. 144

[15] Richard Hill's will is transcribed in Stahlschmidt, *Surrey Bells*, pp. 49–51.

[16] 1422, Hill was a feoffee in St Bride's parish, Fleet Street, where one of the witnesses was described as John Hill 'junior', possibly a son who predeceased his father, CLRO, HR 152 (59); Hill witnessed deeds involving land in St Botolph's parish in 1437, PRO E 326/4406, CLRO, HR 165 (41); he was an executor of Alexander Sprott and was involved in establishing a chantry for him in St Botolph's church in 1438–39, CLRO, HR 167 (15) and BL, MS Cotton, App. XIX, ff. 6v–10v; and see C.J. Kitching, *London and Middlesex Chantry Certificate*, London Record Society (London, 1980), p. 43; 1435–36, Hill assessor, with Dommer, for the subsidy in Portsoken ward, *LBK*, p. 197; 1436, received gift of goods and chattels, *CPMR, 1413–37*, p. 289; 1438, surety for Thomas Morestede, surgeon, *LBK*, p. 223; 1439, common councilman, CLRO, Journal 3, f.13.

[17] Richard Hill's bells are found in the following counties: Bedfordshire (Staughton Parva); Buckinghamshire (Thornton); Cambridgeshire (two at Ufford); Cornwall (Penkivel, recast); Essex (Castle Headingham, St Nicholas Colchester, East Mersea); Gloucestershire (Shipton Mayne); Kent (St Mary Magdalene, Canterbury, Cheriton [recast], Great Chart [recast], Luddesdown, Staple); Northamptonshire (Horton); Rutland (Tixover); Suffolk (Higham, Great Glenham, Ringshall, Washbrook); Surrey (East Horsley, Headley); Sussex (Clayton). I am extremely grateful to Alex Bayliss, who is preparing a University of London PhD thesis on 'Medieval Bells in England', for providing me with this information.

[18] See George Elphick, *Sussex Bells and Belfries* (Chichester, 1970), p. 43; and Cecil Deedes and H.B. Walters, *The Church Bells of Essex* (London, 1919), p. 16. The letters inherited from the Burfords are to be found at East Horsley in Surrey, see Stahlschmidt, *Surrey Bells*, figs 166 and 167. The cross is illustrated, ibid., fig. 165.

FIFTEENTH CENTURY BELL-FOUNDERS' MARKS

1 Richard Hill   2 Johanna Hill   3 John Sturdy
4 Johanna Sturdy

Fig. 6 The foundry marks of Richard Hill, Johanna Hill, John Sturdy and Johanna Sturdy. Taken from drawings to be found in J.C.L. Stahlschmidt, *Surrey Bells and London Bell-Founders* (1884), A.H. Cocks, *The Church Bells of Buckinghamshire* (1897), and H.T. Ellacombe, *The Church Bells of Gloucestershire* (1881).

Richard Hill may have come originally from Rutland. In his will he left 20s. to the fabric of the church of St Andrew in the Rutland village of Glaston, and one of his surviving bells is to be found at Tixover, less than ten miles from Glaston.[19] As we shall see, Richard Hill may have initiated a Leicestershire/Rutland connection for the St Botolph foundry. His wife Johanna may have come from Surrey. In her will she left bequests to the parish churches at Merstham and Banstead. One of Robert Burford's surviving bells is to be found at Merstham. Perhaps young Richard Hill, the leading apprentice in Robert Burford's foundry, was sent to Merstham to hang the Burford bell and while there met Johanna and brought her back to London as his wife.[20]

The substantial nature of Richard Hill's business may be gauged from his will, drawn up in May 1440, the month in which he died. His cash bequests totalled over £20, including 10 marks (£6 13s. 4d.) for daily masses in St Botolph's church for a year following his death. He asked to be buried in the chapel dedicated to the Virgin where the Burfords had been buried, and he (or perhaps his widow) gave a rich vestment of green branched damask to the parish church.[21] But Richard's will is a brief one: he left bequests to the two London parishes of St Mary Axe and St Olave Jewry, as well as to the church at Glaston. These bequests were, however, small amounts ranging from half a mark to one pound. There are no strictly charitable bequests, but it is likely that he trusted his widow, whom he appointed as an executor, to make appropriate provision for his soul which, indeed, she appears to have done.[22] Richard did remember some of the members of his household: each of his four male apprentices was released from the last year of his term and given a sum of money. Two female servants, Johanna Berdefeld and Agnes Heth, each received five marks (£3) for their marriages.[23] Richard's main bequest was a

---

[19] Stahlschmidt, *Surrey Bells* p. 50 and Thomas North *The Church Bells of Rutland* (Leicester, 1880), p. 155 and plates III and VI. The bells now at Glaston were made in the sixteenth and seventeenth centuries, ibid., p. 132.

[20] Johanna Hill's will, drawn up 3 February 1441 and proved 30 May 1441, is to be found in the commissary register, GL, MS 9171/4, ff. 62v–63. Johanna's will also makes bequests to the leper hospital of the Lock 'in Kentstrete' outside Southwark, and she also remembered the prisoners in the two Southwark gaols of the King's Bench and Marshalsea. She would have to have passed the hospital and the prisons on her route to and from Surrey. Her maiden name may have been Payn: she remembered Johanna Payn 'consanguinea mea' in her will, but there are no other references to her family. For Robert Burford's bell at Merstham, see Stahlschmidt, *Surrey Bells*, pp. 81–83.

[21] The vestment survived long enough to be sold off in 1549–50; see H.B. Walters, *London Churches at the Reformation* (London 1939), p. 211.

[22] Hill's executors were William Piggesworth (Pykworth) and John West, both founders. Piggesworth lived in the parish of St Mildred Poultry. By the time of his death in 1458 there is little sign that he was active as a founder; see his will, GL, Commissary Wills, MS 9171/5, f 286. John West died soon after Hill: he drew up his will in October 1442. West was an active bell-founder in the parish of St Margaret Lothbury with two apprentices and a servant, GL, Commissary Will, MS 9171/4, f. 111v.

[23] Hill's will is transcribed in Stahlschmidt, *Surrey Bells*, pp. 49–51. The apprentices were Roger Het, William Bolter, Richard Cresswell and John Wodewall.

hundred marks (£66 13s. 4d.) to his daughter Johanna: all his remaining g[
were to go to his wife. It seems clear that Richard Hill intended that his wid
Johanna, should run the St Botolph foundry and that, in due course, his
daughter would inherit the foundry from her mother.

Richard Hill died in May 1440; his widow drew up her will in February 1441
and was dead by the end of May of that year, so the foundry was only under her
direction for a year. But we know from several sources that she did indeed
actively manage the foundry during the year of her widowhood. In the first
place, on 28 March 1441, 'Johane Hille of London widewe' agreed with five
parishioners of the church at Faversham, Kent, that if the five new 'belles of
accorde' which she had made for them were not 'well sownyng and of good
accorde' for a year and a day, then she would remake any defective bell which
was brought to her workshop in London and transport it back to Faversham
and rehang it at her own cost.[24] Unfortunately, the fifteenth-century bells at
Faversham do not survive, but seven of Johanna Hill's bells do survive
elsewhere in England. Her responsibility for these bells – two at Manaton in
Devon, one at Castlethorpe in Buckinghamshire, one at Norton in Hertfordshire, one in the church (now demolished) of St Nicholas in Colchester, one at
St Mary at Elms, Ipswich, and one at East Preston in Sussex – is suggested by
their marks. All of them carry Richard Hill's distinctive cross and circle shield
but now the shield is surmounted by a lozenge containing a floret (see Figs. 5
and 6). A lozenge-shaped shield is the heraldic indication of womanhood and,
by adding the lozenge to her husband's foundry stamp, Johanna was declaring
her responsibility for the bells produced in that year 1440–1.

Johanna Hill's testament also indicates that she continued actively to run the
bell-founding business.[25] Three of her husband's four apprentices had continued to work for her and she had acquired a new one, so new that she did not
know his Christian name.[26] Johanna Berdefeld was still a member of her
household and received a further contribution towards her marriage, while a
further servant, Agnes Marshall, had been engaged. This Agnes was
bequeathed five marks but, as this was not designated as a marriage portion,
she may already have been married: a Thomas Marshall, servant, was
bequeathed some goods from 'shope me de foundero' (from my foundry
shop). Johanna also left a small bequest of half a mark (6s. 8d.) to Richard

---

[24] This indenture is now in the Maidstone Record Office, MS CCL P 146/7/1. I am most grateful
to Judy Ann Ford, who is currently completing a doctoral dissertation 'The Community of the
Parish in Late Medieval Kent' at Fordham University, for transcribing this document for me. The
contract is also transcribed in Stahlschmidt, *Surrey Bells*, pp. 51–52.

[25] Johanna Hill's will, drawn up 3 February 1441 and proved 30 Mary 1441, is to be found in the
Commissary register, GL, MS 9171/4, ff. 62v–63. Stahlschmidt did not know of this will and so
identified Johanna Hill with Johanna Sturdy (see below) and so made a mistake which has been
copied by all subsequent writers on the subject. For Johanna Sturdy, see below pp. 110–11.

[26] William Bolter, John Wodewall and Richard Cresswell. Roger Het may have completed his
term. The new apprentice's surname was Walbot.

Marshall who may, perhaps, have been the son of Thomas and Agnes. Thomas Marshall was not the only male servant to have joined Johanna's household since her husband's death: there were five others who each received a bequest. Over and above these there were six further male members of the household who included John Bereveyre 'bellemaker' and Jacob Clerk, possibly the scrivener for the business. In all Johanna Hill's household comprised the four apprentices, two female servants and the daughter of a fellow founder, six male servants, four other men whose tasks were not specified, a 'bellemaker' and a clerk. Apart from the three members of the Hill family, the household – that is the home, the foundry and the shop – numbered some twenty people, and Johanna's bequests to them amounted to some £30. It is possible that Johanna's household was enlarged on her husband's death, but it is also noticeable that women's wills are frequently more diffuse than those of men and this would certainly seem to be true of the testaments of Richard and Johanna Hill.

A large household contained within it smaller family groupings. We have already noted the presence of the Marshall family, and the Heths may have formed a similar family group. Richard Hill's leading apprentice was named Roger Heth and one of his two female servants was Agnes Heth who was left money for her marriage. Neither was still working for Johanna Hill a year later, but one of her new servants was a Richard Heth. Perhaps the three Heths were siblings.

Unlike her husband, Johanna did not leave the distribution of her charitable bequests to her executors but, instead, spelled out exactly how she wished her goods to be dispersed. She reiterated her husband's bequests to the two London parishes and to St Andrew's church at Glaston, but she enlarged the bequest to the parish of Glaston by the addition of 20s. to be distributed to the poor there. In London she remembered the prisoners in seven London gaols, the poor in Bethlem hospital, the poor women of Elsyngspittal and the lepers at the Lock hospital in Southwark. In all, these charitable bequests amounted to only about £4, but she left a further £20 for her executors to buy coal and faggots in winter for the poor of St Botolph's parish and the poor of the Founders' company.

In her testament Johanna was careful to specify exactly how her executors were to provide for her soul and that of her husband. Whereas Richard had simply left 10 marks for a year of daily masses in St Botolph's church, Johanna left seventy marks for masses for seven years. She also left £20 which her executors were to spend on a special requiem mass every year for twenty years, to be celebrated on 4 June, presumably the anniversary of Richard Hill's death. This was to be a sung mass 'by note' and the 20s. was to be spent on fees to the parish clergy,[27] and on two wax tapers to burn at Richard's tomb; the

---

[27] The parish chaplain was to receive 6d. and the stipendiary chaplains and parish clerks 4d. each. In 1379–81 the church had one parochial chaplain and a clerk; in 1548 there were three, or perhaps four, stipendiary priests, see A.K. McHardy, *The Church in London, 1375–1392*, London

continued

residue was to be distributed among the poor of the parish and the Founders' company, and among prisoners.

The St Botolph foundry not only made bells but also brass and latten goods. The two Surrey churches at Merstham and Banstead were given five marks each or, alternatively, goods for ornamenting the church to the same value from 'my shop'. The London church of St Olave Jewry was given a pair of processional candle sticks made of latten and a holy water stoup also of latten. Some of the apprentices and servants employed by the Hills were probably turning out brassware of various kinds, but it is quite clear from the Faversham contract and from Johanna's testament that bells were also being made in her workshop. John Bereveyre 'bellemaker' was listed among her servants and apprentices and received one pound, and John Acres 'my servant' was given six marks (£4) on the condition that he remained as a servant with Henry Jordan, Johanna's new son-in-law, and continued to serve him well and faithfully in the art and occupation of 'belmakere'.

Between June 1440 when Richard died and February 1441 when his widow drew up her testament, their daughter, also Johanna, had married Henry Jordan, a member of the Fishmongers' Company. Henry's parents, Giles and Margaret, were fellow parishioners in St Botolph Aldgate so Johanna appears to have married the boy-next-door.[28] But there also seems to be a Leicestershire connection, for Giles and Margaret Jordan, Henry's father and mother, came originally from Loughborough and were commemorated there, so the family links may go back beyond the migrations of the Hills and Jordans to the London parish of St Botolph's.[29] It was clearly Johanna Hill's intention that her daughter and her new husband should continue to manage the Hill bellfoundry. Not only did she leave 'omnia bona mea tam domicilia quam arti mee de belmakere pertinent' (all my goods, both domestic and those belonging to the art of bell-making) to Henry and Johanna, but she also attempted to secure John Acres as their foreman.

What were the domestic goods which Johanna left to her daughter and son-in-law? Compared with many of the widows of London merchants, Johanna's goods were comparatively modest. Her best red gown lined with fur went to Johanna, and her best black furred gown was to go to Isabelle Chamberlain, the wife of the founder, William Chamberlain, who acted as Johanna's

continued
Record Society (London, 1977), p. 6; C.J. Kitching, *London and Middlesex Chantry Certificate 1548*, London Record Society (London,1980), p. 43.

[28] Henry Jordan in his will drawn up in 1468, mentions his parents, Giles and Margaret, and their burial in St Botolph's church. The will is transcribed in Stahlschmidt, *Surrey Bells*, pp. 60–70, see especially pp. 63, 67.

[29] Ibid., pp. 56–59. A much-damaged brass remains in Loughborough church, probably commemorating Giles and Margaret Jordan and referring to their 'sonne Harry late fischmonger of London', Mill Stephenson, *A List of Monumental Brasses in the British Isles*, (1926–38, London; repr. 1964), p. 276.

executor.[30] All her silver plate, two beakers, four cups, two dozen silver gilt spoons and a salt cellar, together with her 'tapserwerk' bed with sheets, mattress and quilt, went to Johanna. It is clear that the newly-weds were to be comfortably furnished, as well as provided with a flourishing business.

Johanna Hill was not concerned exclusively with her own family and the members of her household. Her testament suggest that she had business dealings with other founders whom she remembered charitably: John Bette, founder, was released from his debt to her and given one pound; William Capper, another founder, was also give a pound and a pair of sheets. Johanna Hill was particularly concerned about the family of John Bailly, founder. He also was released from his debts and given bed-clothes and two large pots; his daughter Alice was provided with five marks (£3 6s. 8d.) for her marriage and, in a codicil to her will, Johanna instructed her executors to take particular care of John and Johanna Bailly and their children and to ensure that they were not in need, although she stipulated that if they fell into bad moral habits they would forfeit her bequests. This kind of 'postmortem bossiness' was not unique Johanna Hill and was frequently manifested in the wills of rich London widows. The effectiveness of such contingent bequests would, of course, depend upon the willingness of the executors to keep an eye on the recipients. Finally, Johanna wanted her executors to ensure that Johanna Payn 'consanguinea mea' was provided with woollen clothing, shoes and victuals for the rest of her life.

There is nothing particularly remarkable about Johanna Hill's testament except, perhaps, its length, but it provides an insight into her world. Her thoughts were for her dead husband, her daughter and her new son-in-law, all the members of her diverse household, her home and her shop. She thought about the poor and the sick, and she remembered the parish in Surrey where she was born and the church of her baptism. As death approached, and it came perhaps more slowly than she expected since three months elapsed between the drafting of her testament and the codicil, she painstakingly unpicked the threads from which the fabric of her life had been woven.

What happened to the St Botolph foundry after Johanna Hill died in May 1441? There seems, in fact, to be very little evidence that Henry Jordan and his wife actually ran the foundry. There are no bells which can be certainly attributed to Jordan, and from his will it is clear that his loyalties and legacies were directed towards his own company, the Fishmongers.[31] In documents,

---

[30] For Isabelle and William Chamberlain, see below note 45. Johanna's other executors were John West, founder, and her son-in-law Henry Jordan.

[31] Most nineteenth-century writers mistakenly attributed a large group of over a hundred bells to Jordan, see Stahlschmidt, *Surrey Bells* pp.57–59, 87–88 and figs 186 and 188. A.D. Tyssen, *The Church Bells of Sussex* (Lewes, 1915), pp. 28–38, however, argued against this and attributed these bells to William Chamberlain (see note 45 below). The only possible Jordan bells are Cambridgeshire (Tadlow); Essex (Sturmer); and Suffolk (two at Saxmundham); information from Alex Bayliss, see note 17 above.

and in his will, he described himself as "citizen and fishmonger of London".[32] But he remained as a parishoner of St Botolph and desired burial in the chapel where his parents, parents-in-law and his wife were buried.[33] He also served as a common councilman for Portsoken ward, but by 1468 when he drew up his will he does not refer to any property in the parish.[34] There is some evidence that Henry Jordan may, in the 1440s, have attempted to manage the bell-founding business, but it is very slight. In the late 1450s John Vyncent, described as a bell-maker, complained to the Chancellor that Henry Jordan had, in 1448/9, attempted to persuade him to break his indentures with John Sturdy 'late of London, bell maker' and to work instead for Jordan. To persuade him to leave Sturdy's service, Jordan had lent him 44s. 8d. When Vyncent returned to work for Sturdy in the late 1450s, not surprisingly perhaps, Jordan sued him for debt.[35]

Johanna Hill's foundry seems to have passed, perhaps by sale, to a man named John Sturdy, who is first recorded in London in 1440, the year when Johanna Hill was running the foundry.[36] It is possible that he, like Richard Hill and Henry Jordan, came from Leicestershire/Rutland, for he is described on one occasion as 'John Sturdy alias Leicester'.[37] In 1448-49 he was practising as a bell-maker in London and living in St Botolph's parish.[38] He was certainly dead by 1459, possibly by 1456.[39] About sixteen bells have been found bearing

---

[32] For Jordan's will, see Stahlschmidt, *Surrey Bells*, pp. 60–70. But, as Tyssen pointed out, this will cannot cover the complete disposition of Jordan's estate, but is a devise of certain tenements; primarily those given to the Fishmongers' Company with whom the will is now lodged, Tyssen, *The Church Bells of Sussex*, p. 27. Jordan's will was enrolled in the Court of Hustings, *HW*, ii, pp. 543–44.

[33] Stahlschmidt, *Surrey Bells*, p. 60. Jordan also gave '3 copes of redde Badkyns with lions and flowers' to the church, H.B. Walters, *London Churches*, p. 210.

[34] CLRO, Portsoken Ward Presentments, ref. 242A, rolls for 5 and 6 Edward IV, 1456–57.

[35] Tyssen prints this early chancery petition, PRO, ECP, bundle 26, no. 567, *The Church Bells of Sussex*, pp. 94–95.

[36] *CPMR, 1437–57*, p. 164.

[37] Ibid., p. 180, in 1454.

[38] Tyssen, *The Church Bells of Sussex*, pp. 94–95; J.C.L. Stahlschmidt, *The Church Bells of Kent* (London, 1887), p. 37; CLRO, HR 179 (21), deed dated 5 February 1451. John Sturdy may have been brought to Leicester by Jordan to manage and work the foundry which he had inherited from his mother-in-law. The relations between Jordan, the sleeping partner, and Sturdy, the active bell-founder, seem to have deteriorated by the late 1440s (see note 35 above) and Sturdy may have bought Jordan out and then made bells marked with his own initials. One of the bells at St John the Baptist, Margate was inscribed 'Daudeleon || x S Trinitate Sacra sit hec campana Beata'. Daudeleon died in 1445, so if this is John Sturdy's bell, he was already active as a bell-founder by that date; information from Alex Bayliss, see note 17 above.

[39] Tyssen, *The Church Bells of Sussex*, p. 95; Johanna Sturdy, widow, sealed an indenture, 12 December 1459, Maidstone Record Office, MS CCL P 146/7/2.

John Sturdy's mark, that is a half-groat flanked by the letters I and S (see Figs. 5 and 6)[40] For his inscriptions he seems to have used Richard Hill's letters and one of his crosses had been used by both by Robert Burford and by Richard Hill.[41]

After John Sturdy's death his widow took over the running of the St Botolph foundry, just as Johanna Hill had done nearly twenty years before. Unfortunately, we have no extant wills either for John Sturdy or his widow, but we have evidence of Johanna Sturdy's management in the fourteen bells cast in her foundry, and in the survival of an indenture drawn up on 12 December 1459 between Johanna Sturdy of London 'wydewe' and the mayor of Faversham, the vicar of the parish church there and the three churchwardens.[42] Johanna Sturdy had replaced Johanna Hill's tenor bell at a cost of £9 5s. 3d., and she guaranteed its workmanship and its 'good accorde' with 'the old meen bell' already in the church. If the new bell was found to be defective, especially where harmony with the old bells was concerned, then the churchwardens were to bring it to Johanna Sturdy's 'dwelling-place' in the parish of St Botolph without Aldgate in London. They would pay the costs but Johanna agreed to contribute 10s towards the carriage every time the bell had to be brought to London for tuning.

Presumably Johanna Sturdy marked this bell (no longer extant) with the mark which we find on her other bells (ten extant and three recast);[43] namely, her husband's mark but with the half-groat surmounted by a lozenge (see Figs.

[40] John Sturdy's bells are found in Buckinghamshire (Adstock, Chesham, Stoke Hammond); Dorset (Piddlehinton); Essex (Good Easter, Great Totham [recast], Little Totham, Maldon); Lincolnshire (Tallington); Northamptonshire (Grendon); Oxfordshire (Holton); Somerset (Curry Mallet); Suffolk (Norton [recast]); Sussex (Heathfield [recast], Rumboldswyke – from St Martin Chichester); Warwickshire (Wolfhamcote); information from Alex Bayliss, see note 17 above.

[41] Elphick, *Sussex Bells and Belfries*, p. 45; A.H. Cocks, *The Church Bells of Buckinghamshire* (London, 1897), p. 25. The cross which Sturdy inherited from the Burfords and Hills is illustrated in Stahlschmidt, *The Church Bells of Kent* (London, 1887), fig. 5a.

[42] Maidstone Record Office, MS CCL P 146/7/2. I am most grateful to Judy Ann Ford for making a transcript of this for me. There is a precis of the indenture in Stahlschmidt, *Surrey Bells*, pp. 52–53.

[43] Johanna Sturdy's bells are to be found in Buckinghamshire (Beachampton); Cambridgeshire (Long Stow); Essex (Langford [recast], Layer de la Haye, Wormingford); Hampshire (Southwick, St John the Baptist Winchester); Norfolk (Kenninghall, two at Watlington); Surrey (Stoke d'Abernon); Sussex (Rotherfield [recast]); Warwickshire (Ladbroke [recast]; information from Alex Bayliss, see note 17 above.

5 and 6), the same mark of difference as that used by Johanna Hill, her female predecessor at the foundry.

It is not known when Johanna Sturdy died, but in the 1460s some of the Sturdy's crosses and letters had passed to a founder who used as his mark the shield of the Keble family.[44] The twenty or so surviving bells, marked with the distinctive signs of Johanna Hill and Johanna Sturdy, bear witness, both visually and aurally, to the entrepeneurial skill and managerial ability of artisan widows in fifteenth-century London.[45]

[44] Walters, *Bells of Essex*, pp. 20–21.

[45] Elphick noted five female bell-founders (in fact six because he elided Johanna Hill and Johanna Sturdy); Agnes le Belyetere of Worcester, 1274–75; Christina la Belyetere of Gloucester, 1303–4; Elinor Bartlet, 1632; and Julia Bagley, 1716–19, Elphick *Sussex Bells and Belfries*, p. 113. Heather Swanson noted the case of Margaret Sowreby of York who took over her husband's workshop, *Medieval Artisans: An Urban Class in Late Medieval England* (Oxford, 1989), p. 74. Another possible bell-foundress is Agnes Powdrell, wife of William. His initials appear on a bell at Stowting in Kent, Stahlschmidt, *Church Bells of Kent*, fig. 184; hers on the treble at Little Totham, Essex, see Walters, *Church Bells of Essex*, pp. 18–19, 424. It might be appropriate to add Isabella Chamberlain to this list. She was the wife of William Chamberlain who made over a hundred bells between 1426 and 1456, see Elphick, *Sussex Bells and Belfries*, pp. 55–56. By 1440 Chamberlain was married to Isabella, who received bequests in the wills of both Richard and Johanna Hill (see notes 23 and 25 above). Chamberlain acted as executor for Johanna Hill and also for her son-in-law, Henry Jordan (see note 32 above) and he did not himself die until 1474, see his will proved in the commissary court, GL, MS 9171/6, f.180. His workship was in the parish of St Margaret Lothbury, and he may have taken over the foundry of John West, a founder of that parish who died in 1442, see his will proved in the commissary court, GL, MS 9171/4, f. 111v. When Chamberlain died in 1474 he left his foundry to his wife Isabella and his son Richard and his apprentices were left 3s. 4d. each on condition that they continued to serve with Isabella and Richard. All William's unpaid debts were assigned to Isabella and she was also appointed as her husband's sole executor. Isabella was charged with giving a dozen silver spoons, or a jewel, at her discretion, to the fellowship of William's craft. The value of the gift was to be 20s. We know that Isabella carried out her husband's request, for in 1497 the Founder's Company recorded that they possessed eight silver spoons 'the gifte of William Chamberleyn thelder', Guy Parsloe, *The Wardens' Accounts of the Founders' Company, 1497–1681* (London, 1964), p. 412. Chamberlain also left a bequest to the fraternity of St Clement in the church of St Margaret, which carries the history of the founders' fraternity back at least to 1474, ibid., pp. xiii–xiv. Isabella must have been a notable woman, active as a wife for over thirty years and, in the end, appointed to oversee her husband's will and perhaps to run the bell-making business with, and for, her son who died in 1510 (PRO, PCC wills, 37 Bennett).

9

Joan Buckland (d. 1462)

Jenny Stratford

In the fourteenth and fifteenth centuries, great fortunes made in London were usually invested in land. The wives of a handful of the most successful London merchants in each generation became, at least for part of the year, ladies living on their manors.[1] How did women born and bred in London adapt to their role as landowners and administrators? And how did they sustain their city interests? For the reasons explored in the introduction to this volume, it is notoriously difficult to collect evidence about medieval women during their husbands' lifetime, but the changed legal status of widows makes them more visible. The life of Joan Buckland, who had been a widow for twenty-six years when she died in 1462, may be seen as a case history of a rich woman with roots in both London and the country. In other respects, such as her interest in books and education, she was not typical.

Joan Buckland was the daughter of a London citizen and fishmonger. Her husband, Richard Buckland, also a fishmonger, grew immensely rich as a shipowner, merchant of the Calais staple and royal servant. He was victualler of Calais at the end of the reign of Henry V, and treasurer and victualler of Calais under Henry VI.[2] Richard Buckland died in 1436, leaving part of his fortune invested in land. Because of the prosperity of Joan Buckland's parents and husband, the range of her inherited business and the backlash from her husband's dealings with the crown over Calais, it is possible to find out a good deal about her as a widow.

The background from which Joan came relates in several ways to her life as a widow: in particular her lifelong association with the Fishmongers' Company with its intricate web of relationships, and the influence of her mother, an active and independent widow, who survived her husband by nearly thirty

---

[1] R. Archer, ' "How Ladies . . . who Live on their Manors Ought to Manage their Households and Estates": Women as Landholders and Administrators in the Later Middle Ages', *Woman is a Worthy Wight*, ed. P.J.P. Goldberg (Stroud, 1992), pp. 149–81. The quotation is from Christine de Pisan.

[2] For Buckland, see S. Rose, ed., *The Navy of the Lancastrian Kings: Accounts of William Soper, Keeper of the King's Ships, 1422–27*, Navy Records Society, 123 (London, 1982), p. 232 and passim; J. Stratford, *The Bedford Inventories: The Worldly Goods of John, Duke of Bedford, Regent of France (1389–1435)* (Society of Antiquaries of London, 1993), p. 408, with bibliography.

years. Joan was the eldest daughter and one of four children of Richard
Gifford and his wife, Agnes. Her mother had come to London from Southchurch in Essex, now part of Southend,[3] her father from Gilston, near
Sawbridgeworth in Hertfordshire. The Giffords had lived in Gilston from the
late twelfth century; they seem to have been a close-knit and prosperous
yeoman family and by the fourteenth century were probably educated people.
One of Richard Gifford's uncles was a priest, perhaps a canon of nearby
Waltham Abbey, with which there was a family connection.[4] There is little
evidence about the nature of Richard Gifford's business, apart from a sugges-
tive legacy of a pittance of fish to Waltham Abbey, and his close links with
fellow members of his craft, but fishmongers were often shipowners. In 1381,
already an citizen and fishmonger, Richard Gifford bought his first London
properties with the help of his brother, William Gifford of Gilston. They
consisted of two tenements in Distaff Lane and a shop on the north-eastern
corner of Old Fish Street. These were prime sites not far from St Paul's, in the
parish of St Nicholas Cole Abbey (the Fishmongers' church), and in streets
chiefly occupied by fellow fishmongers. In 1390 Richard bought a third
tenement immediately to the north of his existing holdings.[5] The family lived in
the middle and principle tenement in Distaff Lane, close to the parish church
and not far from St Paul's Cathedral. Richard Gifford participated at least to
some extent in the spiritual renewal which took place at St Paul's at the end of
the fourteenth century. He and his wife left money for building works and for
requiem masses at St Paul's, where they were both buried in Pardon Churchyard, and for lights for four of the shrines most popular with Londoners: the
Rood at the North door, St Mary of Graces, the Virgin in the Lady chapel and
the feretory of St Erkenwald.[6]

---

[3] GL, MS 9171/3, ff. 167r–v; Agnes may have belonged to a family trading in fish through
London and working the lucrative Essex mussel-beds. Southchurch manor was held by John de
Prittlewell, spicer of London, from 1346 to his death in 1385, who was engaged in this trade with
John Seman and other local men (*CPMR, 1364–81*, pp. 29–30); see also J.F. Nichols, 'Southchurch
Hall', *Journal of the British Archaeological Association*, new series, 37 (1932), pp. 106–7. Dr
David Gamester, Medieval and Later Antiquities, British Museum, kindly showed me the
documentation assembled for the recent excavation at Southchurch.

[4] VCH, *Hertfordshire*, iii, ed. W. Page (London, 1912), pp. 319–23; GL, MS 9051/1, ff. 77r–v
(testament of Richard Gifford); GL, MS 9171/3, ff. 167r–v (testament of Agnes Gifford).

[5] CLRO, HR 109 (75), (84), (91), (93), (99), for the tenements, a shop, etc., bought in 1381
from John Frere, son of Thomas Frere, citizen and fishmonger, who received a rent of £4 p.a. for
life; HR 100 (119), for a rent of 12s. on the shop; HR 119 (51), for the tenement bought in 1390. By
1392, the hospital of St Giles had 7s. for a shop belonging to Gifford and St Paul's, 2s., see A.K.
McHardy, *The Church in London, 1375–1392*, London Record Society, 13 (London, 1977), no.
495.

[6] H.H. Milman, *Annals of St Paul's Cathedral* (London, 1868), pp. 144–50; C.N.L. Brooke,
'The Earliest Times to 1485', *A History of St Paul's Cathedral*, ed. W.R. Mathews and W.M.
Atkins (London, 1957), pp. 65–72.

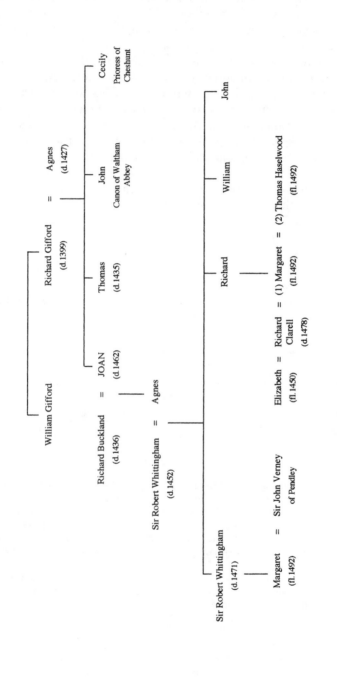

Fig. 7   Joan Buckland's Family.

By 1398, when Richard Gifford made his wills, there were four children, none of them of age. He died in 1399.[7] Among Richard's possessions were a mazer, or maple-wood drinking cup, probably mounted in silver, and another silver cup, evidence of some degree of luxury in the home. The impression of his prosperity is reinforced by his pious and charitable bequests, worth well over £35. He left above average sums for the priests celebrating masses and trentals and remembered the poor, the sick and prisoners.[8] Richard Gifford followed the common practice of appointing his wife his executor. The terms of his testament (concerning the disposal of movables and legacies for the testator's soul), demonstrate that Agnes's appointment was no mere formality. This was recognised by her two co-executors, both fishmongers, when they declined to act over this part of the inheritance, although they agreed to deal with the real estate. Agnes administered a considerable sum of money, £66 13s. 4d., left for her use until the children were of age, and was the residuary legatee. She also inherited a life-interest in the tenements, which were secured ultimately with cross-remainders to three of the four children. The eldest son, Thomas, later a fishmonger, was to inherit the principal tenement and the shop. This could (but need not) mean Agnes carried on her husband's business. Joan was to have the tenement to the south, let to the fishmonger, John Hill, one of her father's executors.

Agnes Gifford lived for another twenty-seven years. To judge both by the arrangements her husband made and by her own two wills, she was an intelligent, active, practical and devout woman.[9] Her long and independent widowhood must have set a pattern for her daughter's. Many features in her own wills are of interest, including her bequests to the four orders of friars. One stands out. Agnes left 10 marks or £6 13s. 4d. to found a chantry in Oxford for herself, her husband, her parents and benefactors and for schools (*ad exercendum scolas*). Although no books are mentioned in Agnes's will, this

---

[7] Both will and testament dated 10 March 1398, and proved 4 July 1399, GL, MS 9051/1, ff. 77r–v (movables), f. 79v (tenements in London), see *Index to Testamentary Records in the Archdeaconry Court of London*, i, *1363–1649*, ed. Marc Fitch, (London, 1979), p. 150. For the tenements, see also CLRO, HR 128 (41), *HW*, ii, *1358–1688*, p. 342. Gifford had presumably been in good health a year earlier, when he acted for a neighbour in an assize of nuisance, see *London Assize of Nuisance, 1301–1431: A Calendar*, ed. H.M. Chew and W. Kellaway, London Record Society, 10 (London, 1973), no. 641.

[8] Over 12,860 London wills survive from 1373–1484. From a survey, Jens Röhrkasten has confirmed that the usual sum for each mass was 1d., and for each trental 2s. 6d. (paper given to the Later Medieval Seminar at the Institute of Historical Research in March 1993, 'Aspects of Piety in Late Medieval London'). Gifford left money for 2,000 masses at 2d and £10 for trentals (cycles of masses), besides money for chantries.

[9] GL, MS 9171/3, ff. 167r–v (movables), dated 12 March 1427, f. 167v (tenement in London), dated 12 June 1423, both proved 14 March 1427, see *Index to Testamentary Records in the Commissary Court of London*, i, *1374–1488*, ed. Marc Fitch (London 1969), p. 79. For the tenement, see also CLRO, HR 158 (33); *HW*, ii, p. 450.

may point to the origin of the interest in books and the universities of Oxford and Cambridge which was later shown by her daughter, Joan.

Nothing is known of Joan's education. The fact that her younger brother became a canon and her sister a nun suggests that she may have received some formal instruction. The date of Joan's marriage to Richard Buckland is also unknown, but it almost certainly took place before 1407, when she was still very young. Joan was not of age in 1398, but Joan and Richard Buckland's only child, another Agnes, was married by 1420 to the successful draper, Robert Whittingham. The minimum age of marriage allowed by the church was twelve for a woman; Agnes must have been born by 1408 at the latest.[10]

At the time of her marriage Joan already had a dowry and some expectations: besides £20 in cash in her father's will, the reversion of the tenement he had allotted to her. Her expectations of other inheritances from her parents may have increased. By 1423 and probably much earlier, her sister, Cecily, was a nun at Cheshunt Priory; by 1426, at the latest, her brother, John, was a canon of nearby Waltham Abbey. Their mother evidently considered Joan the most practical of her children, naming her as one of her two executors and her residuary legatee, in preference to the older son, Thomas, also a fishmonger. Agnes Gifford owned or bought another property, shops and solars in the parish of St Nicholas Cole Abbey, not part of her inheritance from Richard Gifford. She nominated it to endow a perpetual chantry for herself and her husband in the parish church, with music, bell-ringing and lights, but left a life interest to Joan.[11] Joan was to pay the annual dues of 8s. to the church, and also to see that 6s. 8d. went each year to her sister, Cecily, the nun, for clothing. Joan was left to settle the best way of raising money on the property. Half the proceeds were to go to the house at Cheshunt and the other half to Agnes's grandchildren, the children of Thomas and Joan. The endowment of Cheshunt no doubt contributed to Cecily's nomination as prioress before 1436,[12] but it also benefited Joan. Agnes Gifford had died in 1427; Thomas, her son, Joan's brother, in 1435. In a brief will recorded in the commissary court of London, Thomas asked for burial in Pardon Churchyard; he left Joan the remainder of his goods and tried to make her one of his two executors, although for some reason she refused to act.[13] By 1435, therefore, Joan is likely to have inherited

---

[10] CLRO, HR 160 (40); for Whittingham, see *The History of Parliament: The House of Commons, 1386–1421*, ed. J.S. Roskell, L. Clark and C. Rawcliffe, iv (Stroud, 1992), pp. 841–44; Stratford, *Bedford Inventories*, pp. 425–29.

[11] Cf. *London and Middlesex Chantry Certificate, 1548*, ed. C.J. Kitching, London Record Society, 16 (London, 1980), no. 19.

[12] VCH, *Hertfordshire*, iv. ed. W. Page (London, 1914), pp. 426–28. Cecily is called prioress in Richard Buckland's testament of 1436.

[13] GL, MS 9171/3, f. 440v, 6 Oct. 1435. Joan was named principal executor and residuary legatee if anything remained after debts were settled. Thomas Yonge of Kent, gentleman, coexecutor, was associated with the purchase by Richard and Joan Buckland in 1434 and 1435 of the manor of Copthall in Little Wigborough, Essex. See n. 29.

a considerable part of her father's property, as well as her interest in her mother's independent tenement with the charges. The only grandchild by 1435 was Richard and Joan's daughter, Agnes Whittingham.

Whether or not Richard Buckland expected to inherit a substantial amount of city property by his marriage to Joan Gifford, he must have valued highly her close connections with the Fishmongers' Company. One of Richard Gifford's business associates and an executor had been John Hill, fishmonger, the tenant of the tenement left to Joan. John Hill was forwarding Richard Buckland's interests as a fishmonger in the city in the first two decades of the fifteenth century. Other fishmonger connections of Joan's parents were involved with Richard Buckland time and time again in property transactions in the city, while from an early date he formed links of his own with key fishmongers such as William Coggeshall.[14]

Richard Buckland's origins are unknown, although a chantry established in his will at Ottery St Mary suggests he may have had Devonshire connections.[15] He appears as a citizen and fishmonger in the city records by 1409, and was a collector of tunnage and poundage in the port of London in 1415. Later in the same year, he was involved in the transport of the army to France before the battle of Agincourt. At the siege of Harfleur, he lent two ships. He was rewarded with a stake in Henry V's new English colony at Harfleur, an inn called the Peacock. By 1417 he was victualler of Calais and by 1421 treasurer and victualler, where he also controlled the mint and the exchange.[16] His business interests were wide: he had supplied monkeys, a parrot, three salamanders and other animals to Henry V, and was a major supplier of the king's wardrobe and household. Buckland had dealt with Thomas Beaufort, duke of Exeter, and was a councillor of John, duke of Bedford, in England and in France[17] He bought the *Grand Marie* from the navy of Henry V, and had a half share with John Melbourne in the *Antony* of London.[18] Buckland was involved

---

[14] CLRO, Journal 1, f. 7v, Jan 1417, John Hill, fishmonger, elected Richard Buckland. The context is not clear. Hill's name occurs with Buckland's, CLRO, HR 137 (4), 1409; HR 139 (96), 1412. Other names associated with Gifford and Buckland include Esgaston, Lopham, Ragenhill *alias* Seman, Wilford.

[15] For John Buckland, canon of Ottery St Mary, d. 1425, see J.N. Dalton, *The Collegiate Church of Ottery St Mary* (Cambridge, 1917), p. 78.

[16] CLRO, HR 137 (4); *CCR, 1413–16*, p. 410; *CPR, 1413–16*, p. 409: Rymer, *Foedera*, iv (ii) (The Hague, 1740), p. 146; *DKR*, 44 (London, 1883), p. 576; C.T. Allmand, *Lancastrian Normandy, 1415–1450: The History of a Medieval Occupation* (Oxford, 1983), pp. 86–87; R. A. Massey, 'The Lancastrian Land Settlement in Normandy and Northern France, 1417–1450' (unpublished Ph.D thesis, University of Liverpool, 1987), p. 184, citing *DKR*, 41, pp. 5, 22, 23, 691; *DKR*, 44, pp. 626, 629, 631, 634.

[17] *PRO, Lists and Indexes*, xi, *Foreign Accounts* (London, 1900), p. 109, Wardrobe and Household, misceallaneious expenses; Rose, *Navy of the Lancastrian Kings*, p. 130; PRO, E 101/514/22; Stratford, *Bedford Inventories*, p. 408 and passim.

[18] For the *Grand Marie*, a ship of 126 tuns burden, valued at £200, and refitted at a cost of £182 9s. 8d., before being awarded to Buckland in 1423, in satisfaction of tallies worth £148 8s. 11d., see Rose, *Lancastrian Navy*, pp. 53, 65, 66, 109, 114, 153, 207, 249. For the *Antony*, 280 tuns

continued

in the Breton trade, and in the import of arras, perhaps through Calais; he may have been involved in the Baltic trade.[19] In times of war, Buckland profited by 'sea-keeping', in other words capturing prize cargoes. He took figs, raisins, pepper, dates, almonds and wine from a Genoese carrack in Plymouth in 1419. In 1433 the *Antony* and other ships captured two Spanish vessels with cargoes of hides off Dartmouth.[20] Buckland could call on friendships or business connections with his fellow staplers and with the very great: besides those already named, Cardinal Beaufort, Lord Cromwell and William Alnwick, then bishop of Norwich.[21] He had been a member of mercantile embassies to Flanders and the Hanseatic League, and had been instrumental in shipping bullion to the duke of Burgundy,[22] Joan had no doubt been abroad with her husband to Normandy and to Calais. As treasurer, he was lieutenant of Balinghem Castle and had a retinue of thirty-eight soldiers. She knew the duke of Bedford, who gave her an ivory tablet, mentioned in her will. She and her husband were among the largest benefactors of Henry V's new monastic foundation, the Brigittine double monastery at Syon.[23] In short, during her marriage, Joan Buckland was very rich and in the first rank of merchant's wives.

Buckland's death on 10 August 1436 may not have been expected for very long. He had been named an executor of the duke of Bedford less than a year before, and had acquired from the crown valuable salmon-fishing on the River Tweed, which had belonged to Bedford's estate, only in April of the year he died. On the other hand, Buckland's health may have been failing by February, when he arranged for his son-in-law, Robert Whittingham, to succeed him as treasurer of Calais. When Buckland died in August he had not quite had time to finish the process of creating an enfeoffment to the use of Joan in their secondary country manor in Northamptonshire.[24] He made his testament only five days before his death.[25]

---

continued
burden, see ibid., p. 232; see also, C.F. Richmond, 'The Keeping of the Seas during the Hundred Years War, 1422–40', *History*, 49 (1964), 281–98.

[19] PRO, C 1/6/290; C 1/26/522; Rose, *Lancastrian Navy*, p. 232.

[20] *Calendar of Inquisitions Miscellaneous*, vii. *1399–1422* (London, 1968), no. 571. I thank Dr Susan Rose for her help with Buckland and for this reference. Professor Wendy Childs kindly informed me about the 1433 cargo, PRO, E 159/209, recorda, Trinity term, m. 4d.

[21] Buckland bequeathed Cromwell a pair of bottles, silver-gilt, in his testament. Beaufort and Alnwick acted as feoffees of the manor of Edgcote within a month of Buckland's death (PRO, C 140/5/45).

[22] J. Ferguson, *English Diplomacy, 1422–1461* (Oxford, 1972), pp. 93, 188, 206.

[23] BL, Add. MS 22285, the Syon Martyrology, ff. 70–70v. The Bucklands gave £30, £10 more than Archbishop Chichele and the duke of Bedford (who also gave rings and books). Humphrey, earl of Stafford, gave £10. The largest benefaction by far was £200, given by Margaret, duchess of Clarence. This was probably at the laying of the second foundation stone in 1427.

[24] Stratford, *Bedford Inventories*, pp. 42, 427, appendix, no. 12; n. 25, below.

[25] PRO, PROB 11/3, ff. 162r–v, testament proved in the PCC, 5 August 1436, see *The Fifty Earliest English Wills*, ed. F.J. Furnivall, EETS, original series, 78, 1882), pp. 104–8. Buckland died on 10 August, PRO, C 179/172/20. He had also made a will (*ultima voluntas*), shown to the juries at the inquisitions post mortem in Northamptonshire in 1459 and 1462.

Buckland owned lands in London and elsewhere assessed at £100 in the lay subsidy of 1436, putting him among the dozen or so richest Londoners. This may have been a considerable underestimate, and moreover took no account of Buckland's movables such as his ships and his plate.[26] What lands did Joan inherit? By 1436 she held jointure or legal title as joint owner of most of the lands in London and the country. Buckland's main London property was in the parish of All Hallows the Great. It consisted of a waterfront tenement with a quay in Wynges Lane, immediately to the east of the Steelyard, and had belonged to Thomas and Aldmicia Ferrers. Buckland bought it in 1417, the year he became victualler of Calais, creating a trust in 1421, the year he became treasurer. Ten years later, he transferred the tenement into the joint names of his wife and himself; Joan was still the owner of the tenement in 1439.[27] Buckland's main country properties were in Northamptonshire, the county for which he sat as M.P. in 1425 and 1431. These were the manor of Edgcote, north east of Banbury, held jointly with Joan since 1425, and the secondary manor of Sewell (later Seawell), in Blakesley, about eight miles away, both in rich, well-wooded, pasture land. In 1459 and 1462, Edgcote, a manor later owned by Sir Reynold Bray, Thomas Cromwell and Anne of Cleeves, was declared to be worth £20 a year clear, Sewell first £5 and then £6 13s. 4d. Edgcote was perhaps obtained through the Ferrers connection; Aldmicia Ferrers was patron of the living in 1421.[28] From 1434 Richard and Joan also jointly held a manor and advowson in Essex, Copthall in Little Wigborough, belonging to Richard, duke of York's honour of Clare. Joan took the profits of this manor until 1459; it was declared to be worth £26 13s. 4d. in 1460.[29] She may also have enjoyed other income from lands.[30]

[26] J.H.L. Stahlschmidt, *Archaological Journal*, 44 (1887), pp. 56–82; S.L. Thrupp, *The Merchant Class of Medieval London, 1300–1500* (paperback edn, Ann Arbor, Michigan, 1962), appendix B, p. 379.

[27] CLRO, HR 149 (2), (34), 160 (5), (36); CLRO, Roll A 66, m. 9v, where this appears to by Joan's, cf. *CPMR, 1437–57*, p. 20. Buckland may also have acquired property in Distaff Lane in 1424, CLRO, HR 152 (82), and in Warwick Lane in 1433, HR, 162 (76).

[28] PRO, C 139/172/20; C 140/5/45; C 140/8/19; C 140/68/48; PRO, DL 7/3/8, see *Ducatus Lancastriae: calendarium inquisitionum post mortem* (London, 1838), p. 9; J. Bridges, *The History and Antiquities of the County of Northamptonshire*, i (Oxford, 1822–30), pp. 10–11, 117–21, 236; G. Baker, *The History and Antiquities of the County of Northamptonshire*, i (London, 1822–30), pp. 491–501 (ii, pp. 34–35, is incorrect); *The Register of Richard Fleming, Bishop of Lincoln, 1420–31*, i, ed. N.H. Bennett, Canterbury and York Society, 73 (York, 1984), no. 497. Edgcote had been held by Henry V as Prince of Wales and was held in chief, although this was temporarily denied at the inquisition in 1459.

[29] *Feet of Fines for Essex*, iv, *1423–1547*, ed. P.H. Reaney and Marc Fitch (Colchester, 1964), pp. 20, 21, nos 141, 144; PRO, C 139/172/20.

[30] In 1428, Buckland had bought from his fellow M.P. for Northamptonshire, Thomas Chambre, and his second wife, Eleanor, the manors of Napton in Warwickshire, Shankton and Hardwick in Leicestershire and Marcham in Berkshire, *Warwickshire Feet of Fines*, iii, *1345–1509*, ed. L. Drucker, Dugdale Society, 18 (1943), no. 2546, p. 146; J. S. Roskell, *The Commons in Parliament of 1422* (Manchester, 1954), p. 164. Buckland also held property in Calais worth £26 13s. 4d. a year, but this was in the hands of Roger Burgh by 1437 (PRO, C 1/17/106).

Richard Buckland named Joan first of his executors. She was supported by a number of powerful men, headed by Sir John Tyrell of Essex [31] and Master Richard Caudray, dean of St Martin-le-Grand.[32] Other executors included Richard Quatermayne or Quatremains of London and Oxfordshire,[33] and the fishmonger, John Melbourne, both Buckland's partners in shipping ventures, and others with influence far beyond the confines of the city: Thomas Rothwell of Northampton, John Kemplay, Thomas Pound and John Coggeshall.[34] Among the named witnesses were the parish priest of All Hallows the Great, William Lichfield, and two men, who (like most of the executors) had links with Buckland's real estate, the fishmonger, John Ingram, and Thomas Yonge of Kent. Some were no doubt chosen for their knowledge of the finances of Calais and of Buckland's shipping interests. At least two are likely to have been personal friends. Buckland left his purple gown furred with martens and his primer or book of hours to Thomas Rothwell, the only book mentioned in his testament; to John Melbourne he left his scarlet gown, lined with the same very high quality fur. Joan secured the cooperation of the active executors and witnesses for many years, although by the late 1450s these prominent men had been replaced by a more local circle of vicars and others (still including fishmongers), who were her Northamptonshire friends. In almost no time after Buckland's death, she and her fellow executors were heavily involved in Buckland's private and crown business.

The difference in scale between the wealth of Joan Buckland's father, William Gifford, and her husband, Richard Buckland, is well illustrated by

[31] J.S. Roskell, 'Sir John Tyrell', *Parliament and Politics in Late Medieval England*, iii (London, 1983), pp. 278–315; R.A. Griffiths, *The Reign of King Henry VI: The Exercise of Royal Authority, 1422–1461* (London, 1981), pp. 120, 194–95; P.A. Johnson, *Duke Richard of York, 1411–60* (2nd edn, Oxford, 1991), p. 17. As treasurer of the king's household, Tyrell was also treasurer for wars; he had first-hand experience of Calais.

[32] For Caudray, who had links with the council, see Emden, *BRUC*, pp. 126–27. He is known to have been an active executor of the will of John Holland, duke of Exeter, who died in 1447, Westminster Abbey Muniments, 6643; Stratford, *Bedford Inventories*, p. 48.

[33] J.T. Driver, 'Richard Quatremains: A Fifteenth-Century Squire and Knight of the Shire for Oxfordshire', *Oxoniensia*, 51 (1986), pp. 87–103. I thank Dr Linda Clark for her help with Quatremains. Like Buckland, Quatremains had been collector of tunnage and poundage in London, appointed from the accession of Henry VI. His commission specified that he was to write his rolls with his own hand and do no work by deputy (*CPR, 1422–29*, p. 58). For his shipping interests with Buckland, see e.g., *The Overseas Trade of Bristol in the Later Middle Ages*, ed. E.M. Carus Wilson, Bristol Record Society, 7 (Bristol, 1937), no. 76.

[34] Rothwell appears to be the clerk to the treasurer of England, 1450–52, not the M.P. for Berkshire in 1417 and 1420 (*HP*, iv, pp. 235–36; Griffiths, *Henry VI*, p. 616). For Pound, a teller at the exchequer from 1433 who was involved in the wool trade, see provisionally Wedgwood, *History of Parliament: Biographies* (London, 1936), pp. 695–96; he was an associate of Cardinal Beaufort, see G.L. Harriss. *Cardinal Beaufort: A Study of Lancastrian Ascendancy and Decline* (Oxford, 1988), p. 243; John Coggeshall had acted for Buckland in a chancery suit relating to the staple at Calais in 1431, *CCR, 1429–35*, pp. 112–13. Kemplay alone of the executors and named witnesses does not appear to have been active as a feoffee of the Buckland lands after Richard's death.

their pious bequests. Richard Buckland left perhaps ten times as much, well over £340 for masses and chantries, for the poor, the sick, hospitals and prisoners. Joan Buckland's first duties as executor were seeing that these wishes were fulfilled. Much was to be distributed in London, but Buckland also remembered the poor at Edgcote and at Ottery St Mary. He gave £10 for the works of St Paul's, asking to be buried in Pardon Churchyard. Buckland left money to his parish church of All Hallows and to St Nicholas Cole Abbey as well as for numerous sung and said masses and trentals to be paid for at much higher than average rates. Bequests went to two named friars, perhaps confessors, as well as to the four orders of friars in London. Other religious named in Buckland's testament included his brother and sister-in-law, John and Cecily Gifford, the priest who served in his household, the parson of Edgcote and the master of St John's Hospital, Banbury. Several chantries were also established by Buckland; two were to be founded for the term of twenty years. One of these was to be at Ottery St Mary, where the whole ecclesiastical establishment from canons to choristers was to be recompensed on a munificent scale of from 8d. to 2d. for each annual obit; the other (ten times as valuable at £200), was to be at the university of Oxford or Cambridge 'after the discrecion of my wyf & executours'. Joan Buckland's decision about how to bestow this sum was strongly influenced by William Lichfield, parson of All Hallows the Great, the first named of the witnesses to Buckland's testament.

Lichfield, a well-known preacher, was a friend of William Bingham, rector of St John Zachary, and founder of Godshouse, Cambridge, afterwards Christ's College.[35] Bingham's purpose for Godshouse was to educate grammar masters, to supply the want of men to teach in schools. By July 1437, less than a year after Buckland's death, he had the money to buy land for the college. Three benefactors, John Brokley, draper and alderman of London, Joan Buckland and William Flete acted as feoffees. The choice of Godshouse for her husband's chantry was no doubt fully endorsed by Joan. Michaelhouse (refounded as part of Trinity College) may have been an alternative, since Richard and Joan Buckland were remembered there as benefactors.[36] Joan probably had a particular interest in grammar schools. She knew at least two of the four London divines, all bookmen and popular preachers, who successfully petitioned parliament in 1447 on the subject of the lack of grammar schools, even in the city. They were Lichfield himself, Gilbert Worthington, rector of St Andrew's, Holborn, John Coote, rector of St Peter, Cornhill, and John Neel, master of St Thomas of Acre and rector of St Mary Colechurch. Neel

[35] For Godshouse, see A.H. Lloyd, *The Early History of Christ's College, Cambridge* (Cambridge, 1964), chapter 1 and passim; Lloyd's biography of Richard and Joan Buckland, pp. 386–89, contains some inaccuracies. I am very grateful to Dr Caroline Barron for drawing my attention to the Godshouse connection. For Bingham and Lichfield see further, Emden, *BRUC*, pp. 63, 368.
[36] Lloyd, *Christ's College*, pp. 14–16, citing Cambridge, King's College, A 77b; ibid., p. 389.

was remembered in Joan Buckland's 1450 testament; he was to receive the prized ivory tablet which Bedford had given her.[37]

Among the first actions which Joan and her fellow executors had to fight were appeals in two maritime suits in the court of Admiralty over Buckland's shipping interests. Both involved large sums but related to old histories: goods seized from Genoese merchants, [38] and goods confiscated after a collision with the *Antony*.[39] One of Buckland's executors, John Melbourne, had been a partner in both these ventures. No evidence has come to light to show whether or not Joan herself continued in the shipping business, but she was obliged to take legal action over her husband's trading ventures for many years. For example, in 1456 or later, she was still countering charges in chancery that Buckland had failed to pay a Lucchese merchant for arras worth 200 marks or £133 6s. 8d., shipped to London for the duke of Bedford forty years earlier in 1416. After this lapse of time, it is perhaps hardly surprising that her opponent accused her of forgery when she produced an acquittance, a claim she hotly denied.[40] Joan had to prosecute claims and enter defences against other pleas for debt in the King's Bench and other courts at Westminster, but it is probable that she appeared through an attorney, not in person.[41] Perhaps the best evidence of the volume of her continuing business concerns derives from the bequest of a 'flat pece gilt uncovered' (probably a bowl), which she made to her unnamed London scrivener in her 1450 testament. In the city itself, her associates and activities can be traced in the arrangements she made for her mother's London property in 1446 and 1451 and in trusts she created with her executors in 1454.[42]

The greatest worry for Joan and her fellow executors after Buckland's death must have been Calais. The years during which Buckland had been treasurer were no exception to the rule that the expenses of Calais far exceeded the sums provided by the crown. Joan, with the help of the other executors, had to

---

[37] *RP*, v, p. 137; Lloyd, *Christ's College*, p. 11. Besides Lichfield, Coote and Worthington had connections with Godshouse; Neel was an Oxford man (Emden, *BRUC*, pp. 514, 612; idem, *BRUO*, ii, p. 1341). In 1450, some of Joan's goods were stored at St Thomas of Acre.

[38] The case involved goods worth £188 seized before 1435 from the *Calderon* of Santander. They belonged to Genoese merchants. In 1436, Benedict Lombard and others appealed against costs awarded against them in the suit they had brought against Buckland, Melbourne, three other London merchants and John Scot of Calais. A commission was ordered to hear the Genoese appeal in April 1437. This succeeded, but the Buckland syndicate entered a fresh appeal against an order to restore the goods. Commissions were ordered to meet in July and October 1439, *CPR, 1436–41*, pp. 28, 49, 293, 337, 341.

[39] An appeal ordered 16 Oct. 1437, concerned Buckland and Melbourne's seizure of goods worth £250, *CPR, 1436–41*, p. 94.

[40] PRO, C 1/26/522, a-d; petition addressed to William [Waynflete], bishop of Winchester, as chancellor (11 Oct. 1456 to 7 July 1460).

[41] *CPR, 1436–41*, p. 7, 23 Jan. 1437 (£86 12s 9d.); *CPR, 1441–46*, p. 212, 22 Nov. 1443 (£26 0s. 10d.)

[42] CLRO, HR 174 (19), HR 180 (1), (2), (3); *HW*, ii, p. 556 (William Gregory); CLRO, Roll A 79, m. 5, see *CPMR, 1437–57*, p. 181.

account to the crown for the year and a half since her husband had last done so; she had to argue the case for very large sums of money owed to Buckland since 1431, which she needed to pay Buckland's creditors and to counter demands pursued through the courts. The sum the crown eventually agreed to be owing to his estate was over £3,433. As a royal writ put in 1441: 'the said Johane hath be longe tyme gretly occupied, vexed and put to grete coste for the said accomptes'. In 1441 she agreed (as creditors often had to) to forego repayment of 1,000 marks or £666 13s. 4d. in order to obtain payment from the crown of nearly £2,790. In July 1445, she was still owed over £1,100.[43]

A closely related difficulty was the execution of the will of John, duke of Bedford, who had died as captain of Calais, and of whom Richard Buckland had been named an executor. Joan's son-in-law, Robert Whittingham, who had become treasurer of Calais in 1436, had been Bedford's receiver-general. Whittingham was another very active executor of Bedford's and may have been able to protect Joan from involvement in Bedford's complex estate until he died in early November 1452. By 1456, Sir John Fastolf was the only one of Bedford's executors still alive. Joan sued Fastolf in the mayor's court of London through an attorney for a debt of over £1,070 which Bedford had undertaken to pay Buckland in 1434. She claimed damages, asserting that he and Bedford's other executors had consistently refused to pay her and had held up the execution of Buckland's will. She won her suit and obtained in part settlement a magnificent gold and jewelled reliquary cross with images of the Crucifixion and the Resurrection, which Bedford had pledged to Buckland in Calais in 1434 at the time the debt had been incurred. It was valued by two London goldsmiths on her behalf at the large sum of 510 marks or £340.[44]

Given the complexity of Joan's business affairs, it is agreeable to turn to the more positive aspects of her life as a widow. Here the main evidence comes from the inquisitions relating to her country estates in Northamptonshire and Essex, and from Richard's and Joan's testaments.[45] Both Bucklands were much concerned in their wills with Northamptonshire, especially Edgcote, but not obviously with Little Wigborough and Copthall. It would be wrong, however, to assume that Joan took no interest in this manor as a widow, before she ceased to farm it in 1459 or earlier. She may have been at Little Wigborough

[43]   PRO, E 364/72, rot. D; *CCR, 1436–41*, p. 290; PRO, E 404/57/170; E 404/61/250; E 404/61/282; A. Steel, *The Receipt of the Exchequer* (Cambridge, 1954), pp. 25, 185, 203, 207, 217, 248; Stratford, *Bedford Inventories*, p. 264.

[44]   Stratford, *Bedford Inventories*, pp. 425–30 for Whittingham; for the cross, B 194, pp. 334–36 and appendix, no. 18; *CPMR, 1437–57*, pp. 155–56, but the plea was 1456, not 1457.

[45]   For Richard Buckland's testament and lost will, n. 25 above; Joan Buckland's testament of 1450 is calendared from Reg. Chedworth, ff. 55–56, *Early Lincoln Wills*, ed. A. Gibbons (Lincoln, 1888), p. 181, and printed in full, *Lincoln Diocese Documents, 1450–1544*, ed. A. Clark, EETS, original series, 149 (1914), pp. 37–45, where it is collated with the second text, ff. 84v–85v. Her 1462 will, PRO, PROB 11/5, ff. 94v–95, was partly printed in J. Bridges, *The History and Antiquities of Northamptonshire*, ed. P. Whalley, 2 vols (London, 1791), i, p. 118, and G. Baker, *The History and Antiquities of the County of Northampton*, 2 vols in 1 (London, 1822–30), i, p. 492.

within a week of Richard Buckland's death;[46] some unidentified beneficiaries of her 1450 testament could be associated with her Essex manor.

Edgcote was held jointly by Richard and Joan; Sewell was quickly secured to her after Richard's death. The executors acted within a week of Buckland's death to protect the country estates with enfeoffments and a series of similar arrangements in the ensuing months and years were considered an essential protection.[47]

Both Bucklands took great pleasure in their main country estate. Joan must have had experience of all aspects of estate management in her husband's lifetime, given his long periods of absence abroad and in London. Some indication of the scale of farming business is given by Joan's pursuit of a drover through the courts in 1451 for the considerable debt of £20. She no doubt also supervised building works. Richard was accused after his death of diverting bricks and timber from Calais to use in building works in London and at Edgcote,[48] but this accusation does not seem to have spoilt Joan's delight in her house, farms, livestock, male and female servants, and numerous clerical friends. The Buckland's affection was given to their only child and heir, Agnes Whittingham, but Agnes had been married since 1420 and by 1436 may no longer have been very close to them. Agnes Whittingham died in 1456, leaving four sons, Robert, Richard, William and John. The eldest, Robert, a prominent Lancastrian supporter, was knighted after the second battle of St Albans in 1461, went into exile with Margaret of Anjou, was attainted in 1462 and was killed on the battle of Tewkesbury in 1471.

Richard Clarell, merchant of the staple, seems to have been at least as close to both Bucklands as their own daughter. Richard Clarell was almost certainly

[46] PRO, C 139/172/20, 14 Feb. 1460, states that Joan granted the manor and advowson by her charter dated at Little Wigborough, 17 Aug. 1436, to Master Richard Caudray, John Fray (chief baron of the exchequer), John Asshe, Master William Lichfield, John Melbourne, Thomas Pound, John Coggeshall and Thomas Yonge. From 1 March 1459 the profits were taken by Nicholas Sharpe and his cofeoffees.

[47] The initial feoffees for Edgcote were headed by the duke of Bedford and by Cardinal Beaufort. Fresh enfeoffments were made on 17 August 1436, when two men were put in as stopgaps, then on 4 Sept. (Joan Buckland, Thomas Chaumbre, John Melbourne, Thomas Pound, John Coggeshall, William Lichfield, Robert Carleton and Richard Wymark), and 8 Sept. (Cardinal Beaufort, William Alnwick, then bishop of Norwich, Richard Caudray, Sir John Tyrell, William [*sic*] Rothwell, John Ingram, Richard Quatremains, Master John Trotter, parson of Edgcote, and others). In 1457 a much less exalted list of local vicars and merchants took over as feoffees to the use of Joan and subsequently paid a fine. Buckland enfeoffed Alnwick, Thomas Rothwell, Melbourne and his former apprentice, Richard Clarell, with Sewell on 25 May 1436. In March 1437 they enfeoffed Joan, who in May enfeoffed Alnwick, Trotter and Clarell and Nicholas Radford, PRO, C 140/5/45; C 140/8/19; see also the list of inquisitions, n. 28, above.

[48] *CPR, 1446–52*, p. 397; PRO, E 101/193/5, m. 6, Buckland was accused of taking 20,000 bricks worth 66s. 8d., timber for a water-mill and for pews at Edgcote, valued with the workmanship at £20, and making use of two carpenters at the king's wages for six months, at a cost of £12 3s. 4d. See also, *The History of the King's Works*, i, *The Middle Ages*, ed. H.M. Colvin (London, 1963), pp. 431–32; Stratford, *Bedford Inventories*, p. 428.

their former apprentice, speaking of Richard and Joan as his master and mistress. He asked if he died at Edgcote to be buried in the chancel of Edgcote church by the north wall, near to his master's closet (probably the added, north-east, perpendicular chantry chapel, originally built in two stories). If he died in or near London, Clarell wished to be buried at the Charterhouse, where he founded a chantry for his own soul and for those of Richard and Joan.[49] Clarell received bequests in both their wills, relatively small in Richard's in 1436, and large amounts of portable property in Joan's in 1450. He had his own chambers in the house at Edgcote and named his eldest son and daughter Joan and Richard.

Few wills drawn up by medieval women are as vivid as Joan Buckland's testament of 1450. It conjures up a picture of a fifteenth-century manor house, and the surrounding church, parsonages and farms, peopled with servants, tenants and friends.[50] Before giving some account of the contents, two questions should be raised. First, why did Joan draw up her testament, twelve years before she died and being, as she said 'in gode helth thanked be god'? Secondly, how far are these her own words? Neither question can be answered but the testament is dated to early May 1450, in a period of civil unrest which came to a head at the end of the month in Cade's rebellion. This could have some bearing on the contents of the will. Documents drawn up in English and in the first person like Joan's will can be deceptive. The order in which Joan mentioned her possessions and friends is probably her own, but the actual words need not be. At the very least, the listing of her Latin liturgical books probably reflects a preexisting inventory.

The testament begins with bequests to the parish church at Edgcote: plate, vestments, hangings (some for the Easter sepulchre) and books. Seven liturgical books are listed in Joan's will, an unusually large number; she left four to the church: a missal, gradual, breviary and processional, carefully described by the secundo folios or first words of the second leaf. Her more personal service books, a small psalter and a missal with silver clasps, were left to Clarell. She had another large psalter; it is probable that she also had secular books, which are not listed. One book survives, but is not in the will, the collection of theological texts which Joan gave to Syon in return for prayers (now Oxford, Bodley MS 630).

Joan left whole rooms of furnishings to Clarell, to the vicars of Edgcote and Blakesley, and to the master of St John's Hospital, Banbury, beds (sets of hangings), carpets, chests and chairs, described standing in their usual places. Her favourite colour for hangings was red; there are descriptions of the

[49] Clarell's lost epitaph at Edgcote is cited by Bridges, *Northants.*, i. p. 121, and Baker, *Northants.*, i, p. 500; his will, dated 4 June 1478, proved 20 Oct., is PRO, PROB 11/6, ff. 282v–283.

[50] For some aspects of the testament, see E. Power, *Medieval Women*, ed. M.M. Postan (Cambridge, 1975; repr. 1992), pp. 48–50; extracts were printed in R.M. Serjeanston and H. Isham Longden, *The Parish Churches and Religious Houses of Northamptonshire* (London, 1913), pp. 101–2.

furniture and the red and green textiles, which she wished to be left in place in the old chamber, the parlour and the hall, of altar-hangings for the household chapel, and long lists of sheets and fine table linen from Reims. Besides the ivory tablet given to her by Bedford, Joan prized an arras woven with the Annunciation. She had embroideries and a 'stayned' or painted set of hangings. The way of life of the gentry meant she had hot water to wash with and hot food, comforts which she wished her friends and tenants to share. She left some of her spits and racks to be kept in the parsonage 'to her tenants ease perpetual', instructing that indentures for them should be drawn up between the parson and the parishioners.

As a widow, Joan dressed soberly in violet and black. Her best violet gown was trimmed with grey fur; her best black one with martens, that is she wore the fashionable black and brown combination we know from contemporary portraits. These gowns were left to friends and another gown furred with mink was left to the woman attending her deathbed. Alyson Swayn was to have cattle and sheep and to be 'well see to of clothing and bedding that is necessary unto hir and wel rewarded', while Joan's women servants were to share all her other gowns and kirtles. She had prodigious amounts of secular and liturgical plate at Edgcote and in London, some sorted at St Thomas of Acre: silver bowls, basins, saucers and well over fifty silver spoons (those left to Cheshunt were hall-marked), a few pieces of silver-gilt, some with enamel, and at least four chalices. When Joan made her will in 1450, she derived great pleasure, which still leaps from the page, in sharing all these material possessions with her friends, tenants and male and female servants. Named servants (a few already mentioned in Richard Buckland's will), received gifts of carthorses, cows, sheep, while the remaining animals were to be slaughtered, to be 'spended among my tenants in meat'. Each of her tenants was to have an eighth measure of wheat and malt, the residue to be shared out in the surrounding villages. The residue of her linen, pewter and brass was to be distributed among her tenants and servants in Northamptonshire, her furniture among her executors and friends, her clothes among her friends and servants. While the residue of her silver was to be sold, the twenty-six plates and thirty-two saucers she was served with daily were to be 'smytten in koyne and . . . departed amonge poere housebondes here in this Contre after my Executours discrecion'.

The testament Joan had made in London is missing. In the extant testament, she left £20 to the poor men of the fishmongers' craft in London. She made relatively small bequests to the four orders of friars at Oxford, Coventry and Banbury, but made no provisions for her own burial. Clarell and Master John Trotter, the parish priest of Edgcote, who had been provided to the living by Richard Buckland in 1433, were her two executors. In this, as in other respects, she seems to have agreed with her husband's choice of friends.

Clarell's second wife was Margaret Whittingham, daughter of Agnes Whittingham's second son, Richard, and thus Joan's great-granddaughter. As a result of this marriage and the attainder of the direct heir, Robert Whittingham, Clarell succeeded to the Edgcote estate. This seems to have been one of the dearest wishes of Joan's years as a widow. She had arranged in her last will (*ultima voluntas*), made in 1462, shortly before she died, for Clarell to occupy Edgcote for the first two years after her death, and to have a preferential chance of acquiring the estate. If the estate was sold, the proceeds were to be divided into three parts: the first for the 'finding of scolers in the universite of Oxford', the second to mend 'high and perilous wayes', the third to be distributed to the poor, except for an annual sum of 11 marks of £7 6s. 8d., to be used for an annual obit and alms at Edgcote for herself and her husband for the lifetime of the priest in her household when she died.[51]

Joan's mother had set the character of her daughter's widowhood and her piety: open-handed, observant, but robust and practical. Her parents, brother and husband had all been buried in Pardon Churchyard in St Paul's. Because of the nature of the surviving wills, it is not known where Joan was buried, whether in London or at Edgcote. It is likely that wherever she was buried, she was commemorated on the marble monument in Pardon Churchyard her husband had ordered to be set in place in 1436 and to be engraved with his arms and the words 'Mercy and Grace'.[52] For a woman who had so courageously undertaken her husband's affairs throughout her long widowhood, sealing numerous documents with a seal (often mentioned but not surviving), which was perhaps identical with his own, an equal memorial beside Richard Buckland would have been only appropriate.

---

[51] See n. 45.

[52] Baker, *Northants.*, i, p. 493, describes the Buckland arms as argent a fess fretty or between three lions passant gules; as depicted impaled with Whittingam in an early seventeenth-century drawing of the lost glass at St Stephen's Walbrook and on the Whittingham tomb, now St John's, Aldbury, Herts, they incorporate a rebus of buckles, see BL, Lansdowne MS 874, f. 104; Stratford, *Bedford Inventories*, p. 429 and pl. lxvii. Buckland styled himself esquire by 1430, CLRO, HR 159 (44).

10

Alice Claver, Silkwoman (d. 1489)

Anne F. Sutton

Alice's maiden name is not known nor her place of origin.[1] It can be safely assumed, however, that she was apprenticed at an early age by her parents or guardian to a silkwoman of London, the city being the centre of this craft in England, in the solid conviction that a well-trained girl made a better and more useful wife. Her apprenticeship would have lasted for a term of between seven and fifteen years, depending on her age when she was indentured, and from her later career it is certain that she 'graduated' successfully, perhaps brilliantly.[2]

It is probable that she had a good dowry in cash besides her craft for she married well, becoming the second wife of Richard Claver, a well-to-do mercer. Richard had started his own apprenticeship in 1429–30 under Geoffrey Feldyng, mercer and future alderman, and had been admitted to the Mercers' Company in 1438, probably in his early twenties. He came from near Derby, his father being buried in the parish church of Edlaston and his mother in the church of All Hallows, Derby.[3] By 1446 he was a man of substance and, as one of the feoffees of Sir William Estfeld (also a mercer and a past alderman), he was involved in conveyances of Estfeld's property in the parishes of St Mary Aldermanbury and St Lawrence Jewry, both close to the Guildhall and near where Richard lived himself.[4] The association was a matter of some prestige as Estfeld was a considerable benefactor of the city, paying for the completion of

---

[1] This essay is an expanded, and corrected, version of that originally printed in *The Ricardian*, 5, no. 70, Sept. 1980, pp. 243–47, and reissued in *Richard III, Crown and People*, ed. J. Petre (London, 1985), pp. 397–402. The author is most grateful for the permission of the editor and the Committee of the Richard III Society for allowing it to be republished.

[2] For the role of women in medieval London, Sylvia L. Thrupp, *The Merchant Class of Medieval London* (Chicago, 1948), pp. 169–74, and Caroline M. Barron, 'The "Golden Age" ' of Women in Medieval London', *Medieval Women in Southern England*, Reading Medieval Studies 15 (1989), pp. 34–58.

[3] For some of Claver's Derby relatives and several other mercers who either came from Derby or who married into the Derbyshire squirearchy in the later fifteenth century, see the present author's 'William Shore, Merchant of London and Derby', *Derbyshire Archaeological Journal*, 106 (1986), pp. 127, 133 and nn. 5, 24, 53.

[4] Mercers' Company, Biographical Index Cards compiled by Jean Imray et al. CLRO, HR 179 (12). All other details come from Richard's will, see below n. 9.

the water conduit in his parish and the heightening of the belfry of St Mary Aldermanbury.[5]

By his first wife Richard had no surviving children, although he did have a rather grudgingly acknowledged bastard daughter, 'Jone'. When he took Alice as his second wife is uncertain but it was probably not many years before his own death in 1456, when he was probably in his forties and she twenty years younger and fresh from her apprenticeship.[6] As a trained silkwoman she was eminently suitable to be a mercer's wife. Mercers dealt particularly in luxury goods and, with the Italian merchants of London, they were the men from whom the silkwomen bought their supplies. They handled both the raw silk, which the throwsters of the silkwomen's craft converted into yarn, and the already thrown Italian silk thread, as well as the silver and gold threads of Lucca, Venice and Cyprus which the silkwomen wove into ribbons, laces and corses (particularly elaborate silk ribbons).[7] A husband and wife combination of these trades were clearly advantageous and profitable. Alice continued to practice her craft after her marriage and probably did so *sole* with her husband's consent. This meant that she traded in her own right, took her own apprentices and answered for her own debts and transactions as if she were a man and not merely as the chattel of her husband with no legal, separate existence or property of her own, the usual fate of the married woman. Alice would have declared her intention to avail herself of this privilege open to the women of London before the mayor and alderman and sworn to observe the usual regulations for trading and for taking apprentices and to enrol the latter properly before the chamberlain of the city.[8]

In November 1456 Richard Claver died after a long illness leaving his wife

---

[5] Estfeld's will, *HW*, ii, pp. 509–11. He was also the master of Thomas Fyler, one of Alice's acquaintances, see below, and like another acquaintance, John Burton, possessed a large book of the Legends of the Saints.

[6] This assumes he was twenty-five when he was admitted to the Mercers in 1438. Claver appears little in the records of the city or his company. He was on the livery 1439–40, and took a good number of apprentices from 1446–47, including a William Claver in 1452–53 of whom nothing else is heard. His last apprentice, Thomas Cook, was passed over to Roger Copley on Claver's death and admitted to the Mercers in 1462; Copley had been Claver's apprentice 1446–56 and went on to be a warden in 1471. All above details from Mercers' Company Biographical Index Cards. He was trading with the Low Countries 1449–50 (at least), when he paid 45s. 'for the rest of a condyght of the last colde marte' with Ralph Verney and John Lock, Mercers' Company, Wardens' Accounts 1347, 1390–1463, f. 162.

[7] For silkwomen's wares see, E. Crowfoot et al., *Textiles and Clothing, c. 1150–1450: Medieval Finds from Excavations in London* (London, 1992), pp. 130–49, on 'Narrow Wares'; and E.G. Stanley, 'Directions for Making Many Sorts of Laces', *Chaucer and Middle English: Studies in Honour of R.H. Robbins*, ed. B. Rowland (London, 1975), pp. 89–103.

[8] Thrupp, *Merchant Class*, pp. 169–74; Barron, 'The "Golden Age" of Women in Medieval London', pp. 44–48; M.K. Dale, 'London Silkwomen on the Fifteenth Century', *Economic History Review*, 1st series, 4 (1933), pp. 328–29; and see M. Kowaleski and J.M. Bennett, 'Crafts, Guilds and Women in the Middle Ages: Fifty Years after M.K. Dale', *Signs*, 14 (1989), pp. 474–88. K. Lacey, 'The Production of "Narrow Ware" in Fourteenth and Fifteenth Century England', *Textile History*, 18 (1987), pp. 187–89, 192–93. Compare M. Wensky, 'Women's Guilds in Cologne in the Late Middle Ages' *Journal of European Economic History*, 11 (1982), pp. 631–50.

with a young son, also called Richard, to bring up by herself. He had written his will in his own hand on 2 August 1456 and recorded how well Alice had managed to fulfil the medieval ideal of useful housewife and businesswoman, mother and dutiful wife. Despite his obvious affection for and gratitude to Alice, he nevertheless chose to be buried under the same stone in the church of St Michael Bassishaw behind Guildhall where his first wife was buried – but in the event he was buried in the Lady chapel of his current parish church, St Lawrence Jewry. To Alice he left his household goods, 'her own goodys' – an indication that she had been trading in her own right – and £200 of his own goods, a considerable sum. To Richard, their son and his heir, he left 200 marks in money stipulating that if he should die under age Alice should have half the sum and the other half should be spent on poor householders in need. His son was also to have the house and land at Uxbridge which, if he died without heirs, would then pass to the testator's brother and his children. Apparently this was the only piece of property acquired by Richard Claver who must have kept the rest of his wealth in his mercery stock. Was it a small country retreat or just a hardheaded investment? 'Jone', his bastard daughter 'as hit is said', he wrote, was to have £10 for her marriage and a similar sum went to Alison Claver, the daughter of his brother William. Apart from the usual bequests to the Austin and Grey Friars, to the London prisons and to 'Bedlem', he left torches to the high altar of St Michael Bassishaw, the Brotherhood of St Michael (Bassishaw), the Penny Brethren of St Lawrence (Jewry) and to the Brethren of the Rood (in the same church), thereby firmly acknowledging his ties to his local parishes and their fraternities.

His wife Alice, John Stockton, mercer, and a John Burton were to be his executors. Although Claver did not specify Burton's trade it is fairly certain he was the successful mercer of this name; John Stockton was to go on to be an alderman and mayor and like Claver had a wife who was a successful businesswoman in her own right. Between them they were to spend the residue of his estate as they thought best, 'and all waye I praye yowe, tender my wyff well for she hath ben' to me a full luffyng woman en my sekeness ther God reward her en hevyn for that sche hath be to me'. He left his son and his son's goods to Alice's ruling until he came of age, she to find the usual sureties for his estate at Guildhall that London custom demanded. This trust, in itself, was a sufficient indication of her husband's confidence in her business abilities. Only £4 was to be spent on his burying. He concluded his will with the bequests of his gilt standing cup 'and the not' (a coconut cup) to his son, and to each of the two churches of All Hallows, Derby, and of Edlaston, nearby, where his parents were buried vestments worth 5 marks and 40s. to the parish poor. On 28 November 1456 the will was proved in the commissary court of the bishop of London and Alice was granted the executorship.[9]

[9] GL, MS 9171/5 f. 234. In 1461 a pardon for outlawry was granted to William Kyngton late of Uxbridge, Middx., for not answering a charge of debt brought by Richard Claver, citizen and mercer, presumably over four years before, and perhaps connected with Claver's land there, *CPR, 1461–67*, p. 5.

Alice never remarried, although a woman of her trade and wealth must have attracted frequent suitors. Her choice may have been the result of a desire for independence of a state that she had not found to her taste – or an acceptance of the church's teaching that second marriage displayed an unseemly interest in the flesh that was particularly unsuitable in a woman. In the absence of information, the pleasantest conclusion is that her long widowhood of thirty-three years was the result of a genuine and lasting affection for her husband and of her good fortune in having the means and ability to support herself and her son.

Eight years after her husband's death on 31 August 1464 she presented sureties at Guildhall for the payment of the 200 marks due to their son when he came of age, the sureties being Alice herself, John Norlong, William Pratte and Ralph Kempe, all citizens and mercers (to whom we will return). The reason for the eight years delay is not known. Custom dictated that the custody of an orphan (a fatherless child) and his property should be granted by the mayor and aldermen to a suitable person who agreed to look after both until the orphan attained majority; it was insisted that the guardian give a recognisance to the city chamberlain that the inheritance would be paid at the proper time and find three or four sureties to guarantee the debt. The mayor and his brethren continued to oversee the child's welfare through the chamberlain during the remainder of his minority.[10]

Alice's son did not outlive his mother. It seems that he did complete his apprenticeship as a mercer and did take the freedom of the city because in June 1471, as citizen and mercer, he made Alice a gift of his goods and chattels. Such gifts were made for a variety of reasons, mainly as a form of mortgage to secure a loan on the security of the stock of the donor, and it is possible the young Richard was borrowing money from his mother; the gift could also be the basis of a trust for several purposes such as avoiding forfeiture of the goods to a debtor or avoiding the expenses of drawing up and proving a will. It seems most likely that this last alternative was what lay behind Richard's gift – he certainly left no will.[11] By this means Alice received his goods with the minimum of trouble and the house and eighteen acres of land at Uxbridge, Middlesex, as had already been decided by his father, passed to the issue of his uncle William, of whom Alison alone remained at the time of her cousin's death.[12]

[10] *LBL*, pp. 54–55. C. Carlton, *The Court of Orphans* (Leicester, 1974), pp. 13–14, 20–21.

[11] He does not occur in the records of the Mercers' Company. *CCR, 1468–76*, no. 550, p. 142. For a discussion of such gifts, *CPMR, 1437–57*, pp. xxii–xxvi.

[12] Richard had committed the estate, before he died, to a feoffee, Richard Curtayse, to be held to his own use. Curtayse continued to hold to the use of Alison until her death. Alison married Henry Hynede, and according to Henry had persuaded him into marriage by promising him a life estate in the property. Curtayse refused to convey such an estate to Hynede or to sell the reversion to perform her will. Hynede took the case to chancery. The result is not known. PRO, Early

continued

Her son's death was a great blow to Alice – after twenty-five years or so of nurturing. Her compensations and distractions were her friends, her neighbours and fellow parishioners, and above all her work and flourishing business as a silkwoman.

The earliest of her known associates are the men named as executors with her by her husband, John Burton and John Stokton, and a little later John Norlong, Ralph Kempe and William Pratte, her fellow sureties for her son's inheritance. With the exception of the one alderman and mayor among them, John Stokton, all were mercers of the middle rank who remained like Alice in the same area of London near the Guildhall for the rest of their lives: the parishes of St Michael Bassishaw where Richard Claver had lived with his first wife and where the Burtons and Kempes continued to live, St Lawrence Jewry where Alice spent her widowhood and where John Norlong lived, and lastly St Mary Aldermanbury where William Pratte lived with his wife, born Alice Bothe, who was a 'gossep' of Alice Claver. As fellow parishoners and close neighbours they made use of each other as sureties, they took each other's children as apprentices, they witnessed each others' wills and acted as executors. Their parishes were often the focus of their charity. When John Norlong died in 1466 at the early age of forty with only a widow to provide for, he designated William Pratte as one of his executors and left numerous pious bequests which ranged from the painting of the new statue of St John the Baptist in the church of St Lawrence Jewry to the relief of the poor householders of the parish 'in secretewise'. Like John Burton and Richard Claver, who had predeceased him, he did his duty too by the country parish of his birth with vestments, service books and money for the poor, including a sum to alleviate their tax burden.[13]

Some of these men's lives were taken up with the concerns of their company: Pratte in particular was very much involved with the Mercers and Merchant Adventurers from the 1450s till his death in 1486, serving as warden of the former twice; he was a common councilman for the ward of Cripplegate.[14] Stokton's career began in a similar, company-orientated way in the 1450s but by 1461 he had achieved the wealth necessary to become an alderman; he was mayor in the troubled period of the readeption of 1470–71 and was knighted for his part in the defence of the city against the Bastard of Fauconberg;

---

continued

Chancery Proceedings, C 1/58/183, datable to either 1475–80 or 1483–85. The petition calls her 'Alice' but she is clearly the Alison of her uncle Richard's will.

[13] He came from Wybourne (Lincs.), issued from apprenticeship in 1450 and began to take a part in Mercers' Company affairs from 1465, Mercers' Company Biographical Index Cards and Lyell and Watney, *Acts of Court*, pp. 277, 281. His will is impressive both for its charity and the number of his family whom he mentions by name, PRO, PROB 11/5, ff. 96v–98. His third executor was Lady Anne Boleyn; his widow, Margaret, remarried his other executor, William Purchase, mercer and future alderman, and died 1511, PROB 11/17, ff. 30–30v.

[14] For Pratte's career see the present author's 'Caxton was a Mercer: His Friends and Social Milieu', to be published in the proceedings of the 1992 Harlaxton Fifteenth Century Symposium.

he remained an alderman till his death in 1473. His wife, Elizabeth, like Alice Claver, was a trader in her own right and both of them, as well as Elizabeth's second husband, Gerard Caniziani, the renegade representative of the Medici in London who became a mercer of London, are likely to have been among Alice's regular suppliers of raw silk.[15]

The Burtons and Kempes of St Michael Bassishaw are less easy to slot into Alice's life but they were certainly business associates of hers and of William Pratte. John Burton was a well-to-do man in his sixties when he died towards the end of 1460: his daughter Margaret, to whom he left his country retreat in Twickenham, had married his favourite apprentice, Ralph Kempe, and had two thriving sons both intended to be mercers; his other daughter, Katherine, was a nun of Halliwell Priory just north of the city.[16] It is likely that Alice Claver was friends with the Burton and Kempe families: a John Burton received a bequest as one of her two godsons in her will, but his relationship to the elder John Burton is not clear. Certainly they were acquaintances and neighbours, but her closest friend among this group was almost certainly her namesake, Alice Bothe, who came from Derbyshire like Richard Claver.

Alice Bothe had started her London life as a young woman in the household of John Abbot, mercer, in Catte Street, perhaps apprenticed to his wife as a silkwoman; that is conjectural, but she must have been sent south to learn some particular skills. There she had met her future husband, William Pratte, while he was apprentice to Abbot, and it was during these years they began a fifty-year friendship with William Caxton, the mercer and future printer, apprenticed just down the street to Robert Large, and of an age with Pratte. It is not certain when the acquaintance between the two Alices began: it is possible they were apprentices in London at the same time, that Alice Claver also came from Derbyshire, that they just met through their husbands, or that they met through their own considerable female network of parish, charitable and business activities. A couple of years after her friend's death Alice Pratte (née Bothe) still remembered her 'gossep' Claver in her will, the term 'god-sib' indicating that they had had god-children or god-parents in common.[17]

---

[15] Mercers' Company Biographical Index Cards. C.L. Scofield, *Life and Reign of Edward IV* (London, 1923), ii, pp. 420–28. And see Erler, above, n. 37, for the marriage of John Stokton's daughter, Joan, to Richard Turnaunt, the son of Joan Gedney, by her second husband.

[16] Mercers' Company, Biographical Card Index for all these men. Burton seems to have come from Wadworth (Yorks.), to which he made substantial pious bequests; he alleviated the tax burdens of the poor of St Michael Bassishaw, GL, MS 9171/5, ff. 303–304; and the subsequent depositions disinheriting his son, William, a mercer, whom he considered feckless, in favour of Margaret Kempe, ibid., ff. 310v–311. Ralph Kempe's will, PRO, PROB 11/6, ff. 244–244v. Kempe was a warden of the Mercers 1470 and 1476. Henry Bumpstede, another relative of Ralph Kempe, was also a regular associate of both Kempe and Pratte and knew Elizabeth Stokton and Caxton, *LBL*, pp. 99, 167, and Lyell and Watney, *Acts of Court.* p. 81; and see A.F. Sutton, 'Caxton was a Mercer: His Friends and Social Mileiu' to be published in the proceedings of the 1992 Harlaxton Fifteenth Century Symposium.

[17] Ibid. ('Caxton was a Mercer'). Alice Claver's will, see n. 41 below: she had two godsons at the time of her death, John Burton and John Nele.

Another close female relationship in Alice's life was that with the leading silkwoman, Beatrice Fyler, living in the nearby parish of St Mary Magdalen, Milk Street. Beatrice not only ran her own business *sole* but also had a large family by her husband, Thomas Fyler, mercer.[18] The surviving wills of the family show it to have been close and affectionate and capable of providing solid and friendly support for Alice in the 1460s and '70s. In August 1479 Beatrice made her will – which she did with the essential permission of her husband – and Alice Claver was designated executrix with Beatrice's eldest daughter, Joanna, who was almost certainly a silkwoman too, and the wife of John Marshall, mercer. The overseer of their activities was to be Edward, Beatrice's eldest surviving son, another mercer and past apprentice of John Marshall. For her pains Alice was to receive 'a bolyon ryng' of gold (a gold ring with a knob of the metal as an ornament).

Beatrice was a woman with a considerable business, leaving as much as £50 to her eldest son and £30 to each of her unmarried daughters, apart from plate. What happened to her silkwoman's establishment after her death is debatable; possibly she hoped her son Edward would run it, but he died within weeks of his mother and his will was proved before the commissary of London on the same day. It is Edward's will rather than his mother's that may give details of his mother's establishment, as he takes care to give bequests to a number of women, who may have been her employees: Katherine Sergeaunt, 20s.; Agnes Sherman, 20s.; Alice Andrew, 20s.; Anne Dolfynby, 10s.; Isabell Chubbe, 20s.; Joan Stokes, 'shepster', £4. Edward's affection is mainly directed towards his 'maistress and suster', Joan, and her husband, John Marshall, to whom he had been apprenticed; Marshall and Edward's second sister, Isabel, were to be his executors and Joan their overseer.[19] Joan Marshall's own silkwork business – her large role as her mother's executor suggests she had been brought up in her mother's trade – may have continued to provide work for the women who had depended upon Beatrice's acumen and organisation, and so may that of Alice Claver. The executorship of Beatrice Fyler's will was Alice's second experience of such a sad task, her third if her son's death intestate is counted. She was as accustomed to death as Beatrice herself, a bond that may have been as strong as their silkwork: Alice had lost husband and only son, while Beatrice had lost three out of five sons. When Beatrice's husband, Thomas Fyler, died three years later in 1482 only two daughters remained alive out of their eight children.[20]

---

[18] Fyler had been an apprentice of William Estfeld; he was on the livery from 1439–40; in 1475 he was a mercer worth £10 p.a. Mercers' Company Biographical Index Cards; Lyell and Watney, *Acts of Court*, p. 78.

[19] Beatrice's will, GL, MS 9171/6, f. 280v. Barron, 'The "Golden Age" of Women in Medieval London', pp. 38–39. Edward's will, GL, MS 9171/6, f. 280v. None of these women have been identified as silkwomen, see Lacey, 'The Production of "Narrow Ware" ', pp. 200–3.

[20] The full list of Fyler children is given on the flyleaves of San Marino, CA, Huntington Library, MS HM 744 (a collection of religious and didactic pieces, including some autograph Hoccleve, owned and annotated by Thomas and possibly Beatrice too): John died August 1471;

continued

Together with such women as Beatrice Fyler, and possibly Joan Marshall-Fyler and Elizabeth Stokton, Alice must have taken an active part in the politics of her craft. During her working life there were five acts of parliament touching silk work.[21] She was probably least involved in the silkwomen's first petition of 1455 as her husband must have been ill by that date.[22] Its phrases were repeated with few changes in the petition of 1463 from the

> silkewomen and throwesters of the craftes and occupation of silkework within . . . London, which be and have been craftes of women within the same cite, of tyme that noo mynde renneth unto the contrary . . . many a wurshipfull woman . . . have lyved full honourably, and theirwith many good housholdes kepte, and many gentilwomen, and other in grete nombre, like as there nowe be moo that M, have been drawen under theym in lernying the same craftes . . . full vertuously unto the plesaunce of God . . .

Lombards and other unspecified aliens were accused of destroying the livelihood of silkwomen by importing poorly-made thrown silk, ribbons, laces and corses. Merchants, both aliens and denizens, were forbidden to import these goods for the next five years on penalty of a fine of £10, of which half went to the prosecutor.[23] Twenty years later, at the parliament of January 1483, it was necessary to seek a new restraint: the importing of thrown silk made by the women of Cologne was presented as a particular grievance. This time the petition came from both the men and the women of the mystery of silkwork – perhaps these were men who ran silkwomen's businesses with their wives, the latter either not finding it necessary to trade *sole* or not being permitted to do so by their husbands. The destroyers of the craft were now defined as Jews, Saracens and undefined alien merchants; again the embargo of four years fell on alien and denizen importer alike, but the penalty was changed to forfeiture

continued
Joan (the Ioha[nnes] of the *Guide* should read Ioha[nna]; Thomas died 1473; Robert; Edward; Margaret (left £30 for her marriage by her mother); William. This book also contains what must be Thomas Fyler's merchant's mark and an inventory of 1463 of 'my place in litill Barw', C.W. Dutschke et al., *Guide to the Medieval and Renaissance Manuscripts in the Huntington Library* (San Marino, CA, 1989), ii, pp. 247–51; the inventory is given in full by 'W' in *The Retrospective Review*, new series, 1 (1853), pp. 101–2. Thomas did not remarry and died 1482, desiring to be buried with Beatrice in the Pardon Churchyard of St Paul's; his will is mainly concerned with bequeathing lands he had bought in Willinghale Andrew, Willinghale Spain, Little Baddow, and nearby, in Essex, to his two surviving children, Joan Marshall, and Isabel who had married John Marshall's brother, Robert, a haberdasher, GL, MS 9171/6, ff. 335–335v. The paucity of wills for the Fyler daughters and their husbands means that firm evidence of their activity as silkwomen and of the fate of the family is lacking.

[21] Dale, 'London Silkwomen', pp. 342, 332, and her 'Women in the Textile Industries and Trade of Fifteenth Century England', (unpublished M.A. thesis, University of London, 1946), pp. 37–46. And see Lacey ' "Narrow Ware" ', pp. 193–94.

[22] An embargo on importing of silkwomen's work for four years was secured, the corses of Genoa excepted, with a penalty of £20, *RP*, v, p. 325; *Statutes of the Realm*, ii, pp. 374–5.

[23] *RP*, v, p. 506; *Statutes of the Realm*, ii, pp. 395–96 (3 Edward IV, cap. 3; reinforced cap. 4).

of the goods.[24] This act was extended in 1484 by ten years, and in 1485 by twenty years to 1505.[25]

The denizen merchants restrained by these acts included mercers, silkwomen's wares being by definition mercery. It is therefore a matter of conjecture how these men, so often the husbands of silkwomen, collaborated on these petitions to parliament. It might be supposed the members of the Mercers' Company were the natural protectors of silkwomen but in fact the top mercer-importers may have had little interest in, or sympathy for, the predicaments of their poorer brethren and sisters running silk-workshops and faced with a flood of foreign imports. It must have often been the energy and ability of a very few leading practitioners, such as an Alice Claver or a Beatrice Fyler, that made the problems of the craft heard among the mercers and before parliament.

Mercers, however, always kept a jealous eye on anyone other than themselves importing mercery into the country, and they especially hated the privileges of the Italians and the Hanse: in 1480, for example, several mercers, including Alice's friend, William Pratte, were busy preparing a 'book' on the offences of the Hanse in this matter to go before the king's council.[26] In the early 1480s it is therefore possible that the Mercers' opposition to the Hanse contributed to the success of the silkwomen's petition of 1483 against foreign goods which included products of Cologne, one of the Hanse cities, and also that Pratte's expertise in preparing reports for the royal council was available to the silkwomen, among whom was his friend, Alice Claver.

Alice's workshop must have been a substantial one by 1480 when she was supplying goods to King Edward IV through the great wardrobe. She sold the department sewing silk, silk corses, 'streyte' (narrow) ribbon, single and double laces, as well as a mantle lace of blue silk with buttons for the garter robe of the duke of Ferrara. She also made sixteen laces, tassels and buttons of blue silk and gold for garnishing various books of Edward IV.[27] In 1483 she was supplying much larger quantities of silk and gold fringe, sewing silk and ribbon, the last costing 14d. the ounce if made from silk thrown in England and 2s. the ounce if made from Venetian thrown silk. She made twelve tufts of silk and gold thread which were used to decorate the coronation gloves of Richard III, and the great laces of purple silk and gold thread of Venice, with their tassels and silk buttons, for the purple velvet coronation mantles of Richard and his queen, for 63s. 2d. each. For the white silk and gold lace to tie the queen's mantle worn during the coronation vigil procession through the streets

---

[24] *RP*, vi, pp. 222–23; *Statutes of the Realm*, ii, p. 472 (22 Edward IV, cap. 3). Compare Wensky, 'Womens' Guilds in Cologne', pp. 639–50.

[25] *RP*, vi, p. 263: *Statutes of the Realm*, ii, pp. 493–94, 506 (1 Richard III, cap. 10; 1 Henry VII, cap. 9).

[26] Lyell and Watney, *Acts of Court*, pp. 136–37.

[27] Great wardrobe accounts for 1480, BL, MS Harley 4780, ff. 9v–10, 21–21v. These were edited by N.H. Nicolas, *The Privy Purse Expenses of Elizabeth of York: the Wardrobe Accounts of Edward IV* (London, 1830), but the original is clearer for Alice's work.

of London she was paid 60s. 7d. Her own labour on the three laces cost 2s., but the hours she spent are not specified.[28] The prestige of working for the king and queen would have undoubtedly increased her business, there being always citizens and their wives, quite apart from courtiers, eager to patronise those who supplied royalty. In the parish of St Lawrence Jewry she was equally well placed to catch the custom of the rich civic officials, the lawyers, merchants and representatives of livery companies and wards who had to have regular recourse to the Guildhall and the administration of the city. She continued to sell goods to the great wardrobe in the next reign: a mere six ounces of red silk ribbon for Henry VII's coronation and, between 1486 and 1488, points (laces used to attach doublet to hose) and fringe made of silk and Venetian gold thread.[29]

She probably sold other mercery and haberdashery goods besides these specifically silkwomen's wares, including perhaps expensive, worked linen of which the 'fyne table cloth diapre' of ten yards and the 'towell diapre' of twenty-five and a quarter yards which she gave to the Founders' Company may have been examples.[30] Such goods were standard imported mercery from the Low Countries but any well-trained housewife and needlewoman like Alice and her employees could make up elaborate table-linen themselves. She could also have dealt in embroidered goods and items such as gloves decorated with silk fringes and tassles, or girdles of silk and gold thread.

A little can be gleaned about her workforce and household from her will of 1489, although its text never in fact refers to her trade and she (or the scribe) only describes herself as widow of Richard Claver, mercer of London. Elizabeth Bertram, her servant, perhaps an ex-apprentice in her craft now working for her, was a 'cosen' of her late husband and important enough to her to merit a bequest of 10 marks. An Elizabeth Atkynson was another servant, again possibly an ex-apprentice, who received the lesser sum of 53s. 4d. Margaret Taillour is the only woman specifically described as her apprentice and she received 20s. Other employees would have presumably worked in their own homes and done piece-work. Her main, possibly only, male servant seems to have been Thomas Porter, to whom she left £6 13s. 4d. on top of his wages, with the request that he collect in the debts owing to her; a task which neatly explains the need any female merchant had for at least one responsible male servant if she was to operate successfully. Small tasks about the household may have been done by Alice, her 'mayde that was gevyn me to find of almes', to

---

[28] Great wardrobe accounts 1483–84, edited in A.F. Sutton and P.W. Hammond, *The Coronation of Richard III* (Gloucester, 1983), pp. 114–17, 132–33. And see A.F. Sutton, 'The Coronation Robes of Richard III and Queen Anne Neville', *Costume*, 13 (1979), pp. 8–16.

[29] L.W. Legg, *English Coronation Records* (Westminster, 1911), p. 208, where her name is mistranscribed as Clance. W. Campbell, ed., *Materials for a History of the Reign of Henry VII*, Rolls Series, (London, 1877), ii, p. 491, where her name is mistranscribed as Claverer.

[30] G. Parsloe, ed., *The Wardens' Accounts of the Founders' Company, 1497–1681 (London, 1964), p. 413.

whom she left 40s., and perhaps a few errands were run by Edward whom 'I finde in almes for Goddis sake called my childe', the recipient of another 40s.; both of these children would have been suitably educated at Alice's expense. Other boys in the household who had moved on before her death were a John Benet, whom she had apprenticed to Master Byllyston, possibly Thomas Bullesdon, founder, and a Robert she had apprenticed to Master Bukland, a founder.[31] Another woman who was in the Claver household for some time in the 1480s was a Katherine Hardman who received a bequest in 1491 from Alice Pratte.[32] Katherine and her two daughters had become objects of charity in the neighbourhood of Guildhall after she was widowed in the late 1470s.[33] At some date Alice Claver took her in and presumably found work for her.

Most important in her shop and household was Katherine Champyon, another 'servant', who received the residue of her goods and was to be her sole executrix. Katherine must have been her prize apprentice, a well-loved and suitable heiress for the flourishing business. She seems to have taken to using her mistress's name, a not uncommon practice among apprentices: she must be the Katherine Claver who sold a little ribbon and thread to the great wardrobe in both 1483 and 1485.[34]

In so far as it is possible to assess it, Alice led a particularly active life in her parish and the fraternities of its church. Like her husband she was a member of the Penny Brethren of St Lawrence Jewry, leaving one of her burial torches to its altar; she was also, more unusually, a sister of the fraternity of the Founders' Company and left it 40s. in her will for their prayers.[35] There were many founders in the neighbourhood of Guildhall, and perhaps their fraternity was more congenial and welcoming to a hardworking widow than the Mercers' and Merchant Adventurers' fraternity of St Thomas Becket of which her husband had presumably been a member. (She did, however, scrupulously remember the master of the Hospital of St Thomas of Acre, the church where the Mercers worshipped, with 40s., for his prayers, in her will). Membership of a parish fraternity was a safeguard against old age and sudden failure of fortune, for

---

[31] *Parslow, Wardens' Accounts of the Founders' Company*, contains no details of either of these men. See J.H. Baker, ed., *The Notebook of Sir John Port*, Selden Society, 102 (1986), pp. 48–53, for Bullesdon (dead by 1495).

[32] She was paid 13s. 4d. and described as 'late resorting towards my gossep Claver', PRO, PROB 11/8, f. 321v.

[33] William Power, yeoman of the Guildhall, left her daughters 13s. 4d. each, in 1477, the money to be in the keeping of their mother and to be set against the debt of 6 marks that she owed the testator, GL, MS 9171/6, f. 206.

[34] Sutton and Hammond, *Coronation of Richard III*, pp. 114, 116. Legg, *Coronation Records*, p. 207.

[35] Alice's will (see n. 41) is specific that her bequest is for the Founders' fraternity in St Lawrence Jewry, although their fraternity of St Clement is known to have been in St Margaret Lothbury, see Parslow, *Wardens' Accounts of the Founders' Company*, pp. xiii–xiv, and see pp. xliii–xliv.

they provided for their indigent and aged brothers and sisters. This considera-tion must have prompted Alice's membership as much as the local conviviality and goodwill the fraternities aimed to promote.[36] In the event Alice never had to ask for anything, it was she who gave: the almschildren mentioned in her will were surely given to her to care for by either parish or fraternity, as were the succession of boys – and presumably there had been girls as well over the years – whom she had brought up and then apprenticed to a good master. The taking in of Katherine Hardman, widow, was apparently another act of local almsgiving. Alice's charity was in the most recommended vein because it was sustained and regular and not the result of whim. In her will she rounded it out with £11 worth of the conventional bequests chosen by dying Londoners in her day: 40s. to poor householders and 40s. for poor girls' marriages in her parish; and 20s. to relieve prisoners in each of the London prisons.[37]

There is a certain austerity about the image of Alice that survives, although it does not negate the love that took in the poor. Apart from the gold ring left her by Beatrice Fyler, there is no record of any of her personal possessions or books. But it is unlikely she was without pious reading matter at the least. John Burton had had a 'grete Inglissshe booke' of the lives of the saints, a *Golden Legend*, which he had left to his daughter the nun and then in perpetuity to Halliwell Priory.[38] The Fylers owned a compendium of religious and didactic texts in English, including some by Richard Rolle, the *Seven Workes of Mercy Bodily*, and some of Thomas Hoccleve's religious poems and prayers, as well as his *Letter of Cupid* and a ballade to Henry V all written out by the poet himself in the 1420s.[39] They recorded the births and deaths of their children in its Easter table and presumably read its texts. They also had a *mappa mundi* at their house at Little Baddow in Essex.[40] William Pratte owned a copy of Jacques Le Grand's *Livre de bonnes meurs*, a book of moral advice which he gave, shortly before his death in 1486, to William Caxton to translate and print and thereby encourage people to live better lives.

By the time Alice made her will, on 27 June 1489,[41] all the friends and associates of her own generation were dead except for Alice Pratte, who was now a widow herself. The £33 she left to persons went to her household, dependents and two godsons. She spent just over £21 on prayers, including the

---

[36] C.M. Barron, 'The Parish Fraternities of Medieval London', *The Church in Pre-Reformation Society: Essays in Honour of F.R.H. Du Boulay*, ed. C.M. Barron and C. Harper-Bill (Wood-bridge, 1985), pp. 13–37.

[37] John Burton made similar bequests to his London parish and the London prisons, but on a much larger scale, and so did John Norlong and William Pratte; Ralph Kempe omitted the poor householders.

[38] Now Oxford, Bodleian Library, MS Douce 372.

[39] See note 20. H.C. Schulz, 'Thomas Hoccleve the Scribe', *Speculum*, 12 (1937), pp. 71–81.

[40] See n. 20

[41] PRO, PROB 11/8, ff. 189v–190. Proved 10 July 1489. The only person whom she fails to define by his relationship to her is John Spencer who received 20s. to pray.

usual request to the several orders of friars in London for their prayers, the single most expensive investment being two years of prayers in St Lawrence Jewry for her soul and those of her husband and son. Like William Pratte, she took the advice of the *Book of Good Manners* (bk. 5, ch. 6) seriously and directed that her burial and month-mind be without 'pompe or pryde'. Her executor and heiress, Katerine Champyon, and her overseer, William Banknot, a mercer with a reputation for both competence and charity,[42] had a comparatively simple task to perform, a tribute in itself to Alice's business ability and character. In the first days of July 1489 Alice joined her husband in his tomb in the chapel of Our Lady in St Lawrence Jewry.

There are no frivolities to be discovered about Alice except that so many of the products she made and sold were luxury items and only available to the rich. Perhaps that fact in itself encouraged her to turn some of her profits into charity: she could have heard William Pratte expound on the estate of merchants from the *Livre de bonne meurs* (bk. 4, ch. 13), likening the evil businessman to the phoenix consumed by his greed on the pyre of his hoarded goods. In memory of Pratte she could have read with his widow its translation, the *Book of Good Manners*, by their friend, William Caxton, together with Caxton's prologue remembering his 'synguler frende and of olde knowlege'.[43] Alice Pratte survived Alice Claver by two years and Caxton outlived Alice Pratte by a few months.

Alice comes over as an impressive and likeable character. She had the forcefulness to make a career of her own and accept over thirty years of widowhood in a society that expected widows to remarry rapidly. She did not, apparently, feel the need to endorse her widowhood or protect herself by becoming a vowess. Her friends and business associates seem to have been of a type that made that unnecessary: she was already protected by them, her own talent for business and her role in her parish as a householder providing practical charity. Her life is particularly conspicuous for its revelation of female networks of apprenticeship and employment as well as friendship and support, independent of, and existing alongside, the more visible business networks of their male relatives. She was extremely close to Beatrice Fyler, a fellow silkwoman – between them they must have been acquainted with every silkwoman in the city – and Alice did Beatrice the final service of acting as one

---

[42] Banknot received £5 for his labour. He issued from apprenticeship to Roger Bonyfaunt 1462–63, so he was approximately fifty-two in 1489; warden of the Mercers once in 1495, Mercers' Company, Biographical Cards. Appointed to carry out responsible tasks for the company from 1486, Lyell and Watney, *Acts of Court*, pp. 295, 183, 588, 657. In his will of 1485, Richard Wise, mercer, of Alice Claver's parish, left a child, Alice Bishop, to the care of Banknot and Thomas Fabian, mercer, his son-in-law, expecting them to apprentice her to a 'good woman' sometime, GL, MS 9171/7, f. 7. In 1488 Banknot was also executor of Richard Hill, mercer, PRO, PROB 11/8, f. 105.

[43] N.F. Blake, *Caxton's Own Prose* (London, 1973), pp. 60–61, for the prologue. Caxton's translation has never been reprinted.

of her executors. She had a long standing friendship with Alice Pratte, probably sharing godchildren and certainly sharing concern for another woman, Katherine Hardman, struggling alone to bring up two daughters. Lastly, she left her business to a younger woman whom she had trained herself. Alice channelled considerable affection and energy into her network of female friends, her large household of apprentices, trained silkwomen or 'servants' waiting to get married and set up their own households and workshops, and what appears to have been a long line of children taken in for charity and prepared for apprenticeship and adult life. Underpinning all her activities were Alice's talents for her craft and for business which attracted the patronage of three kings and a queen of England.

11

Margaret Croke (d. 1491)

Kay Lacey

Margaret Croke, who died in 1491, is unique among the widows considered in this volume because she is the only one who is vividly described by one of her contemporaries. In the early days of her widowhood Margaret on several occasions met Thomas Betson, who was soon to marry her grand-daughter, Katherine Ryche. Katherine's mother and Margaret's daughter, Elizabeth, now married to Sir William Stonor, got on very well with her future son-in-law, and he enjoyed writing her lively and amusing letters from London while she was in the country at Oxfordshire. Margaret Croke could be difficult and Thomas Betson's portrait of her is not an attractive one. 'I spake unto my lady your modyr on Seynt Thomas daye [21 December 1477] and she wold scarsely oppyn hir mouth unto me: she is displesid and I know nat whereffore, with owte hir old sekenes be fallen on hir agayn: God send hir ones a mery countenaunce, and a ffrendly tonnge, or else shortly to the mynnorres [Minories], whereof she waxhith wery now, as it was told me but late'. Six months later, Thomas wrote again in a similar vein that he had seen Elizabeth's mother, 'and God wote she made me right sulleyn chere with hir countenaunce whyles I was with hir: me thought it longe till I was departid . . . I had no joye to tary with hir. She is a ffyn mery woman, but ye shall know it not yit ffynd it, nor none of youres by that I se in her'.[1] It would seem that Margaret, widowed eight months before this letter was written, was suffering from reactive depression, which left her family baffled and exasperated. The solution, as Betson saw it, was for Margaret to take herself off to live at the house of the Minoresses, as several widows did. But she chose not to follow that course and, as it happened, outlived both her daughter Elizabeth and the cheery Thomas Betson. Who was Margaret Croke?

Margaret Croke was the daughter of William Gregory, a skinner and alderman who was mayor in 1451–52. Probably Gregory's third wife, Joan, was Margaret's mother; Margaret recorded in her testament that her parents were

---

[1] C.L. Kingsford, ed., *The Stonor Letters and Papers, 1290–1483*, 2 vols, Camden Society, xxix–xxx (1919); for Thomas Betson's letter, ii, p. 28, no. 185, 224. I have dated this document to 1477, as Margaret is a widow.

buried together in the church of St Mary Aldermary.[2] She was probably born sometime before the end of the 1430s and, with her sisters Cecily and another Margaret, probably spent her childhood in their father's house in the parish of St Mary Aldermary. They were brought up in a wealthy and privileged environment. Their father who came from Mildenhall in Suffolk had land and yeoman relatives there. Gregory maintained links with his former parish and requested in his will that an obit be kept for him in Mildenhall church. He was active in London from the 1430s both in his livery company and as an alderman. The evidence for his involvement in foreign trade is slight but he supplied the royal household with furs.[3]

Margaret's social status in the city of London probably derived more from her father, who had been mayor, than from the man she married. The date of her marriage to the skinner John Croke is unknown but, as he acquired his great mansion house in 1441 it is possible that they were married at this time. John Croke was born about 1416 and it is likely that his wife Margaret was younger than him.[4] When Margaret first met John he was probably already a skinner with contacts in the parish of All Hallows Barking. By June 1434 he was involved in a transfer of land with John Poutrell, skinner, and John Bacon, woolman, who were parishoners of All Hallows Barking.[5] In 1441 Croke and Poutrell with other feoffees bought a property in this parish from James Swettenham, which stood east of Mark Lane; this great house was to become

---

[2] Gregory's executors were his daughter, Margaret, and her husband, John Croke, gentleman. John Snype, skinner of London, the first named executor had died in July 1465, PRO, PROB 11/5, f. 108 (PCC 14 Godyn). Gregory's will was proved 23 January 1466, enrolled in Hustings 8 February 1472, J. Gairdner, *Historical Collections of a London Citizen*, Camden Society, 17 (1876), pp. iv-viii, xvii. Skinner's Company of London, Catalogue of Deeds, no. 203. E. Veale, *The English Fur Trade in the Later Middle Ages* (Oxford, 1966), p. 183. For Margaret Croke's will see PRO, PROB 11/9, ff. 44–45v. (PCC 6 Dogett).

[3] Gregory's cousin, Master Thomas Sygo was left 13s. 4d. Members of the Sygo family lived in Mildenhall and Bury St Edmunds, V.B. Redstone, ed., *Calendar of Pre-Reformation Wills, Testaments, Probates, Administrations, Registered at the Probate Office, Bury St Edmunds* (Ipswich, 1907), pp. 48, 98, 127, 150, 174. PRO, E 101/409/2; CP 25 (1) 2/24 (12 Henry VI). Walter Rye, *A Calendar of the Feet of Fines for Suffolk* Suffolk Institute of Archaeology and Natural History (Ipswich, 1900), p. 295.

[4] He is unlikely to have married before the age of twenty-six (*c.* 1436). This suggests a date of birth *c.* 1407 or earlier, and of death at sixty-eight or older.

[5] PRO, C 54/295, m. 9v (12 February, 13 Henry VI). Croke, and two others were to deliver seisen of lands in Hertfordshire and Middlesex, belonging to John Tasborough, stockfishmonger and John Whitwell, chaplain, to Poutrell and John Bacon, Henry Barton, alderman of London, and John Carpenter, common clerk of London. Bacon was active in the parish of All Hallows Barking as was John Poutrell's father-in-law. He died in 6 May 1437. A brass depicting him and his wife Joan is in the church. His will was proved on 6 June 1438 by John Poutrell and Thomas Claidich, scrivener, his executors. Bacon left the residue of his goods and lands in Bermondsey to John Poutrell and his wife Margery. G.R. Corner, 'Memorials of the Principal Persons Interred in the Church of All Hallows Barking' *Transactions of the London and Middlesex Archaeological Society*, 2 (1862), pp. 226, 236–38; CLRO, HR 266 (2). There are few references to Croke's activities with other skinners, but see, *CCR, 1454–1461*, p. 400.

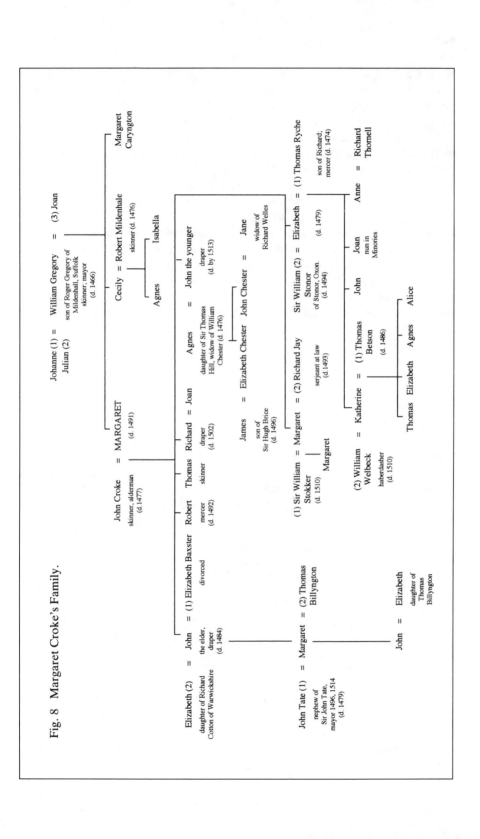

Fig. 8 Margaret Croke's Family.

John Croke's and Margaret's own residence. Later it is known that this mansion and the two adjacent tenements contained shops, cellars, solars, vaults and warehouses. Neighbours in Mark Lane included Thomas Babham, a grocer and his wife, Margaret; Richard and Anne Cely of the family of Calais merchants; and Lady Margaret, the widow of the alderman and grocer Sir William Taylor. In the same parish of All Hallows Barking lived the Tate family which was to be linked with the Crokes in succeeding generations. It was a pleasant, comparatively open part of the city, and was the home of several successful and wealthy merchants, particularly those involved in the wool trade through the staple at Calais.[6]

John Croke's career as a London citizen and liveryman was unusual as he was also a royal official in the exchequer and a tax collector. From 1445 until his resignation in 1470 he was a foreign apposer (a clerk and officer of the court of the exchequer), at an annual salary of £10. From 1447 until 1464 he was also deputy to the chamberlain of the exchequer, with a salary of £5 with fees. He became clerk of the receipt, an officer of the receipt of the exchequer from the 18 July 1467 to the 25 February 1469 at £15 a year. His friend and business associate John Poutrell was also employed in the exchequer.[7]

It was possibly through his connection with Poutrell, who had become a collector of the customs and subsidies in the port of London in 1442, that Croke received his commission of appointment as a collector for exported woollen cloths (the petty custom) with Peter Caldecote in December 1446. Croke's father-in-law, William Gregory, served as collector with Caldecote the following year and may have been recommended to the exchequer by Croke and Poutrell. In 1449 John Croke purchased the farm of the subsidy and alnage of cloth in Hertfordshire with George Tromy for ten years. Croke then became controller of the London subsidy of tonage and poundage in 1450 and in the following year he was granted the farm of the Hertfordshire cloth alnage

---

[6] CLRO, HR 170, (26, 48, 67). The great house with a garden adjacent to it was in the parish of All Hallows, and two smaller messuages were annexed to it on the north side were in the parish of St Olave's, Tower Street. For the Celys, see A. Hanham, ed., *The Cely Letters, 1472–1488* (Oxford, 1975) p. xiii, and idem, *The Celys and their World: An English Merchant Family of the Fifteenth Century* (Cambridge, 1985) pp. 317–18.

[7] PRO, C 60/255, mm. 15–16 (26 October 1447); C 60/254, m.15 (21 December 1446). Customs accounts: Poutrell, PRO, E 122/75/34; E 122/75/37; E 122/75/38; E 122/73/19; E 122/75/39; E 122/76/41; E 122/75/42; E 122/73/26; E 122/74/28; E 122/73/28; E 122/76/45a; E 122/76/47; E 122/213/8; E 122/75/48; E 122/75/49; E 122/75/37; E 122/73/42; E 122/73/37; E 122/73/32/ Gregory, E 122/75/43; E 122/75/44; E 122/74/29; E 122/74/45; Croke, E 122/75/41; E 122/76/43; E 122/73/25/ E 122/76/43; E 356/20; E 356/22. A John Croke was collector of the tronage and poundage of wool in Southampton in 1456, C 60/264, m.16. For careers, J.C. Sainty *Officers of the Exchequer* List and Index Society Special Series, 18 (London, 1983) pp. 78, 82. See also PRO, C 60/255, mm. 3, 4, 15 (24 October 1447, 27 November 1452). *CFR, 1445–52*, p. 175 (25 June 1450), p. 267 (15 November 1451). Poutrell was foreign apposer from 1431 to 1433, and from 1437 to 1460 he was one of the four tellers of the exchequer. He was then made clerk of the receipt from October 1460 until December 1461 and was reappointed from August 1463 to October 1464. Poutrell remained a collector of the wool custom until 1465.

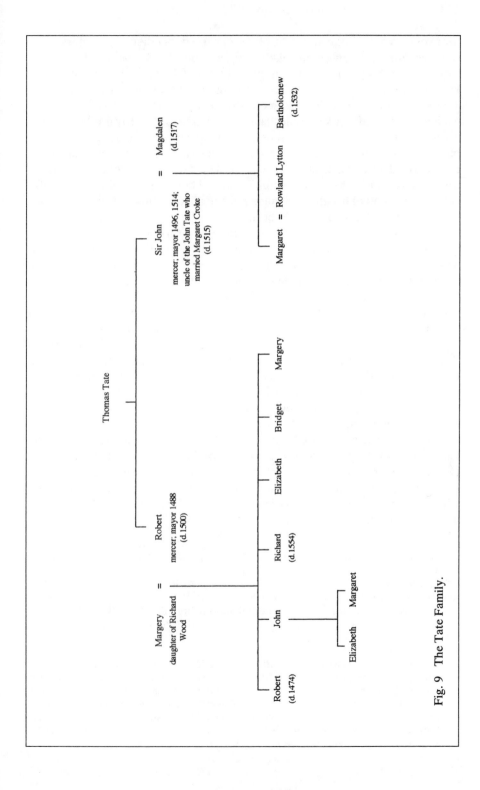

Fig. 9   The Tate Family.

for twenty years. Croke and Poutrell never served together as collectors of the same custom, although their relationship was obviously close, and they both worked in the customs house at the Old Wool Quay in the parish of All Hallows Barking, very near to Croke's house in Mark Lane.[8] Their friendship continued after Croke had ceased to serve as a customs collector. As an exchequer official Croke would have been based in the royal offices of the receipt, situated in the lower part of the exchequer house on the east side of the palace of Westminster, and he probably maintained a counter in Mark Lane for the conduct of his trade as a skinner. The careers of Croke and Poutrell followed similar paths until Poutrell's death. Poutrell suffered financial difficulties at the end of his life, and made a gift of all his goods and chattels in 1461 to Croke and other exchequer officials.[9]

John Croke does not appear to have imported furs and skins into London, nor did he do business with the royal household. From the 1460s, however, he was an exporter of wool and fells. As a merchant of the staple he would frequently have visited the Staplers' Hall in Westminster and probably also the Leadenhall, where wool arriving in London was weighed. It is probable that he sometimes also travelled to Calais where he had storehouses for his wool and fells, but there is no evidence to suggest that his wife accompanied him. From 1461 to 1473, he leased two woolhouses and a cottage near 'le postern' in 'Hempstreet' in Calais, at 2s. a year.[10] This may mark a growing commitment to his dealings in wool. Towards the end of his life Croke was primarily a wool trader, although he also imported madder, oil and wine. In 1464, 1470 and 1472, when he was pardoned by the crown, he was described as a gentleman, stapler and denizen.[11]

John Croke worked in close cooperation with another family of skinners, the Chesters, who also dealt in wool. John exported wool and fells to Calais with a London stapler, woolman and bell-founder, William Chester, with whom he seems to have had a joint-stock company, and he had other business dealings with William and his brother Richard Chester. William Chester was knighted in 1467, nine years before his death.[12] Croke also had business dealings with

---

[8] London County Council, *Survey of London*, xv, *The Parish of All Hallows Barking* (London, 1934), p. 33.

[9] *CPMR, 1458–82*, p. 157. John Poutrell made a grant of his Bridge Street property formerly of John Bacon woollen draper 30 July 1461, to John Croke and William Chester. Poutrell and his wife Margaret Bacon, Croke and Chester released this property for £100, PRO, C 1/88/33–35.

[10] Croke and other staplers were pardoned, 26 April 1464, *CPR, 1461–67*, pp. 351, 502; *CFR, 1461–21*, p. 69.

[11] *CPR, 1467–77*, pp. 212, 316.

[12] For the customs accounts, PRO, E 122/73/32; E 122/73/37; E 122/128/1. The enrolled customs accounts for London from 23 Henry VI to 19 Edward IV have provided only three 'Croke' entries, E 356/22, m. 31 (John Croke, Chester, Stokker and Tate), 33 (John and Thomas Croke); *CPR, 1467–77* p. 347. William Chester was the elder brother of Richard, citizen and skinner of London, described as a chapman and woolman of Stowe St Edward, Gloucestershire. He was an alderman and became a sheriff in 1484–85, PRO, PROB 11/6, f. 177 (PCC 23 Wattys). J.J. Howard and J. Gough Nichols, ed., *The Visitation of London, 1568*, pp. 2–5.

the London merchants of the Staple, John and Robert Tate, and he shipped wool in association with other exchequer officials, Hugh Fenne, Humphrey Starky, Robert Stoke, Walter Blount Lord Mountjoy and Thomas Kent in 1468.[13] John employed agents in the Cotswolds who bought wool for him.[14] In August 1468 Croke was exempted for life from holding offices and serving on juries. This included posts such as alnager, searcher, gauger, mayor, sheriff and tax collector.[15] This marks the end of his activity as a royal official and of his increased association with the merchants of the Staple.

Croke shunned most forms of public office and does not seem to have desired to make a name for himself in the city, he was active to a certain extent in city politics and, in December 1464, with two others, nominated John Tate, then alderman of Bridge ward, to be elected to Tower ward, in which Mark Lane was situated. Aldermen had always been men of substantial means and from 1468 were required to own goods and possessions worth in excess of £1,000. Yet to be regarded as a gentleman it was only necessary to have an income of £10 a year.[16] It was often difficult for wealthy London citizens to avoid civic office, the office of alderman being both onerous and expensive. In 1469 Croke became master of the Skinners' Company, and the following year he was finally elected an alderman for Bishopsgate ward on the nomination of William Stokker, his future son-in-law, John Barnwell and Thomas Staughton, and he later transferred to Lime Street. Very soon, however, in November 1470, he was exonerated from office on the grounds of age and infirmity and paid a fine of £50. Thereafter he was called by the title of alderman and was accorded the dignity of someone who had served the city in high office. Croke's new social standing within the city provided his wife Margaret with greater status and dignity.[17]

Although he seems to have done his best to avoid civic office, Croke was active in his parish and before October 1452 had provided a frontal of white tartarin with garters and two curtains for the high altar. He served as a warden of the fraternity of the Blessed Virgin in the chapel fo the Blessed Mary in the churchyard of All Hallows Barking. This fraternity became a royal chantry in 1465 when Edward IV appointed the scholar John Tiptoft, earl of Worcester as master, and John Tate, John Croke, Sir John Scot, and Thomas Colt as wardens.[18]

[13] *CCR, 1468–76*, pp. 9–10.

[14] PRO, C 1/66/442; C 1/64/1048; E 122/73/32; E 122/73/37; *CPR, 1467–77*, p. 347. One example of John's dealings in wool has survived, PRO C 1/66/442, date either 1441/ 1447, 1452, 1458, 1469 or 1475.

[15] For Croke's exemption from office see, *CPR, 1467–77*, p. 108.

[16] S.L. Thrupp, *The Merchant Class of Medieval London* (Chicago, 1948), pp. 17–18, 64–65, 71–72, 80–81, 127; *LBL*, p. 85.

[17] *CPR, 1467–77*, pp. 108, 212, 316. CLRO, Journal 8, f. 1b, 7, f. 213. *LBL*, pp. 91, 92. Beaven *Aldermen*, i, pp. 44, 35, 175, 227. John Croke resigned his exchequer office in 1470. He attended the court of aldermen on twenty-nine occasions from the 28 March to 13 October 1470.

[18] *CPR, 1461–67*, p. 428. The chantry statutes were confirmed on the 10 December 1476; it was dissolved in 1547, PRO, E 36/110. Two chaplains celebrated for the souls of Edward IV and his

continued

Although Croke became wealthy through crown employment and his trading activities as a merchant of the staple of Calais, he continued to live in the
same house in Mark Lane which he had acquired in 1441. His parentage is a
mystery and we do not know if he ever inherited property, but he seems to
have invested his wealth in the purchase of lands and tenements. By the time of
his death he had acquired a considerable property portfolio.[19] John Croke had
a tenement in Calais called 'Le Shewhous' (where his wools were kept), and an
inn in London called 'Le Royall' in the parish of St Thomas the Apostle in the
ward of Vintry which, until 1476, had been owned by Robert Mildenhale,
Croke's brother-in-law; also a brewhouse called 'Le Cuppe' next to the wharf
calle 'Le Newe Wolle keye' (near the customs house, at Old Wool Quay) in the
parish of All Hallows Barking, another brewhouse in Tower street, called 'Le
Swanne', and other tenements, in that area one of which had once belonged to
his father-in-law, William Gregory. Croke also had tenements in the western
suburbs of London. Further afield, he had properties and lands in Tottenham
and Edmonton in Middlesex. The Tottenham property 'Croke's Farm', he had
acquired in 1455–56, probably from John Drayton, who held 180 acres of land
in the parish. In Buckinghamshire he had properties in Drayton, Solham, Iver
and Isenhampsted.[20] It seems likely that Croke's properties were used to

continued

family. Croke's altar frontal was listed in inventories in 1506 and 1512. A priest celebrated in All
Hallows for the Tate family and Robert Tate lived in a great tenement in Tower Street, *The Survey
of London*, xii, *The Parish of All Hallows Barking* (London 1929), pp. 75, 77, 81.

[19] PRO, C 54/296, m. 19v (1446). Various gifts of goods, chattels and property were made to
Croke from 1462 to 1468: C 54/314, m. 20v; C 54/319, m. 26v; C 54/337, m. 10v; C 54/316, m. 21v;
C 54/316, m. 26v; C 54/320, m. 12v; *CCR, 1461–68*, pp. 38, 144–42, 234, 241–42; 1468–76, p. 38.
1476–85, p. 401; *CPR, 1461–67*, p. 502.

[20] The enrolled exchequer accounts for Calais are insufficiently detailed to record Croke's lease
from the Crown, PRO, E 364/118. The crown possessed seven shewhouses and other property
which was let for £13 6s. 8d. p.a., E 364/119, m. 2 (Trin 1 R.111); PROB. 11/7, ff. 252v–254v (PCC
33 Wattys). The Croke properties included lands near Coldharbour which had been acquired by
John Croke and Robert Tate from the executors of Henry Brounflete, Lord Vescy, d. 1469, PROB
11/5, ff. 203v–204 (PCC 26 Godyn). This was to pass to Thomas Croke, with remainder to John
Croke the elder and, if he had no heirs, it was to pass in similar fashion to Robert, Richard and
John the younger. Other lands and tenements in Tower Street were acquired from Walter Vitull,
armourer, and John Hurst, skinner. Thomas was to inherit these after Margaret's death. If he had
no heirs they were to pass to John Croke the elder, and thence in similar fashion to Robert,
Thomas, Richard and John the younger. A tenement in Westcheap in the parish of St Giles called
'Athelstrete' beside London once belonged to William Gregory. Richard was to inherit this and if
he had no heirs then it was to pass John the elder etc. as before. There were tenements in Wood
Street and Silver Street. Croke had two tenements in Fleet Street, one in 'Aldrichgatestrete',
another in Bridge Street, and crofts in 'Lyverlane' and 'Bradfordbridge', Holborn, and a house in
Chelsea. Margaret Croke inherited these properties, except the Chelsea house which passed to
John Croke's daughter, Margaret, the wife of Sir William Stokker. For the Tottenham and
Edmonton lands see, VCH, *Middlesex*, v (Oxford, 1976), p. 332. After Margaret's death these
properties were to pass to Croke's son John the elder; if he died without heirs, then his brother
Robert was to inherit, with similar defaults to Thomas, Richard and John the younger, PRO,
PROB 11/7, f. 27 (PCC 4 Logge). In 1453 A John Croke with Thomas Burgoyn acquired property
in Northamptonshire and London. *CCR, 1447–54*, pp. 483–84.

provide him with a rental income, for all the evidence suggests that he only lived in the Mark Lane house.

Margaret and John Croke were probably married between 1441 and 1443. Margaret seems to have spent the remainder of her life in the Mark Lane house and it is probable that all of her children were born there. By November 1465 she had five sons (John the elder, Robert, Thomas, Richard, John the younger), and two daughters (Margaret and Elizabeth) all of whom survived to adulthood. She may in fact have borne twelve children in all, as this number are depicted on the Croke memorial brass in the church of All Hallows Barking.[21] Margaret seems to have spent most of her married life bearing and rearing her children, caring for her godchildren and sons-in-law, and maintaining her household.

Margaret's father, William Gregory, died in 1466 and she was appointed one of his executors. Together with her sister Cecily, the wife of Robert Mildenhale, also a skinner, she inherited 'Le Coppidhall' and five shops in the parish of St John Walbrook with a property in Candlewick Street. Gregory left Margaret £10, of which half was for her to use to pray for his soul, and the remainder she was to give to poor men and women at her discretion. To each of Margaret's children, five sons and two daughters who were all unmarried, Gregory left 5 marks.[22] Three of Margaret's sons entered the freedom of London as drapers, John the elder and John the younger in 1486, and Richard in 1490. The last two seem to have been apprenticed to Sir William Stokker, an alderman and one of those who had proposed their father as alderman of the Tower ward in 1470 and was to marry their sister Margaret. Robert, the second son, appears to have been a mercer. Thomas was the only son who entered the freedom in his father's company of the skinners. Richard, Robert, and Thomas became merchants of the staple at Calais.[23] Richard married a woman called Joan and died in 1502, John the younger, married Agnes, the widow of William

---

[21] Gairdner, *Historical Collections*, pp. iv–viii.

[22] In 1482 Margaret and her sister finally devised the tenements they had inherited from their father to Richard Chester. Margaret's sister Cecily married a Robert Mildenhale whose will was proved 24 March 1476 PRO, PROB 11/6, ff. 210–211v (PCC 28 Wattys). He left Cecily his wife and Agnes one of his two daughters the house in which they all lived. He owned properties in Southwark, and St James Garlickhithe. When he died he was living in Kingston-upon-Thames. Cecily was one of his executors, PRO, C 4/1/36. Margaret's Croke's children may have been quite young when her father died, the third son Thomas was about ten, having been born in 1456–57.

[23] P. Boyd, ed., *Roll of the Drapers Company of London Collected from the Company's Records and Other Sources* (Croydon, 1934); *LBL*, p. 268; PRO, C 66/571, m. 16 (4); *CPR, 1485–94*, p. 344. A Thomas Croke was free of the Draper's Company in 1479 and was still alive in 1509. Thomas, the skinner was still alive in 1504 and was a merchant of the staple of Calais in 1509, Draper's Company Register, vol. C, deeds AXV 9/3, AV11 99 and 288. PRO, C 241/270/25; C 241/275/91. John the younger was made free as a draper in 1486, and Richard in 1490, Draper's Company Register, vol. C. William Chester died in 1476, PRO, PROB 11/6, f. 117 (PCC 23 Wattys).

Chester. She was the daughter of Sir Thomas Hill, grocer, alderman and mayor. Robert and Thomas do not appear to have married.[24]

We know something of the steps John the elder took to get married. In 1477 he wrote to his brother-in-law, William Stonor, and thanked him for his kindness and labour in promoting a match with a gentlewoman. John said that he had spoken to his father about this matter and his father had been very content with the proposal.[24] John the elder in fact married an unknown woman, Elizabeth Baxster, but then within six months took the unusual step of having the marriage annulled to marry Elizabeth Cotton, the daughter of Lady St George. His only child, a daughter called Margaret, was probably the child of his brief first marriage.[25]

Margaret and Elizabeth, Margaret Croke's two daughters, both at first married London merchants but then, as widows, remarried outside the merchant class. Margaret married Sir William Stokker, a draper, wine importer and merchant of the staple, who had been elected an alderman in 1470 and was to serve as a mayor in 1485. As a young man in 1440 and 1441 Stokker had commanded a contingent of the army sent to Calais. He was considerably older than Margaret and died on 28 September 1485, of the sweating sickness, two days after being sworn as mayor to replace Thomas Hill who had himself died of this illness of 23 September.[26]

Some time before 1465 Margaret Croke's second daughter Elizabeth married Thomas Ryche, a woolman and son of a wealthy mercer, and they had four children. On the advice of his father-in-law, John Croke, Thomas directed that no month's mind was to be kept for his father, who had died in 1464, and the money was given instead to the poor. Thomas himself died in August 1474 and his widow Elizabeth then married William Stonor of Oxfordshire the following summer. As a result of this marriage members of the Croke family are mentioned in the surviving correspondence of the Stonor family.

---

[24] *Stonor Letters*, ii, no. 183. Elizabeth Hill, mother of Agnes, PRO, PROB 11/12, f. 186 (PCC 23 Moone).

[25] John the elder made his will on the 8 February 1484 and was dead within six days. His daughter and heir Margaret married John Tate the son of John Tate who died in 1479, and who was the nephew of Sir John Tate, the alderman and mayor of London who died in 1515, PRO, PROB 11/8, f. 25 (PCC 4 Holder). Margaret and John, had a son, John, who married Elizabeth the daughter of Thomas Billyngton of North Mimms, Hertfordshire. See PRO, C 1/20/36. Writs of diem clausit extremum were sent to the escheators of London, Middlesex, Buckingham and Kent, C 60/302, m. 1 (27); *CFR, 1485–1509*, no. 366. Margaret Billyngton, formerly Tate, was ultimately to own all of Margaret and John Croke's lands, PRO, PROB 11/41, ff. 82v–84 (PCC 50 Noodes).

[26] Sir Thomas Hill, died 1485 and his wife Elizabeth in 1501. It is possible that Agnes was dead by 1501, as she is not mentioned in her mother's will. On 13 December 1490 John Croke received Agnes Hill's patrimony, *LBL*, p. 249 n.3. Stokker was sworn as mayor two days after Hill's death, *The Great Chronicle of London*, ed. A.H. Thomas and I.D. Thornley (London, 1938), pp. 239, 438. For Stokker as a commander of the Calais army, see PRO, C 81/1322–24. Sir William Stokker was living in two buildings by the 'new alee' in the parish of St Michael's Cornhill when he died, PRO, PROB 11/7, ff. 198–198v (PCC 26 Logge). Stokker's executors, including Margaret, sued five Londoners, PRO, CP 40/923 Attorn recept., rots 6v, 13v.

The letters which mention the Crokes and their extended family were written by Elizabeth Stonor herself, her brother John the elder and Thomas Betson, a family friend who was to marry Elizabeth's daughter, Katherine Ryche. Elizabeth, who was shrewd and affectionate, comes vividly to life in her letters, delighting in her acquaintance with the duchess of Suffolk and her visit to court. There are hints that William Stonor's relatives regarded Elizabeth as a social climber who had led her husband into extravagance. The marriage to a London woman was probably advantageous to William, who was a sheep grazier with great sheep runs on estates in the Chilterns and Cotswolds and needed a London outlet for his wool.[27]

In October 1476, when Elizabeth Stonor received a gift of venison and rabbits from her husband, she gave a half haunch and a couple of rabbits to her father and mother; such fresh meat was a delicacy in London. Elizabeth also sent her father a tench for his supper.[28] As well as showing kindness to her parents Elizabeth also sought to arrange for the future of her children by Thomas Ryche. In the December following the gift of venison, Elizabeth Stonor had dined with her father and mother in London and met some guests who were the friends of a child who was interested in marrying one of her daughters.[29] Thomas Beston, merchant of the staple and stockfishmonger, who had worked with Elizabeth's first husband Thomas Ryche and from 1475 had been employed by her second husband, Sir William Stonor, was destined to marry Ryche's daughter Katherine. In June 1476 he wrote a famous letter to his young betrothed, urging her to grow up quickly so that he could marry her, which he finally did in August 1478. After Elizabeth's death the following year, however, Betson's association with Stonor was broken over a business debt. Betson himself died in the spring of 1486, after he and Katherine had had four children; she then married William Welbeck, haberdasher (d. 1510).[30] Of Margaret's seven children, two appear not to have married and one of those who did had no children. Of the remaining four, two only had one child, John

---

[27] *Stonor Letters*, ii, nos 168–70, 172–73, 175–76, 180, 183, 204, 208, 226, 229, 237. William Stonor was knighted in 1478. Thomas Ryche died 1475, PRO, PROB 11/6, ff. 117v–118 (PCC 20 Wattys). He inherited £200 and lands in Islington and Ratcliffe from his father in 1464. His widow was bequeathed her part according to London custom and her father was left £13 6s. 8d. to the intent that he would be an executor, with Sir Robert Love priest.

[28] *Stonor Letters*, ii, nos 172, 170, and 175.

[29] Ibid., ii, no. 176. *LBL*, pp. 268–69. Elizabeth Stonor's daughter, Anne, married Richard Thornell, mercer, who died in 1501, PRO, PROB 11/13, f. 51v (PCC 5 Blamyr).

[30] *Stonor Letters*, ii, no. 166. Betson had been factor and servant to the stockfishmonger John Fenn who died in 1474 PRO, PROB 11/6, ff. 125v–126v (PCC 17 Wattys). Betson and Katherine's children were Thomas, Elizabeth, Agnes, and Alice. He was buried in All Hallows Barking. Although his named executor was Sir Robert Tate it was Katherine who acted as the administrator, PROB 11/7, ff. 184–184v (PCC 24 Logge) 25 September 1485, proved 12 May 1486. E. Power, *Medieval People* (London, 1924), ch. 6. Kathryn Betson PROB 11/16, f. 212 (PCC 27 Bennett). William Welbeck d. 1510, PROB 11/16, f. 211 (PCC 27 Bennett). *Stonor Letters*, ii, nos 168, 172, 175, 180. Veale, *The English Fur Trade*, p. 184.

the younger had two, and Elizabeth Ryche had four, thus making eight grandchildren in all. Although the girls, Margaret and Elizabeth, made quite suitable and prestigious marriages, only John the younger, of the sons, married a well-connected woman. Could this have something to do with the fact that whereas daughters were likely to have marriages arranged for them, sons were more inclined to take matters into their own hands?

Margaret Croke became a widow on the 4 October 1477. A year later (5 October 1478, a Monday) Elizabeth Stonor wrote to her husband Sir William, informing him that on Sunday last past (i.e., 4 October) she had gone to her father's *dirige* (the annual obit) and had stayed with her mother for the night. Elizabeth unfortunately does not tell us which church she attended, but All Hallows Barking had been her father's parish church. John Croke had asked in his will to be buried in this church and requested a sung anniversary obit, with *placebo* and *dirige* by vigil, and a requiem mass.[31] A purbeck marble altar tomb, with a canopy on which is inscribed the holy name, on the north wall of the north aisle in All Hallows Barking, has been ascribed to John and Margaret Croke. It is possible that Margaret, who was her husband's executor, had this constructed as the inlaid brass (see fig. 12) includes a man kneeling at a prayer desk with seven sons and a woman with five daughters. This, if it is the Croke brass, suggests that Margaret may have borne twelve children in all, only seven of whom we know to have survived into adulthood.[32]

After John's death Margaret was accorded the honorary title of 'Dame', probably because Croke had been an alderman for a brief period. Margaret was his principal beneficiary, his testamentary estate being divided into three parts according to London custom (for wife, children who were not yet

[31] John Croke made his will 6 September 1477, proved 19 November 1477. His testament was proved 19 November 1481. I have been unable to identify most of the legatees. On the 5 October 1478 Dame Elizabeth Stonor writing to her husband informed him that she had attended her father's church remembrance and said 'my modyr and my broodyr Stooker recomaunde hem both right hartely unto you: and ffull ffayn they wold [th]at ye had bene here, yff it myght have bene your ease'. *Stonor Letters*, ii, nos 229, 250, 267, 282.

[32] Margaret Croke in her will, 14 December 1490, PRO, PROB 11/9, ff. 44v–45 (PCC 6 Dogett) said that her husband, John, was buried in the church of All Hallows Barking. But according to the will of John Croke the elder, proved in 1484, his father had been buried in the Blackfriars, London, and he asked to be buried near him, even though his parish church was St Clement's Danes, PRO, PROB 11/7, f. 159 (PCC 21 Logge). A 'Croke Gent', occurs in the nave section of Blackfriars, BL, MS Harley 6033, f. 10 (*c.* 1590). In the north aisle of the choir of All Hallows Barking was a 'very godly tombe' much defaced, with an inscription, ' . . . Staple fuit seniorum, & unius Londoniis habitans, sermone fidelis, cum Margareta Domina castaq' beata. Hunc rapuit Michael ad coeli gaudia lati & c', J. Stow, *The Survey of London* (London, 1618), p. 253, and this has been identified as John Croke's by e.g., *Royal Commission on the Ancient and Historical Monuments and Constructions of England*, (London, 1929), iv, p. 179. The arms ascribed to John Croke are a fess engrailed between three spread eagles or. I would like to thank Mr William Hunt of the College of Arms for his help in trying to identify the Croke heraldry. W.H. Turner, ed., *The Visitations of the County of Oxford Taken in the Years 1566, . . . 1574, . . . and in 1634*, Harleian Society, 5 (1871), p. 238.

married or of age, and soul). Margaret was to provide surety for the portion of his estate which was to come to his sons who were not yet twenty-one.

John Croke's will, although fairly straightforward, took a considerable time to prove. Probate was finally granted on 19 November 1481 to Dame Margaret, Henry Woodcock and Thomas Asshford.[33] Margaret inherited John's Middlesex and Calais lands and tenements and some of the London properties for her life, but the revenues from these were to be used to provide a chaplain to celebrate mass at the altar of St Nicholas in All Hallows Barking, as well as 'anniversary masses'.[34] Margaret established the Croke chantry in All Hallows which survived until the Reformation, and she administered her husband's estate well and in accordance with his wishes. In widowhood Margaret probably lived on the income from her husband's rental properties and lands. She kept a considerable amount of plate which could be used to raise cash if necessary.

John, the eldest son, was left his father's London properties in Wood Street and Silver Street and his Buckinghamshire properties in Drayton, Solham,

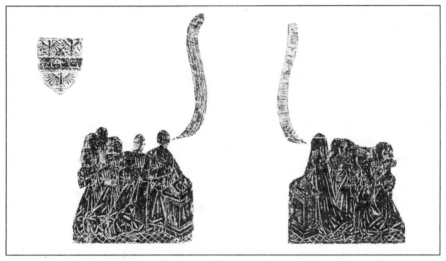

Fig. 10   The brass of John (died 1477) and Margaret Croke (died 1491), with their large family of twelve children, in All Hallows Barking by the Tower.

[33]   Sir William Stonor died 21 May 1494 *Stonor Letters*, i, p.xxx; ii, nos 267–68; PRO, PROB 11/10, f. 157 (PCC 20 Vox), not proved.

[34]   After Margaret's death her properties passed to the vicar of All Hallows Barking, to sustain a chaplain at the altar of St Nicholas to celebrate divine service and pray for her, her husband and his parents. The chantry was suppressed in 1548. If All Hallows failed to maintain this obit then the properties were to pass to the church of St Olave. The Croke endowments were seized by the royal commissioners and the great house in Mark Lane was bought by Thomas Mildmay, of Moulsham, Essex. J. Maskell, *Collections in Illustration of the Parochial History and Antiquities of the Ancient parish of All Hallows Barking, in the City of London* (London, 1864), p. 16; *The Survey of London*, xii, *The Parish of All Hallows Barking*, pp. 34, 36.

Iver and Isenhampsted.[35] After Margaret's death, John Croke's lands in Tottenham and Edmonton in Middlesex eventually passed to Thomas Croke the second son, who inherited them after John, the eldest, died without male issue.[36]

John Croke made various bequests to the church of all Hallows Barking in his will, which included £40 towards the making of the Rood, £40 for a set of vestments, and 40 marks to mend and purvey books for the church. To the fraternity of the Blessed Virgin in Barking Chapel, where he had been a warden he left £2, and to the Skinners' fraternities of Corpus Christi and the Blessed Virgin £5 and £2. He specified that 100 marks be given to friaries, prisons, hospitals and leper hospitals. For his burial and his funeral exequies he left 100 marks. Croke left various sums to his apprentices, former apprentices, and servants. His son John the elder received £100 and his four Ryche grandchildren £10. None of his legatees was of the London office-holding class, and only the bequest of £20 to John Strangeways' 'armiger', indicates any connection with the exchequer.[37]

Settling John Croke's estate proved to be a protracted affair both for Margaret and the co-executors, her son-in-law Sir William Stokker, her neighbour the mercer Robert Tate and William Essex, the King's Remembrancer at the exchequer. Probate of his testament was not obtained until more than three years after his death. Margaret continued to administer her husband's business affairs which were primarily concerned with the trade in wool and woolfells.[38] A court case heard in Bergen op Zoom on 17 December 1477, two months after Croke's death, reveals that Robert Michel, Margaret's factor, was forced at gunpoint to pay £111 5s. 0d. Fl. to Thomas Abot, the factor of William Welbeck, another merchant of London, and this was probably related to John Croke's business activities.[39] Margaret is to be found shipping fells, in the right of her husband, as a 'merchant of the staple of Calais' in the London customs account covering the period from 5 July 1478 to October 1479. On the 24 July 1478 Margaret is again listed as exporting of wool and woolfells in various vessels.[40] This was common practice for staplers' widows and their exports were usually consigned to a single year.

---

[35] See n. 25 for descent of these lands.

[36] Thomas Croke sold these lands to Sir Thomas Lovell but John Tate claimed them in right of his wife, Margaret, and leased them in 1505 for thirty years to George Henyngham, who was then expelled by Lovell. Tate sued Henyngham in the common pleas for debt whilst Sir Thomas Lovell was overseas on the king's business, PRO, C 1/321/10. See also n. 67.

[37] PRO, PROB 11/7, f. 26. (PCC 4 Logge). Skinners' Company Deeds, nos 136, 137, 138.

[38] PRO, PROB 11/7, ff. 26–28v (PCC 4 Logge); PROB 11/7, ff. 252–53.

[39] Robert owed this sum to Thomas on two bills of exchange which were due on the previous 30 November and 4 December. These bills, it was stated, had been forcibly taken from Thomas on the 14 November between Mardike and Dunkirk. H.J. Smit, *Bronnen tot de geschiedenis van den handel met Engeland, Schotland, en Ierland, 1150–1585* (R.G.P. The Hague, 1928), i, 2, *1435–1485*, no. 1822. I would like to thank Livia Visser-Fuchs for bringing this document to my attention.

[40] PRO, E 122/73/40, mm. 7v, 8, 11, 12v, 12, 13v, 14v, 16, 17v.

There is no other evidence that Margaret shipped fells to Calais in her own name. Her sons John the elder and Thomas were also staplers. They shipped fells and wool both jointly and singly in the 1478–79 account. Neither Margaret nor her sons shipped on the other sailings to Calais which took place on 9 October 1478, 13 February and 27 March 1479. John and Thomas Croke shipped again on 18 May 1479.[41]

Some time fairly soon after the death of her husband, Margaret was sued in the staple court at Calais by William Waren for a debt of £13 12s. 5d. which he was owed from the estate of Thomas Ryche, John Croke's son-in-law, for whom he had acted as executor. Margaret, styling herself widow and late wife of 'John Crooke merchant', together with her husband's executors, petitioned the Chancellor about the activities of William Waren. Margaret claimed that she had 3,000 woolfells at Calais 'of her own proper goodes' which she was unable to sell because they had been arrested 'to her great hurt'. These fells may have been some of the 6,532 woolfells which Margaret had shipped to Calais the previous July. Margaret explained that William Waren was very powerful within the company of the staple and she was likely therefore to lose her woolfells because of this debt. She claimed that, in his lifetime, her husband had fully settled Thomas Ryche's estate and that at the time of her husband's death they were not in possession of any of Ryche's goods. She had sealed probate documents to prove this. Margaret explained that, using an attorney, she had pleaded this case in the staple court at Calais but the court had not accepted it. 'William Waren', argued Margaret, 'undersands oratrice is in greate age and also advowesse not p[ro]posing to deale w[i]t[h] the world trustyng also that she for so small a some woll not do the coste to send ov[er] to Caleys the p[ro]ves of her said property of the fells for as much as the costs of the sending of her proffs be as great a charge as the said demande amonts to'.[42] Whether Margaret was successful in persuading the chancellor to support her against William Waren and the staple merchants is unknown.

It was during these months, when Margaret was coping with her bereavement and also struggling to settle her husband's business affairs, that Thomas Betson encountered her in London and wrote of her so unsympathetically to her daughter, his friend Elizabeth Stonor. But although in December 1477 and July 1478 Thomas's letters clearly describe a woman who was depressed, she

---

[41] PRO, E 122/73/40 mm. 42, 44, 45v, 47, 48v, 50, 51v. Customs accounts consulted: (Sandwich). E 122/126/16; E 122/128/1–16; E 122/129/1; E 122/129/3–5; E 122/129/8; (London) E 122/73/37, E 122/73/32; E 122/73/40; E 122/194/25; E 122/194/17; E 122/75/41. Writs for warrants and issues of Privy Seal C 81 and C 82, Extents for debts C 131, and Statute Staple recognisances C 241 have been examined for the reigns of Edward IV, Richard III and Henry VII, but no other evidence for the trading activities of Margaret have been found. Random sampling of the Common Plea rolls (CP 40) has yielded evidence of Margaret prosecuting for debt mostly as an executor. Veale, *The English Fur Trade*, p. 184, n. 8.

[42] PRO, E 122/73/40; C 1/64/1048.

evidently had some brighter periods during that time.[43] In June 1478 Thomas wrote, 'My Lady, your modyr, is in good helthe and ffareth well, and she s[endyth] you Goddes blissyng and hirs'.[44] For part of this time Elizabeth's daughter Anne lived with her grandmother in London, but after her sister married Thomas Betson in 1478, Anne went to live with them. A year later Thomas Betson, Katherine's new husband, was very ill in Stepney and Margaret Croke went to visit him and took with her a physician, Master Brinkley.[45]

In the years after John's death, Margaret may have found solace in religion. By the time she was widowed she was probably about fifty years old: she had borne at least seven and possibly twelve children and she had no desire to remarry. As she explained in her petition to the lord chancellor in 1478, she had taken a widow's vow of chastity 'not p]ro]posing to deal with the world'. She had considered going to live in the Minoresses' house, but she seems, in fact, to have remained in her house in Mark Lane. The brass in All Hallows church shows her dressed in the mantle, wimple and head dress of a vowess. But, in spite of her protests to the chancellor, she continued, to some extent, to deal with the world. She was still John's executor and she carried out this task diligently. In 1481 together with Sir William Stokker and Robert Tate as executors, she sued Robert Kele, gentleman of London, for a debt of £27 14s. 4d.[46] Two years later they pursued further actions against John Palmer of Dagenham, gentleman, and his wife Anna. In 1486, together with Robert Tate, Margaret initiated numerous actions for debt in the court of common pleas.[47]

---

[43] *Stonor Letters*, ii, nos 185, 224. Betson wrote to Elizabeth Stonor informing her that he had seen her mother 'and God wote she made me right sulleyn chere with hir countenaunce whyles I was with hir: me thought it longe till I was departid. She brayke unto me off old ffernyeres, and specially she brayke to me off the tayll I told hir betwene the vicar [th]at was and hir: she said the vicar never ffared well seth, he tooke it so mych to hart. I told hir a lyght amswere ageyn, and so I departid ffrom hir. I had no joye to tary with hir. She is a ffyn mery woman, but ye shall nat know it nor yit ffynd it, nor none of youres by that I se in her.'

[44] *Stonor Letters*, ii, no. 217.

[45] Margaret had taken her bereavement badly and was probably suffering from reactive depression. Even though her granddaughter Anne Ryche was living with her Margaret had difficulty in speaking and, by the report of 'modyr mydwiffe' would only say to her 'Godes blissynge have ye and myne' and then she would 'goo hir waye fforthe as thow she had no joye off hir'. Sir Wiliam and Margaret Stokker avoided visiting Margaret. The visit to Betson took place on Thursday 30 September 1479. A Master Brinkley of Cambridge qualified in 1473. C.H. Talbot and H.A. Hammond, ed., *The Medical Practioners in Medieval England* (London, 1965), p. 26.

[46] The Kele debt case of 1481 was on a contract made in London on 31 August 1469 and concerned the collection of a tenth and fifteenth in Lincolnshire. PRO C 1/60/133; CP 40/878, rots 218, 472, 472v, 537, 538. Attorn recept., rot. 10 (21 Edward IV); CP 40/879 rot. 1, (21 Edward IV); CP 40/880, rot. 447 (21 Edward IV).

[47] The Palmer case was examined in May and October 1483, PRO, CP 40/881 rot. 520; Attorn recept., rot. 7 (22 Edward IV); CP 40/882, rots 12, 22v (22 Edward IV). In 1486 Margaret prosecuted John Horton, the abbot of the monastery of St Mary of Stanley in Wiltshire, William Pyers, of Clayden, Suffolk, John Newman, dyer, of 'Chellesworth', Suffolk, Richard Fox, of Buckingham, draper, John Grove, of Burford, Oxfordshire, and Nicholas Kyrton, of Cricklade,

continued

Some time after her husband's death Margaret was sued in chancery by the executors of John Welles for a debt which John Poutrell had owed to him. John Croke had acquired Poutrell's goods by a deed of gift in 1461. According to Margaret, Poutrell had owed her husband £600 when he died, but his goods were in fact only worth 100 marks. Margaret told the court that since Poutrell's wife Margery, and her daughters Elizabeth and Alice, had no means of support, John Croke of his 'pite' lent them all the goods which had been Poutrell's. When Margery died, Margaret inherited the remaining goods which had been appraised at no more than £30. The plaintiffs counter-claimed that after John Croke's death Margaret had inherited John Poutrell's lands, which were worth twenty pounds a year.[48]

Margaret for her part successfully sued a substantial Southampton merchant, John Walker, for a debt of £16 17s. $9\frac{1}{2}$d. contracted on 3 June 1480. There is nothing to indicate what the debt was for; the contract may not originally have been made with Margaret, since bills were often transferred to other people. But there is, however, some evidence to suggest that Margaret administered her own affairs, for in 1481 and 1482 she started debt cases in her own name against several men who were probably her tenants in Edmonton and Tottenham.[49]

Margaret had also inherited lands in Kent as her husband's heir; these lands comprised seven messuages, four gardens, two dove-cotes, 400 acres of land, thirty acres of meadow, 300 acres of pasture, 400 acres of wood and 2s. rent, worth 20 marks in fee, in Dartford, Sutton, Wilmington, Hill St Margaret, Horton, Southfleet, Bexley and Crayford (Earde).[50] Margaret was sufficiently

---

continued

tallowchandler. PRO, CP 40/896, rot. 18(1 Henry VII); CP 40/897, rot. 64 (1 Henry VII); CP 40/897, rots 24v, 25, 457, (1 Henry VII).

[48] Poutrell was still alive in 1465, PRO, C 1/88/33–35.

[49] Margaret claimed debts of 40s. each from John Tayllour and Peter Toppesfeld of Edmonton, husbondmen, and William Padyngton of Tottenham, brewer. Toppesfeld had broken into her close in Edmonton and had cut and taken away wood and underwood to the value of 40s. He was distrained to appear by the seizure of chattels worth 12d. She sued two Londoners, Thomas Wakelyn, pinner, and Roger Copland, for 40s. each. PRO, CP 40/878, rots 278, 378 (21 Edward IV); CP 40/880, rot. 366 (22 Edward IV); CP 40/881, rots 28, 28v, 429v, 479; Attorn recept., rot. 7v (x2 entries) (22 Edward IV); CP 40/878, rots 35, 218v, 218, 277v, 284, 284v, 377 (21 Edward IV); CP 40/880, rot. 461 (22 Edward IV); CP 40/881, Attorn recept., rot. 7v (22 Edward IV), not found in rots. I wish to thank Miss Rosalind Murrell of Exeter College, Oxford, for several of the Receipts of the Attorney's references in CP 40/878, 879.

In 1501 John Croke was described as the late free tenant of Pembroke's manor in Tottenham. In the same year customary lands in Tottenham were described as lately belonging to a Margaret Croke. They comprised 4 acres and 1 rod in Pembroke's manor, 3 acres and 3 rods in Longcroft, half an acre in Westlees, 5 acres and 1 rod in Redeland, part of Daubeney's Manor, and 2 acres in Redeland and Goseherne. These rental of these lands was 5s. 10d. p.a., PRO, SC 11/457, mm. 2, 9.

[50] These lands reverted to Margaret from John Chester, the son of William Chester, who had inherited them after John Croke's death. He enfeoffed Dame Margaret Croke, the bishops of Worcester and Chichester, Robert and John Tate, aldermen of London, Richard, Thomas and John Croke and Henry Woodcock, to the use of Margaret and her heirs. Dame Margaret held these lands of Sir William Stonor, the archbishop of Canterbury, the prior of St John of Jerusalem

continued

interested in her Kent lands and tenements to have initiated court actions for their recovery, shortly before she died.[51]

During her widowhood Margaret lent money to her family when they were in financial difficulties. Her son-in-law Sir William Stokker borrowed considerable sums of money from her. He and his brother John borrowed £39 to pay their custom and subsidy when they were at Calais, and Margaret of Burgundy repaid £9 9s. 6d. of this sum.[52] In 1483 Margaret had lent Sir William £60 in gold for the city of London's loan to King Edward IV, and on his behalf she lent the abbess of the Poor Clares in the Minories £11 when her granddaughter, Joan Ryche, was professed.[53] Stokker also acquired thirty-three pounds which had been owed to her by the London ironmonger Henry Nevill.[54] Stokker remembered these acts of kindness in his will and instructed that she was to 'be well and truly paide agen of all the money' that she had lent him, and he left her ten pounds and his 'standing cupp w[i]t[h] a columbyne'. Most of the money she lent to Stokker was unpaid at the time of her death, six years after his death in 1485, and his estate owed her a total of £133 11s. 0d.[55] Margaret instructed her executors to pardon Stokker's debt of 200 marks; a sum which she and her husband had lent him from her father's goods, because of the kindness and love which she 'found in Maister Richard Jay serjent of the law', her daughter Margaret's second husband. Her decision to do this had been declared 'unto them by mouth in the dwelling place of the said Master Jay without Newgate of London the Friday which was the 3rd day of Juyn the 6 yere of the Reigne of Kyng henry the viith [i.e., 1491] in the presence of my

continued

and John Pecche. After Margaret's death these lands then descended to Thomas Croke, PRO, C 142/8 (40); E 150/461 (10). London Lambeth Palace Library, Estate Document 233, ff. 1, 2.

[51] The Kent lands were recovered from the heirs of Thomas Pulter. Pulter's lands were to be sold for the benefit of her sons, if Margaret had not disposed of them in her lifetime. Pulter died on 27 May 1488. He held the manor of Down, in the parish of Down, and in Sandhurst, Cowdam and Keston, Kent, from the Prior of Christchurch, Canterbury. His heir was Richard Pulter, the son of Thomas the elder's son Thomas the younger. PRO, PROB 11/9, ff. 44–45v (PCC 6 Dogett). PRO, C 142/53; E 150/459 (4). See also, PRO, C 82/18/31 (21 & 25 November 1485).

[52] The money was probably borrowed before 1480 when they were at Calais. Margaret of York, duchess of Burgundy, sister of Edward IV visited England from June to September 1480. Margaret Croke was probably repaid during this visit. C. Scofield, *Life and Reign of Edward IV* (London, 1923), ii. pp. 283–97.

[53] London loaned Edward IV £2,000 on 22 February 1483, to which each alderman was expected to contribute 50 marks. Eightly commoners were asked to donate £15 a piece. Scofield, i, p. 363. PRO, PROB 11/7, ff. 198–198v (PCC 26 Logge). The abbess of the Minories told Margaret Croke to seek repayment of the Ryche dowry from Master Stokker, because he had £60 of Joan's goods. PRO, PROB 11/9, f. 45 (PCC 6 Dogett).

[54] Henry Nevill, PRO, PROB 11/8, f. 219v (PCC 28 Milles).

[55] Sir William and John Stokker his brother died of the sweating sickness. Sir William's will, 20 September 1485, named his wife Margaret, Dame Margaret Croke, John Croke his brother-in-law, and John Thornborough as his executors. John Thornborough was the attorney for the staple. Stokker's widow and the other executors gained probate on 16 September 1486; in the Michaelmas term 1489 they took out actions of debt against twenty-four men, PRO, CP 40/910, rots 24, 395v, 90v, 222 (5 Henry VII); CP 40/910, rot. 147v (5 Henry VII); C 81/1321/44.

sone John Croke [the younger] and of Henry Wodecok scryvener. And for the more clering of the saime I have sens that time delyv[ere]d unto the said Master Jay the seyd byll.'[56] Dame Margaret clearly helped her daughter after her husband, Sir William Stokker's death and bought his Cornhill property from her some time after 1485, since Stokker had requested that it should be sold to provide masses for him.[57]

Margaret's son, Richard, also suffered financial difficulties and was in debt to his mother. He may have been pursued by creditors, for on 8 October 1490 he made a grant to his mother, Dame Margaret, and his brother John, the younger, of all his movable goods, because he was 'endetted unto' his 'moost dere moder dame Margaret Croke of London wedow in divers sumes of money for p[ro]ftis loones and other divers thinges which of hir tender moderhode afore this tyme she' had lent to him 'and doone' for him. His 'dere brother' at his desire had agreed to be bound to other persons for different sums of money on his behalf, and to recompense them he had sold them 100 tons of gascon wine, 100 weys of bay salt, and thirty bales of Tolouse woad which had been purveyed for him by his factor and attorney in Bordeaux.[58]

Margaret's other sons also had financial problems. In 1485 Robert mortgaged all his goods, wares and debts due to him to William Vernon, grocer, Joan Clement, singlewoman and Richard Wood, mercer and merchant of the staple.[59] John Croke the younger was also in debt at the time of his death. Margaret was not particularly assiduous in collecting debts, and it was only when her husband's testament had received probate that she finally gathered in the sums owing to the estate of her father, William Gregory. The reason for her delay is unknown, but perhaps during her husband's lifetime she left the task to him. Many of the debtors were skinners. In 1481 and 1482, as her father's executor, she initiated actions against five men in the court of Common Pleas.[60]

Margaret died on 17 August 1491, when she was perhaps sixty-five years old. She had made her testament and will on 13 December 1490 and specified that she wished to be buried in the convent church of the friars preachers or Dominicans, the Blackfriars, before the image of 'Seint Sithe'. She left 40 marks for her 'burying place to be had' and for prayers for her soul and that of

[56] Richard Jay, who had married Sir William's widow acted as co-executor. He came from Hampshire, had been previously married and lived in Chelsea. He died in 1493 and his wife, Margaret, inherited property in Bassing and Shirborne, in Dorset. Richard had messuages in the parishes of St Edmund the Martyr and St Peter Cornhill, London. PRO, PROB 11/10, ff. 52v–53 (PCC 7 Vox); PRO, PROB 11/9, ff. 44v–45 (PCC 6 Dogett).

[57] PRO, PROB 11/7, ff. 198–198v (PCC 26 Logge). In her will Margaret Croke directed that the Cornhill property was to be sold after her death if she had not already sold it to provide leagacies for her sons.

[58] PRO, C 54/351, m. 1; *CCR, 1485–1500*, no. 533; *CPR, 1485–94*, p. 344. *LBL* p. 249.

[59] *CCR, 1476–85* p. 147.

[60] In 1481 and 1482 Margaret sued five men: John Acclom (or Acclond) of Kingston-on-Hull, armiger, for 25 marks; Thomas Preston, of London, gentleman, for £12; Edward Cheseman of

continued

her husband.[61] In choosing a friary for her place of burial Margaret had regard to the spiritual well-being of her soul, which is an indication of her piety and devoutness. No direct evidence has survived to indicate that Margaret was active in her parish church, but she bequeathed to All Hallows Barking her 'grete chales of silver and gilt' which had once belonged to the church. Unusually, she did not leave specific requests for torches, torch bearers, black gowns, memorial rings and other trappings normally associated with the funerals of wealthy Londoners. Margaret left the details of her funeral service to the discretion of her executors but specified that 40s. was to be given in alms to the poor both at her burial and at her month's mind.[62] Margaret left various sums to the London friaries but the house of the Dominicans was singled out. She left them two table cloths and two diaper towels. Margaret's 'little lowe cupp p[ar]cel gilt covered' and a little salt, which she said 'I am wont to occupy daily', she bequeathed to the prior Dr Winchelsea, with 40s. The sub-prior, Master Philip, received 20s., a former friar of the house, Richard Hayes, now the prior of Guildford, received 6s. 8d. Each priest was left 2s. and all other friars 12d. each.[63]

Margaret made particular provision for her female relatives and friends. Dame Joan Ryche, her grand-daughter, a nun in the Minories, was left 20s. To her daughter Margaret Jay, 'wt whom', Margaret said, 'I have moderly and right largely departyd', she bequeathed 'goddes blessing and myn, my cup callid the shepard and those [£10] of money which Sir Willyam Stokker Knyght late her husband bequethid and assigned me in his testament remaynyng yit in her hands'. Margaret had settled her gifts to her daughter before her death and her inheritance was concluded. Margaret left a ring to her cousin Agnes Bell, 10s. to Dame Agnes Cole, and a cup to the wife of Master John Rede, notary. One of Margaret's five godchildren, her grand-daughter Katherine Welbeck, widow of Thomas Betson, was bequeathed a cup worth 10 marks and a 'gyrdell' of Margaret's own wearing which was to be chosen for her by the executors. Another godchild, Margaret Tate the daughter of Master Robert Tate, former mayor of London, was left a gold ring. The two sons of Tate's brother John the alderman were also godchildren and were to receive 20s. a piece. Another godson, the son of Master John Rede, notary was to have 6s. 8d.

continued

London, skinner, Stephen Bettenham, of Cranbrook, Kent, gentleman; and William Deryng, of London, skinner, for 40s. each, PRO, CP 40/878, rots 214, 214v, 282 (21 Edward IV); CP 40/879, rot. 35, 282v; Attorn recept., rot. 10v (22 Edward IV).

[61] Margaret Croke's will, PRO, PROB 11/9, f. 44–45v (PCC 6 Dogett). Although this 'Saint Sithe' has been identified as St. Osyth it is more likely that she was St Sitha, the patron saint of housewives and domestic servants who was invoked especially when keys were lost or there was danger from rivers or crossing bridges. Her feast day was 27 April. D.H. Farmer, *The Oxford Dictionary of Saints* (Oxford, 1978), pp. 418–19. For the identification of St Osyth, J.C. Adams 'The Conventual Buildings of Blackfriars, London, and the Playhouses Constructed Therein', *Studies in Philology*, 14 (1914), pp. 65–67.

[62] PRO, PROB 11/9, f. 44v (PCC 6 Dogett).

[63] Ibid.

Margaret's two servants, Elizabeth Browne and Thomas Bostok, were left 26s. 8d. and £2 respectively. Peter, a charity child brought up in her house, if he was still living with her when she died, was to receive £2 and was to be made free of the city in a craft of the executors' choosing. Each servant living with her when she died was to have a feather-bed or mattress and a pair of blankets and sheets with a coverlet. Margaret's former servants William Brakeshawe and Elyn Mallery were given 6s. 8d. and ten shillings. Her last 'common servant' Agnes was left £1 6s. 8d. John Dunwich, Richard Boner, and Mother Johan were each left 20s. Anthony Goldsmyth and his wife received 13s. 4d. and enough cloth for two gowns.[64]

Margaret's remaining goods were to be divided into two parts: one half was to be given to her sons Richard and John, the other to pious uses for the benefit of her soul, and for the souls of her husband, parents, friends and benefactors. To her sons, Margaret left legacies to be paid half in money and half in plate, to Thomas £20, to Richard £50 and John £100, with the proviso that 'fforseen alwey yt of such dett as eny of them at the tyme of my deceese shall owe unto me euy mannys pairt of redy money of his owne dett be taken & payd if it come so moche to and else as moche therof as the dett shall amont to'. The plate to Richard and John was to include her two cups called 'the grapes'. If her son Robert was 'goode in demenyng' towards her executors 'without vexyng or troblying them' or annoying them for any other or more of her goods then he was to have £20 in money and ten marks in plate. Margaret's personal gifts, excluding her religious disbursements, totalled £41 10s. 0d. and in addition she left a total of £160 in money to four surviving sons.[65]

Margaret asked her executors to obtain an 'ornament or garnishment' for the church of Our Lady Aldermary beside Watling Street, where her father William and her mother Joan were buried. To the poor of this parish she left £2, so that the parishioners there would remember to pray for them and so provide their souls with greater release and comfort.[66]

Margaret may have owned lands in London, Middlesex and Buckingham-shire when she died, but the returns of the escheators have not survived. The inquisition into Dame Margaret's lands in Kent was held at Welling on 30 August 1492. Her properties were inherited by her sons in accordance with her husband's wishes, the Mark Lane house was leased and continued to provide an income for Croke's chantry in All Hallows church. Margaret's executors, her son John Croke the younger and Henry Woodcok, scrivener of London, were left twenty marks to perform their duties. Her overseer, Master John

[64] PRO, PROB 11/9, f. 45v. Henry Wodecock was left a silver-gilt standing cup and his wife a similar cup with a ring of gold and 5 marks in money. Roger Smalwoode, 'plommer' of St Botulph's Bishopsgate, was granted 6s. 8d. to pray for her. Alice Smalwoode, his wife, inherited tenements outside Aldrichgate, a tenement in Woodstreet, and others in Abchurch and Pudding Lanes. PRO, PROB 11/1, ff. 317v–318 (PCC 39 Horne), made 23 Feb. 1497, proved 4 Nov. 1499.

[65] Robert Croke was dead by 16 January 1492. Writs of *diem clausit extremum* sent to the escheators of London and Buckingham *CFR, 1485–1509*, nos 367, 460.

[66] PRO, PROB 11/9, f. 44v

Tate, alderman, was to have 10 marks. They were not as diligent in their office as she had been for her father, her husband and her son-in-law Sir William Stokker. They never proved her will and in 1493 were in mercy in the court of Common Pleas for failing to reply to a claim by Margaret Croke, the daughter and heir of John Croke the elder, that they owed her a box containing various writings and charters.[67]

Dame Margaret outlived not only her father and mother but also her husband, her eldest son John, her daughter Elizabeth and two sons-in-law. Her children did not prosper after her death and most of the lands they inherited were sold to pay their debts. Margaret's surviving sons seem not to have made wills and appear to have fallen in social status.

The few surviving references to Margaret in the *Stonor Letters*, taken out of context, would leave an unfair impression of a difficult, miserable, sullen, surly old lady, who did not take pleasure in her grandchild, and who was avoided by members of her family; yet Margaret was an exceptionally generous and kind mother, a thoughtful employer and a dutiful godparent. Although it seems clear that at her husband's death she wished, as far as possible, to retire from the world, she still worked hard to execute her husband's will and to collect up his debts. She lent money to all her children when they were in need. To set against the 'sulleyn chere' observed by Thomas Betson during the first year of Margaret's widowhood, we should note the 'tender moderhode' gratefully acknowledged by her son Richard, and the loving relationship between Margaret and her only surviving daughter Margaret 'wt whom I have moderly and right largely departyd'. Thomas Betson's cheerful and brash comments allow us to see how one widow survived a period of acute depression to find a purposeful and significant role as a loving mother and grandmother of an extended, and by no means always successful, family. Thomas Betson unwittingly enables us to observe a London woman coming to terms with the pain of widowhood.

---

[67] PRO, C 142/8 (40); E 150/461 (10). Henry Woodcock, scrivener, had property in Lewisham, Lambeth, Streatham, 'the Coppidhall' parish of St Swithun's London, tenements in the parish of St Benet Shorehog and St John Walbrook in London, and a messuage in Buklersbury in St Benet Shorehog in which George (his son) lived, PRO, PROB 11/18, ff. 102–102v (PCC 13 Holder). John Croke, Sir William Taillour, Sir William Stokker, Robert Tate and John Tate, held three messuages in Wood Street, and five in Silver Street, in the parish of St Alban, Cripplegate ward; these properties descended to Margaret, the daughter of John Croke the elder, on 1 June 1487; the property evidences had been looked after by Dame Margaret Croke, PRO, CP 40/923, rot. 306, Attorn. recept., rot. 9 (8 Henry VII); CP40/1041, rot. 519 (Buck). Properties in parish of St Bride, Fleet Street, Aldrich Street, in parish of St Botulph without Aldrichgate and parish of St Margaret Bridge Street were inherited by Margaret Tate, wife of John Tate, daughter and heir of John Croke the elder. 'Crokes farm' had also been inherited by Margaret Tate. For the suits over these lands into the sixteenth century: CLRO, Journal 7, f. 87; PRO, C 1/61/486; C 1/366/69; C 1/582/27; C 1/605/21; C 1/360/25. Drapers Company deeds, AVII, 288/2796 (1509); AVII, 99/3250 (1509); AVII, 3481 (1511); AVII, 255/3255 (1511); AV, 282/3590; AVII, 97/3251; AVII, 249/3249 (31 Dec 1461); AVI, 283/3590 (20 May 1504); AVII, 127/3252; AVII, 129/3244; AVII, 288/2796 (1509); AVII, 3250 (1509); AVII, 255/3255 (1511); AVII, 256/3254 (1512); AVII, 25/3480 (1526).

12

Three Fifteenth-Century Vowesses

Mary C. Erler

From the fourteenth century to the Dissolution of the monasteries, names survive of women who chose a life containing elements of both religious and lay states. This life was elected, for the most part though not entirely, by widows: it constitutes the familiar 'mantle and ring' of medieval literature. The term which such women most often use to describe themselves, beginning in the late fifteenth century is 'vowess', and the significant vow was one of perpetual chastity. Like nuns, vowesses were clothed and veiled at an episcopal ceremony; unlike nuns, these women did not promise either poverty or obedience. Indeed their state remained formally a lay one, with physical freedom to come and go, and economic freedom to dispose what were sometimes considerable holdings of land or goods. The vow did not imply a rule of life, like that of a third order, and no particular spiritual regimen was specified. Though some vowesses affiliated with communities of religious women, others did not.

Before examining the form which the vowess vocation assumed in three London lives, some general consideration of its nature will be useful. The vowing ceremony is preserved in several pontificals,[1] among them a London volume owned by Thomas Bele, who served as suffragan to Cuthbert Tunstall between 1522 and 1530.[2] Its rubrics specify that at a ceremony preceding the Gospel at mass, the woman should approach the seated bishop, wearing ordinary dress, carrying dark clothing over her left arm and led by two honest

---

[1] Contemporary pontificals which provide the service include that of Edmund Lacy, bishop of Exeter, 1420-55, and Christopher Bainbridge, archbishop of York, 1508-14. Several other women discussed in this volume were also vowesses. The *Calendar of Entries in the Papal Registers*, for instance, gives Elizabeth de Burgh an indult to enter houses of the Minoresses 'she having made a vow of chastity' (iii, p. 113); see also the essays in this volume by Carole Rawcliffe and Kay Lacey. I am grateful to Caroline Barron for long-continued and invaluable assistance in examining both the vowess vocation and individual vowess lives.

[2] For Bele's pontifical, see F.C. Eeles, 'Two Sixteenth-Century Pontificals Formerly Used in England'. *Transactions of the St Paul's Ecclesiological Society*, 7 (1911-15), pp. 69-90. The book is now London, Lambeth Palace Library, MS 1509. N.R. Ker, *Medieval Manuscripts in British Libraries*, 4 vols (Oxford, 1969-92), i, pp. 106-7, spells the owner's name 'Bale', and gives his dates of service as 1522-28.

men of her relationship. Kneeling, she first placed the paper with her vow (*cedula professionis*) at the bishop's feet, then read the vow from it. If illiterate she might be helped by the bishop who led her in reading it (*vel si illiterate fuerit episcopo docente sic dicat*). Then she marked the document with a cross upon the seated bishop's knee and gave him the paper for safe-keeping.

The words of profession, whether in French or English – and even the vowess's mark – were sometimes copied by the scribe into the episcopal register. Use of the mark should not be regarded as unequivocal evidence of illiteracy. It has been suggested that in various contexts the mark's invocation of the holy cross signalled the signer's piety and that it was in fact equivalent to an oath, and documents survive which are both signed and marked.[3]

The ceremony proceeded with an episcopal blessing and asperging, first of the clothes, then of the ring, with which the woman was then invested. Vowess clothing seems to have been indistinguishable from that of widows. Besides the veil, mantle and ring mentioned in the rite, the widow's wimple was worn – often, though not always, in its pleated form, the *barbe*.[4]

Mass resumed with the offertory, and at the mass's end the woman received the bishop's blessing and kissed his ring. When women of elevated status made profession, the registers sometimes recorded the names of official witnesses or noteworthy guests. The ceremony's location was most often the chapel of an episcopal manor. It was sometimes preceded, at some distance in time, by an examination – or at least by some assessment of the prospective vowess's suitability, set in motion by the ecclesiastical authority.

Some women's vows mention the rule of St Paul the Apostle. The reference is to 1 Timothy 5:3-16, written in the early second century, though no longer thought to be composed by St Paul. This text describes an order of widows whose members were to devote themselves to a life of prayer in this ecclesiastically recognized vocation. Most commentators believe that a formal vow of enrolment is suggested by the passage.[5]

The conventional and traditional nature of this vocation is illustrated by evidence, based on the *ordo*'s frequent appearance in pontificals, that it was ecclesiastically sanctioned, and by the ceremony's resemblances to female religious profession. Like a nun's profession, in fact, the vow was a public one,

---

[3] For discussion of cross-marks, Samuel Schoenbaum, *William Shakespeare: A Compact Documentary Life* (New York and Oxford, 1987), pp. 37, 295n. A.G. Dickens cites a 1534 abjuration of heresy, for instance, which is both signed and marked, 'In witnes whereof . . . I have subscribed my name and sette the signe of the crosse. Gelen Vanbellaer +', *Lollards and Protestants in the Diocese of York, 1509-1558* (Hull, 1959; repr. London, 1982), p. 21.

[4] Muriel Claydon, *Catalogue of Rubbings of Brasses in the Victoria and Albert Museum* (London, 1915), p. 25.

[5] The literature on the subject of early Christian widows is substantial. An overview is provided by Roger Gryson, *The Ministry of Women in the Early Church* (Collegeville, MN, 1976); more recent and more specific is Bonnie Bowman Thurston's clear summary, *The Widows: A Women's Ministry in the Early Church* (Minneapolis, MN, 1989). See also Jouette M. Bassler, 'The Widow's Tale: A Fresh Look at 1 Tim. 5:3-16', *Journal of Biblical Literature*, 103 (1984), pp. 23-41.

accepted by the church's representative in the name of the institution; hence papal permission was necessary in order to dispense from it. The *Calendar of Papal Letters*, which records such appeals to Rome, affords the best glimpse of failed vows.[6] Occasionally, female motives are revealed: in requesting to be freed from their vow some women cite the desire to be mothers, while other petitions reveal that occasionally birth had already occurred.[7]

For the great majority of women who remained under their vows, however, motives varied as widely as did those underlying female religious profession. In some cases husbands' wills promised specific economic benefit if the wife vowed chastity. Even when such particular inducement was not present, the vow offered the opportunity for female control of temporal resources, free from male intrusion in the form of pressure to remarry. Secular advantage could include the maintenance of inheritance patterns as well. Spiritually the vow of chastity placed the woman in a state which, though less valued than virginity, was more elevated than the marital one. In some instances widows' literature of counsel recognises a tradition of vowed widowhood, semi-secluded and prayerful. Finally, though some vowed women lived with or near nuns' communities, for others the maintenance of domestic life provided a psychologically satisfying continuum which, at the same time, acknowledged a fresh direction.

The three vowed London widows discussed here lived at the opening, the middle, and the end of the fifteenth century. The earliest of these women, Alice Lynne, was married to a wealthy woolman and grocer; some records of his business ventures survive.[8]

Her reasons for taking the vow are very clear: William Lynne's 1421 will left her his quay and messuage called the Wool Wharf, and also lands and tenements in three London parishes, for life as long as she remained

---

[6] Interesting cases are summarised in John A.F. Thomson, ' "The Well of Grace": Englishmen and Rome in the Fifteenth Century', *The Church, Politics and Patronage in the Fifteenth Century*, ed. R.B. Dobson (Gloucester and New York, 1984).

[7] In 1419 Edynna Clerck stated that she was still young and desired to be a mother (*Calendar of Papal Letters*, vii, p. 120) and in 1482 Margaret Singleton had had offspring after her vow of chastity (*CPL*, xii, pt 2, pp. 835-36); both quoted in Thomson, pp. 106, 113.

[8] In 1405, after shipwreck of Lynne's wool cargo, the Dover customs officials were ordered to allow him to reload and take the wool to the Calais staple without a second customs payment. *Calendar of Close Rolls, 1402-5*, pp. 427-28. Eight years later a vessel of Lynne's was taken at sea by a Calais ship and brought to Sandwich; the order for release of the vessel is recorded in 1413. *CCR, 1413-19*, pp. 16-17. See also *CCR, 1403-9*, pp. 263, 359; *CCR, 1409-13*, p. 201; *Calendar of Plea and Memoranda Rolls, 1413-37*, pp. 63, 86.

The Lynnes were apparently from Kent, since William's will leaves money for repair of Rochester Bridge, and one of the supervisors of his will was William Sevenoke, grocer, mayor in 1418, of Sevenoaks, Kent.

unmarried.[9] The Lynnes' five children were all under age at their father's death and the wife's response was not long delayed. The will is dated 6 August 1421; on 31 October Alice Lynne vowed chastity before Henry Chichele, archbishop of Canterbury, in the chapel of his manor of Lambeth.[10]

Though Alice Lynne's subsequent career shows her as well off, some cash shortage perhaps necessitated the widow's and executors' pledge, nearly a year after William Lynne's death, that the five children's patrimony which totalled £1,750 would be paid in two years. When it was received in January and March 1424, guardianship of her two sons was given to Alice, of her two daughters Alice and Margaret to Thomas Catworth (later mayor 1443-44), and of her daughter Beatrice to William Trymnel, mercer.[11] These negotiations in the mayor's court, which show the widow as a functioning member of London's governing class, were common to all three vowesses, as we shall see.

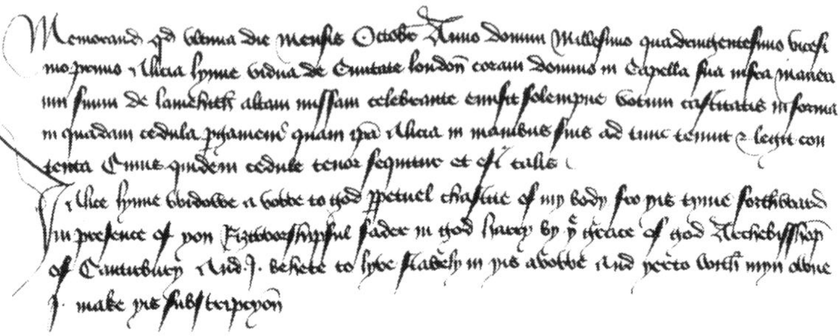

Memorandum that on the last day of October A.D. 1421, Alice Lynne, widow of the city of London, before the lord [archbishop] in his chapel in his manor of Lambeth celebrating high mass, took a solemn vow of chastity according to a certain schedule of parchment which the same Alice held in her hands then and read the contents, of which schedule the tenor follows and is such.

I, Alice Lynne widowe a vowe to god perpetuel chastite of my body fro yis tyme fortheward in presence of you riȝtworshipful fader in god, Harry by ye grace of god Archebisshop of Cantirbury, and I behete to lyve stavely in yis avowe, and yerto withe myne owne [hand] I make yis subscripcyon.

Fig. 11   Alice Lynne's vow of perpetual chastity. (*Lambeth Palace Library, Register of Henry Chichele, Archbishop of Canterbury 1414-43, f. 343v*).

---

[9] PRO, PROB 11/2B, ff. 189v and 202v-204, made 6 August 1421, proved 4 December. The will was also proved in the court of Husting, but not until over two years after Lynne's death, 23 November 1423, *HW*, 152 (20), p. 433. Of wills proved both in PCC and the court of Husting, see E.F. Jacob, ed., *The Register of Henry Chichele, Archbishop of Canterbury, 1414-1443*, 4 vols, Canterbury & York Society (Oxford, 1937-47), ii, p. xv, who says 'the testators are mostly of the highest municipal standing'.

[10] Ibid., iv, p. 221.

[11] *LBI*, pp. 268-69; *LBK*, pp. 25-27, 171.

Before his death William and Alice Lynne had purchased together a house variously called 'le Wollewharf' or 'le Weyngehous', where the compulsory weighing of wool for duty assessment (tronage) took place. Situated on 'le Newe Wool Wharf' off the present Lower Thames Street, the house was used for 'the convenience of the customers [customs employees], controllers, clerks, and other officers'. In return the crown granted a fee of four pounds yearly to the owners of the customs house, and in 1423, two years after William's death, Alice received this grant.[12] Fifteen years later, in 1438, it was renewed in the names of Alice Lynne and her son John,[13] and one more renewal was extended in 1462, though at this time the grant was made simply to Alice Lynne, her heirs and assigns.[14]

This house on the river lay only two blocks south of Alice Lynne's dwelling, a tenement in Mincing Lane. She was occupying her home still in 1470, when a contemporary document describes a property as lying 'between the tenement of Dame Alice Lynne on the north and the tenement late of Thomas Horsham on the south' in the parish of St Dunstan in the East.[15] Her very long widowhood extended in fact until the end of this decade: her will, made in 1458, was not proved until 6 October 1480.[16] It is solely concerned to dispose the properties in which she held a life interest and which, after her death, her husband William's will had specified should support a chantry.

During these years Alice Lynne's enviable financial position is confirmed by her appearance in the 1436 London lay subsidy roll. Among fourteen women identified as London widows, the richest, Margaret Berkeley, had an estimated income of £160 yearly, while Alice Lynne stood fourth in this group with £43 annually.[17]

---

[12] A new building for the weighing of wool was erected on the site by John Churchman in 1382, with an addition in 1383, *CPR, 1381-85*, pp. 149, 299. The freehold passed to a group perhaps representative of the Grocers' Company, one of whom was John Shadworth from whom the Lynnes acquired it. London County Council, *Survey of London*, xv, *The Parish of All Hallows Barking*, pt 2 (London, 1934), pp. 33-34. Alice Lynne's 1423 grant is *CPR, 1422-29*, pp. 142-43. Excavations at the site in 1973 revealed what were probably the foundations both of Churchman's original building and his addition containing 'a small chamber for a latrine and a sollar'. 'It is an interesting thought that the most famous controller of customs, Geoffrey Chaucer, may have used this latrine', Tim Tatton-Brown, 'Excavations at the Custom House Site City of London, 1973', *Transactions of the London and Middlesex Archaeological Society*, 25 (1974), pp. 117-219; the reference is on p. 141.

[13] *CPR, 1436-41*, pp. 225-26, 231.

[14] *CPR, 1461-67*, p. 92. John Lynne was still living, since his name appears on a manorial grant in 1464 (ibid., p. 323). See also *LBL*, p. 58, where he is party to a bond in March 1465.

[15] *CPMR, 1458-82*, pp. 65-66.

[16] *HW*, ii, p. 580; roll 210 (13).

[17] Sylvia Thrupp, *The Merchant Class of Medieval London* (Chicago, 1948), appendix B. In 1412, about ten years before his death while his career was still on the rise, William Lynne's income from land in London had been assessed at 40s. annually, J.C.L. Stahlschmidt, 'London Subsidy temp. Henry IV', *Archaeological Journal*, 44 (1887), pp. 56-82.

Perhaps the most intriguing element in Alice Lynne's life is her connection with John Shirley, the well-known scribe and bibliophile. A.I. Doyle has shown, through Shirley's will with its appointment of 'my benyngne Moder in Lawe Dame Alice Lynne Widow' as an overseer, that Shirley's second wife was Alice Lynne's daughter Margaret. Doyle dates the marriage before 1441. It is likely to have taken place after 1428 when, with his employer Richard Beauchamp, earl of Warwick, Shirley returned to England from Calais. Since 1414 Beauchamp had been captain of Calais where Shirley served as his secretary, and Calais may have provided the connection between the wool-trading Lynne family and the book-loving, book-circulating Shirley. In addition, Alice Lynne's grant of royal fees from the customs house indicates that she continued to move in the same world as Shirley, who was appointed in February 1432 as controller of the subsidy of tunnage and poundage, this appointment being replaced in March by an appointment as controller of the petty custom.[18]

Margaret Lynne Shirley's name remains in a notable manuscript of Hoccleve's and Lydgate's work (Huntington Library, MS EL 26.A.13) where Shirley has lettered together the names 'Margarete & Beautrice' above his own. Beatrice Lynne, Margaret's sister, married Avery Cornburgh, a career official who rose to become keeper of the great wardrobe. Beatrice outlived her husband: her inscription survives in a fifteenth-century psalter which she gave to Dame Grace Centurio of the London Minoresses, and after her death to the use of the house.[19]

Alice Lynne's third daughter, another Alice, seems to have possessed unusual qualities of loyalty and strength. In 1430 she married John Knyvett: one of their daughters was Christian, wife of Henry and mother of John Colet. In a protracted inheritance struggle which recalls the Pastons' difficulties over the Fastolf will, Alice Lynne Knyvett and her husband claimed their right to Buckenham Castle in Norfolk. On one occasion Alice refused entry to the royal commissioners. With fifty men she raised the drawbridge asserting 'I woll

[18] A.I. Doyle, 'More Light on John Shirley', *Medium Aevum*, 30 (1961), pp. 93-101, discovered what is currently known about Shirley's life. More recent on Shirley's books is Julia Boffey and John J. Thompson, 'Anthologies and Miscellanies: Production and Choice of Texts', *Book Production and Publishing in Britain, 1375-1475*, ed. Jeremy Griffiths and Derek Pearsall (Cambridge, 1989), pp. 279-316. Shirley's grants are given in *CPR, 1429-36*, pp. 188, 183.

[19] Huntington Library, San Marino, MS EL 26.A.13 also bears Avery Cornburgh's name, see *Guide to Medieval and Renaissance Manuscripts in the Huntington Library* (San Marino, CA, 1989), i, pp. 35-39. The psalter is described in Margaret M. Manion, Vera F. Vines and Christopher de Hamel, ed., *Medieval and Renaissance Manuscripts in New Zealand Collections* (Melbourne and New York, 1989), no. 135. Beatrice Cornburgh's 1501 will is PRO, PROB 11/15, f. 56r–v. In it she leaves Dame Christian Colet, wife of Henry Colet, knight, 'my cowsyne' (i.e. her niece, see note following) her best black gown furred with marten and her girdle of black harnessed with gold. The overseer and supervisor is Master John Colet, D.D., parish priest of Stebenheth (Stepney). Grace Centurio does not appear in the Minoresses' pension list at the Dissolution.

nott leve the possession of this castell to dye therfore . . . lever I had in such wyse to dye than to be slayne when my husbond cometh home, for he charget me to kepe it'.[20]

While Alice Lynne took the vow of chastity early, and after only a single marriage, the career of Joan Gedney, in both its marital and financial aspects, exhibits a more complex character and a more ambitious scope. Married four times as her 1462 will shows, she took the vow after her third marriage to Robert Large, the mayor of London, and broke it to marry John Gedney, whose London and career and honours echo Large's.

Cloth-trade networks perhaps underlie at least her last three marriages. Although nothing is known about her first husband, John Gade, save for his mention in her will, her second, Richard Turnaunt, a fuller, was M.P. for Winchester five times beginning in 1416, and was twice mayor of the city. Derek Keene calls him 'one of the wealthiest Winchester clothiers of his day'. Keene's work allows us to see him amassing an estate of seven properties and to locate these precisely. Cash legacies in his 1433 will amounted to over £400. He and Joan Gade were married at least by 1427, as their son Richard was born in 1428. Like Joan's subsequent husbands, Turnaunt must have been considerably older than his wife, since he had been previously married between 1410 and 1417 to Juliana, widow of Gilbert Forster, another Winchester clothier through whom Turnaunt acquired substantial property.[21]

Nothing is known of Joan from 1433 until she appears in the 1441 will of her subsequent husband Robert Large, London mercer, mayor, M.P., and perhaps best-known as William Caxton's master.[22] Here she was left the huge sum

[20] Roger Virgoe, 'The Earlier Knyvetts: The Rise of a Norfolk Gentry Family', *Norfolk Archaeology*, 41 (1990), pp. 1-14. In part 2 of this article, *Norfolk Archaeology*, 41 (1993), pp. 249-78, Virgoe says that Alice spent 'at least part of her later years in residence at Carrow Abbey apart from her husband' (p. 250). Alice Knyvett's 1461 exploit is recounted in *CPR, 1461-67*, p. 67. *The Visitation of Cambridgeshire*, ed. J.W. Clay, Harleian Society, 41 (London, 1897), p. 102, states that Alice Lynne Knyvett's brother John Lynne married Margaret Knyvett, sister of Alice's husband John Knyvett. A Knyvett manuscript, now Cambridge, Trinity College, MS O.5.2, carries arms commemorating the marriage of Alice Lynne Knyvett's grand-daughter Anne Knyvett, *c*. 1480-90; see Derek Pearsall, 'Notes on the Manuscript of *Generydes*', *The Library*, 5th series 16 (1961), pp. 205-09.

[21] Derek Keene, *Survey of Medieval Winchester*, 2 vols (Oxford, 1985), i, p. 161. Turnaunt's career is summarised, ibid., ii, p. 1371. Of the many references to Turnaunt in these volumes the following are particularly interesting: i, pp. 132, 161, 218, 224, 227, 307, 418; ii, pp. 792-93.

By her first husband, John Gade, Joan had a daughter, Denise, who was remembered in Turnaunt's will. For this information and knowledge of Turnaunt's previous marriage I am indebted to Dr Linda Clark who generously allowed me to see her biography of Turnaunt before publication: *The History of Parliament: The Commons, 1386-1421*, ed. J.S. Roskell, L.S. Clark and C. Rawcliffe, 4 vols (Gloucester, 1992), iv, pp. 675-76. For Richard Turnaunt the younger's birthdate, see Daniel Lysons, *Environs of London*, 4 vols (London, 1792-96), iii, p. 526, n. 61, who says that at his mother's death in 1462 Turnaunt was thirty-four.

[22] Robert Large's will is PRO, PROB 11/1, ff. 120v-121v and 145. It is incomplete, breaking off at the bottom of f. 121v and concluding on f. 145. It was printed and translated by William Blades,
continued

of 4,000 marks in lieu of her legal one-third of Large's estate and was named one of the executors. If dissatisfied, she was to have only the portion to which she was legally entitled. Richard Turnaunt, Large's stepson, received a legacy of twenty pounds. (For comparison, Large left his apprentice William Caxton twenty marks.)

Large died in April 1441.[23] His widow took the vow of chastity sometime between her husband's death and 13 August 1442 when *Letter Book K* refers to her as *domina* (English 'dame'). The records' editor, Reginald Sharpe, observed that since Large was neither knight nor baronet 'the title of *domina*, here applied to his widow, is somewhat strange',[24] but clearly its use means that Joan Large vowed sometime in this fifteenth-month period. Search of the relevant episcopal register, that of Robert Gilbert, bishop of London, for 1436-49 (GL, MS 9531/6), and of the register (1414-43) of Henry Chichele, archbishop of Canterbury, has not uncovered the document, but the detailed form of words provided by William Blades, Caxton's biographer, indicates that he saw it:

> I, Johanna, that was sometime the wife of Robert Large, make mine avow to God and the high blissful Trinity, to our Lady Saint Mary, and to all the blissful company of Heaven, to live in chastity and cleanness of my body from this time forward as long as my life lasteth, and never to take other spouse but only Christ Jesu.[25]

The scandal of Joan Large's broken vow and remarriage is first recorded in Bodleian Digby Roll 2, a London chronicle, where it appears under the year of Thomas Catworth's mayoralty, 1443-44:

> Also in this year John Gedney, draper alderman of London [omission] which was Robert Large wife late mayor of London which was sworn chaste and had take the mantel and the ring and should have kept her a godly widow time of her life. And anon after the marriage done they were troubled by holy church because of breaking of her oath and were put to penance both he and she.[26]

John Stow likewise records these events, in terms so similar as to suggest his dependence on Digby Roll 2, and the story is found again in the eighteenth-

---

continued

The Life and Typography of William Caxton (2nd edn, London and Strassburg, 1882), pp. 153-58. The translation in this second edition, however, has had its pages scrambled and the text is not reliable. Large's career is summarised in Alfred B. Beaven, *The Aldermen of the City of London*, 2 vols (London, 1913), ii, p. 7, and more recently in Thrupp, *Merchant Class*, p. 352.

[23] Although Beaven gives the death date as 24 April 1441, the date of the will's making was 11 April, and in 1459 a writer of the court hand, Robert Bale, testified that he had made a copy of 'the last will of the said Robert Large dictated the day before he died' (*CPMR, 1458-82*, p. 9). If this is correct, Large died on 12 April.

[24] *LBK*, p. 273n.

[25] Blades, *Caxton*, p. 11.

[26] Caroline Barron provided the chronicle reference, knowledge of Joan Gedney's will and references to her in the *Letter Books*. Thomas Catworth was guardian of Alice Lynne's daughters Alice and Margaret.

century antiquarian William Cole's collections (now BL, MS Add. 5808).[27] Since London mayors were both elected and inaugurated in October, Joan Large married John Gedney between October 1443 and October 1444.[28]

She had taken the vow of chastity soon after Large's death, as Alice Lynne did after her husband William died, and their reasons too may resemble each other. Though only the final paragraph of Large's real estate bequests survives, later legal records reveal that, like Lynne's bequest to Alice, Large left Joan his Essex manorial lands on condition she remain unmarried.[29]

Here, as in Alice Lynne's case, the vow was evidently felt to stabilise a potentially volatile situation. Once vowed, the woman would retain an unchanged legal/ecclesiastical status for the rest of her life, one which offered no challenge to the husband's testamentary desires. The troubling possibility of female remarriage with the complexities of additional children, or at the very least with the attendant need to redevise land or property, would be eliminated.

Robert and Joan Large had no children together. After his death guardianship of his son Robert went to Thomas Staunton, one of Large's executors, while, as his will specified, Joan assumed guardianship of his sons Thomas and Richard, each of whose patrimonies of £1,000 she held and gave legal surety for in the mayor's court. Robert and Thomas were dead by 1448, and in 1452 Large's remaining son, Richard, now aged twenty-four, acknowledged receiving from Joan his patrimony of £1,000[30] and legacies consequent on the death of his brothers. By 1450 Richard was in possession of his father's Essex property – the lands which had been left to Joan if she did not remarry – since he was party to a bond in that year which identifies him as 'Richard Large of Thakstede, Essex, esquire'. Weever records the 27 March 1458 tomb inscription of a Richard Large at Thaxted, Essex, and cites a tradition that the dead man was brother to the London mayor.[31] That this was Large's last surviving son, however, is made clear by Thomas Staunton's claim in the following year, 1459, to this manor left him by Large consequent on the death of all Large's children.[32]

---

[27] C.L. Kingsford, *A Survey of London by John Stow*, 2 vols (Oxford, 1908), i, p. 186. For Cole, ibid., vii, f. 191v. I am indebted to Marilyn Oliva for this reference.

[28] For mayoral year, see Beaven, *Aldermen*, ii, p. xxviii; *LBK*, p. 280.

[29] *CPMR, 1458-82*, p. 9. The manor, called in the document Horham, and glossed by its editor 'Horham Hall, near Thaxted', had been devised by Large to Joan for life, as long as she remained unmarried, with remainder to her sons.

[30] For these transactions during the ten years after Large's death from 1442 to 1452, see *LBK*, pp. 272-73, 279, 280 (two entries), 281 (two entries), 282. Also *CPMR, 1437-57*, pp. 110, 114.

Large's will gave guardianship of his daughter Elizabeth and her patrimony of £500 to Stephen Stichemersch and this was done (*LBK*, p. 281); she later married the son of Simon Eyre (Thrupp, *Merchant Class*, p. 352). Large's daughter Alice was left £100 'to be spent in the purchase of furniture and utensils most necessary for her house' (Blades, *Caxton*, p. 154), which, since she was under twenty-one, perhaps implies she was then engaged or recently married.

[31] *CCR, 1447-54*, p. 238.

[32] John Weever, *Ancient Funerall Monuments* (London, 1631), p. 628 (STC 25223). See n. 29 above.

Joan Large remained in the vow for about three years. In breaking this socially and ecclesiastically sanctioned public pledge, she not only incurred social and religious censure, but sustained the loss of Large's Essex lands. Such a considerable economic loss could perhaps only have been justified by a parallel gain.

Since about 1427 John Gedney had been negotiating the acquisition of the four sub-manors which together comprised the manor of Tottenham, Middlesex. (Londoners' purchase of Tottenham lands for investment had begun as early as John of Northampton's 1392 acquisition.) Like Large's, Gedney's career was an elevated one and they were personal friends, Gedney serving as one of Large's executors. Each was master of his company, the Drapers and the Mercers respectively, and served as alderman, as M.P. for London, and as mayor (Gedney twice). Gedney died in 1449; his will does not survive.[33]

Douglas Moss has traced the immense changes which Gedney's tenure brought to Tottenham. Surpluses of over £100 per year are continuous in all surviving accounts between 1443 and 1449. These years saw the building of first one fulling mill and then a second, to join the older water mill; sales of hay supplementing earlier sales of timber; and the operation of a brickworks. Gedney raised rents, leased the demesne either in one piece or in large parcels, and in summary, treated the manor like 'a business run for profit'.[34]

Reference to 'Joan Large widow' in some Tottenham conveyances indicates she too was involved with the ownership of these Middlesex lands before 1443-44,

---

[33] For the most recent and most inclusive summary of Gedney's career, see Carole Rawcliffe's biography in *The History of Parliament: The Commons, 1386-1421*, iii, pp. 170-73. Dr Rawcliffe kindly let me see her work before publication.

Gedney's appearance in the notable stained-glass of Long Melford church, Suffolk, is explained by his earlier marriage to Elizabeth, sister of John Clopton, the man responsible for this splendid assemblage of family and friends and Gedney's executor. For Gedney's earlier marriage, see Sir William Parker, *Handbook to the . . . Glass in the Church of . . . Long Melford* (Ipswich, 1888), p. 29.

Arrangements for Gedney's chantry in St Christopher le Stocks where he was buried were not completed until 5 February 1483, when one John Plonket, shearman, composed a document headed 'The testament of John Plonket Sherman of the lands and tenements for the Sowle of John Gedney etc to the ayed of the dead bequethed'. Acting 'at the special request and instance of John Clopton Esquier Executour', he specifies the lands and tenements which will support the chantry. The document concludes with a description of the ceremonial confirmation of these arrangements, held 14 February at St Christopher's in the presence of various named drapers, *Wills, Leases and Memoranda in the Book of Records of the Parish of St Christopher le Stocks*, ed. Edwin Freshfield (London, 1895), pp. 9-12. In this document Gedney's wives are specified as Alice, Elizabeth and Joan; a son, John, is also named.

[34] 'The Economic Development of a Middlesex Village', *Agricultural History Review*, 28 (1980), pp. 104-14. Further evidence is provided in Douglas Moss and Ian Murray, 'Signs of Change in a Medieval Village Community', *Transactions of the London and Middlesex Archaeological Society*, 27 (1976), pp. 280-87; the quoted phrase is on p. 286. Turnaunt was likewise a clothier-entrepreneur, though on a smaller scale than Gedney. He held the fulling-mill at Easton at farm from the cathedral priory in 1430; compare Gedney's building of two fulling-mills in the 1440s.

when she married Gedney and took his name. Lysons reports that at the sub-manor of Bruses, the first manorial court of Joan Large, widow, was held in 1444, and later the same year, the court of John Gedney and Joan his wife.[35] Although the complex land transfers of various feoffee groups make assignment of actual ownership difficult, if Joan Large was indeed lady of the manor of Bruses and John Gedney was enfeoffed of the remaining sub-manors, union of their Middlesex interests may have represented possibilities even more substantial than those Large and Turnaunt had left her. Gedney's wealth was, in fact, greater than Large's: for instance in the 1436 lay subsidy Gedney's assessment was £120, Large's £15.[36]

After Gedney's death in 1449, the Tottenham lands went to a group of six feoffees of whom Joan was one. In the following decade her continuing efforts to acquire these manors for herself were notable. In 1451, 1455 and finally 1458 she negotiated a series of quit-claims which gradually left the whole manor in her possession for life. In this decade, when the manor's ownership was in more or less constant transition, Moss notes that three surviving accounts show the manorial surplus falling somewhat and large arrears reappearing. 'Even so, much was being spent on repairs to the fulling mills and on a new oven for the brickworks, – decisions in which Joan Gedney must have played a part. After the final 1458 release to her she commissioned a terrier or rent-roll of all the Tottenham lands in 1459. Here she is styled lady of the entire manor (her will left the parish church of Tottenham the appropriately large sum of £10).[37]

Upon her death in 1462 the lands passed to her son Richard Turnaunt, and then to Joan's granddaughter Thomasina Turnaunt and her husband Sir John Risley, where they facilitated Risley's career as a Middlesex J.P. and courtier to Henry VII.[38] This formation of the estate is recalled in one of the transactions of the 1480s, which specifies that the lands may eventually be sold and the purchase money distributed in works of piety for the souls of Thomasina and John Risley, Richard Turnaunt and Elizabeth his wife, and Joan Gedney.[39] Thomasina's grandmother is thus recognised as responsible for the acquisition of substantial familial wealth and security.

---

[35] See *CCR, 1447-54*, pp. 89-90. Daniel Lysons, *The Environs of London*, 4 vols (London, 1792-96), iii, p. 523n.

[36] Thrupp, *Merchant Class*, pp. 381-82.

[37] *CCR, 1447-54*, p. 263 (1451); *CCR, 1454-61*, p. 58 (1455); *CPR, 1452-61*, pp. 474-75 (1458). Moss, 'Economic Development', p. 112. The terrier is London Borough of Haringey, Bruce Castle Collection, M.R. 75. It is discussed in Douglas Moss and Ian Murray, 'A Fifteenth-Century Middlesex Terrier', *Transactions of the London and Middlesex Archaeological Society*, 25 (1974), pp. 285-94.

[38] For the grant to Richard Turnaunt and his wife Joan, daughter of John Stokton, Mayor of London, dated 17 August 1462, *CCR, 1461-68*, pp. 118-19. Richard and Joan had to sue her father (PRO, C 1/28/50) and received a quitclaim from him 24 March 1464 (*CCR, 1461-68*, p. 241).

[39] For Sir John Risley, see J. Wedgewood, *History of Parliament*, 2 vols (London 1936), i, pp. 717-18. Roger Virgoe's recent work on him has illuminated much Turnaunt history: 'Sir John Risley (1443-1512), Courtier and Councillor', *Norfolk Archaeology*, 38 (1982), pp. 140-48. For instance Virgoe notes that when her father Richard Turnaunt died in 1486 Thomasina was twenty-

continued

In 1512, failing direct heirs, the lands escheated to the crown. The family of John Gedney had held the manor since about 1427, approximately eighty-five years. In this narrative of determined entrepreneurship we may recognise not only Gedney's administrative skill but also the role played by Joan Large's broken vow, her marriage to Gedney, and her own decade-long effort in the 1450s to acquire Tottenham for herself and her own descendants.

During the years of her final widowhood, two further examples demonstrate the extent of her wealth. She was one of a group of distinguished people, including the archbishop of Canterbury, to whom a royal loan was repaid in 1451: in her case the amount was £200. In the year of her death, 1462, she was receiving annual payments on a large debt of £236, money owed her originally by Thomas Eyre, probably the husband of Large's daughter Elizabeth.[40]

In her will, which left over £500 in money bequests, she remembered particularly her only grandchild, the two-year-old heiress Thomasina, who on her marriage was to receive 600 marks, half Joan's jewelry and napery, and other valuables. She directed her son to give security for these in the mayor's court (as she herself had done for the patrimony of Large's sons). The same tendency which Alice Brice's will shows to control legatees' behaviour through gifts is illustrated in Joan's stipulation that if Thomasina married against her advisers' wishes she should receive only as much of her legacies as father and advisers thought appropriate, the rest to be disposed in pious works.

Joan Gedney requested burial in St Christopher le Stocks with her last husband. She designated 100 marks for a priest to pray for her soul and those of her first three husbands, for ten years. Interestingly, her tenement 'le ledenporche' which fronted on Threadneedle Street, was next to the tenement of an earlier vowess, Margery de Nerford (d. 1417), also a parishioner of St Christopher's.[41]

continued

six; hence at her grandmother's death she would have been only two. Virgoe discovered that Thomasina was alive in 1505, dead by 1507. Risley, seventeen years older than she, died in 1512. Thomasina had been first married to Richard Charlton, probably the son of their Tottenham neighbour Sir Thomas Charlton. *The History and Antiquities of the Parish of Tottenham*, H.G. Oldfield and R.R. Dyson (London, 1790), p. 47. In 1474 Risley and Thomasina, then fourteen, sued Charlton for return of Joan Gedney's bequests, conferred at the marriage. Particularly mentioned, both in suit and will, was a covered cup of Paris gold weighing 26 ounces, worth over £47. (PRO, C 1/66/286-87). The accompanying list of gifts Richard Turnaunt gave Thomasina at her wedding includes a woman's saddle covered with red velvet and harnessed with copper and gilt, price £5. Acknowledgement of Joan Gedney's role in acquisition of the Middlesex lands appears in *CPR, 1485-94*, pp. 228-29.

[40] *CPR, 1446-52*, p. 452. The suit for debt, PRO, C 1/29/455, offers a personal glimpse of Joan as the debtors, Richard Quatermayns and William Hampton, who assumed the debt of Thomas Eyre, visited her at Candlemas 1462 and were told the document was with one of her servants 'not then present'. She died probably at the beginning of July.

[41] Joan Gedney's will is GL, MS 9171/5, f. 326v, made 28 June, proved 10 July 1462. In it the Tottenham lands are referred to as 'Herber', the name of a section of them sometimes used for the whole. For locations of both tenements, Margery de Nerford's 'Worm on the Hoop' and Joan Gedney's 'Le Ledenporche', see H.L. Hopkinson, 'Ancient Bradestrete Identical with Threadneedle Street', *London Topographical Record*, 13 (1923), pp. 23-28.

The career of Alice Brice, widow and 'avowes' as she calls herself in her 1499 will,[42] although less sensational resembles Joan Gedney's at some points. She married three times, the last time to London sheriff Henry Brice, and was firmly situated in this upper-class world. Her first husband Roger Steynour is known only from mention in her will, but her second, John Crichefeld, was a skinner who died in 1454.[43] By Crichefeld, to whom she was married at least by 1445, she had two children. Her son John Crichefeld was renter warden of the Goldsmiths' Company in 1486/87 and died in that year, making her his sole executor. The language of his will is perhaps uncharacteristically intimate. After a very few bequests he leaves the residue of his estate to 'Dame Alice Brice my mother of whom I had the substance of my goods and my upmaking', and he asks that she dispose of his goods in works of charity and mercy 'as she would that I would do for her in like case'.[44] This latter formulation is frequently found, but 'upmaking' is an unusual word for which *O.E.D.* gives only physical examples from the construction trades. By analogy, John Criche-feld seems here to recognise his mother's nurturing role in his own formation.

Alice Brice's relation with her other Crichefeld child, her daughter Alice, provides some insights into female religious life at the end of the fifteenth century. In her will the vowess leaves a silver and parcel gilt basin valued at £5 to Halliwell nunnery 'where my daughter Alice is a nun professed', if the prioress and convent there 'suffer my said daughter Alice to have the reason-able occupation of the said basin as long as she shall live and be abiding within the said place'. Alice Crichefeld had been at Halliwell at least since 1462, in which year, aged fifteen and a half, she and prioress Joan Sevenok appeared before the mayor's court in the Guildhall to acknowledge receipt of Alice's patrimony.[45] Hence Alice's birthdate was 1446; in the year of her mother's will, 1499, she would have been fifty-three. The conditional nature of her mother's bequests, in consequence, is somewhat surprising. The will mentions 'certain plate which she [Alice Crichefeld] hath of mine in keeping' which is now given to her outright 'as long as she dwells in the said place'. If she leaves Halliwell, the plate is designated for Alice Brice's other daughter, Joan. Again, all the mother's lands and tenements in the parish of St Nicholas Acon

---

[42] PRO, PROB 11/11, f. 238r–v, made 15 February, proved 4 March 1499.

[43] His will, PRO, PROB 11/1, f. 86v, names as executors his wife Alice and John Cole, who was later to hold the office of King's Skinner beginning in 1461; see Elspeth M. Veale, *The English Fur Trade in the Later Middle Ages* (Oxford, 1966), p. 207. That Crichefeld was young is suggested by the rather modest amounts (£10 each) which he left his two children, but he employed the standard form, specifying that the £20 should remain with Cole 'under sufficient surety as the manner and form is for the ward of orphans'.

[44] PRO, PROB 11/8, f. 79Ar–v, made 29 September, proved 8 October 1487. At some point, probably between 1483 and 1485, John Crichefeld brought an action of trespass against Alice, wife of John King, grocer, for complaining to the chamberlains of London about his treatment of her son, his apprentice (PRO, C 1/66/215).

[45] Although *LBL* in 1462 calls her 'a nun of Halliwell' (p. 8), she is listed as a novice in the prioress's election of 1472, at which time she would have been twenty-six (GL, MS 9531/7, f. 5v, Register Thomas Kempe 1450-89). Seven nuns and ten novices were present.

are to go to Joan on condition that she pay yearly to Alice 53s. 4d. (13s. 4d quarterly) as long as Alice remains at Halliwell. Should she leave, her annual income would be reducèd by half. Much as we would like to know whether this method of financial control succeeded, the next prioress was not elected until 1534, when Alice Crichefeld's name does not appear.

The vowess's ability to act within the legal system, suggested by her probable role in paying her daughter Alice's patrimony, is witnessed by the record of a chancery suit in which she appears between 1475 and 1485. Two complainants state they agreed to purchase from Alice Brice three pieces of broad cloth, price £21, though the 'acqueyntance' of Sir Hugh Montague, chaplain. Though they assert they paid the debt, part to Alice and part to Sir Hugh, the latter had fled the country 'for diuers faults' and Alice was suing them in the mayor's court for the whole sum.[46]

This wealthy vowess thus maintained some involvement in trade. Her third husband's civic career had been cut short by his death in 1467 while serving as sheriff; he left her £1,000 in his will and his (or their) children Henry and Joan Brice received £500 and 500 marks respectively.[47] The son is not mentioned in Alice Brice's will but, like her half-sister Alice Crichefeld, Joan appears in her mother's will in a fashion remarkably personal.

After specifying the usual honest priest who will pray for her soul (in this case for three years at a salary of ten marks a year), Alice Brice continues: 'And I will that the said priest shall be attending upon my son in law Henry Kebell and my daughter Johane his wife upon their reasonable desire when they ride or go on pilgrimage or into the country upon their sporting or my daughter lying in childbed and other times convenient'. She adds: 'the said priest always praying for my soul and other souls aforesaid'.

That this attempt to bequeath services was not peculiar to Alice Brice is shown by the 1488 London will of Richard Gardener, who stipulates 'prouided allwey that if my seid wyfe for a monith or ij in the yere be owte of the Cite of London That than if she wyll the seid priest assigned to syng In the church of seint Bartholomew aforesaid shall awayte/vpon hyr for the seid tyme/Soo alweys that he pray and syng for my sowle and other sowles aforseid . . .'[48] In

---

[46] PRO, C 1/64/962. Alice told Sir Hugh she had 'noo trust nor confidence' in the two complainants and refused to make an obligation with them directly, insisting that Sir Hugh also be involved.

[47] For Brice's career, Beaven *Aldermen*, ii, p. xxxix; Thrupp, *Merchant Class*, p. 326, under Hugh Brice. His will is PRO, PROB 11/5, f. 153v-154v.

[48] See Kristine G. Bradberry, 'The World of Etheldreda Gardener', *The Ricardian*, 9 (1991), pp. 146-53, esp. p. 14. Richard Gardener's will reference, PRO, PROB 11/8, f. 277-280v, comes from Caroline Barron. Perhaps Gardener's and Brice's wills should be compared with other wills which stipulate that their chantry priests shall assist with parish work and services, thus enriching and diversifying parish religious life, though they nevertheless suggest the perception that chantry priests had considerable unoccupied time.

Since Joan Brice Kebell was born before 1467, when she was mentioned in her father's will, she must in 1499 have been at least thirty-two (probably slightly older), so childbirth would certainly have been a possibility.

thus disposing their clerical employees' time both Richard Gardener and Alice Brice were pursuing traditional testamentary aims: to protect and serve those left behind.

Henry Kebell's career was a flourishing one: lieutenant of the staple of Calais in 1485, elected four times as master of the Grocers' Company beginning in 1502, alderman continuously for fifteen years beginning in that year, sheriff in 1502-03, and mayor in 1510-11.[49] The wealth displayed in his 1517 will (PCC 30 Holder) which lists properties in Warwickshire, Northamptonshire, Kent and Oxfordshire, recalls Alice Brice's provision for him and her daughter Joan 'when they ride . . . into the country upon their sporting'. Kebell's magnificence is remembered particularly through his £1,000 gift for the rebuilding of St Mary Aldermary, although Stow notes that his bones were not allowed to rest there but were moved in 1545 to make room for two later mayors.[50]

The vowed life was familiar at the highest level of London's mercantile elite. Though all these women were connected with wealthy cloth-trade merchants,[51] perhaps particular guild membership is less important than the level of economic activity it reveals. No characteristic pattern emerges in the relation of marriage and vow. Alice Lynne married once, took the vow in response to her husband's initiative, and lived as a vowess for almost all her adult life – nearly sixty years. Joan Gedney married four times but vowed after her third marriage. Her tenure as a vowess was about three years, after which she spent about five more years as a wife and thirteen as a widow. Alice Brice married three times, vowed sometime after her last husband's death and lived the rest of her life, probably for over thirty years under the vow.

The lives of these women do not allow us to glimpse a particular spirituality. To some extent we may blame the legal and financial nature of the surviving records, though on the other hand the language of their wills and the nature of their bequests do not illustrate the fervent piety which such documents sometimes reveal.

Other contemporary London vowesses differ from them in this respect. Margery de Nerford, for instance, who died in 1417 and whose origins were

---

[49] Alison Hanham, *The Celys and their World* (Cambridge, 1985), p. 241. Beaven, *Aldermen*, ii, pp. 20, 168. *List of the Wardens of the Grocers' Company from 1345 to 1907* (London, 1907), pp. 15-16, and T.F. Reddaway, *The Early History of the Goldsmiths' Company, 1327-1509* (London, 1975), p. 339.

[50] Stow, *Survey*, i, p. 253, cited in Beaven, *Aldermen*, ii, p. 168. A sixteenth-century St Mary Aldermary verse epitaph for Kebell is printed by Baron Heath, *Some Account of the Worshipful Company of Grocers of the City of London* (London, 1869), pp. 238-40. His executors included John Colet (who also served as overseer for Beatrice Cornburgh) and Sir Henry Wyat, perhaps the father of the poet.

[51] William Lynne, woolman and grocer; Richard Turnaunt, fuller; Robert Large, mercer; John Gedney, draper; John Crichefeld, skinner; Henry Brice, fuller. In addition son-in-law Henry Kebell, though a grocer, was a merchant of the staple of Calais, as also William Lynne probably was.

somewhat more aristocratic, had a private chapel with several sets of vestments, plate and service books. During her lifetime she had commissioned a chapel in St Christopher's and in her will she expressed the wish to be buried in this chapel where she was accustomed to sit in front of the image of the Virgin.[52] Emma Cheyne and her husband William separated, he to live as a recluse at Bury St Edmund, she to become the anchoress of St Peter Cornhill. In 1449 she was described as being 'professed for twenty-two years in the order of widowhood'.[53]

Such ardent spirituality is nowhere in evidence here. Rather what is illustrated is the continuance of an active life as an economic agent. These women share familiarity with the legal system, and particularly with the London courts: Alice Lynne and Joan Gedney and Alice Brice all safeguarded their childrens', step-childrens' or grandchildrens' inheritances through the mayor's court. In addition Alice Lynne used this court to litigate for money belonging to her son John,[54] while Alice Brice employed it in a trade dispute.

In addition all continued to work, to some extent, in the world of money. Alice Lynne received her annual tronage fees, Alice Brice dealt in cloth (to how large an extent it is impossible to say), while Joan Gedney, perhaps at a higher level than either, lent money and accumulated land. Such mercantile activity seems to preclude a spiritual impetus as primary.

What then impelled these women? Despite its spiritual form, the vow might be seen as itself an element in a mercantile exchange. In some cases – certainly not in all – the woman who took the vow traded the sexual and economic possibilities inherent in future marriage for a clearly-defined present economic good. In vowing, the woman not only made a public promise to the representative of the institutional church, but a private one, by implication, to her dead husband. In return for what seems, usually, considerable economic support, she promised stasis, the absence of unsettling change – a kind of personal, rather than legal, mortmain, in which the husband's 'dead hand' continued to exert its grip.

The vow of course was not only an economic bargain but also an emotional response and a religious statement. If Alice Lynne and Joan Gedney vowed in response to financial coercion, Alice Brice, in her impenetrability, makes us acknowledge the complexity of motive which must have figured in every such decision. Nevertheless, if a vowed spirituality can be traced in some women's

---

[52] Margery de Nerford's will is printed in Edwin Freshfield, ed., *Wills, Leases and Memoranda in the Book of Records of the Parish of St Christopher le Stocks* (London, 1895), pp. 8-9, from GL, MS 4424.

[53] For Emma Cheyne, see *CPR, 1446-52*, p. 304. The record of her husband's enclosure can be found in BL, MS Add. 14848, f. 79v, the register of William Curteys, abbot of Bury St Edmund. It is dated 6 March 'MCCCC vicesimo nono', i.e. 1430.

[54] *CPMR, 1437-57*, pp. 39-40.

lives, it is not visible here. Instead these three well-connected, propertied women allow us to view female manipulation of legal, ecclesiastic and economic counters in an elevated urban setting.

Table 5

Some London Vowed Women 1367–1537

6 Jan. 1367	Elizabeth Talleworth, widow. Vowed before Simon Langham, archbishop of Canterbury, in chapel at Lambeth. A.C. Wood, ed., *Registrum Simonis de Langham* (Oxford, 1956), p. 144.
Before 7 July 1376	Margery, widow of Thomas Broun. CLRO, HR 109 (89), her will.
18 Oct. 1379	Isabel, widow of Thomas Burgh. Form in English; Isabel, widow of John Golafre, 'chivaler'. Form in French. Vowed before William Wykeham, bishop of Winchester, in chapel of his manor of Southwark. T.F. Kirby, ed., *Wykeham's Register*, 2 vols (London, 1896–99), ii, pp. 307–8.
4 May 1383	Margery de Nerford. Form in French. Vowed before Robert de Braybrooke, bishop of London, in chapel of bishop's palace. GL, MS 9531/3, f. 325v.
Week after Palm Sunday, 1387	Margery Ittelcote, widow. GL, MS 9531/3, f. 334v.
16 Jan. 1396	Katherine Brokas, widow of London. Form in French. Anchoress. Vowed before Edmund Stafford, bishop of Exeter, in chapel of his London house. F.C. Hingeston-Randolph, ed., *Register of Edmund Stafford* (London, 1886), p. 39.
26 Aug. 1397	Margaret, widow of Adam Bamme, mayor of London. GL, MS 9531/3, f. 346v.
6 Oct. 1401	Alice Carlill, widow. GL, MS 9531/3, f. 352v.
9 April 1407	Elizabeth Willford, *vidua.* In 1412 lay subsidy, see below, husband, Thomas Welford. Vowed before Nicholas Bubwith, bishop of London, in chapel of manor of Fulham. GL, MS 9531/4, f. 14v.
26 June 1407	Alice Langhorne, widow. Form in English. Vowed before Nicholas Bubwith, bishop of London, in chapel of his dwelling in St Clement Danes. GL, MS 9531/4, f. 14v.
1 Nov. 1416	Isabella, widow of Thomas Bridlyngton. Commission to suffragan to receive vow. E.F. Jacob, ed., *Register of Henry Chichele*, 4 vols (Oxford, 1937–47), iv, p. 38.
19 Feb. 1418	Lady Alice Salvan. Letter of Henry Ware, vicar general of bishop of London, allowing Thomas Langley, bishop of Durham, to receive vow in London diocese. *Testamenta Eboracensia,* iii, p. 323: 'Salvin'.

31 Oct. 1421	Alice, widow of William Lynne. Form in English. Vowed before Henry Chichele, archbishop of Centerbury, in chapel of the manor of Lambeth. *Register Henry Chichele*, iv, p. 221.
1427	Emma Cheyne, anchoress of St Peter Cornhill, wife of William Cheyne, recluse of Bury St Edmunds. *CPR, 1446–52*, p. 304. 'Professed for twenty-two years in order of widowhood' in 1449.
Between 12 April 1441 and 13 August 1442	Joan, widow of Robert Large, mayor of London. Stow, *Survey*, i, p. 186; Bodleian Library, Digby Roll 2.
Between 20 June 1467 and 1499	Alice, widow of Henry Brice, sheriff of London. PRO, PROB 11/11, f. 238r–v, her will.
8 Feb. 1473, date of will	Katherine Rippelingham, 'Videwe Advowes', widow of William Southcote. PRO, PROB 11/6, ff. 116v–117, her will.
Between 4 Oct. and 21 Dec. 1477	Margaret, widow of John Croke. *Stonor Letters*, ii, p. 28.
28 March 1482	Joan, widow of Robert Byfeld, ironmonger, sheriff of London. PRO, PROB 11/7, ff. 36v–39v, his will; PROB 11/9, ff. 166–167v, her will; *Cely Letters*, no. 147.
1499	Margaret Beaufort, countess of Richmond and Derby. C.H. Cooper, *The Lady Margaret* (Cambridge, 1874), pp. 97–98.
Before 23 April 1510	Kathryn, widow of Henry Langley, esq. GL, MS 9531/9, ff. viii–x (third series).
13 July 1511	Katherine, countess of Devon, widow of William Courtenay, earl of Devon. Vowed before Richard Fitzjames, bishop of London. GL, MS 9531/9, f. 30v.
2 Dec. 1537	Margaret Raynkynne, widow. Previous tenant, lease in parish of St Helen Bishopsgate, London. PRO, E303/8/16.

I am indebted to Caroline Barron for the names of Elizabeth Willford and Alice Langhorne; to Catherine Paxton for Margaret Raynkynne; to Carole Rawcliffe for Margaret Bamme; to Kay Lacey for Margaret Croke.

Margery de Nerford, Alice Carlill, Elizabeth Willford (or Welford) and Alice Langhorne all appear in the 1412 London lay subsidy list, where their annual incomes are given, respectively, as £6; £5 6s. 8d.; £44 9s. 11d.; and £13 18s. 0d., J.C.L. Stahlschmidt, 'London Subsidy temp. Henry IV', *Archaeological Journal*, 44 (1887), pp. 56–82, ref. p. 64. In the subsidy of 1436 (Thrupp, *Merchant Class*, p. 385), Alice Carlill, £5 6s. 8d.; Elizabeth Wellford, £60; Alice Lynne, £43.

2. The door of the Grammar School at Week St Mary, Cornwall, founded by Dame Thomasine Percyvale, 1508. (*Woolf/Greenham Collection*)

13

Dame Thomasine Percyvale, 'The Maid of Week' (d.1512)

Matthew Davies

The activities and achievements of wealthy urban widows were frequently remarkable, and often left a lasting impression upon the collective memory and indeed the physical fabric of the urban community in the middle ages, an impression which was often as durable as that made by prominent men. The subject of this essay is one such widow, Thomasine Percyvale, who after marrying three husbands, all members of the Tailors' Company of London, continued to play an active role in civic life and founded a free grammar school in the parish of her birth, Week St Mary in Cornwall, before her death in 1512. Richard Carew's remarkable account of her life, contained in his *Survey of Cornwall*, first published in 1602, is the starting-point of this inquiry: as a piece of evidence it can be tested against the surviving sources for her life, including her will and those of her three husbands as well as records concerning the foundation of her school.[1]

S. Marie Wilke
This village was the birth-place of Thomasine Bonaventure, I Know not, whether by descet, or event so called: for whils in her girlish age she kept sheepe on the fore-remembered moore, it chanced, that a London marchant passing by, saw her, heeded her, liked her, begged herof her poore parents, and carried her to his home. In passage of time, her mistres was summoned by death to appeare in the other world, and her good thewes, no less than her seemely personage, so much contented her master, that he advanced her from a servant to a wife, and left her a wealthy widdow. Her second marriage befell with one Henry Galle; her third and last with Sir John Percival, Lord Maior of London, whom she also overlived. And to shew, that vertue as well bare a part in the desert, a fortune in the meanes of her preferment she employed the whole residue of her life and last widdowhood, to works no lesse bountiful than charitable: namely, repayring of high waies, building of bridges,

[1] I am grateful to Caroline Barron for reading and commenting upon earlier drafts of this essay, and for her valuable suggestions on a number of points. The careers of Thomasine and her three husbands are considered below with reference to their wills, the records of the Merchant Taylors' Company and the excellent accounts of the foundation of Thomasine's school written by P.L. Hull, 'The Endowment and Foundation of a Grammar School at Week St Mary by Dame Thomasine Percyvale', *Journal of the Royal Institution of Cornwall*, new series, 7 (1973), pp. 21-55, and by Nicholas Orme in his *Education in the West of England, 1066-1548* (Exeter, 1976), pp. 173-82.

endowing of maydens, relieving of prisoners, feeding and apparreling the poore &c. Amongst the rest, at this S. Mary Wike, she founded a chauntery and free-schoole, together with faire lodgings, for the schoolemasters, schollers and officers, and added twenty pounde of yeerely revenue, for supporting the incident charges: wherein as the best of her desire was holy, so God blessed the same with al wished success, for divers the best gent. sonnes of Devon and Cornwall were there vertuously trained up in both kinds of divine and humane learning, under one Cholwell, an honest and religious teacher which caused the neighbours so much the rather and the more to rewe, that a petty smacke onely of Popery, opened a gap to the oppression of the whole by the statute made in Edw. the 6 raigne touching the suppression of chaunteries.[2]

Yet Carew's account is also important in another sense, that of its role as the progenitor of a legend, comparable in many ways to that which developed around the person of the three-times mayor of London, Richard Whittington.[3] The similarities are marked: both were supposedly poor immigrants who 'made their fortunes', one through commerce, the other through marriage, culminating in the achievement of mayoral status. Furthermore, both were to leave their mark through charitable activity, Whittington through his foundation of a college for priests and an almshouse, and Thomasine through her foundation of a grammar school in the parish of her birth. Perhaps the main difference is that Thomasine was 'rescued' from poverty as a result of the favourable impression made by her 'seemly personage' on a visitor to her parish, whereas the Whittington of legend made his own way to the capital, and was subsequently befriended by a cat.[4] Subsequent accounts of Thomasine's life, produced by Cornish antiquarians in the nineteenth century, contain marvellously fanciful descriptions of her meeting with a 'tall and portly merchant', with 'a broad beaver, or as it was then called, a Flanders hat, shading a grave and thoughtful countenance, wherein shrewdness and good humour prevailed'.[5] The heroine, 'a damsel in the blossom of youth', stood leaning on her shepherd's staff on a 'green and rushy knoll', and her Celtic origins are emphasised by 'her eyes of violet-blue and abundant hair of rich and radiant brown'. By contrast, her dwelling-place is described in unflattering terms, 'all within and without bespoke extreme poverty and want', exaggerating the contrast between her humble origins and the physical and moral qualities which so attracted the visiting merchant and induced him to persuade her parents to allow him to take her back to London as his servant. The

[2] Richard Carew, *The Survey of Cornwall* (1602), ff. 119-119b.

[3] See Caroline M. Barron, 'Richard Whittington: The Man behind the Myth', in *Studies in London History Presented to P.E. Jones*, ed. A.E.J. Hollaender and W. Kellaway (London, 1969), pp. 197-250.

[4] A seventeenth-century invention, ibid., pp. 197-98.

[5] R.S. Hawker, *Footprints of Former Men in Far Cornwall*, ed. C.E. Byles (London, 1903), p. 141. Other 'Former Men' include 'The Botothen Ghost' and 'Antony Payne, a Cornish Giant'. From this description it would seem that Chaucer's merchant, with his 'Flaundryssh bever hat' was Hawker's model for Thomasine's suitor: 'General Prologue', line 272, *The Canterbury Tales*, ed. F.N. Robinson (Oxford, 1948).

ascription, by Carew, of the surname 'Bonaventure' to Thomasine and her parents could scarcely be more appropriate in view of what was to come.[6]

How accurate is the legend as described by Carew and his successors? Before considering the details of Thomasine's life it is important to consider the evidence for her origins, and the manner of her departure for London, the common themes which run through the accounts of her life. First, it is clear that her family name was indeed Bonaventure. In the second of her wills, dated 26 March 1512, she mentions a brother, John Bonaventure, as well as her parents, John and Joan.[7] Thomasine's origins, like those of Whittington, were in fact far from humble. Little is known of her father, but on her mother's side Thomasine was certainly well connected, her mother and aunt in fact being the heiresses of a John Westlake, a man of armigerous status.[8] The will of another of Thomasine's brothers, Richard Bonaventure, proved in 1499, sheds further light on her family, indicating that she had at least two sisters, Margaret and Alice, as well as her brothers, Richard and John.[9] Richard can probably be identified as the Oxford graduate of the same name listed as a canon of Chichester and prebendary of Mardon from 1478, who became rector of Stisted in Essex and Herne in Kent.[10] From 1463 until his death, Richard was also rector of the parish church of Chelsfield in Kent and it is possible that one of his duties as rector may have been the burial of his own parents: the many donations made by Thomasine in her will of 1512 included a cope, vestments, a chalice and a mass book to the value of £20 to be given to the church at Chelsfield 'whereas my fader and moder lieth buried'.[11] John and Joan Bonaventure had evidently kept in touch with their children, and may even have followed Richard to Kent to live out their last years close to both son and daughter. Thomasine's will reveals the affection which she evidently still felt towards her own family, over fifty years after she left Cornwall.

John Bonaventure, Thomasine's other brother, appears to have been the eldest son. He remained in Cornwall and is almost certainly to be identified as the John Bonaventure who was chosen mayor of Launceston in 1512.[12] The Bonaventures were also connected to an important Devonshire family, the Dinhams of Lifton. This connection was established by the marriage of Thomasine's maternal aunt, Elizabeth Westlake, to Nicholas Dinham and was

[6] Hawker, *Footprints of Former Men*, pp. 139-58.
[7] PRO, PROB 11/17, ff. 218-220.
[8] Barron, 'Whittington', pp. 197-99; Hull, 'Endowment of a Grammar School', pp. 37-39.
[9] PRO, PROB 11/11, ff. 318v-319. Thomasine's third husband, John Percyvale, is named as the overseer of the will in which Thomasine herself was bequeathed 'my best pair of shetis'.
[10] Emden, *BRUO*, i, p. 216.
[11] Richard asked to be buried 'in the body of the church of Chellifeld before the crucifix', PRO, PROB 11/11, ff. 318v-319; Hull, 'Endowment of a Grammar School', p. 37; PROB 11/17, f. 220v (codicil of same date as will).
[12] John Bonaventure of Knoll in the parish of Week St Mary is listed as one of the witnesses to a deed of 1506, forming part of the process of the foundation of Thomasine's school, Hull, 'Endowment of a Grammar School', p. 26; ibid., p. 37.

strengthened subsequently by the marriage of Thomasine's niece Margery, daughter of her sister Margaret, to John Dinham, son of Nicholas, Thomasine's cousin.[13] As will be shown, the foundation of Thomasine's school owed much to the strength of her ties with her family. In her will of 1512 Thomasine left John Dinham the residue of her estate and made him responsible for the final arrangements for the establishment of her school and other complex *post obit* arrangements.[14] Thomasine's widowhood was evidently a period during which her gentle origins became an asset, despite the wealth she had accumulated as the wife of an important London citizen.

It is possible now to place Thomasine's journey to London in context. The fact that her origins were not as humble as Carew supposed makes the scenario he suggested, whereby she came to London as a servant, equally if not more likely. As Dr Goldberg has shown, women in northern Europe tended to marry later, around their middle twenties in the case of urban women, frequently after undertaking a period of service or an apprenticeship. Surviving wills often include bequests of bedding and other household items to female servants, as if anticipating their marriages and the establishment of households of their own. Thomasine herself was particularly generous to her female servants: Margaret Lawson, for instance, received bequests amounting to £33 6s. 8d.[15] It is entirely possible that Thomasine came to London as a servant before marrying for the first time.

We know from the fortunate survival of the wills of Thomasine's husbands that all three were London tailors, and that Henry Galle, noted by Carew as her second husband, was in fact her first.[16] As far as the circumstances of her meeting with her future husband are concerned, there is nothing implausible about the notion of a London tailor such as Galle travelling to Cornwall on business. The evidence from the pardons for outlawry contained in the patent rolls suggests that London tailors in the fifteenth century had wide-ranging business contacts outside London. In all, 175 cases of debts owed to tailors are recorded between 1400 and 1500, of which ninety-eight involved individuals of gentry rank or above. Moreover, the geographical distribution of the gentry cases shows that the south west as a whole was particularly well represented, accounting for twenty-five of the cases. Remarkably, twelve of these involved

---

[13] Hull, 'Endowment of a Grammar School', pp. 37-39 and Orme, *Education in the West of England*, p. 173. John Dinham was one of four sons of Nicholas Dinham and Elizabeth Westlake (Thomasine's aunt).

[14] PRO, PROB 11/17, ff. 220, 221.

[15] P.J.P. Goldberg, 'Marriage, Migration and Servanthood: The York Cause Paper Evidence', in *Woman is a Worthy Wight: Women in English Society, c. 1200-1500*, ed. P.J.P. Goldberg (Gloucester, 1992), pp. 1-15. In Mediterranean Europe women frequently married earlier, and service was viewed as an occupation associated with low status; PRO, PROB 11/17, ff. 219v, 221.

[16] Unfortunately, the illegibility of much of the first page of Galle's will, proved on 7 April 1466, makes it difficult to say whether or not Thomasine was in fact his second wife, as Carew suggested, GL, MS 9171/6, f. 1r-v (commissary court of London).

Cornish gentry.[17] Henry Galle himself was not among those pursuing debts and, as will be shown, his business activities were centred upon a different part of the country. This does not of course rule out the possibility that Galle did indeed meet his future wife while in Cornwall, taking her back to London with him as a servant. The available evidence, however, points to a more subtle variation of Carew's story, involving yet another London tailor as well as Thomasine's clerical brother, Richard Bonaventure.

Richard, who was beginning his ministry in Kent in the early 1460s, had at some stage entered into a friendship with Richard Nordon, a prominent tailor and one time sheriff of London.[18] Nordon, like several of his fellow tailors, had established strong trading links with the south west, particularly Devon and Cornwall, before his death in the early 1460s.[19] His executors included Bonaventure and John Markwyck 'clerk' and, soon after Nordon's death, the two men attempted to recover debts owed to him, including one of £4 11d. owed by the vicar of Lanreath in Cornwall.[20] Thomasine herself knew Markwyck and Nordon well: Markwyck was subsequently chosen alongside Bonaventure to assist her in carrying out the last wishes of Thomasine's second husband, Thomas Barnaby. Forty years later both Markwyck and Nordon were listed among those to be remembered in the prayers of the priest and scholars of her new school.[21] It seems reasonable to suggest that Thomasine came to London as a result of her brother's connections with Nordon, and that her good fortune began with a period of service in the latter's household, before his death in 1463-64 left her free to proceed to the first of her marriages.

The earliest firm evidence for Thomasine's life as a Londoner is as the wife, first of Henry Galle (d.1466) and secondly of Thomas Barnaby (d.1467), both tailors and both parishioners of the church of St Dunstan in the West in Fleet

---

[17] *CPR, 1399-1509*, passim. A high proportion of these cases were doubtless the result of the trading activities of the London tailors. This was not confined solely to the production and sale of items of clothing: several prominent tailors can be found supplying cloth, most notably to the great wardrobe, in the fifteenth century. William Tropenell, for example, was tailor to Henry V, but can also be found elsewhere in the accounts of the great wardrobe as a 'pannarius', supplying large amounts of cloth alongside Robert Fenescales another prominent tailor/draper: PRO, E 101/407/1, f. 3 (1422-23).

[18] Nordon was chosen as master of the London tailors in 1422, and was elected sheriff in 1442, see C.M. Clode, *The Early History of the Guild of Merchant Taylors of the Fraternity of St John the Baptist, London, with Notices of the Lives of Some of its Eminent Members*, 2 vols, (privately printed, London, 1888), ii, p. 337; *LBK*, p. 274.

[19] *CPR, 1429-36*, pp. 310, 430 (both involving Gloucestershire gentlemen); *1436-41*, pp. 5 (gentlemen of Cambridgeshire), 6 (unknown), 10 (clerk of Devon), 13 (gentlemen of Cornwall), 103 (two Cornishmen), 216 (gentleman of Cornwall); *1452-61*, p. 131 (esquire of Devon). Nordon's increasing involvement in Devon and Cornwall is illustrated by a dispute with another Devonshire esquire over cloth worth £20 1s. 6d. (*c.* 1455), PRO, C 1/18/61.

[20] *CPR, 1461-67*, p. 317 (3 Nov. 1464); *1467-77*, pp. 3-4 (3 July 1467).

[21] GL, MS 9171/6, ff. 31v-32; Hull, 'Endowment of a Grammar School', p. 44 (the foundation deed dated 10 July 1506); *CPR, 1494-1509*, p. 604 (mortmain licence dated 6 November 1508).

Street.[22] The parish itself provided what was in many ways the ideal social context for Thomasine's early years in the capital, and in particular as the wife of three London tailors. The evidence from the surviving fifteenth century wills of London tailors suggests that a remarkable number of wealthy members of the craft lived in the parish of St Dunstan's or in the neighbouring parish of St Bride's Fleet Street.[23] These included nine men who at some point in their careers attained the office of master of the craft, one of whom, William Galle, was Thomasine's brother-in-law by her first marriage.[24] Such a concentration was doubtless encouraged by the profusion of wealthy potential customers in the area; the admission to the tailors' fraternity, dedicated to St John the Baptist, of high-ranking clergymen with large town houses along Fleet Street, may well have been a product of the strong relations built up between the craft, the parish and its important residents.[25] The parish of St Dunstan itself also had strong links with the tailors' fraternity, with three rectors of the parish admitted as brothers between 1435 and 1443.[26]

---

[22] Their wills were both enrolled in the commissary court of London: GL, MS 9171/6, ff. 1-1v (Galle), ff. 31v-32 (Barnaby).

[23] Although tailors were not generally concentrated in any one geographical area of London, these two westernmost parishes appear to have attracted the most successful practitioners of the craft. Sixty-five of 409 tailors whose wills were proved between 1388 and 1512 chose to be buried in the parishes of St Dunstan and St Bride, with forty-three preferring St Dunstan's. References to tenements, membership of fraternities and other inhabitants indicate that the attachment was a real one, PRO, PROB 11/1-11: GL, MS 9171/1-9 (commissary court), GL, MS 9051/1 (arch-deaconry court) and *HW*, ii, passim. For the geographical distribution of tailor taxpayers in the late thirteenth and early fourteenth centuries, see E. Ekwall, *Two Early London Subsidy Rolls* (Lund, 1951).

[24] John de Bury (elected master in 1423), William Chapman (1428), Geoffrey Guybon (1431), Richard Skernyng (1441), William Knotte (1453), William Person (1462), Thomas Burgeys (1467), William Galle (1471), and William Hert (1491). See Clode, *Early History*, ii, pp. 337-38.

[25] Two bishops of Salisbury, Robert Neville and Richard Beauchamp, were admitted in 1436-7 and 1458-9 respectively, with two bishops of Exeter, George Neville and John Booth, becoming members in 1459-60 and 1469-70, Merchant Taylors' Company, Accounts, i (1398-1445), f. 280; ii (1453-1469), ff. 152, 173; iii (1469-1484), f. 6, hereafter referred to as Accounts, i, ii, etc. The original records are kept at Merchant Taylors' Hall, but a microfilm copy is available at Guildhall Library. I am grateful to the Clerk of the Merchant Taylors' Company for the loan of a copy of the microfilms of the accounts and other records of the London tailors. These form the basis of my doctoral thesis on the tailors of London and their guild in the period 1300 to 1500. The tailors possessed perhaps the most successful of the craft fraternities of late-medieval London, admitting over 1,200 non-tailors, including more than 150 clergy, in the period covered by the accounts. Several inns along Fleet Street belonged to prominent clergy, such as the bishops of Exeter, Salisbury and Bath and Wells, see *The British Atlas of Historic Towns*, iii, *The City of London from Prehistoric Times to c. 1520*, ed. M.D. Lobel (Oxford, 1989), maps 1 and 2.

[26] John Wybbe in 1435-36, John Plungar in 1437-38 and George Adyff in 1443-44, Accounts, i, ff. 267, 294, 373. George Adyff was almost certainly related to a tailor, Richard Adyff, who presented his first apprentice in 1458-59, and subsequently went on to join the livery of the craft in 1460-1, ibid., ii, ff. 151, 193v. For Adyff and the other rectors of St Dunstan's see G. Hennessy, *Novum repertorium ecclesiasticum parochiale Londinense* (London, 1898), p. 137.

There is little doubt that for Thomasine the opportunities for the establishment of social contacts during the early years of her life in London were particularly good, not only among members of the craft, but also in the great houses and inns which dominated the topography of the westernmost parishes. Thomasine seems to have become part of a close-knit community centred around St Dunstan's: William Barnaby, brother of Thomasine's second husband, became the apprentice of William Person who, along with John Markwyck, was an executor of the wills of both Henry Galle and Thomas Barnaby.[27] The shortness of Thomasine's first widowhood (Galle's will was proved on 7 April 1466 and Barnaby's was dated 15 March 1467) may owe much to these local craft-based connections. Thomasine may have got to know Thomas Barnaby through this social network; William Person, a successful tailor and former master of the Tailors' Company, appears to have stood at the nexus of these social relations.

In considering the careers of Galle and Barnaby it is clear, judging from the evidence of their wills and the records of the Tailors' Company, that both men, though successful tailors, died when their careers were still at a relatively early stage. Galle, for instance, enrolled his first apprentices, Robert Harryson, Thomas Lassell and Henry Cort, in 1457-58, only ten years before his death. He subsequently presented another six apprentices, the last of whom, Henry Whitefeld, was enrolled in 1465-66. Barnaby too was active in establishing a thriving workshop – he presented six apprentices during his career, beginning in 1455-56 with Richard Barnaby, possibly a younger brother or cousin.[28] Given that the average number of apprentices enrolled by a tailor over the course of a career was of the order of three in the fifteenth century, the activity of both men in a relatively short period of time is significant.[29] In addition, both Galle and Barnaby had been recently admitted to the livery of the craft, the first step along the *cursus honorum* within the Company.[30] We know little of Barnaby's business activities beyond the evidence provided by his will and the records of the London tailors, but there is firm evidence that Galle at least was the owner of a very successful business. The household accounts of Sir John Howard, later duke of Norfolk, indicate that Galle's workshop was the largest single supplier of clothes to Howard and members of his family in the mid 1460s. At one point nine separate orders, totalling just over £6, were

---

[27] Accounts, ii, f. 3v.

[28] Accounts, ii, f. 125 (1457-58). Galle enrolled Richard Smythmede and Richard Jenkinson in 1460-61, Thomas Leven and Thomas Carter in 1462-63, John Ascote in 1464-65 and Henry Whitefeld in 1465-66, ibid., ii, ff. 192v, 227v, 253v, 276v; ibid., ii, f. 62. Barnaby subsequently presented Richard Cuttelford in 1456-57 William Smyth in 1459-60, Edward Bouth in 1462-63, William Dedge in 1465-66 and Thomas Newton in 1466-67, ibid., ii, ff. 99, 172, 227, 276, 293.

[29] William Person, elected master of the craft in 1428, enrolled fifteen apprentices during his career, but that took place over a period of thirty-five years, Accounts, i-iii, passim.

[30] Accounts, ii, ff. 193v, 278.

received and executed by the workshop in less than two years.[31] What is perhaps most significant is that the workshop continued to produce apparel for the Howards after the death of Galle in April 1466. Payments were made instead to 'Herry Galles man' on six occasions between April 1466 and 5 July 1467.[32] The shortness of Thomasine's first widowhood makes it difficult to say whether it was Thomasine herself who kept the business going, but there is every reason to suppose that she was capable of doing so, particularly given the provisions of Galle's own will. Particularly striking is his bequest of £100 worth of cloth from his shop to Thomasine as well as the terms of his apprentices and £100 in cash. This was evidently an attempt to pass on the business to Thomasine, which may well indicate that she had some knowledge of her husband's craft.[33] The will of Thomas Barnaby, proved on 15 March 1467, indicates that Thomasine had successfully carried out the wishes of her first husband, before transferring the business to Barnaby. Henry Whitefeld, originally one of Galle's apprentices, had since gone on to serve Barnaby, who remitted the last six months of his apprenticeship and exhorted his own executors to continue to carry out the 'ultima voluntatem Henrici Galle nuper mariti Thomasine uxoris mei'.[34] The shortness of Thomasine's first widowhood precludes judgement as to her capabilities and success as a businesswoman, but it is clear that Galle's confidence in her ability to ensure the survival of the business was well-founded.

Other aspects of the wills of Galle and Barnaby deserve consideration. In both cases, Thomasine was the sole beneficiary of the residue of their estates, which, insofar as a judgement can be made of wealth from testamentary evidence, were typical of many middle-ranking craftsmen. Barnaby, for instance, was able to provide 30 marks to fund a chantry for three years, either in St Dunstan's or else in the church at Kirton-in-Holland, Lincolnshire, possibly his birthplace. The chaplain was to be a cousin, William Castre.

---

[31] *The Household Books of John Howard, Duke of Norfolk, 1462-1471, 1481-1483*, ed. A. Crawford (Gloucester, 1992), i, p. 299; ii, pp. 321, 356, 375-76, 411-12, 596, 606, 618. The largest commission consisted of eighteen gowns, a hood, and the repair of two more gowns; the cost of this came to £4 11s. 2d., ibid., ii, pp. 411-12.

[32] Ibid., ii, pp. 356, 375-76, 411-12, 596, 606, 618.

[33] GL, MS 9171/6, f. 1. It is important to note that it was the terms of the apprentices which could be bequeathed or even sold, rather than the apprentices themselves. Testamentary bequests of the terms of apprentices were fairly common among craftsmen, but there was a general recognition that widows in particular did not necessarily go on to follow their husbands crafts: in his will proved in 1446 one tailor, William Chapman, left 100s. and the terms of his apprentices to his wife Alice as long as she continued to follow his craft, PRO, PROB 11/3, ff. 240-240v. In the event that she did not, the terms of the apprentices were to be made over to one of Chapman's executors, another tailor, John Gyffard, who was a former apprentice of his who had since established his own business, cf. Accounts, i, ff. 193 (1428-29), 342 (1441-42).

[34] GL, MS 9171/6, ff. 31v-32. Barnaby also remitted one of his own apprentices, William Smyth, the rest of his term, and asked his executors to present Smyth at the city chamber for admission into the freedom of the city.

Barnaby left further bequests to the altars of three parish churches, including St Dunstan's, as well as to two parish fraternities, and both men left 20s. to the tailors' own fraternity.[35] This reinforces the impression of men whose careers were cut off at an early stage, leaving Thomasine a relatively young, if increasingly wealthy, widow. The deaths of two husbands within a year of each other was doubtless perceived as a great misfortune by contemporaries. The claims of writers much later than Carew that both died of the 'sweating sickness' or another plague-like disease should be taken seriously in view of the recently suggested stagnation, or even decline, in London's population during the greater part of the fifteenth century, caused by frequent outbreaks of plague.[36] It is reasonable to assume that many London women in the 1450s and 60s were widowed prematurely as a result of epidemics of one kind or another.

As well as the familial attachments exhibited by both Henry Galle and Thomas Barnaby in their wills, Thomasine's influence and even her personality can be glimpsed in Barnaby's choice of supervisors to oversee the work of his executors. Whereas Galle had appointed two tailors, his brother William and John Stodard, Barnaby opted for his wife's brother, Richard Bonaventure, as well as Philip Stevenson, described as a gentleman but who was probably also a citizen of London.[37] It was perhaps only logical to have the same executors as Galle, given that the administration of the latter's estate was apparently not yet complete, but in the matter of supervisors more freedom was possible. As a result, Barnaby was able to express attachments different from those to his craft and parish already discussed; this focus on Thomasine's family was to surface again in the provisions of her own will.

It is not clear how soon after 1467 Thomasine married her third husband, John Percyvale, another tailor and a future alderman and mayor of London. In

---

[35] GL, MS 9171/6, ff. 31v-32. Galle's will, though badly damaged indicates a similar level of wealth through his bequests to relatives, and to the poor of St Dunstan's parish.

[36] Hawker, *Footprints of Former Men*, pp. 141-56; D. Gilbert, *The Parochial History of Cornwall*, 4 vols (London, 1838), i, p. 133; D. Keene, 'A New Study of London before the Great Fire', *Urban History Yearbook* (1984), pp. 18-19. On the London plagues, see J.M.W. Bean, 'Plague, Population and Economic Decline in England in the Later Middle Ages', *Economic History Review*, 2nd series, 15 (1963), pp. 429-31. Such outbreaks often resulted in apprentices being granted permission by their masters to leave the city and return to their families in the country until the plague abated. A tailor's apprentice, Thomas Bygham, obtained such leave from his master Edward Davy 'in the tyme of pestilence' to return to Hereford 'till it were seassed', PRO, C 1/61/478. This document, a petition submitted to the royal chancery, it not dated, but the tailors records show that Bygham was enrolled as an apprentice by Davy in 1456-57, Accounts, ii, f. 99v.

[37] GL, MS 9171/6, ff. 31v-32. Stevenson appears to have been connected with a number of London citizens in the 1450s and 1460s, *CCR, 1454-1461*, pp. 253, 363, 294, 461; *1461-68*, pp. 62 and 455. For such 'urban gentry' see Rosemary E. Horrox, 'The Urban Gentry in the Fifteenth Century', in *Towns and Townspeople in the Fifteenth Century*, ed. J.A.F. Thomson, (Gloucester, 1988), pp. 22-45 Thrupp, *Merchant Class*, pp. 234-87.

several respects it marked the beginning of a very different phase in her life. In the first place, her life was thereafter centred first upon the parish of St Martin in the Vintry, and then on St Mary Woolnoth: John Percyvale was elected first as alderman of Vintry ward in 1485 and then of Langbourn ward in 1496.[38] Secondly, Percyvale's career pattern differed markedly from that of either Galle or Barnaby. The diversity of his interests was apparent at an early stage through his career as a mayoral official in the early 1460s. This is documented in both the city records and in the records of the Tailors' Company, where he appears as a much valued contact within the city government. In 1460-61, three years after first being appointed to the office of serjeant-at-mace, he was granted a livery suit by the tailors as his predecessor had been.[39] In 1464-65 Percyvale was called upon by the tailors to extricate Henry Clough from Newgate prison after the latter had uttered *verbis inhonestis* to certain members of the Skinners' Company.[40] It is likely that Percyvale's admission to the livery of the craft in 1468-9 was as much a product of his civic prominence as his business activities. This view is strengthened by the fact that, unusually, he did not present his first apprentice until the year after his admission to the livery. This raises some interesting possibilities. We know from Percyvale's will that he was born in Macclesfield in Cheshire, but there is no record in the tailors' accounts of his being bound as an apprentice to a member of the craft.[41] It is conceivable that he was not a tailor by origin or training, but that his contacts with the tailors in the early 1460s encouraged the development of his business affairs in this direction. By 1467 Thomasine was a well-connected widow of two successful tailors, and would have enjoyed the status of a member of the livery of the craft, although she was not admitted in her own right until the mastership of her future husband. It is an attractive scenario, therefore, that Percyvale's admission to the livery and his belated enrolment of apprentices was a product of his marriage to Thomasine, and the taking on of Barnaby's business.

The major landmarks in John Percyvale's career on the civic stage and as a member of the Tailors' Company are clear and well known to historians of city politics in the later fifteenth century. Although we know nothing of him during the 1470s, apart from an apprentice presented in 1471-72, he had advanced sufficiently in the craft to be elected master of the Tailors' Company

[38] Thomasine subsequently came to own properties in both parishes, *HW*, ii, p. 605; Beaven, *Aldermen*, ii, p. 17.

[39] Percyvale was appointed in December 1457, CLRO, Journals 6, f. 188. References to Journals 1-6 were obtained from the card index compiled by Caroline M. Barron which is deposited in the Corporation of London Record Office; Accounts, ii, f. 199. For the role of the mayor's serjeant-at-mace see Betty R. Masters, 'The Mayor's Household before 1600', in *Studies in London History*, ed. Hollaender and Kellaway, pp. 95-114.

[40] *CPMR, 1458-82*; Accounts, ii, f. 261. Percyvale received two payments two years later for his efforts on behalf of two more tailors, John Benet and William Hert, ibid., ii, f. 299v.

[41] PRO, PROB 11/13, ff. 191v-193v.

in 1485, the year in which he also became an alderman.[42] The next year Percyvale was elected as one of the sheriffs, and in 1487 was knighted by Henry VII.[43] If all this appears to have been an almost effortless rise to prominence, his election as mayor in 1498 was much less straightforward. Percyvale had in fact been nominated by the Tailors for the mayoralty as far back as 1489, and the author of the *Great Chronicle* put down his next recorded failure in 1493 to the 'hote apetyte which he hadd yerely to that offyce'.[44] When he was eventually elected in 1498, apparently with the support of the king, the chronicler again rehearsed the reasons for his earlier exclusion by the other aldermen: 'ffor as much as It was thowgth by theym that he was verray desyrous to have It, In othir maner than othir of his predecessours mayris beffore hym'.[45] It is perhaps difficult to attribute the opposition to Percyvale entirely to dislike of an excessively ambitious alderman. Percyvale was the first tailor to hold the office of mayor, and so in many ways represented the civic ambitions of the craft which culminated in 1503 in the obtaining of a charter from Henry VII, which allowed them to call themselves *Merchant* Tailors and to acquire new powers which were perceived as threatening to the rights and established privileges of the other companies.[46] John Percyvale died in 1503, after having acquired considerable wealth through his dealings as a general merchant whilst continuing to run a tailoring business.[47] In 1487 and 1488, for instance, Percyvale was granted licences to export 500 quarters of corn and to import 100 gallons of wine from Gascony. He also had dealings with a Spanish iron merchant, Ochoa Martines de Orindo, who came to owe Percyvale a large sum of money.[48]

Of Thomasine's life during her third marriage we know very little. It is possible, however, using her will of 1512 and that of her husband (1503), to reconstruct something of their life together and their relationship with each other and their circle of friends, relatives and acquaintances. It is clear that the

[42] Accounts, iii, f. 34v; Clode, *Early History*, p. 338.

[43] *LBL*, p. 235; Beaven, *Aldermen*, ii, p. 17; Stow in his *Survey of London*, ii, pp. 178-79 asserts that Percyvale was 'made knight in the fielde by King Henrie the seventh'.

[44] CLRO, Journals 9, f. 239; *The Great Chronicle of London*, ed. A.H. Thomas and I.D. Thornley (London, 1938), pp. 245-46.

[45] Ibid., p. 288.

[46] For the dispute over this charter, see H. Miller, 'London and Parliament in the Reign of Henry VIII', *Bulletin of the Institute of Historical Research*, 35 (1962), pp. 128-31.

[47] James Wilford, alderman until 1511, was described by the author of the *Great Chronicle* as a former apprentice of Percyvale (probably in the period c.1470-80), *Great Chronicle*, p. 378. In his will of 1503 Percyvale mentioned several apprentices to whom he left 40s. each, PRO, PROB 11/13, ff. 191v-193v.

[48] Clode, *Early History*, ii, p. 15; PRO, PROB 11/13, ff. 191v-193v. For the iron trade between Castile and England, see Wendy R. Childs, *Anglo-Castilian Trade in the Later Middle Ages* (Manchester, 1978), pp. 112-19. The debt was still owing when Thomasine died in 1512, when it is described as consisting of the monetary value of 55 tons, 3 quarters and 1 pound of iron, probably of the order of £280 at 1487 prices, ibid., p. 114 and PRO, PROB 11/17, ff. 218-221v.

Percyvales were connected with some important individuals: as early as 1486-87, John Percyvale lent Thomas, earl of Ormond, £20 for which Ormond offered six silver bowls as security.[49] In their wills both named prominent churchmen as overseers: John Percyvale chose Thomas Savage, then archbishop of York and a fellow Cheshire man; Thomasine selected William Warham, archbishop of Canterbury.[50] It may well be significant that both Savage and Warham were former bishops of London; the tailors enjoyed good relations with the see, admitting the bishops as members of their fraternity on a regular basis and celebrating services in a chapel in St Paul's dedicated to their patron, St John the Baptist. The tailors themselves and their company provided an important social milieu for both Thomasine and her husband. Following her husband's election as master in 1485, she was a member of the livery of the craft in her own right, although as suggested above, her earlier marriages to two liverymen must have given her a certain status within the company. The Grocers' Company was doubtless not alone in allowing the widows of liverymen to attend their annual feast, though they had to pay double the usual fee.[51] Similarly, as the widow of a former master of the Tailors' Company, Thomasine would have enjoyed the status accorded to her husband. In 1490, for example, the tailors' court established a more relaxed policy of admission to the livery of the craft for those men who had married the widows of former masters or wardens of the Company.[52]

Thomasine's business activities, previously hidden by the activities of her husbands, can be seen for the first time during her final widowhood. Her will mentions eight former apprentices and servants as well as Thomas Roche, John Husbonde and Ralph Walker 'whiche be nowe apprentices with me'.[53] Hence Thomasine appears to have been capable of training tailors in her own right, using skills that in all probability she had learned informally from her husbands. A parallel case is that of Isabel Sampson, the wife of a cordwainer, who taught a male apprentice the art of tailoring before being sued by the boy's mother who questioned the standard of the instruction her son had received.[54] Rather than diversify into a related craft, both Isabel and Thomasine may have preferred to learn tailoring skills informally and to assist in the running of their

---

[49] *Calendar of Ancient Deeds*, C 3016, dated 8 Nov. 2 Hen. VII.

[50] PRO, PROB 11/13, ff. 191v-193v, 11/17, f. 218-221v. As will be shown, Savage appears to have encouraged Percyvale in the foundation of his school in Macclesfield. For his career see Emden, *BRUO*, iii, pp. 1046-47.

[51] *LBL*, p. xxxi, n.5.

[52] Merchant Taylors' Company, Ancient MS Books, xxxvii, f. 22. Such men could be admitted at any point during the year instead of just at the annual feast on 24 June.

[53] PRO, PROB 11/17, f. 219v. Roche, Husbonde and Walker received 20 marks each, with the former apprentices and servants receiving 10 marks.

[54] CLRO, Calendar of Mayor's Court Bills, 1/50. I am grateful to Caroline Barron for this reference. Isabel may well have been, like Thomasine, the widow of a tailor, who despite learning the craft informally, achieved a sufficient level of skill to be able to train others after her first husband's death.

husbands' workshops. Many other wives of tailors, by contrast, acting as *femmes couvertes*, became silkwomen, and trained up female apprentices who were nominally indentured to both husband and wife.[55] In Thomasine's case it was probably essential for her to be competent and to be able to supervise the running of the business given her husband's mercantile activities and his involvement in civic affairs. Thomasine was also expected to run a large urban household which would have emphasised, as one historian has put it, 'the centrality of administration to daily life'.[56] Although the greatest opportunities came with widowhood and the acquisition of the status of a freewoman, there must have been a very real sense in which businesses were run as partnerships between the husband and wife, even though these were rarely expressed in formal terms.[57] As a widow, Thomasine continued to look after the business affairs of her husband. On one occasion her vigorous pursuit of a debt of £10 she claimed was owed to her late husband brought her into conflict with Beatrice Snow, another widow, whose husband had evidently done business with John Percyvale.[58] Around the same time, Thomasine appears to have fallen victim to a 'forced loan' of £1,000 imposed on her by the crown. No details of this survive other than a list of those 'pardoned', but the wealth and prestige she had acquired over many years may have made her an easy target. It may be that Thomasine managed to avoid paying this huge amount; it does not appear to have affected the plans for her school or any of the other provisions she was to make in her wills.[59]

[55] M. Bateson, ed. *Borough Customs*, i, Selden Society, 18 (London, 1904), pp. 229-30. Recognition of the reality behind the indentures can be found in a proclamation of 1415-16 addressed to 'every man and woman having apprentices', *LBL*, p. 200. In a deed of 1454-55, Elizabeth Eland, daughter of a Lincolnshire esquire, was apprenticed to John Langwith, citizen and tailor of London, and Elene his wife, silkwoman, for seven years to learn Elene's trade, PRO, E 210/D1176.

[56] Rowena E. Archer, ' "How Ladies . . . who Live on their Manors Ought to Manage their Households and Estates": Women as Landholders and Administrators in the Later Middle Ages', in *Woman is a Worthy Wight*, ed. Goldberg, p. 149. Christine de Pisan also emphasised the necessity for women to be able to supervise the shop and its workers when the husband was away, see Margaret Wade Labarge, *Women in Medieval Life: A Small Sound of the Trumpet* (London, 1986), pp. 144-47.

[57] Such informal partnerships are by definition only implied by the sources, as witnessed by the arrangements made by Stephen Piers concerning the transfer of the family tailoring business to his son John between 1467 and 1471. It was only in the final indenture that Julian and Margaret, the wives of the two tailors were mentioned alongside their husbands. Merchant Taylors' Company, Ancient MS Books, xxxvii, ff. 21v-22. Agreements were occasionally more formal: Erika Uitz cites the case of a Basel couple who formed a cloth company and swore to stand by their agreement 'through profit and loss', in her *Women in the Medieval Town* (London, 1990), p. 41.

[58] PRO, C 1/166/5. Beatrice, the widow of Richard Snow a merchant haberdasher (d.1506-7), petitioned the chancellor for a writ of *certiorari*, claiming that the debt had in fact been paid to John Percyvale's servant before her husband's death, and that neither John nor 'my lady Tomesyn his wife sithen his deces demaunded never a peny of dette'.

[59] 'For the pardon of Lady Percivall 1000 lib'. The document (BL, MS Lansdowne 160, f. 311) is dated 17 November, 23 Hen VII and is printed in *Archaeologia*, 25 (1834), pp. 390-93. Hall

continued

Both John and Thomasine Percyvale expressed a deep regard for their craft in their wills. This was manifested in three ways. First, John bequeathed 'grete potts' and Thomasine 'grete bollys wrought with vynes' to the tailors, with John favouring 'the hole body of my felawship of taillours' and Thomasine the Bachelors' Company which comprised those freemen of the craft outside the livery.[60] In the second place, twenty-four and sixteen wax torches were to be made for the funerals of John and Thomasine respectively. These were to be carried to church by poor householders of the parish or of the ward of Langbourn, of whom as many as possible were to be tailors. Each was to be provided with a black gown and hood as well as some rosary beads, John specifying that the name of Jesus was to be picked out on the right sleeve 'a spanne from the hande'.[61] This combined expression of loyalty to craft and locality is echoed by the choice of burial place, on the south side of the chapel dedicated to St John the Baptist, the patron saint of the tailors' fraternity, in St Mary Woolnoth.[62] Lastly, and perhaps most significantly, the Tailors' Company was to be responsible for the administration of the chantry established by John Percyvale in St Mary Woolnoth. This was achieved through the gift of twelve messuages in Lombard Street to the Company, the rents from which were to be used to pay the salaries of two priests and to fund a yearly anniversary and other services in St Mary's. Five years after the death of her husband, Thomasine evidently found that the arrangement was working well as she chose that moment to make over five more tenements to the Tailors, this time in the parish of St Martin in the Vintry, in return for an increase of 26s. 8d. in the salaries paid to the priests and the establishment of an anniversary for herself.[63] The early dates of these testaments (21 February 1502 and 12 February 1508) as compared with their wills (4 March 1502 and 26 March 1512) indicate the specialised nature of such arrangements and the methodical approach adopted, particularly by Thomasine. As we shall see, such planning was characteristic of her approach, to be seen again in the arrangements for the foundation of her school. As the chantry certificate of 1546 shows, the tailors appear to have administered the endowment efficiently, repaying the trust placed in them by John and Thomasine; the properties themselves generated

continued

condemned the forced loans 'by whose meanes many a ryche and welthy person, by the extremyte of the lawes of the realme, were condempned and brought to misery', *Hall's Chronicle*, ed. H. Ellis (London, 1809), p. 502.

[60] PRO, PROB 11/13, ff. 191v-193v; 11/17, ff. 218-221v.

[61] This interest in the Name of Jesus was associated with the cult of the five wounds which, as shown below, both John and Thomasine express a deep regard for in their wills, see R.W. Pfaff, *New Liturgical Feasts in Later Medieval England* (Oxford, 1970), p. 84. For a discussion of John Percyvale's piety see Colin Richmond's article, 'The English Gentry and Religion *c.* 1500', in *Religious Belief and Ecclesiastical Careers in Late Medieval England*, ed. C. Harper-Bill, (Woodbridge, 1991), pp. 126-27.

[62] PRO, PROB 11/13, f. 191v.

[63] *HW*, ii, pp. 605 (dated 21 Feb. 1502), 618 (12 Feb. 1508).

an income of £47 *per annum* which, after the payments for the priests' salaries and the other services, resulted in a 'profit' of £26 4s. 1d.[64]

We have seen that both Thomasine and John Percyvale united together successfully their loyalties to both parish and craft through their funerary and their post obit arrangements. These were very elaborate, particularly so in the case of Thomasine who displayed piety of a very conventional kind. Thomasine's arrangements utilised a number of short, medium and longer term strategies to provide for her soul. Immediately after her death, a trental of masses was to be said and sung in St Mary's for the souls of all three husbands, and John and Joan 'my fader and moder'. Distributions to poor householders of the parish were then to take place within three days of her death, during which time her body was to remain in her house. Poor men and women of the parish who came to her house during this period were to receive bread, drink and 'mete both sodde and roste as the tyme requireth'. Echoing this concern for food appropriate to the phases of the ecclesiastical year, poor elderly men and women were also to receive 'hole mete goode and holsom be it fisshe or flesshe as the season requireth' as well as 'good thre halpeny ale'. After the funeral, distributions to the poor were to continue until the month's mind, with bequests to poor prisoners, almsmen and lepers also taking place during this period. Nine London monasteries, including three nunneries, also received bequests of 20s. enabling them to say a dirge and a mass for her soul, with two others also being required to say a trental of masses. Although three nunneries (Clerkenwell, St. Helen's and Halliwell) were among the nine institutions, Thomasine's interest in female foundations was not particularly striking, although greater than that of her late husband who remembered six male institutions in his will. The timescale then enlarges to five years: on the anniversary of her death, prisoners in four jails were to receive beef, mutton and bread, and a priest was to be employed to say mass daily at 'Scala Celi' in Westminster Abbey during this period.[65]

Conventionality did of course encompass new developments in lay piety and perhaps most striking in the wills of both Thomasine and John is their interest in the cult of the Five Wounds, and the associated devotion to the Name of Jesus. Although not developing into a feast in England as it did on the Continent, the Mass of the Five Wounds appeared in this country in the early fifteenth century and drew particular strength from having a definite subject,

[64] PRO, LR 2/241, ff. 10-12. The 1548 return also indicates the healthy state of the chantry and the tailors' finances, see *London and Middlesex Chantry Certificate, 1548*, ed. C.J. Kitching, London Record Society, 16 (London, 1980), pp. 87-88.

[65] PRO, PROB 11/17, ff. 218-19. 'Scala Coeli' was an indulgence, celebrated at the main altar of the Lady Chapel of Henry VII, and which attracted bequests for masses to be sung at the nearby chapel of 'Our Lady of the Pew': see H.F. Westlake, *Westminster Abbey*, 2 vols (London, 1923), ii, p. 332. Westlake cites the will of William More of London, who in 1521 left money for a trental of masses 'at [the time of] Scala Celi at the Chapell of the Pewe before our lady next St Edward Chapell at Westminster'. I am grateful to Dr Gervase Rosser for his advice on this point.

as distinct from other votive mass offerings such as the Gregorian trental.[66] Both John and Thomasine displayed a keen interest in, and devotion to, the Five Wounds: five masses were to be said by a priest in Thomasine's house while her body remained there 'in the worship of the v wounds of our saviour crist Jhesu'; both required five lighted torches to be placed around their bodies in St Mary's, with John asking for five more to be held by poor householders 'in worship of the five joyes of our lady'.[67] This devotion was, therefore, something which both shared. Perhaps the main difference between the wills is that while John specified fewer definite arrangements, concentrating on the details of the funeral and the twenty-four torch-bearers, Thomasine outlined a lengthy programme of services and distributions for her soul. This may well indicate that he and Thomasine had already agreed on further *post obit* arrangements which she would administer after his death, and shows a degree of trust which Thomasine was perhaps not able to place even in John Dinham, her cousin and principal executor. John's regard for, and confidence in, his wife is also apparent in his instruction to his executors that the garments to be made for poor women were to be 'after the fasshion of my wiffs sloppe'.[68]

Both John and Thomasine were immigrants to London: Thomasine as we have seen had come from Cornwall; John was born in Macclesfield. Their wills testify to their affection first for their families and secondly for their birthplaces. The distribution of the torches used at the funerals is an interesting indicator of their loyalties: John left torches to his own parish church of St Mary Woolnoth, St Christopher le Stocks where his mother was buried, St Dunstan in the West (where Thomasine's first two husbands' were buried) as well as the parish of Chelsfield in Kent, where Thomasine's brother Richard was rector until his death in 1499.[69] Thomasine, whilst remembering her brother's parish (three torches) left the other thirteen torches to London parishes including, once again, St Dunstan in the West (two), St Christopher's (two) and St Mary Woolnoth (five). A link with John's nephew and the heir to part of his estate, Richard Percyvale from Ipswich, is also revealed in Thomasine's will through her bequest to his parish church of St Mary at the Key in that town, as well as £20 to him personally.[70] Whilst no expressions of personal

---

[66] Pfaff, *New Liturgical Feasts*, pp. 84-91.

[67] PRO, PROB 11/13, ff. 191v-193v; PROB 11/17, ff. 218-218v.

[68] PRO, PROB 11/13, f. 193. Unlike Thomasine, John Percyvale asked for his clothing, jewelry and so on to be sold 'by discrete persons' of which one was to be a goldsmith, one a tailor and one a skinner, a further example of the meticulousness which characterised the arrangements made by both.

[69] PRO, PROB 11/13, ff. 191v-193v. Richard Bonaventure asked to be buried 'in the body of the church of Chellifeld before the crucifix', PROB 11/11, ff. 318v-319.

[70] PRO, PROB 11/17, f. 220v. Richard Percyvale was aged at least twenty-eight on the death of John, and was to have tenements in Lombard Street after Thomasine's death, see G.S. Fry ed., *Abstract of Inquisitions Post Mortem Relating to the City of London*, 3 vols (London, 1896), i, pp. 19-20. The original document is PRO, C 142/17/42. He was appointed collector of customs and subsidies for Ipswich in 1502 and died in 1529: *CFR, 1485-1509*, pp. 336-37, PRO, PROB 11/23, ff. 52-v.

sentiment accompany these bequests, it seems fair to conclude that John and Thomasine were on good terms with each others' families. Similarly, both seem to have had a great affection for their birth-places. This found its ultimate expression in the founding of schools by both John and Thomasine but, in the provisions of their wills themselves, a high degree of local concern was also manifested. John, for example, left more torches and copes to two Cheshire parishes (Macclesfield and Stockport) and torches to a church in Derbyshire. Thomasine cast her net more widely through her bequests, and looks to have been much more adventurous than John: she left a gilt goblet and cover with 'a blue floure in the bothom' to the vicar of Liskeard in Cornwall; six silver bowls to the priory of Bodmin; three of her best goblets to the priory of Launceston (close to Week St Mary); 20 marks to the church of St Stephen's in Launceston for the new tower; and £20 to the priory of Cornworthy in Devonshire.[71]

The most important links with Cornwall were provided by her surviving relatives and Thomasine displayed her affection for them in her will: she made substantial bequests to her brother John Bonaventure and his wife, her cousin John Dynham and his son William, and to her niece Margery Dynham. These and other bequests make it possible to gain an insight into Thomasine's life as the wife and later the widow of John Percyvale. Great wealth is indicated by the cash bequests, which alone totalled over £700, augmented by lists of clothing and the details of 'my mansion' in Lombard Street. To Margery Dynham, for instance, Thomasine left some fine items including gowns, bonnets, damask tablecloths and one of the two side-saddles 'of blewe velwet' mentioned in her will, together with a bridle and horse-harness.[72] Thomasine, as one might expect, was head of a large household: as well as the three male apprentices whom she was evidently still teaching as a widow, Thomasine had several female servants, including Margaret Lawson who was undoubtedly a much loved retainer and who received a total of £33 6s. 8d. from her mistress. Thomas Hethcott, who was a servant first to John and then to Thomasine, received due recognition of this from his mistress in addition to the bequests which her husband had already left him. All the household servants were permitted by Thomasine to continue to live in her house for six months after her death, 'they to lye in the grete chamber over the gate and none other chamber'. Thomasine's piety as much as her status is indicated by her employment of 'Master Wolf my chaplain'. Robert Wolf, as he is listed elsewhere in the will, was an equally valued member of Thomasine's household, and received her 'litell salt of silver and gilt which I was wont to be served with daily at my borde'. His duties were not finished however, for he was to sing mass daily for her soul and those of her husbands and her parents for seven

[71] PRO, PROB 11/17, ff. 220v-221. It seems highly likely that, as Nicholas Orme suggests, Thomasine Dinham, prioress of Cornworthy from c. 1470-1519, was a relation of Thomasine Percyvale, *Education in the West of England*, p. 173.

[72] PRO, PROB 11/17, ff. 218-221.

years, at an annual salary of £10 including 'mete and drink'.[73] It is possible that Wolf was the Oxford graduate of the same name who became vicar of Poughill in Cornwall in 1504, and in 1520, eight years after Thomasine's death, became rector of North Tawton in Devon. The choice of Wolf reinforces the impression of a woman whose high standards and regard for her homeland were exhibited to great effect in the foundation of her school.[74]

Thomasine's household was not simply made up of servants and a chaplain. Perhaps the most striking aspect of her life as a widow, and one which is particularly distinctive, is the active role she played in the educating of poor children within her own house. Thomasine was closely involved with five such children, three boys, William Bonefortune and Robert and William Peny-father, 'which i have brought up of almes', and two girls, Denyse and Barbara, 'maide childen whiche I have also brought up'. All five were to continue to have 'mete drynk & lernyng': the boys until twenty-one if they were 'disposed to be men of the churche' or else until appropriate masters could be found to take them on as apprentices; the girls were to continue to be provided for until the age of fourteen when Thomasine's executors were to find them each a good master.[75] Hence, like Thomasine perhaps, they were to be well brought up and introduced into a good household prior to marriage. At twenty-one the girls were to receive 10 marks (probably towards their marriages) and the boys five marks. In addition, Thomasine had an interest in the fortunes of several other children, including three sons of Edward Dernyck (Nicholas, Philip and John), who were also to be provided with board and education by her executors.[76]

It is in the context of Thomasine's zeal for the educating of young children that we should view her foundation of a grammar school in Week St Mary where she was born. It is clear that this enthusiasm was shared by her husband, whose school in Macclesfield provided the exemplar for Thomasine's own foundation. John Percyvale was certainly concerned that 'many children for lak of such techyng and draught in conyng fall to Idleness And so consequently live disolately all their daies', but it seems unlikely, given his other duties and activities, that he took as active a role as Thomasine in teaching children in his own home.[77] There was nothing particularly exceptional about the Percyvales' charitable bequests as a whole, but the foundation of schools was still at this time a relatively unusual event. This was particularly so in the case of Thomasine, who may have been the earliest non-noble female founder of such

[73] Ibid. John Skevyngton, merchant tailor and one of the witnesses to her will, was to administer the payments.

[74] Emden, *BRUO*, iii, p. 2076. Wolf was ordained in 1496 and received his M.A. in 1504.

[75] PRO, PROB 11/17, ff. 218-221.

[76] Ibid.

[77] From the foundation deed of John's school, dated 25 January 1503, cited in C. Stella Davies, *A History of Macclesfield* (Manchester, 1961), p. 211. A transcript of the deed can be found in G.E. Wilson 'A History of the Macclesfield Grammar School in the County of Cheshire, 1503 to *c.* 1890'. (unpublished M.Ed. thesis, University of Leeds, 1952).

a school.[78] The process of founding the school at Week St Mary has been described by both P.L. Hull and Nicholas Orme, but certain aspects of it are particularly important as regards Thomasine, her relationship with her husband, and her life as a widow. Although it is clear that the idea of the school originated with John Percyvale, the school he founded at Macclesfield in 1503 was the product of his association with a number of men who, like himself, were born in Cheshire.[79] In the first place, John claimed to have been 'much stirred' by consultations with Thomas Savage, the overseer of his will who was then archbishop of York.[80] Savage, born in Chifton in Cheshire, was not a noted benefactor of education, but had enjoyed a successful ecclesiastical career during which he studied at Oxford, Bologna and Padua, before his appointment as bishop of Rochester in 1492.[81] Another Cheshire man, Sir Richard Sutton, co-founder of Brasenose College, Oxford, was also involved in the foundation.[82] John Percyvale's school was established by a foundation deed dated 25 January 1503 which provided for lands to be made over to eighteen feoffees. The master of the school, who also acted as the chaplain of John's chantry in Macclesfield church, was to be a university graduate which was still at that time a relatively unusual requirement.[83]

Many of the phrases and provisions of the Macclesfield deed were subsequently used by Thomasine in her own deed of foundation, dated 10 July 1506. Like John, Thomasine cited a lack of teachers which led many children to 'fall to idlenesse & diuerse other vices', as well as a need for priests in the nearby parish church.[84] Nineteen feoffees were to be appointed of whom four were to act as the governors of the school for the purpose of hiring the priest and the other employees. Once again the master was to be 'sufficiently lerned in Gramer Graduated in one of the vniversities of Oxford or Cambriege So that he be a maister of Arte or a maister of Grammer atte least', with the combined duties of teaching children, free of any charge, and saying mass and other daily

[78] Hull, 'Endowment of a Grammar School', p. 30. The only other female founders of schools before 1509 appear to have been Margaret Tudor (grandmother of Henry VIII) at Wimborne, and Lady Katherine Berkeley at Wotton-under-Edge.

[79] Davies, *A History of Macclesfield*, pp. 211-12 and J.P. Earwaker, *East Cheshire*, 2 vols (London, 1880), ii, pp. 511-12.

[80] Davies, *A History of Macclesfield*, pp. 210-11.

[81] Orme, *Education in the West of England*, p. 176; Emden, *BRUO*, iii, pp. 1046-7; Helen Jewell, 'English Bishops as Educational Benefactors in the Later Fifteenth Century', in *The Church, Politics and Patronage in the Fifteenth Century*, ed. R.B. Dobson, (Gloucester, 1984), p. 157.

[82] Orme, *Education in the West of England*, p. 176. For Sutton see Emden, *BRUO*, iii, pp. 1826-27 and R. Churton, *The Lives of William Smyth, Bishop of Lincoln and Sir Richard Sutton*, (Oxford, 1800).

[83] Orme, *Education in the West of England*, p. 176.

[84] Hull, 'Endowment of a Grammar School', p. 43. A transcript of the foundation deed of Thomasine's school is printed on pp. 43-48, and is MS AD.405 in Cornwall Record Office, Truro.

services.[85] Not only did the school not charge fees, it also provided accommodation for the scholars as well as the master. The chantry commissioners of 1546 were enthusiastic about the school, claiming that 'they that list may sett their children to borde there & have them taught freely'.[86]

Whereas John's school was founded close to his death in 1503, Thomasine took much longer over the process of foundation, indicating that, although she had access to her husband's deed and was doubtless cognisant of the processes involved, she wished to make sure that the endowment was placed in safe hands. This began as early as May of 1506 when Thomasine purchased the manor of Simpson and 220 acres of land in Holsworthy, Devon, from Sir John Lisle for £220. These lands were then to be handed over to three trustees who were to convey the lands to the nineteen feoffees on her death.[87] This did not constitute the endowment of the school in its final form. The next burst of activity took place in 1508 when Thomasine secured a royal licence, dated 6 November, for the foundation of a chantry at Week St Mary and, on 1 December, granted a schoolmaster, John Andrew, possession of the manor of Simpson.[88] Andrew had been educated at Winchester, and at New College, Oxford, before returning to Winchester as usher of the school. With this combination of education and teaching experience he was a good choice as the first master of Thomasine's school.[89]

To all intents and purposes, therefore, the school had been founded by the close of 1508, the year in which Thomasine also made her first will, dealing with the augmentation of her husband's chantry in the church of St Mary Woolnoth.[90] Possibly she feared that she had not long to live, but the evidence of her will suggests that any such fears were shortlived since she evidently continued to train apprentices, bring up and educate her alms-children, and run a large household. It is likely that the school, under the guiding hand of John Andrew who was named in the deed of 1506, was up and running well before Thomasine's death in 1512, despite the fact that the endowment was not yet in the hands of the nineteen feoffees. Thomasine's will is itself ambiguous on this point, but her words do seem to indicate that she was merely asking her cousin to keep an eye on what was an already functioning school:

---

[85] Orme, *Education in the West of England*, pp. 176-77; Hull, 'Endowment of a Grammar School', pp. 21, 43-48.

[86] PRO, E 301/15, f. 47.

[87] Hull, 'Endowment of a Grammar School', pp. 21, 43-48; Orme, *Education in the West of England*, p. 176.

[88] *CPR, 1494-1509*, p. 604; Hull, 'Endowment of a Grammar School', pp. 28-29. A subsequent grant by Thomasine in a codicil of 1512 made over the manor of Brodworthy in Devon, purchased in 1507, to her executors, part of which came to be applied to the school, see Orme, *Education in the West of England*, p. 177 and PRO, PROB 11/17, f. 221v (10 April 1512).

[89] Emden, *BRUO*, p. 34.

[90] *HW*, ii, p. 618.

And as for all things concernyng my chauntry and gramer scole at Saint Mary Wike in the Countie of Cornwall I comitte only to the discression of my said cosyn John Dynham requiringe hym to see every thinge concernynge the same to be parfite and sure as nigh as he can accordyng as he knoweth my mynde.[91]

How successful was Thomasine's school? Carew certainly saw the school and its master as performing an essential function in the local community. But whereas John Percyvale's school survives to this day, Thomasine's was to last only half a century before being moved to Launceston, a process which involved the breaking up of the endowment.[92] The chantry certificates of 1546 and 1548 shed light on the state of the school, though their conclusions differ markedly. The commissioners of 1546 found a successful school which was 'a grete comfort to all the countre'. William Cholwell is named as the incumbent assisted in his teaching by the manciple (not named).[93] Two years later the Edwardian commissioners found that Cholwell was 'a man well learned and a greate setter forthe of Gods worde', yet were sceptical about the future of the school as a whole, remarking that 'The said scole [is] in decay by reason yt standith in a desolate place And far from the markett for provision of the said scolers'. [94] The school was transferred to Launceston following suggestions, apparently made to the commissioners by the citizens, that as the towns were only seven miles apart, 'thys ys a very meate place to have the foundacion of the said scole removed unto'.[95] The chantry buildings were seized and sold in 1549, the manciple and laundress were pensioned off and the feoffees lost all their rights concerning the school and its master.[96] Cholwell was kept on at Launceston and was still teaching in 1556, but was no longer master of the school.[97] Thomasine's decision to found her school in the place of her birth was a product of the same conventional piety which lay behind her other post obit arrangements and bequests. Yet, as with her other activities, this was conventionality of a high quality, shown in the meticulous planning and endowment of the school, the appointment of a well-qualified graduate as master, and the relatively unusual decision to found a free school. It is probable that, as Orme suggests, the high standard of education provided by the school was, at first,

[91] PRO, PROB 11/17, f. 221.

[92] Orme, *Education in the West of England*, pp. 180-181.

[93] PRO, E 301/15, no. 73, ff. 46v-47, 'The Chauntry called dame Percyvalls chauntry'. A laundress was also employed at a cost of 13s 4d. *per annum*. The yearly income from the chantry lands was £15 14s. 8d. with expenses amounting to £15 7s. 7d., of which Cholwell received £12 6s. 0d.

[94] PRO, E 301/9, no. 6, f. 3. The certificate also indicates that the services were held 'at the awlter of Seynt John Baptyst in the Northe yete within the same church', possibly another reminder of the craft practised by Thomasine's three husbands.

[95] Launceston chantry certificate, 1548, PRO, E 310/9/7. This was endorsed by 'worshipfull of the shere', E 301/10/9.

[96] PRO, E 301/9, no. 7; *CPR, 1548-49*, pp. 34, 362, 364-65; Orme, *Education in the West of England*, p. 181. See also A.F. Robbins, 'John Aylworth and the Launceston Free School', *Notes and Gleanings for Devon and Cornwall*, iii (Exeter, 1896), pp. 167-77.

[97] PRO, LR 6/104/3; LR 6/1/3.

able to offset the difficulties inherent in its establishment in a parish of only 150 communicants.[98] By 1548 these difficulties had become more serious and the quality of the teaching provided by Cholwell was no longer able to attract sufficient scholars to the school.

The physical destruction of Thomasine's highly personal foundation at Week St Mary was rendered all the more complete by the fact that the school doubled as a chantry, designed to nurture the memory of its founder in the prayers of the scholars, a function which lapsed after 1548. Fortunately, the memory of Thomasine's life and her foundation was kept alive through the legend which expressed the affection with which Thomasine appears to have been remembered in Cornwall. Thomasine was, however, also a Londoner, and it was through her life in the capital and her marriage to three of its citizens that she came to acquire the wealth sufficient to realise her ambitions. Her importance as a London citizen is shown by John Stow's inclusion of a brief account of her school foundation in his *Survey of London* first published in 1598; significantly, the name of Carew, a fellow member of the Society of Antiquaries, is noted in the margin as the source of his information.[99] As the wife successively of three tailors, and of the first tailor mayor of London, Thomasine was undoubtedly a well-respected member of the tailors' fraternity: along with other important tailor widows such as Rose Swan, Margery Materdale and 'Maistres Champernoun', her name is recorded in an inventory of 1512 as a donor of plate, in her case a 'standyng cup, gilt with a cover and a columbyn on the pomell'.[100] The Percyvales were also important parishioners and property-holders in the London parish of St Mary Woolnoth. Thomasine was far from being simply the wife of a prominent liveryman, parishioner, alderman and mayor; she not only shared John Percyvale's interests in education and in business, but was able to develop them much further during her nine-year widowhood. The free grammar school she founded, although modelled on her husband's foundation in Macclesfield, was very much her own creation: the process of foundation was typically methodical and was focused around her life rather than that of her husband, first through the prayers offered for the souls of her parents and her husbands, and secondly through its location in the small parish of Week St Mary in Cornwall, where she had been born. The fact that Thomasine did not have any children of her own from any

---

[98] Orme, *Education in the West of England*, p. 178.

[99] Stow, *Survey of London*, i, p. 111; Carew was elected a member in 1598, the year before the completion of Stow's *Survey*, see M. McKisack, *Medieval History in the Tudor Age* (Oxford, 1971), pp. 140-42, and *Richard Carew of Antony, The Survey of Cornwall*, ed. F.E. Halliday (London, 1953), pp. 15-68. Carew was also a close associate of William Camden, who cited him in his *Britannia*.

[100] Printed in C.M. Clode, *Memorials of the Merchant Taylors' Company* (London, 1875), p. 89. Hugh Champernoun joined the livery of the craft in 1437-38 and died in 1464; John Materdale was master of the tailors in 1479 and John Swan in 1470. Accounts, i, f. 294v, GL, MS 9171/5, f. 350v and Clode, *Early History*, ii, p. 338.

of her three marriages may well have been a factor in her enthusiasm for the education and training of children and apprentices in her own home, perhaps the most notable aspect of her widowhood. The lack of children of her own would also have meant that she was better able to make financial provision for her school. The legend which later grew up around her foundation is very much a Cornish one, starting with her meeting the mysterious merchant and ending with the establishment of her school. This is highly appropriate since Thomasine was so attached to her own family throughout her life, yet it was London which provided the context for the development of her wealth, her ideas about the importance of education and the loyalties which shaped her life and her distinctive benefaction.

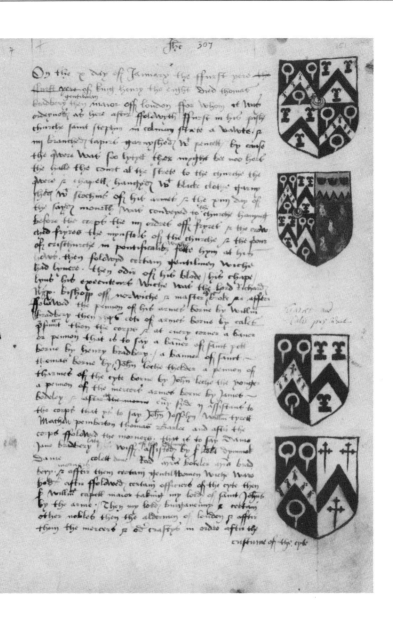

3. The account of Thomas Bradbury's funeral 10 January 1510 by Calais Pursuivant, showing the coats of arms displayed: Bradbury and Rokell, Bodley and an unidentified coat. BL, Add. MS 45131, f. 151 (*By permission of the British Library*)

14

Lady Joan Bradbury (d. 1530)

Anne F. Sutton

Wife, widow, sister and matriarch are all words defining a woman solely in her relationship to other persons, and they are all entirely appropriate to Joan Bradbury. She spent most of her life carrying out the wishes of two husbands and a brother, and providing for her children. Only as the wealthy widow of a lord mayor of London and a potential benefactress was she personally able to command attention from a livery company, and only as the wealthy sister of the vicar of Saffron Walden was she able to play a conspicuous part in the campaigns that bought the town self-government and rebuilt its church. It was her good relations with certain male relatives and considerable wealth in her own control that enabled her to operate successfully. A discussion of her life as a series of dependent relationships therefore represents both the actual facts of her female life and its chronology, but it is very far from being the whole truth. It was Joan who personally bonded her natural family to those of her first and second husbands. She managed to be a Leche, a Bodley and a Bradbury with equal spirit. It was her own talents that brought her so much success despite the severe social restrictions imposed on her sex – if she had been a man she would have been lord mayor herself, and not had to make one out of her second husband. She set up two endowments – a chantry and a school – with exemplary care, she bought herself a landed estate and she disposed of her wealth to her surviving children and grandchildren, leaving neither quarrels nor despairing trustees behind her.[1]

The Wife: Marriage to Thomas Bodley, Children and First Widowhood

Lady Bradbury was born Joan Leche, about the year 1450, the daughter of Denis Leche of Wellingborough, Northamptonshire, and Elizabeth, his wife.[2] She had at least three brothers, Henry, Thomas and John, of whom John, considerably her senior, was educated at Winchester, Oxford and Cambridge,

---

[1] The research on Lady Bradbury was started at the request of Mr S.K.M. Powell when Master of the Mercers' Company, 1982-83, and the Clerk, Mr G.M. Wakeford; it owes much to the encouragement of the Company.

[2] *The Visitation of Hertfordshire 1572*, ed. W.C. Metcalfe, Harleian Society, 22 (1886), p. 129,

continued

and became a priest.[3] That Joan's father, of whom nothing is known, was able to educate one son in this way and dower Joan well enough to secure her a match with a prosperous citizen of London indicates that the Leche family were in comfortable circumstances.

About 1470-75 Joan was married to Thomas Bodley, a citizen and tailor of London who came originally from Devon.[4] They lived in the parish of St Botolph Billingsgate, and so did Thomas's brother, Richard, a grocer. Thomas and Joan had two boys and two girls, while Richard had four sons and three daughters. Both brothers made their wills within a month of each other and died within eight months of each other, between November 1491 and July 1492, when most of their children were still minors.[5] Taken together, their careers and wills give considerable information about the social milieu of Joan Leche's first marriage and the degree of interest taken in religion and education by their families.[6] Both of them had served as warden of their respective companies within a year of each other;[7] both were below the aldermanic class, but might have attained it had they lived. Thomas left the larger movable estate, over £1,000, but Richard had the more impressive civic relations, including a brother-in-law who was an alderman (from 1478).[8] Both brothers

continued

is confirmed by the obit arranged by Joan for her parents at Wellingborough, and the obit of her brother, John, which names both parents (see below). Her birthdate is conjectural, based on the known dates of her brother John's career, the fact that she had four children who were minors in 1495, and had no children by her second husband.

[3] Henry and Thomas are mentioned in the 1510 will of Thomas Bradbury as 'my brothers', PRO, PROB 11/6, f. 202v (PCC 26 Bennett). For John, see Emden, *BRUO*, s.n. John Leche, and VCH, *Essex*, ii, ed. W. Page and J.H. Round (London, 1907), p. 518. For other Leches, see below.

[4] The same family as the founder of the Bodleian Library and bearing the same arms: gules, five martlets argent on a chief indented or three crowns azure. A fairly accurate pedigree of these Bodleys (but with the wrong arms) is in *Visitations of Surrey 1530, 1572 and 1623*, ed. W. Bruce Bannerman, Harleian Society, 43 (1899), p. 147. The present essay relies on the evidence of wills. F. Troup, Biography of John Bodley, father of Sir Thomas Bodley', *Transactions of the Devonshire Association*, 35 (1903), pp. 167-97, does not go back far enough to reveal the antecedents of the London Bodleys.

[5] Of Richard's children, one daughter was married at the time of her father's death: Isabel married William Butler, grocer, future alderman and mayor. Thomas, the eldest was to go to King's Hall, Cambridge (where his mother's relative, William Claryvaunce, was a fellow), and become vicar of South Weald, Essex, 1499-1537; William became a grocer and had children, see below, n. 12; John died young; Ellis became vicar of Beckenham, Kent, and St Stephen Walbrook; Elena married (1) William Copland, merchant taylor, (2) William Gresham; Emma married (1) – Pratt, (2) Sir Christopher Askew, lord mayor, 1534-35. For Ellis, see G. Hennessy, *Novum repertorium ecclesiasticum parochiale Londoniense* (London, 1898), p. 386.

[6] Richard Bodley: PRO, PROB, 11/9, ff. 5v-6 (PCC 1 Dogett), sealed 27 October 1491, no date of probate; his will and the surety for the estate of his children (£100) give their names, *LBL*, pp. 313-14. Thomas Bodley: PRO, PROB 11/11, f. 211v (PCC 27 Dogett), 27 Nov. 1491, proved 1 Aug. 1492.

[7] Richard, 1488-89, GL, Grocers' Company, MS 11592, f. 154; Thomas, 1489-90, C.M. Clode, *Early History of the Merchant Taylors' Company*, ii (London, 1888), pp. 23, 338.

[8] Richard married Joan Warde of Hinxsworth: her brother Robert was the heir, Thomas was a mercer, and John was a grocer, alderman (1478-1501), sheriff, M.P. and mayor (1485), Thrupp, *The Merchant Class*, pp. 372-73, and Beaven, ii, p. 15.

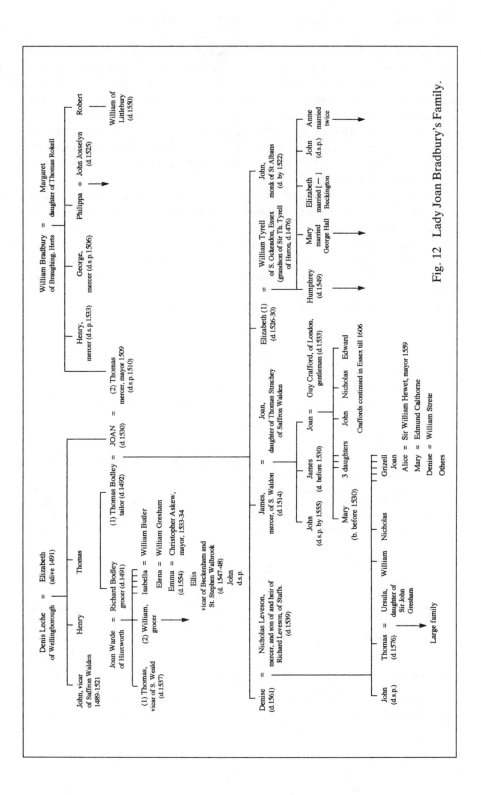

Fig. 12 Lady Joan Bradbury's Family.

wanted to be buried in the Trinity chapel of their parish church and both wanted two-year chantries there,[9] Thomas specifically requesting Master Thomas Driffield to be his priest if he was free, at 11 marks the year.[10] Richard had several primers, a psalter and two sets of beads to leave, while Thomas bequeathed a mass book, a private altar and its furnishings. That the Bodley families were genuinely involved in their religion, and not merely observing social conventions, may be borne out by the fact that of Richard's four sons, two became priests, including the eldest, and of Thomas's two sons, one became a monk of St Albans.

Richard's will also provides a few details about the level of interest in education in the family group. Before his death Richard had planned that his son Thomas should go to King's Hall, Cambridge, where a relative of his wife was a fellow.[11] Apart from his psalter and 'finest' primer bequeathed to edify his two daughters, he had English books, one of which contained lives of Christ and St Katherine, to leave to his son, William, who was to be a grocer like his father.[12]

The will of Joan's husband shows that she had been taken into his affections, along with her mother and brother. Joan was left the third of his movable estate (£362), to which she was entitled by the custom of London, the residue,[13] and a life interest in Thomas's lands in Southwark so long as she 'peaseably suffyr Elizabeth Leche hire moder to have and to hold to hire assignes during hire lif all that my tenement' in the parish of St Margaret. (Joan's mother survived to share Thomas Bradbury's great house and her

---

[9] Richard's chantry paid £3 6s. 8d.; he also asked Giles, the anchorite of London Wall, for prayers leaving him his two best gold rings. The Bodley descendants of Richard maintained their connection with St Botolph Billingsgate, see below.

[10] Driffield was the priest who took Richard Hunne to court over a mortuary fee; he had been at Winchester and Oxford like Joan's brother John (although later) and may have been known to him. At the time of Bodley's death he appears to have had no ecclesiastical post, having vacated the bursarship of Eton College in 1490 and the rectorship of Wakerly, Northants., in 1488, so he may have been glad of the chantry, Emden, *BRUO*, s.n. Driffield. S. Brigden, *London and the Reformation* (Oxford, 1990), pp. 99-100.

[11] A sister of Joan Warde married a Claryvaunce and Richard Bodley specifically left beads to William Claryvaunce, fellow of King's Hall, Cambridge, where his son, Thomas, was to be educated. See Emden, *BRUC*, and Thrupp, *Merchant Class*, pp. 372-73.

[12] William married (1) Elizabeth, the widow of William Masset, grocer, (2) Beatrice Sadler. He and Beatrice lived in the messuage 'the Ball' and 'the Bell' in St Botolph Billingsgate, possibly part of his father's property. See their wills: William (1540), PRO, PROB 11/28, f. 132v (PCC 17 Alenger); Beatrice (1557), PROB 11/42A, ff. 139-140 (PCC 18 Welles). A volume of Nicholas Love's *Life of Christ* and a life of St Katherine, probably made in London in the 1480s, inscribed: 'Thys Booke ys Wylliam bodleys & Elizabethe hys wyffe', and 'Thys ys betrys beverleys book' may have originally been one of Richard Bodley's books, now Cambridge, Corpus Christi College, MS 142. Another may be a very fine London made book of hours, which records the birth of Francis, son of William and Beatrice, C.R. Borland, *A Descriptive Catalogue of the Western Mediaeval Manuscripts in Edinburgh University Library* (Edinburgh,1916), MS 39.

[13] This is probably why there are so few objects bequeathed by Thomas, apart from a few clothes and his altar, so less can be said about his home and tastes.

room there was still being referred to as hers by Joan in 1530.) Joan's brother, John, vicar of Saffron Walden since 1489, acted as one of Thomas Bodley's overseers[14] and received his private altar with its apparel, vestments, candlesticks and mass book.[15]

To his children, Thomas left the customary third of his estate, and a further £50 each when they came of age or married.[16] They were all minors: John, James, Elizabeth, probably the eldest, and Denise, a baby. He chose one executor, his wife Joan (and two overseers), and expected her to make all the arrangements for his chantry, and if Thomas Driffield was unable to be his priest she was to find someone else; she was also to arrange his funeral in the Holy Trinity chapel of St Botolph Billingsgate and to see to everything according to his earlier, verbal instructions. In the event, Joan was to take far better care of his soul than Thomas can have thought possible, with four children and a widow to provide for from his estate.

As a widow with four young children Joan was comparatively well off. There is no precise evidence that she continued to run her husband's business, but it is probable that she did. It was not a small household: there were at least two apprentices, several 'covenanted' servants, both 'men kynde' and 'women kynde'. It is only the size of his estate and lands which indicates that he was more of a merchant than a craftsman tailor.

Well-provided widows did not have to stay unmarried for long in medieval London: they might marry younger men eager to make their way in the world and in need of a rich wife. If Joan was ambitious she might be able to use her wealth to move nearer the centre of civic life. Joan's final choice is an interesting one: it was not one she made in a hurry. Enough is known of the circumstances, for certain conclusions to be drawn about her ambitions, her sense of responsibility to her children and the respect and love she engendered. She was now in her forties and the man she chose, after about three years of widowhood, was Thomas Bradbury, a wealthy mercer and a bachelor, aged between fifty and fifty-six years. Neither of them was marrying in haste. They probably married about March 1495 when Thomas and his younger brother, George, also a mercer, with Christopher Elyot, an overseer of Thomas Bodley's will, stood surety for the sum of £362 14s. 5d., the estate of the Bodley children, all still minors. About the same time Thomas Bradbury

---

[14] Christopher Elyot, goldsmith and first assayer of the Goldsmiths' Company under the regulations of 1478, was the other overseer. He seems to have been a friend: he received a furred gown and hood, and his wife, Philippa, and children, 40s. Elyot was married to the sister of Elizabeth, the wife of the goldsmith and mayor, Bartholomew Rede: Bartholomew was an associate of Thomas Bradbury and 'Dame Rede' a life-long friend of Joan. T.F. Reddaway and L. Walker, *The Early History of the Goldsmiths' Company, 1327-1509* (London, 1975), pp. 164-65, and see below.

[15] The almsmen and women of Saffron Walden received 12d. to pray for Thomas's soul.

[16] Also small bequests he was holding for them from his mother.

took one of his step-sons, James, as his apprentice.[17] It is possible Joan's brother, the vicar, was the matchmaker: Littlebury was the main home of the Bradburys and just down the road from Saffron Walden, and a vicar eager to finish an expensive new church needed to know all his wealthy neighbours. Joan's new husband was never to show any signs of regretting his acquisition of a ready-made young family so late in life; if the middle-aged bachelor had belatedly decided that he wanted children of his own he could have found a younger woman more likely to provide him with them. All the evidence suggests that it was a marriage of mutual esteem and affection.

The Wife: Marriage to Thomas Bradbury, Lady Mayoress and Second Widowhood

Joan left the Bodleys' parish of St Botolph Billingsgate,[18] down by the river, for her new husband's parish of St Stephen Coleman Street in the centre of the city, and she made it her home. Neither she nor her young children ever looked back, though she never forgot her first husband. She took on a new house, a new set of relatives and exchanged the trading customs of the tailors for those of the mercers.

Thomas Bradbury had been born about 1439, in Braughing, Hertfordshire, a younger son of William Bradbury and his wife, Elizabeth Rokell. The family was armigerous and reasonably prosperous. All the younger sons, Thomas, George and Henry, became mercers of London and apparently only Thomas ever married. Their elder brother, Robert, inherited the family lands and one sister, Philippa, married well among the local gentry.[19]

---

[17] *LBL*, p. 305. A fourth surety was Richard Thornell, mercer, and husband of Anne Rich, grand-daughter of Bradbury's old master, Richard Rich.

[18] Bodleys buried in the Trinity chapel of St Botolph: the brothers, Richard and Thomas; William Holybrand, second husband of Joan Warde, Richard's widow; Richard's son, William, under the door of the chapel with his wives, Elizabeth and Beatrice; Thomas, Richard's son, deserted South Weald, his parish of thirty-eight years, for the 'presyncte' with his parents. All of Richard Bodley's children, but not those of Thomas, remembered the parish in some way in their wills: e.g. Ellis made bequests to the poor and sent three spice cakes and three buns to every house; Emma Askew left 20s. to repair the church. Wills: W. Holybrand, 1505, PRO, PROB 11/15, ff. 5v-6 (PCC 1 Adeane); T. Bodley, 1537, PROB 11/27, ff. 53-53v (PCC 7 Dyngely); W. Bodley, 1540, PROB 11/28, f. 132v (PCC 17 Alenger); Ellis Bodley, 1547, PROB 11/32, ff. 35-35v (PCC 5 Populwell); Emma Askew, 1554, PROB 11/37, ff. 60v-63 (PCC 8 More); Beatrice Bodley, 1557, PROB 11/42A, ff. 139-140 (PCC 18 Welles).

[19] Bradbury referred to his birthplace in his will – he maintained contact with it through Holy Trinity Aldgate which held manor and advowson. The home of the family moved to Littlebury, Essex, with Robert. Pedigrees in *The Visitation of Hertfordshire 1572*, ed. W.C. Metcalfe, Harleian Society, 22 (1886), p. 129, and *The Visitation of Essex*, ed. W.C. Metcalfe, Harleian Society, 13-14 (1878-9), i, p. 28 (inaccurate), p. 224 (confirmed by will evidence). *VCH Hertfordshire*, iii, ed. W. Page (London, 1971), pp. 308-9, 316. Details of apprenticeships from the Mercers' Company, List of Members from 1347; there is no entry fee for Thomas in the company's accounts which end in 1464; Henry's trade is only known from his will; George was Thomas's apprentice.

Thomas served his apprenticeship with the wealthy Richard Rich,[20] probably issuing from his term before Rich died in 1464.[21] In his master's household Thomas met some very important citizens: Riche's sons-in-law included a recorder, a mayor and an alderman. Thomas maintained contact with his master's heir, Thomas, another mercer (died 1474), and Elizabeth, Thomas's widow, an active merchant in her own right.[22]

The personality of Joan's new husband can be surprisingly well delineated. A letter to Elizabeth Rich from Bradbury shows him busy at his trade of mercer:

> Madame, the sarcenet is verry ffyne. I thynke most profytable and most worshipfull for you, and shall [last] you your lyff and your chyldes after you, wher as harlatry of xl.d. or xliiij.d. a yerd wold nat indure too sesons with you: Therfor for a lytill more cost, me thinketh most wysdom to take of the best. In certen I have bought the most part of the sarcenet, for I had nat I-now to perfourme yt. I wynne never a peny in that &c.[23]

Two episodes from the records of his company show him to have been an independent man, impatient in interference, particularly when it concerned his money. When, in January 1475, he assisted the wardens of the Mercery to list mercers of sufficient wealth to contribute towards the expenses of Edward IV's expedition to France, he saw fit not to include his own name; his name had to be added to a second list.[24] In 1481 he declined to take up the livery of his company, a rank that meant more demands would be made on both his time and his money, 'for divers consideracions and specially for obstinacie', wrote the Mercers' clerk. He was sufficiently important for the wardens to debate whether they would admit him, despite himself, or 'spare hym to an other season'.[25] At some date he was duly admitted to the livery and he played a modest role in company affairs in the 1480s, being elected to his first wardenship in 1489.[26]

---

[20] Riche's will, PRO, PROB 11/5, f. 32v *et seq.* (PCC 4 Godyn). He had Herts. connections, J.E. Cussans, *History of Hertfordshire* (London, 1870-3), ii, pt. 2, p. 274.

[21] The length of a mercer's apprenticeship was about ten years which puts his birth about 1439 if he issued before 1463 – he is not referred to in Riche's will.

[22] She married (2) Sir William Stonor of Oxfordshire, and continued to trade. After her death in 1479 Bradbury became a surety for the estate of the orphans of John Fenne, stockfishmonger and relative of the Riches, the youngest of whom had been in the care of Elizabeth Riche/Stonor from 1477. (The Bradbury/Fenne association continued through George Neville, Lord Abergavenny, see below.) C.L. Kingsford, ed., *The Stonor Letters 1290-1483*, Camden Society (1919), i, pp. xxvi-xxxi. See also Lacey, above.

[23] *Stonor Letters*, ii, ppp. 90-91, and see also pp. 122-23. Thorn has been rendered as *th*.

[24] L. Lyell and F. Watney, ed. *The Acts of Court of the Mercers' Company, 1453-1527* (Cambridge, 1936), pp. 78, 84. He was living in Coleman Street ward in 1475; he does not appear to have owned the house next to St Stephen's Coleman Street until after 1500; information from Derek Keene.

[25] Lyell and Watney, *Acts of Court*, p. 141.

[26] Ibid., pp. 147-48, 175-76, 183, 204-7, 237-41.

Little is known of Bradbury's trading or business activities at any time during his lifetime.[27] Only the names of his associates and fellow sureties suggest the range of his business: Sir Henry Colet,[28] the Rich family, already mentioned, some of the Nevilles, and Sir Thomas Thwaites, treasurer of Calais and merchant of the Staple as well as a mercer.[29] He was undoubtedly involved in financial dealings and loans as well as overseas trade.[30] His eight known apprentices taken from about 1471 onwards may be only a small proportion of those he trained.[31] What is certain is that by the time he married he was as prominent in the Merchant Adventurers as he was in the Mercers.[32]

From 1495, the year of his marriage, Bradbury's public career took off, and it is reasonable to ascribe this to his new wife and her influence. He had dragged his heels over joining the livery of his company and, for a wealthy man of fifty-five, he had held few offices. In Joan he had someone who was able to take full charge of his business in his absence; as his wife she had the authority and position to do this far more effectively than any employee.

In 1495 Bradbury was elected to parliament, in 1496 he was again a warden of the Mercers, and in 1498-99 he served as one of the city's sheriffs. For 1502-3 he was master of the Mercers, and during this term he was selected alderman of Aldersgate ward, removing to his own ward of Coleman Street less than a year later. He was now in his middle sixties, worth at least the £1,000 in goods that was expected of an alderman and, as he had already served as sheriff, he was eligible for the mayoralty. Thomas and Joan Bradbury were now among the most worshipful of the citizens of London.[33]

---

[27] Bradbury hardly occurs in the few surviving customs accounts for London, and the entries merely show that he traded in cloth, worsted, silk and buckram, as one would expect, PRO, E 122/194/26, ff. 9, 10 (23 Edward IV-1 Richard III), 78/7, ff. 1, 1v, 2v (3-4 Henry VII). I am indebted to Kay Lacey for these references and the information that he does not occur in the surviving wool customs accounts or in the other main categories of public records dealing with trade; nor does Joan.

[28] E.g. *CIPM Henry VII*, 3 vols (London, 1898-1956), ii, no. 917, iii, nos 55, 63.

[29] Thwaites' offices made him an invaluable associate in the cloth and wool trade: Bradbury was involved in Thwaites' transactions over his house leased to Sir Thomas Lovell and stood surety for him, with Thomas Rich, in 1495 when he was accused of treason. CLRO, HR 225 (21), and *CCR, 1485-1509*, no. 895; J.C. Wedgwood, *History of Parliament, 1439-1509*, ii, *Biographies* (London, 1936), p. 855.

[30] See his relationships with the Nevilles and *CCR, 1485-1509*, no. 605.

[31] His brother, George, 1471; his step-son, James Bodley (admitted to the Mercers 1510); John Harrison, possibly a relative of the Lancelot Harrison who married a daughter of William and Beatrice Bodley, greatniece of Joan Bradbury (admitted 1502); Thomas Miles, who acted with him over land in Hertfordshire; Richard Shore; Thomas Cross; William Thinkhill; and Richard Austyn. Mercers' Company, List of Members from 1347 – this is the only source available and is not complete.

[32] 1487 discussing the interdict on trade with the Low Countries, Lyell and Watney, *Acts of Court*, pp. 299-300.

[33] Beaven, i, pp. 109, 273, ii, p. 20. Lyell and Watney, *Acts of Court*, pp. 259-60, 593-610; CLRO, Journal 10, f. 285v, and R.R. Sharpe, *London and the Kingdom* (London, 1894), i, p. 337; *RP*, vi, p. 542; CLRO, Repertory 1, f. 174, Repertory 2, ff. 42, 43.

It was just six months into the reign of Henry VIII when it was announced to the Mercers' Company, on 15 October 1509, that Thomas Bradbury had been elected mayor: he asked for their 'good myndes and assistens', and they prayed God send him 'good fortune and muche worsshipp'. They immediately elected eight bachelors to oversee the company's barge during the mayoral procession and serve at the mayoral banquet and chose them blue gowns and black sarcenet hoods so that 'worship' should accrue to them and their mayor. Later in the year the company gave him £48 for ray gowns of the livery of his mayoral household at Christmas.[34] Otherwise nothing is known of his inaugural ceremonies and nothing of Joan's part in them.

As mayor he was kept busy by complaints and quarrels of the Merchant Adventurers and of the Calais Staplers, the death of one of his sheriffs in office and, in January 1510, the likelihood of parliament giving the new king a retrospective grant of the customs duties from the death of his father.[35] It is doubtful, however, that Thomas took much notice of this last threat: he fell ill at the beginning of January, made his will on the 9th and died the next day.

He was buried in the Lady chapel of St Stephen Coleman Street before the image of the Virgin, as he wished, and with all the pomp appropriate for a lord mayor who died in office. His widow, too, spared no effort and their relatives turned up in force to make it a family event. The church was so small that no hearse could be used, so the hall and courtyard of his house (which was next to the churchyard) and the street from the house to the church was hung with black cloth garnished with his coat of arms. The body was fetched to the church between four banners: that of St Paul carried by his brother, Henry Bradbury; that of St Thomas Becket carried by John Leche the elder, a relative of his widow;[36] the arms of the City of London borne by John Leche the younger; and lastly the arms of the Mercers. The pennon of his own arms was borne by his nephew, William, now the head of the family and his male heir, and his coat

---

[34] Lyell and Watney, *Acts of Court*, pp. 335-38, 345. The list of contributors is headed by the 40s. of Thomas Semar, 'second' warden, who came from Saffron Walden, where his relatives were closely involved with the town's affairs and its vicar, Joan's brother.

[35] Lyell and Watney, *Acts of Court*, pp. 342-6. CLRO, Repertory 2, ff. 75v, 76v.

[36] A lawyer, John Leche, gentleman, can be found acting in various records, e.g. 1515 in London, CLRO, HR 238 (14). He was left a life interest in lands in Lambourne, Essex, by George Bradbury and was his executor, in 1506 (see below). The relationship between the elder and younger John Leches and Joan's immediate family has not been established. They may be of the Carden family, G. Ormerod, *A History of the Country Palatine of Cheshire*, ed. T. Helsby (2nd edn, London, 1882), ii, pp. 700-3. (The Leche family of poulters in London does not appear to be a connection of Joan.) The Leche family is made more mysterious by the arms displayed at Thomas Bradbury's funeral: (1) Bradbury quartering Rokell, the whole differenced by a crescent (Rokell was his mother's family); (2) No. 1 above impaling Bodley; (3) Bradbury impaling Rokell; (4) Bradbury impaling argent, a chevron sable, between three crosslets fitche also sable. No. 4 might justifiably be thought to include Joan's arms but this coat is a common one worn by several families and cannot be associated certainly with her or the Leches. It seems possible she was not of an armigerous family, or that her mother's arms were preferred to those of her father, if he had any.

of arms by John Joyner, Calais Pursuivant,[37] who had made most of the funeral arrangements. Behind the corpse followed the funeral 'assistants': John Josselyn, the husband of Thomas's sister, Philippa; William Tyrell, the husband of his wife's daughter, Elizabeth; Mathew Pemberton, a friend;[38] and Thomas Barley.[39] The chief mourners behind them were Joan herself, supported by Sir Robert Dymok, the hereditary champion of the kings of England, who was perhaps another friend, Dame Christian Colet and Dame Rede, widows of business associates and friends, Sir Henry Colet and Sir Bartholomew Rede. Then came Mistress Butler, wife of alderman William Butler (Isabel Bodley, niece of Joan), and William Bradbury's wife. Behind came the rulers of the city, the Mercers' Company and George Neville, Lord Abergavenny, another old associate of Thomas Bradbury and a friend of the family.[40] The prior of Holy Trinity Aldgate, alderman of Portsoken, said the service, singers were in the rood-loft and torches burned in the gallery; all the crafts filed past their deceased mayor, the Mercers last of all. After the *dirige* everyone gathered for spiced bread, cheese, comfits, sweet wine and hippocras in the Bradbury house. The next day saw three masses, the third being one of requiem taken by Richard Nix, an old friend of Bradbury. Joan offered the mass penny supported by Sir Robert Dymok; William and Henry Bradbury offered the coat of arms; Richard Broke, the under-sheriff and one of Bradbury's executors, with John Josselyn offered the shield of arms; and William Tyrell with John Leche the helm and crest, of which the silk and velvet had been supplied by Joan out of her husband's stock. During the mass 'gret dole' was given to the poor at the nearby Prince's Wardrobe and throughout the city; thirty poor men carried torches, and four more held tapers round the tomb. The ceremonies were concluded by 'a gret and sumptyeux dyner' arranged by Joan, with 'right honest messes of mete and allsoo wyne' sent to the lodgings of those who could not stay.

The dignified funeral provided consoling rituals for Joan: it marked her transition from the status of wife and all the agreeable pomp of being lady mayoress to that of widow. She would be rich, but as a widow she was shut off from any direct access to the centre of civic power – unless she were to marry again. The rest of Joan Bradbury's life, however, was to show that one way for a widow of character and wealth to retain some sort of position in her own right in the exclusive male world of civic government was to become a benefactress.

---

[37] H. Stanford London, *The College of Arms*, Monograph of the London Survey Committee, by W.H. Godfrey and others (London, 1963), p. 109. Joyner's description of the funeral provides all the details used here, BL, Add. MS 45131, ff. 151-152v.

[38] See below n. 103

[39] Probably the gentleman of Hertfordshire (BL, Harley MS 6166, p. 112), a relative of the Josselyns. See also, *Essex Feet of Fines, 1423-1527*, ed., P.H. Reaney and M. Fitch, Essex Archaeological Society (1964), p. 80.

[40] See below nn. 48, 100.

During the fifteen years of Joan and Thomas's marriage there had been changes in both their families. Joan's mother had died, but she still had three brothers alive: the beloved John, vicar of Saffron Walden, and the obscure Thomas and Henry Leche – presumably back in Northamptonshire – both of whom were remembered with a gown as 'my brothers' in Bradbury's will. Thomas's eldest brother, Robert, had died in 1500,[41] and the head of the family was now his nephew, William, who lived at Littlebury, Essex. Of his younger brothers, George and Henry, both mercers and neighbours in the parish of St Michael Bassishaw, George had died in 1506.[42] Henry, however, outlived Joan and died in 1533.[43]

Joan's Bodley children had largely been provided for by the time of Thomas's death, and she and Thomas had had no children. James had been apprenticed to Bradbury himself and was to be admitted to the Mercers' Company later in 1510, so he was now about twenty-five years old.[44] John had become a Benedictine monk at St Albans and was studying for his mastership in arts at Oxford before proceeding to canon law studies.[45] The youngest daughter, Denise, was still unmarried and was left the manor of Westcourt in Gillingham, Kent, as her marriage portion by her step-father, after the life interest of her mother. The eldest daughter, Elizabeth, had been married for some years to William Tyrell of South Ockendon, Essex, a member of a large and influential family, and she already had several children including a son and heir, Humphrey.[46] Bradbury seems to have paid a lot for this marriage and to

[41]   Robert had been a minor character in county government, linked briefly on commissions with such notables as Sir Thomas Montgomery and John Fortescue (some of their lands were to pass through Joan's hands), and William Tyrell who married Joan's daughter; J.P. in Cambridgeshire, 1486 till death; no will. *CPR, 1485-94*, pp. 162, 164, 165, 181, 214, 241, 348, 482; *1494-1509*, p.32; *CFR, 1485-1509*, nos 686, 692.

[42]   Neither Thomas or Joan Bradbury were mentioned in George's brief will, PRO, PROB 11/ 15, f. 58v (PCC 8 Adeane), sealed 6 June, probate twelve days later. Property in the Barbican (acquired 1498, CLRO, HR 225 (49)), St Margaret Lothbury, and Ware, Hertfordshire, went to his sister Philippa Josselyn and her daughter, Joan Hannys, with life estates to his brother Henry and to John Leche, gent., the last two being his executors. For this John Leche, see above n. 36.

[43]   Buried like his brother George in the chapel of Our Lady in St Michael Bassishaw; all his goods to his 'cousin' Mary, wife of William Woodham, citizen and tailor; she was executor (and possibly his daughter), GL, MS 9171/10, f. 223. 'Aunt Woodham' also occurs in William Bradbury's will of 1550. Nothing has been discovered about the Bradbury sister who married a man called Illesley and to whom Thomas left £7 or more, at Joan's discretion, and £40 for the marriage of her daughters.

[44]   Mercer's Company, List of Members from 1347. James must have been born about 1480; he was playing an important role in his uncle's town of Saffron Walden by 1513.

[45]   Only *Visitations* record his monastery. Emden, *A Biographical Register of the University of Oxford, 1501-1540* (Oxford, 1974), s.n. John Bodley.

[46]   Bradbury probably assisted Tyrell to retrieve some of his inheritance: Tyrell's mother, Elizabeth Bruyn had been a coheiress with her sister, Alice, and both of them married several times leaving a disputed inheritance. The Harlestons were the heirs of Alice, represented by Sir Clement Harleston in 1531 when the manor of South Ockendon was finally divided. The manor of Beckenham, Kent, was divided much earlier between the Tyrells and Harlestons, the Tyrell

continued

have helped William Tyrell financially. He and Joan had hopes that Humphrey Tyrell and Joan Josselyn, the daughter of Thomas's sister, Philippa, would one day marry and unite the Bradbury and Bodley families: he promised them the manor of Bawdes after the life estates of his brother-in-law and Joan, as an inducement.[47]

Thomas's will is conventional in its remembrances: as a mercer he thought naturally in terms of velvet, silks and embroidery, so suites of vestments went to the parish of his birth, Braughing, Hertfordshire, to Stansted Montfichet, Essex, where his grandmother was buried, and Manuden, Essex, one of his manors. He remembered the poor of several parishes and his tokens of family affection or duty took the form of sums of money, black gowns and rings. He mentioned no books, plate or any treasured possessions, all of which presumably passed to his wife with the residue of his estate. Outside the family, Robert Blagg and Thomas Stokes received black gowns and rings, and as they were both of the exchequer, these were presumably tokens of a past association that had been both amicable and profitable.

Thomas's depositions of land will be dealt with later for everything went first to Joan for her life, and how she augmented her estate and amended his depositions is a subject in itself. The only exception was his grant of the manor of Bawdes, Essex, to John Leche, vicar of Saffron Walden, for his life; a grant undoubtedly made in the knowledge that its profits would be mostly spent on charity and rebuilding Saffron Walden church. It is clear that John had endeared himself to Joan's second husband as effectively as he had to her first.

Joan's life estate consisted of a spacious mansion fronting Catte Street (now Gresham Street), adjacent to the churchyard of St Stephen Coleman Street and lying between Coleman Street and Basinghall Street; one Essex manor, two in Kent and another in Hertfordshire; an annuity of £60 out of the manor of 'Haryngfeld' paid by George Neville, Lord Abergavenny,[48] and another of

---

continued

moiety being further complicated by Elizabeth Bruyn's second marriage into the powerful Brandon family represented by Charles Brandon, Duke of Suffolk, in 1531. The precise transactions have not been discovered but the marriage arrangements for William and Elizabeth Bodley may have involved the purchase of the Tyrell moiety by Bradbury and a bailing out of Tyrell during his conflict with the Brandons. Bradbury owned the moiety at his death and bequeathed it to Humphrey, son of William Tyrell after Joan's life interest. *Visitations of Essex, 1552-1634*, pt 1, ed. W.C. Metcalfe, Harleian Society, 13 (1878), p. 114, and P. Morant, *History and Antiquities of Essex* (London, 1768), ii, p. 100. C.F. Richmond, *John Hopton* (Cambridge, 1981), pp. 238-39, n. 316, and VCH, *Essex*, vii, ed. W.R. Powell (London, 1978), p. 119. E. Hasted, *The History of Kent*, (2nd edn, Canterbury, 1797-1801), i, pp. 530-2. I am grateful to Kent Archives Office for confirming that there are no manorial rolls for Beckenham to elucidate the descent.

[47] Expressed in his will and in an indenture of 1513, BL Add. Charter 27442.

[48] Bradbury's will seems to be the only source (PRO, PROB 11/16, f. 203) for this annuity out of the manor of 'Harringfield': the £60 was covenanted to Thomas and Joan by Abergavenny for their lives and, so long as it was paid, certain, unspecified lands were to be held to the use of Thomas Neville (presumably Abergavenny's younger brother, citizen and goldsmith, and husband of Elizabeth Brice). If the annuity was not paid the lands were forfeit to the Bradburys.

£20 from the prior of Holy Trinity Aldgate.[49] She also received the residue of the estate which included a prosperous mercery business, 'at her free will'. Bradbury, no more than Thomas Bodley, thought of trammelling his widow in her freedom either to remarry or to manage her business affairs. Joan was executrix with Richard Broke, the under-sheriff (soon to be recorder) of London, and Richard Nix, bishop of Norwich, an associate of Thomas of at least twenty years standing. Thomas had only made the barest requests for prayers and directions for his funeral in his will, because the main arrangements had been made verbally with Joan: he only needed to suggest which properties were to be used to set up the chantry they had planned together, in St Stephen's Coleman Street where he was buried.[50] This was a trust that Joan regarded with the utmost seriousness, just as she had for her first husband – she was not one of Stow's 'forgetful' widows – and the way in which she carried it out gives us her measure as a person. The responsibility of setting up a sound endowment also meant that one aspect of her immediate future was settled: she had to remain active or fail in her trusts.

Apart from these duties, she had several options. She was now about fifty-five: her wealth might attract another husband even higher up the social scale than a lord mayor, but widowhood would allow her to be her own mistress. She could choose either to manage or to wind up her husband's mercery business, and she in fact seems to have done the latter, although possibly not till after the death of her mercer son in 1514.[51] The resulting cash could be converted into lands to increase her income as a rentier. She was certainly going to need large amounts of cash to purchase the lands and licences for her chantry. She had an extensive family to engage her interest and she could augment her lands for the benefit of her children. She also had the option of the role advocated as the most becoming for a widow, that of religion and an obscure retirement. Religious observance and charity seem to have been important to Joan, but there is no sign that she ever wanted a religious life or felt the need to take a vow of chastity, like several of her female contemporaries and social equals. She never adopted a severe regimen, dressed in widow's weeds and barb

---

[49] The Holy Trinity Aldgate annuity may have been the result of Bradbury assisting the priory in its considerable financial difficulties at this time. It held the manor and advowson of his birthplace, and the prior was an alderman. M.C. Rosenfield, 'The Disposal of the Property of London Monastic Houses, with a special study of Holy Trinity Aldgate' (unpublished Ph.D. thesis, University of London, 1961), esp. pp. 28-30. Joan had corrody there, *L&P HVIII*, ii, pt 1, p. 39.

[50] Bradbury never specifically refers to a chantry in his will, PRO, PROB 11/16, ff. 202v-203 (PCC 26 Bennett). John Stow saw the monument on the north side of the choir after it had been defaced by reformers, *A Survey of London*, ed C.L. Kingsford (Oxford, 1908), i, p. 284. Joan's freedom compares favourably with some of the other widows in this book, and see A.J. Kettle, ' "My Wife shall have it". Marriage and Property in Wills and Testaments of later Medieval England', in *Marriage and Property*, ed. E.M. Crick (Aberdeen, 1984), pp. 97-102.

[51] Within two months of Bradbury's death she agreed that John Aleyn, mercer and friend, should take over William More as his apprentice, Lyell and Watney, *Acts of Court*, pp. 358.

unnecessarily or mortified the flesh. There is in fact every reason to believe that, after her initial grief, she maintained a nice worldly pomp and relished a good meal even as she dispensed charity, encouraged prayer and education and enjoyed the conversation of a good, honest priest.

The Widow: The Bradbury Chantry in St Stephen's Coleman Street and the Mercers' Company

The details of the setting up of the Bradbury chantry provide the most personal picture of Joan that exists apart from her own testament. She already had the experience of setting up a two-year chantry for her first husband, dealing with a chantry priest, paying his wage and choosing the most efficacious prayers. She now had the means to do something more permanent and prestigious and to include Thomas Bodley in the arrangements for Thomas Bradbury.

The size of the endowment must have been decided before Bradbury died, for he suggested that the reversion of his great dwelling-house, worth about £10 a year in rent, be used, as well as the annuity paid by Lord Abergavenny, *but only as his wife thought best*. The average cost of endowing a perpetual chantry around this date has been estimated at £200, but Joan spent more than that on the lands alone. It was to be a 'service' chantry with a priest whose salary came from an endowment of land granted to trustees, who would collect the rents and appoint and supervise the priest, pay him and keep the surplus for their fee. The trustees held by 'divine service' and could be prosecuted for negligence. Licences had to be obtained from the crown to alienate into mortmain, at a cost of several times the annual income of the land; the local bishop had to approve; reliable trustees had to found who were prepared to take on the burden; land with a clear, unencumbered title had to be secured; and lastly ordinances setting out the priest's and the trustees' duties had to be drawn up and approved.[52] It was to take fourteen years.

Within a year of Bradbury's death Joan had bought the ideal land with a clear title: twenty-nine acres in the parish of Marylebone and 120 acres in Westminster and the parishes of St Giles and St Martin in the Fields, Middlesex, from John Fortescue of Punsborne and his wife, Philippa Spice, paying in the region of £260.[53] The pipes of the city's water supply from Tyburn crossed this land and any new owner was an object of interest to the civic

---

[52] K.L. Wood-Legh, *Perpetual Chantries in Britain* (Cambridge, 1965), pp. 16-20, 39, 46-50. Alan Krieder, *English Chantries: the Road to Dissolution* (Cambridge, MA, 1979), pp. 81-82, on the severity of the fines paid to the crown.

[53] The Fortescues had held the land for a considerable period, leasing the city water rights at £5 a year. It was to produce an income of £13 14s. 8d. Joan's feoffees for the purchase were: Richard Nix, Richard Broke, John Leche, her brother, James Bodley, her son, Robert Blagg of the exchequer, and Thomas Ashby and Andrew Edmund, two lawyers. PRO, CP 25/2/27/178, nos 6, 7, 8 (feet of fines for Middlesex, Nov. 1510 to Feb. 1511).

authorities – Joan's proposals for the land would have been regarded with complete approval.

She could now approach her chosen trustees, the Mercers' Company. From this date she appears regularly in her own right in the company's acts as 'Lady' Bradbury: the title was a tribute to her position as a benefactress of the company as well as that of widow of a lord mayor. On 10 April 1511 the court of assistants was told:

> that my lady Bradbury was disposed to gyve unto this Compeny her hous that she dwellith yn & for to put us in possession as shortly as she can, to thentent we shuld make therof oure Hall & there to kepe oure assembles.

The house was conveniently near the company's existing headquarters in the Hospital of St Thomas of Acre and abutted to its west on property owned by the company's Whittington estate. At this time the company had no proper hall and was engaged in lengthy negotiations with the Hospital for land on Cheapside so that they could build one large enough for their annual feast on St Thomas's Day. A house that could be used in the meantime was a very attractive offer: the company lost no time in choosing a high-ranking deputation to wait upon Lady Bradbury.[54]

The terms were that the house was a free gift, void if they failed to perform the charges laid on the Middlesex lands held in trust for the chantry, the annual obit and bequests to the parish poor. The Mercers had long experience of trusteeship and there is no doubt that they were from the start prepared to accept a trust that gave them £10 a year profit.[55] The profit was so great that it seems likely that Joan was aiming to make her second husband's company a gift as well to ensure that the chantry was well cared for.

The use of her house by the Mercers resulted in Joan playing a role in the Mercers' affairs not usually open to a woman: in June 1511 it was announced that, at her request, the company would keep their St Thomas Tide banquet in her house and that it would be more 'chargeable' than usual because of the 'Company of Gentilwemen that she myndeth to have'; £15 was allowed out of the common box. In July 1512 this diversion was repeated, and in September the whole company was formally informed about the obit and lands and duly consented to all decisions that the wardens and court of assistants might make in concluding the matter.[56] While steady progress was made over the slow and

---

[54] Lyell and Watney, *Acts of Court*, pp. 378, 384, 387. For the general use of this title for the widows of mayors, E. Miller, 'Rulers of Thirteenth Century Towns: The Cases of York and Newcastle-upon-Tyne', *Thirteenth Century England*, ed. P.R. Coss and S.D. Lloyd (Woodbridge, 1986), p. 140.

[55] They were expert at assessing the viability of a trust, Lyell and Watney, *Acts and Court*, pp. 185-86, Wood-Legh, *Perpetual Chantries*, pp. 34, 42-3.

[56] Lyell and Watney, *Acts of Court*, pp. 391, 403. By this time Joan had received preliminary licence to establish the chantry and acquire lands worth £9 13s. 4d. p.a., *L&HVIII*, i, item 833, no. 166.

expensive acquisition of the necessary royal licences, the banquets attended by Joan and the 'gentlewomen' continued.[57] The first check occurred in January 1518 when everything was complete and all Joan had to do was seal the documents.[58] The delay seems to have been of her making and to have been caused by the conveyance of her house. Her life had changed since her initial intention to make it over to the Mercers' as 'shortly' as possible: she had come to enjoy having the Mercers' assemblies and banquets in her house, and her favourite daughter, Denise, had married Nicholas Leveson, a mercer, and lived in London.[59] Joan now had every reason not to give up her great house.

The Mercers continued to use it for their banquet over the next four years because their new hall was still not finished, but in 1522 they were sufficiently irritated to 'abate' the guests and the ladies at the banquet and only spend £10.[60] Joan's son-in-law, Nicholas Leveson, was called into the negotiations and on 2 March 1524 the final indenture was sealed. As a sweetener, the company agreed to Joan's request that the profits of the house should go to her executors for one year after her death to perform her will, because of her 'good benevolent mind' towards the company, and further agreed to abide by her lease of one tenement in the property to her grandson-in-law, Guy Crafford.[61]

Despite the delays the Mercers knew very well they had a generous agreement and a worthy benefactress and that celebrations were in order: in 1525 the St Thomas Tide banquet went off in style, £20 being spent and the wives of the wardens and court being present.[62] It is not known if Lady Bradbury attended, but if she did not she could at least derive satisfaction from the knowledge that the banquet was being held again in the manner *she* had instituted fourteen years before and would continue to be so held for some considerable time.

[57] Lyell and Watney, *Acts of Court*, pp. 413, 422, 428, 438, 446. *L&P HVIII*, i, item 1732 (4); ii, pt 1, item 359. See also Wood-Legh, *Perpetual Chantries*, pp. 310-11.

[58] 24 Oct. 1514, licence in mortmain received, (*L&P HVIII*, ii, pt 1, item 359); May 1516, Joan's feoffees granted the Middlesex lands to the Mercers, the conveyance to take effect on her death. An indenture recording the requirements of the chantry was drawn up (the date of this conveyance is recorded in the final indenture of 1524, Mercers' Company, Register of Benefactors' Wills, i, ff. 55v-59, and see Lyell and Watney, *Acts of Court*, p. 751); Jan. 1518 the deeds granting the house were ready and so was the will of Richard Fielding, mercer declaring the use (ibid., p. 451).

[59] They lived in Lime Street in the parish of St Andrew Undershaft where they were buried.

[60] Lyell and Watney, *Acts of Court*, pp. 456, 474, 532, 543. This was a time of bereavement for Joan as her brother died in 1521. Some of the Mercers' vexation sprang from the cost and delay of the building of their hall.

[61] Indenture between Joan, the Mercers and the Hospital of St Thomas of Acon (who received the house if the Mercers were negligent), Mercers' Company, Register of Benefactors' Wills, i, ff. 55v-59. Thomas Draper's will declaring the use, CLRO, HR 241 (30). Lyell and Watney, *Acts of Court*, pp. 672, 675-76. There is no sign of the Crafford lease after her death.

[62] Ibid., *Acts of Court*, p. 696. The same sum was spent each year up to 1531 and presumably ladies were always present, ibid., pp. 726, 747 Mercer's Company, Acts of Court 1527-60, ff. 13, 20v, 29v, 47, 62.

Through the precise ordinances of the chantry in St Stephen's Joan could express her own religious needs and those of her husbands and ease the passage of their souls through purgatory. Each mass had its own particular value as did the annual giving of alms at the founder's obit, the latter securing the valuable prayers of the poor who benefited.[63] Conclusions as to her piety, however, are not easy to reach for the chantry is typical of its kind. Her requirement for masses was undemanding, compared to some other founda- tions, in that she only stipulated a requiem mass on three days a week, wisely avoiding the danger of too much repetition, and left her priest free to choose the mass on the other days. Her choice of the requiem mass was an obvious one: it was the one most frequently asked for, and it was held to be particularly efficacious. The choice of prayers was equally conventional. If the ordinances of her chantry do not reveal her piety as anything but what could be expected of a woman of her background, their detail, the list of beneficiaries and the generous treatment of its trustees say a great deal about her foresight and character: she loved her family and friends and she knew the Mercers would be the better trustees if they profited handsomely from their duties. (The Mercers were to spend £11 13s. 4d. of the rent from the Middlesex lands on the annual obit, of which 10s. was for their 'potation' and 16s. 8d. for their rewards – and of course the profit from her great house was pure profit.) She intended the chantry to carry her name and those of her brother, husbands, all their parents and benefactors and friends, into the prayers of future generations and it was not going to fail through any error or parsimony on her part.[64]

The Sister: Benefactress of Saffron Walden

Joan had a second life that centred on Saffron Walden in Essex where her brother, John Leche, was vicar from 1489 till his death in 1521. It was a prosperous wool and cloth town with a Mercers' Row in its market place. Joan had other ties with the area too. The main line of the Bradbury family was settled nearby at Littlebury and had extensive property in the county including shops in Saffron Walden.[65] Also her son James Bodley, the mercer, had married Joan, the daughter of Thomas and Joan Strachey of Saffron Walden, before 1510.[66] The Stracheys were part of the town's ruling clique which exercised its power mainly through the chantry guild of Our Lady of Pity which

[63] Wood-Legh, *Perpetual Chantries*, pp. 305-310.

[64.] Mercers' Company, Register of Benefactors' Wills, i, ff. 57-59. See Wood-Legh, *Perpetual Chantries*, pp. 202, 212-213, 243, 281-290.

[65] R. Griffin, Lord Braybrook, *History of Audley End* (London, 1836), p. 159; PRO, PROB 11/ 33, ff. 205v-206 (PCC 26 Coode).

[66] Visitations are the main source for this marriage, but it is borne out by other evidence. Visitation of 1623 for Surrey in *Surrey Archaeological Collections*, 10 (1891), and *Visitations of Surrey 1530, 1572, 1623*, Harleian Society, 43 (1899), p. 147.

administered the town's almshouses.[67] James swiftly became part of this clique: he became 'Jamy Bodley of Chepyng Walden' and apparently preferred provincial life, leaving London to his mother and his sister, Denise.[68]

All three of them were closely involved in one of the most important ventures in the history of Saffron Walden: its campaign to achieve self-government. It was part of the king's duchy of Lancaster and as a consequence it had several charters of privileges but no corporate status. From the 1490s its trade had increasingly suffered from royal enforcement of manorial rights of toll which drove traders to patronise the rival market of Newport. In 1513 John Leche, Joan, her son James, his father-in-law and other leading townsmen failed in a petition to Henry VIII offering to redeem the tolls for a substantial sum of money: the king's rights could not be bought. On advice it was decided that a new religious guild of the Holy Trinity should be set up to which the tolls and other manorial rights could be granted by the king. The new guild would be able to operate just as if it was the town incorporate and its basis would be the chantry already envisaged by Katherine Semar, a wealthy widow of the town.[69] The king's licence directed to Thomas Strachey, James Bodley and two others, permitting the establishment of a Holy Trinity guild in the church of Saffron Walden with land worth 20 marks a year, arrived in March 1514 – Joan's chantry in London was being planned at this time and personnel and expertise were used to the common benefit of the two projects, James Bodley being an energetic factotum in both.

The list of those to be prayed for and the lavish decoration of the licence sets out graphically and precisely who had contributed most to the 'freedom' of the town and what position Joan occupied in this hierarchy. Katherine Semar headed the list (after the king, queen and Wolsey), Joan came second, followed by John Leche,[70] Thomas Strachey and his wife, James Bodley and his

---

[67] For the government of the town and its first guild, F.W. Steer, 'The Statutes of Saffron Walden Almshouses', *Transactions of the Essex Archaeological Society*, new series 25, pt 2 (1958), pp. 162-63, 192-203. Its bederoll records some of the benefactors of the guild and the town; the 'John clerk, late vicar of Walden' must conceal John Leche, a major benefactor, and not John Hodgkin, vicar for only 1540-44, as glossed by Steer; there are several Semars including Sir Thomas, the London mercer and associate of the Bradburys; Joan's name does not occur.

[68] The name he used in his will, Essex Record Office, D/ACR 2/22, ff. 22-22v.

[69] The king's profit on the transaction was undoubtedly the same! For some reason the existing guild of Our Lady of Pity was not used. Katherine Semar's will of 1510 had provided for the endowment of a chantry to pray for the souls of herself and a large number of relatives and friends. The gift was made good in her second will of 26 May 1514, James Bodley and his father-in-law being two of the witnesses, just as they had been trustees in her earlier will. Her will of 1514 is given by J. Clarke, 'The Guild of the Holy Trinity Saffron Walden', *Transactions of the Essex Archaeological Society*, new series 3, (1889), pp. 285-86. (Her dead husband, Thomas Semar, must not be confused , as he often is, with Sir Thomas Semar, mercer and associate of the Bradburys: their wills make this clear; he was however, a considerable benefactor of Saffron Walden, especially its almshouses, PCC 31 Hogen.) C.B. Rowntree, *Saffron Walden Then and Now* (Chelmsford, 1951), pp. 11-14 (no references).

[70] John Leche and Katherine Semar paid £20 each towards buying a further grant of tolls, a court of pie powder, the king's wind and malt mills, etc., Rowntree, *Saffron Walden*, p. 14.

wife, and then a long list of others, both alive and dead, including Thomas Bodley. The border was decorated with a picture of St Katherine for Katherine Semar, the arms of the Bodley family, the maid's head of the Mercers' Company, and a merchant's mark, perhaps that of Joan Bradbury. The cross of St George, the Holy Trinity, a picture of St Ursula and her companions on whose feast day the new guild was licensed to hold a fair, and lastly the blue saffron crocus of the town completed the chosen motifs.[71]

The same year saw the death of one of the youngest and most energetic campaigners for this licence: James Bodley, who left three children, all minors, to the care of his wife and executrix, Joan Strachey. He asked his mother to be overseer of his will, leaving her a pound of saffron as a token payment.[72] Joan had lost a son who had been one of her active business representatives.

John Leche and his sister, Joan, not only contributed money and time to the civic and business prosperity of Saffron Walden, they also spent generously on beautifying its church and the education of the neighbourhood. The fine church still stands as a visible reminder of John Leche's involvement with his parish. The composer of the epitaph that runs round his plain altar tomb, who had benefited personally from his charity, placed him among the best of his profession.[73] His vicariate saw the completion of the new clerestory and crypt, the north and south aisles, the south porch and its upper chamber, the north porch (*c.* 1500) and the corner towers (1512-15):

> With many a gift the sacred shrine he filled,
> Prompt to design and sedulous to build.

Joan made considerable financial contributions as well, and the profits of the manor of Bawdes that John received from Thomas Bradbury in 1510 must have largely gone to the church works. John did not live to see the church finished (about 1526), but Joan did.[74]

---

[71] *L&P HVIII*, i, item 2772 (57). The town clerk of Saffron Walden kindly allowed the author to see the original licence. The merchant's mark is close to one on a seal to a deed (BL, Add. Charter 64102) to which Thomas Bradbury was a party. The one seems to incorporate a TB and the other a JB; wives often used their husband's mark with a difference. It could also be James Bodley's mark, but that would mean Joan is completely unrepresented.

[72] Dated 27 Oct. 1514, no probate clause, Essex Record Office, D/ACR 2/22, ff. 22-22v. Bequests to the church's 'next newe worke,' and to the new guild, and more if all his children died. His eldest son, John, got his 'corner house' against the market cross.

[73] Braybrook, *Audley End*, p. 213, gives Latin text; an English translation hangs in the church.

[74] Neither the accounts nor the bederoll survive to show precisely how much Joan and John contributed to this project. The main architect employed during Leche's life was John Wastell who also worked on King's College Chapel, Cambridge. Emden, *BRUC*, s.n. John Leche. Notes including a history of the church, *Transactions of the Essex Archaeological Society*, new series, 21 (1933-4), pp. 374-77. W.J. Fancett, *The Story of Saffron Walden Church* (rev. edn, Saffron Walden, 1983). J.H. Harvey, *English Medieval Architects: A Biographical Dictionary down to 1550* (London, 1954), s.n. Wastell.

From at least 1517 John Leche wanted to endow the new Holy Trinity guild with the means to support another priest who would be a schoolmaster. An agreement of that year mapped out his proposals for the employment of a 'profound grammarion' to teach grammar after the manner of Eton or Winchester. He was also to pray, 'for as much as there is nothing in this world so behoveful for the soul health as is prayer' for John and others, including 'my lady Dame Johanne Bradbury the which hath been special benefactrix in the purchasing and obteynyng the said lettres patent', and James Bodley, his nephew 'speciall laborer for the patent' (i.e. for the guild). The schoolmaster would live and teach in the house on the corner of Castle Street and Vicar Lane rebuilt for the purpose by John and his sister.[75]

In the event John found that his lands were insufficient for his purpose, but he continued to discuss the project and agreed before he died that the prayers demanded of the priest be set aside and that he should 'applye [to] the techyng of his scolers and to syng masse' only. John died on 8 November 1521 in his eighties,[76] trusting in his sister to establish the school in a more lavish way than he could afford.

For the third time in her life Joan was carrying out the wishes of the dead. She acted with all speed, perhaps aware of her own advancing years. She immediately found a suitable schoolmaster and paid his salary herself, and then she turned to the problems of the endowment. Within the year she had bought a royal licence that the guild of Holy Trinity might acquire lands worth £10 a year to support the schoolmaster to teach 'grammer and good manners and literature' and to pray for, among others, Richard Nix, bishop of Norwich, and Richard Broke and his wife (fellow executors of her second husband), and the now dead, John Leche, Katherine Semar, Thomas Bradbury, and Thomas, John (her monk son) and James Bodley.[77] She then granted to the guild a rent charge of £12 out of her manor of Willingale Spain, of which £10 was for the salary of the schoolmaster and £2 for an obit for herself and her brother. The whole scheme was finalised by a tripartite indenture on 18 May 1525, similar to that with the Mercers, between herself, the guild and the nearby abbey of Walden (which would intervene if the others failed in their duties). The boys were to be drawn from the neighbourhood of her brother's vicarages, her kin

[75] VCH, *Essex*, ii, p. 518. Rowntree, *Saffron Walden*, pp. 14-15.

[76] His will does not survive; his executors were Joan and Nicholas Leveson, Greater London Record Office, Bishop of London Vicar General's Book i, f. 21. It is likely he was the John Leche who owned, signed and annotated four books now in Oxford, Trinity College, MSS E14, Munshull's *Nominale*; D16A, *Prick of Conscience*; F13, hymns and prayers; D49, *Canterbury Tales*. See J. Griffiths in G. Cigman, ed., *Lollard Sermons*, EETS original series 294 (1989), pp. xiv-xvii; I am grateful for Dr Griffiths' advice. All the books suit what is known of Leche's interests. The annotations in the *Tales* show he owned it as a boy.

[77] VCH, *Essex*, ii, p. 519. Krieder, *English Chantries*, p. 63. *L&P HVIII*, iii, pt 2, no. 2993.

and her tenants; teaching was to be free, though a registration fee could be accepted; the curriculum was to be that of Eton or Winchester as her brother had wished.[78]

The establishment of the school was the last work of endowment that Joan undertook: it was the last act of a long, loving friendship with a brother and cleric who must have been an amiable and charming as well as an energetic, charitable and pious man. John had endeared himself to the two families into which Joan had married and helped her to cement them into a whole.

The Matriarch

Joan's role as a matriarch can be studied in almost as much detail as her roles as benefactress and founder. The day to day management of her estate is not known,[79] but her larger transactions can be traced with the guidance of her detailed and immaculately thought out will. During the twenty years of her second widowhood she more than doubled her substantial jointure, and these purchased lands were her own to bequeath as she pleased for the benefit of her dynasty. She made two changes in her two husbands' dispositions which accorded with her own wishes and took account of the alterations that had occurred among their descendants.[80] All her married children had given her grandchildren. At some date after Bradbury's death her youngest daughter, Denise, had married Nicholas Leveson, a younger son and eventual heir of Richard Leveson of Staffordshire. Nicholas was a mercer and a merchant of the Staple; he became a warden of the Mercers and sheriff.[81] The match was suitable and it turned out to be a great success. Her eldest grand-daughter, who was named for her, the daughter of James Bodley, had also married well to Guy Crafford of London, 'gentleman', a lawyer.

The lands that Joan held from her first marriage were small compared to those she acquired later. The three messuages at Battle Bridge in Southwark

---

[78] VCH, *Essex*, ii, pp. 519-20. Rowntree, *Saffron Walden*, p. 15. T. Wright, 'Rules of the Free School of Saffron Walden,' *Archaeologia*, 34 (1852), pp. 37-41. There is little sign that she was influenced by St Paul's School recently founded by Dean Colet and administered by the Mercers' Company, except possibly in the registration fee. Colet's school had little influence, see N. Orme, *English Schools in the Middle Ages* (London, 1973), pp. 113-14. John's obit was duly observed by the Holy Trinity Guild as 'our founder', as was that of Katherine Semar, but Joan's does not appear in the Saffron Walden Guild Accounts, 37-38 Henry VIII, p. 5 (in the care of the town clerk). In 1513 John had also arranged for an obit at St Catharine's, Cambridge. Compare the school foundation by Thomasine Percyvale, above.

[79] There are few surviving court rolls, see n. 88.

[80] The main source for the descent of the lands are the wills of her husbands and herself.

[81] *Visitation of Kent 1574 and 1592*, Harleian Society, 75 (1924), pp. 133-34. Mill Stephenson, *A List of Monumental Brasses in the British Isles* (London, 1926): St Andrew Undershaft, brass showing eighteen children. Beaven, *Aldermen*, ii, p. 171. He was sheriff 1534-35, and died in 1539; his widow never remarried and her will shows that she continued the business until her death in 1561, see n. 97.

were profitable and they duly passed by her will to the Bodley male heir, John, son of James. Not so the messuage in St Margaret's Southwark, however, which she left to Thomas, the second son of her daughter, Denise Leveson, charged with a 20s. annuity to his cousin Elizabeth Tyrell.[82] The lands Joan had from her brother John were even less significant – the copyhold lands at Newport and Widdington, Essex, which had proved insufficient to endow his schoolmaster. Before she died she transferred them to feoffees for the use of her grand-daughter, Mary Tyrell, and her husband, George Hall, with remainder to the Levesons.

Thomas Bradbury died possessed of five manors, besides his great house in London and his two annuities of £60 and £20: Bawdes and Manuden in Essex, Westcourt (in Gillingham), and a moiety of Beckenham, in Kent, and Horwellbury in Kelshall, in Hertfordshire. Several of his dispositions were intended to benefit Joan's children after her life estate: the Beckenham moiety was to go Humphrey Tyrell, her grandson,[83] and the manor of Westcourt was to be Denise Bodley's marriage portion.[84] Joan interfered with neither of these bequests nor with that to his nephew, the son of Philippa Josselyn, of his manor of Manuden (with lands in Stansted Montficet and other places),[85] and indeed probably could not have done so. It may have been his financial problems that enabled Joan to buy William Bradbury's reversionary rights in the manor of Horwellbury, Hertfordshire,[86] along with those in the manor of Bawdes and in the mill that Bradbury had in Essex, for £160 in 1513. This left her free to sell Horwellbury and to leave Bawdes to her grand-daughter Joan Bodley and her husband, Guy Crafford.[87]

---

[82]　Surveys of 1555 show that these properties lay between Fishmongers' Alley and another alley off the west side of St Margaret's Hill: two tenements 'being olde inheritances' were owned by Francis Bodley (the son and heir of William Bodley, and the sole male heir of both Thomas and Richard Bodley); a house owned by 'widow Leveson' (i.e. Denise) – the survey erroneously says it had formerly belonged to Richard (and not Thomas) Bodley. See M. Carlin, 'The Urban Development of Southwark, *c.* 1200 to 1550', (unpublished Ph.D. thesis, University of Toronto, 1983), pp. 121, 166, and fig. 8.

[83]　Worth £20 p.a., see William Tyrell's will, GL, MS 9531/11, f. 124 (1534). Remainder to the heirs of Philippa Josselyn, Thomas's sister.

[84]　Bought from John Thorpe. Hasted, *A History of Kent*, ix, p. 232.

[85]　With remainder to his other nephew, William Bradbury. Bought in 1509 for £400 from Henry Wodecok, executor of Henry Gardiner. Bradbury used as his feoffees, his old associates, the bishop of Norwich and Lord Abergavenny, with Sir Edward Poynings and his brother-in-law, John Josselyn. Extensive documentation, Essex Record Office, D/DGI TI/1-9, showing the involvement of Richard Broke and John Leche. See also *Essex Feet of Fines 1423-1527*, p. 128. The earlier history of manor is given in E.W. Ives, *The Common Lawyers of Pre-Reformation England* (Cambridge, 1983), pp. 120-21; by 1539 it was held by the Crawley family, P. Morant, *History and Antiquities of the County of Essex*, 2 vols (London, 1768), ii, p. 619.

[86]　Bought by Thomas Bradbury in 1507 from William Paston, *The Paston Letters*, ed. J. Gairdner (London, 1875), iii, p. 403.

[87]　Bradbury acquired Bawds from Sir Thomas Bawd, the husband of a sister of the John Fortescue of Punsborne who was to sell so much land to Joan. It seems likely from the text of her will that she bought yet more land from Bawd near the manor. BL, Add. Charter 27442 (the feoffees were the bishop of Norwich, Sir Edward Poynings, Thomas Miles, mercer and a past

continued

Joan also built up an extensive estate of her own which was entirely hers to dispose of as she wished. She must have invested the proceeds of the Bradbury mercery, cloth and commercial business in this way, or continued to run it for some time while investing the surplus – a rough estimate shows she spent in the region of £5,000 on her land and projects. James Bodley may have also profited from the business before his death in 1514: he had possibly acted as a factor among the clothiers of Essex for his step-father during the early years of his Saffron Walden marriage, as he certainly acted as feoffee and agent for his mother's Essex lands, performing such tasks as taking fealty at a manorial court.[88]

Joan's largest purchases were from John Fortescue of Punsborne and his wife Philippa Spice and cost her over £1,000: the Middlesex acres for her chantry for about £260, and the extensive manors of Willingale Spain and Black Notley with the latter's smaller companions of White Notley and Staunton, for a total bordering on £800.[89] She acquired further land in White Notley from a William Aylnoth of Chelmsford.[90] Apart from the comparatively small annual charge on her manor of Willingale Spain for her school, all these lands went to her daughter, Denise and Denise's heirs, of whom there was an abundance.[91] Joan also allowed the Levesons to profit from two other purchases of hers, her house at Stratford, where she presumably stayed when travelling between London and Saffron Walden, and the manor of Tendering in West Thurrock, bought from Sir Richard Fitzlewis, a connection of the

continued
apprentice of Bradbury, and Robert Bowman). VCH, *Hertfordshire*, iii, p. 243. Morant *Essex*, i, p. 121, who is aware that Bawdes was held by Craffords till 1606 but ignorant of the connection between them and Bradbury. Joan made the bequest to the Craffords on the condition they did not procure 'busines of russeling by any maner sute in the lawe' – Crafford was a lawyer.

[88] Essex Record Office, Court Roll of Black Notley 1513, T/A 469/23 (microfilm of rolls held at North Riding Record Office): he took her tenants' fealty there at her first manorial court on 15 July 1513. The only court rolls surviving for Joan's manors during her life appear to be those for this manor, 1513-39.

[89] The Middlesex lands were Fortescue lands, but all the rest represented the inheritance of Philippa, from her grandfather, Clement Spice and his wife, Alice, the sister and coheiress of Sir Thomas Montgomery (d. 1489). Morant, *Essex*, ii, pp. 48, 123-24 (Morant is always mystified by Lady Bradbury because he expects her *eldest male* heir to succeed to her Essex lands). *Essex Feet of Fines, 1423-1527*, pp. 121, 128, 158. Lord Clermont, *The Works of Sir John Fortescue* (London, 1869), ii, pp. 163-65, and his pedigrees for the links between the Tyrells, Bawds, Fitzlewises, Fortescues and Stonors that may have facilitated these sales.

[90] The only source for this purchase seems to be her will.

[91] Remainders went to (1) her grandson, Humphrey Tyrell; (2) Joan Crafford; and lastly if all heirs failed, to the Mercers who were to sell everything and spend the proceeds on repairing the roads of Essex, taking £10 for themselves. Joan's will refers to a previous indenture about these lands between herself and the Levesons made on 18 Jan. 1526, since when her other daughter, Elizabeth Tyrell, had died, an event which had necessitated the specification of Humphrey as the next reversioner rather than his mother, presumably to prevent his father acquiring any of his dead wife's inheritance and using it for children by his second wife. For their descendants, Morant, *Essex*, ii, p. 124, and G. Leveson-Gower, *The Pedigree of Gresham* (London, 1883), p. 11 (unaware of Lady Bradbury).

Fortescues and Tyrells.[92] The latter was near South Ockendon; Joan kept cattle there, as did Nicholas Leveson after her. He bought the manor from Joan's executors, with her specific permission, so long as he paid the full market price without 'covin.'[93] The money went to perform her testament.

Her sense of family and her knowledge of its members is apparent in all that she did. The order of reversionary rights on her own lands after the main bequest to Denise sets out her dynastic preferences: the heirs of Denise and Nicholas, the heirs of Denise, her grandson Humphrey Tyrell, and then her grand-daughter, Joan Bodley-Crafford. She pointedly ignored the male heir of the Bodleys – John already had property in Saffron Walden from his father, but at Joan's death he only got what his Bodley grandfather left and nothing more, not even a remembrance.[94] What Joan's decisions would have been if James, her son, had lived, we cannot know; the death of her daughter Elizabeth only changed some reversionary rights. Joan clearly did not feel blindly bound by notions of male primogeniture. She did have a sense of dynasty, however, and did not bestow freedom of action upon her heirs: she specified in her will that her male heirs might make life estates to their wives from her lands but no more. She wanted the lands *she* had bought to stay in the family *she* had selected to be *her* dynasty.

At bottom her choices were governed by affection and reasons of personality. A comparison of the wills of Joan and her daughter, Denise, reveal that they were chips off the same block and it is not surprising that Joan wanted to benefit this daughter with whom she got on so well. Joan's experienced eye may have also consciously chosen the best stock: she preferred adults who were married and had children rather than the doubtful products of male primogeniture. Not only did she ignore the Bodley male heir but she specifically excluded the eldest son of the Levesons, and both these young men in fact failed to marry and have children. Joan's choices were good ones and she became the ancestress of a wealthy and prolific dynasty.

Joan did not neglect her other younger descendants and recognised her responsibilities to the less well-off. She remembered the three Tyrell daughters of her dead daughter Elizabeth, whose husband had remarried so quickly and

[92] The only reference to this house is in her will (see n. 110); its precise location is unknown. Tendering was acquired before Sir Richard died in 1528, H.L. Elliot, 'Fitz Lewes of West Hordon,' *Transaction of the Essex Archaeological Society*, new series, 6, pp. 43-46, *Essex Feet of Fines, 1423-1527*, p. 171. The manor was held from the prior of St John's (Morant, *Essex*, i, pt 2, p. 98), remembered in Joan's will.

[93] Both references to cattle come from their wills; Joan's will shows considerable concern over the repair of the waterworks and ferry at West Thurrock. Tendering continued in the Leveson family, although Morant, *Essex*, ii, p. 98, says it went to John Bodley – a statement that seems to result from his conviction that all Joan's lands *should* have gone to her male heir.

[94] James Bodley's other son must have been dead by 1530. John Bodley died without issue, see above nn. 72, 82; he was trading with the Low Countries in 1530s, H.T. Smit, *Bronnen tot de geschiedenis van den handel met Engeland, 1485-1585* (The Hague, 1928), ii, pp. 453, 488, 607.

already had more daughters by his new wife.[95] Mary Hall received the copyhold lands of John Leche, Anne £100 worth of plate when she married, and Elizabeth a 20s. annuity. All the Crafford children, including the one in the womb, received £30 between them, and the eldest, Mary, an extra £10 in witness of the pleasure Joan took in her first great-grandchild. Predictably the Leveson children did much better, with £20 each, except for the eldest boy, John, specifically excluded, in marked contrast to the gift of a Southwark messuage to his brother, Thomas.[96]

The twenty-two wills that survive for Joan Bradbury's extensive family between 1491 and 1561, the majority before 1540, give innumerable examples of the use made of blood or marriage connections when choosing executors, lawyers and advisers or finding a loan.[97] The family could be a useful unit if kept together by a strong personality, such as Joan. One example of Joan's exploitation of a not particularly close relationship, was her choice of a serjeant-at-law, Richard Norwich, as the supervisor of her will: he was married to a cousin of William Tyrell of South Ockendon.[98] Expressions of affection in words are comparatively rare but the endless small bequests of gowns and rings and the large numbers of godchildren show that neither affection nor responsibility of the richer for the less well-off were lacking within the group.[99]

Joan Bradbury's role as a good example and source of benefit must have counted for a good deal in the family: the wealthy 'Lady' and benefactress of London and Saffron Walden.

Herself: The Pleasures of Life, Friends and Possessions, and the Care of her Soul

We are indebted to Joan's own testament for all personal details. Friends are the most elusive, as the dividing lines between friend and mere acquaintance

---

[95] He died 1534; his will, GL, MS 9531/11, ff. 123-124v, makes no mention of his first wife and does not include her in his chantry.

[96] John Leveson was to be killed in Kett's Rebellion 1549, information from Mary Edmond,

[97] Those consulted and not previously referenced are: Sir William Butler (1528, proved 1534), PRO, PROB 11/25, ff. 62v-64 (PCC 10 Hogen); Nicholas Leveson (1539), PROB 11/27, ff. 250v-252 (PCC 31 Dyngely); Sir Christopher Askew (1539), PROB 11/27, ff. 239v-240v (PCC 30 Dyngely); Humphrey Tyrell (1549), PROB 11/32, ff. 339-339v (PCC 44 Populwell); William Bradbury (1550), PROB 11/33, ff. 205v-206 (PCC 26 Coode); Guy Crafford (1553), PROB 11/36, ff. 35-35v (PCC 5 Tashe); Lady Emma Askew (1554) PROB 11/37, ff. 60v-63 (PCC 8 More); Denise Leveson (1561) PROB 11/43, ff. 463-466v (PCC 60 Mellershe).

[98] Husband of Julian, daughter of Humphrey Tyrell of Warley and East Horndon and Elizabeth Walwyn (to whom he was also executor) and cousin of William Tyrell of South Ockendon, PRO, PROB 11/21, ff. 162-163 (PCC 21 Bodfelde).

[99] E.g. wills of Joan, Denise and Ellis Bodley (a particularly delightful will) are full of remembrances; Denise provided for the education of William Barret, son of Anne Tyrell (Denise's cousin) by her second husband, at £5 p.a.; Ellis lent to his brother William. Compare J. Murray, 'The Perception of Family by Clergy and Laity', *Albion*, 20 (1988), pp. 369-85.

or useful contact are rarely defined. A few can be picked out with certainty because they occur both in her testament and elsewhere. An old friend was George Neville, Lord Abergavenny, relative of the Fenne children Bradbury had stood surety for in 1481, and a nobleman who never forgot his city connections even after he became a friend of Henry VIII. Bradbury had probably lent money to George or his family. He was younger than Joan and is one of the few who dined at her table whose homely features, done by Holbein, we can still see clearly. Joan was godmother to his daughter, Mary, to whom she bequeathed her device or collar of gold weighing seven ounces with 'god blessing and mynde'.[100] City friends of long standing were Sir William Butler, Sir John Aleyn, and their wives; Elizabeth, the widow of Sir Bartholomew Rede; and Dame Christian Colet (died 1524),[101] Other old friends were Nicholas and Clemence Rutland, prominent citizens of Saffron Walden. Nicholas was a public notary and the equivalent of Joan's family solicitor, drawing up her will and remembered in her chantries.[102] Her friendship with the Pemberton family went back at least thirty-five years: Matthew (died 1518) assisted at Bradbury's funeral and his widow received one of Joan's own lined gowns, a token of a close relationship.[103]

Her friends were all from the affluent world of rich mercers, aldermen and tailors, with the occasional member of the upper class. She had enough money to live in London at a level where the boundaries between trade and gentility were hazy and intermarriage frequent. She also travelled between city and country town with ease, having her own position and friends in each. She was 'my lady' in the city and 'dame' in the country. There were no members of the county gentry of Essex in her testament, however, and her main social contact with that class appears to have been her relatives, the Bradburys of Littlebury and the Tyrells of South Ockendon, despite her extensive manorial holdings in the county.

As already mentioned, Joan's house was next to the churchyard of St Stephen Coleman Street and large enough to be used for banquets by the Mercers' Company. When she died she had a clear idea of its contents down to the last diapered linen tablecloth. It had several commodious chambers available for guests, one of which was used by the Craffords, to whom its

[100] *DNB: Complete Peerage*, i, pp. 31-33; Thrupp, *Merchant Class*, p. 262. His mother was a Fenne.

[101] Joan and the other women were all widows of mayors and all associated with the foundation of schools. See above n. 14. Thrupp, *Merchant Class*, p. 269. W. Herbert, *The Twelve Great Livery Companies* (London, 1836), ii, pp. 209-10. J.H. Lupton, *A Life of John Colet D.D.* (London, 1887), pp. 13-14.

[102] He also supervised the will of Sir William Butler, whose first wife had been a Bodley.

[103] Mathew's parents had been Hugh, merchant taylor and alderman (d. 1500; of St Martin Outwich) and possibly an associate of Joan's first husband, and Katherine who, like John Leche, had established a chantry at St Catharine's, Cambridge. H. Philpott, *Documents Relating to St Catharine's College in the University of Cambridge* (Cambridge, 1861), pp. 42-49, 68-70. Mathew's will, PROB 11/19, f. 43-43v (PCC 6 Ayloffe).

bedding, hangings and furniture was left. There was also what Joan called the 'sparversilk' chamber where the bedding included a silk sparver (canopy) and a coverlet 'with the parke', presumably embroidered with the scenes of a country park, which went to her nephew, Humphrey Tyrell. The 'apparell' of her own chamber may have been finer but she did not describe it. There was other bedding and linen in abundance, including six pairs of sheets in the chest next the window in her maid's chamber. Her tables were equally well furnished with carpets, diapered linen and other napery.

There was plenty of plate and she described some of the finer pieces: Humphrey Tyrell received her gilt cup decorated with pomegranates and the coffer kept 'in my dry larder hous beneath'; Joan Crafford got her covered 'mawdelyne goblet', the parcel silver-gilt salt used daily by her, and a dozen silver spoons with 'sleppis' (slip-ended). Two silver 'pottal' pots and six silver-gilt covered bowls, already in Nicholas Leveson's possession, went to him and his wife, as well as the chest in which Joan stored her plate. Perhaps the 'tune' or ton of silver and gilt that 'Dame Jane Bradbury my mother gave to me' and which Denise bequeathed in her turn to her daughter, Alice, wife of Sir William Hewet, lord mayor 1559-60, was among these items.[104]

Joan dressed to suit her station and not in widows' weeds. Joan Crafford got two of her best, lined gowns, while Denise got her best gown furred with foins and bordered with martin, her gold rosary beads and her 'dymyseut' (*demi-ceinte*, girdle) of gold and pearls with a little ruby in the middle. Her aristocratic god-daughter, Mary Neville, received her device or collar of seven ounces of gold, and her friend, Dame Rede, one of her gold rings.

She mentioned no books in her testament, but it can be assumed she had something more than the usual service books and account books. Her interest in education must be inferred from the inclusion of her kin and her tenants among the pupils of her school, and her bequest of 25s. for four years to pay for the education of William Bradbury's son and heir.

Joan was a housewife in the grandest sense and she was just as interested in her pewter ware and certain prized kitchen utensils: 'my great ketell wherin I have usid to sethe my brawn, my new great bras potte and ij of my bras pottes beying next in valew to other, two beyng the best pottes' went to Denise, as tokens from one majestic householder to another.[105]

The composition of her household can only be sketched. She had several men and women servants and two almschildren: 'my litell maide', Joan Herrat, was left 20 nobles for her marriage if she 'use herself honestly as a good maid ought to do till able to be married'; and Stephen, 'my lad', who was to be freed from his 'bondage' by her executors and given 40s., when of man's estate. Both children were passed on to the Leveson household. Her 'extended' household included two former female servants now living in Peckham and Stratford,

---

[104] PRO, PROB 11/43, f. 463.
[105] The similarity of their wills leads to this conclusion.

tradesmen she had dealt with in Saffron Walden, her schoolmaster and the almsmen there, as well as her regular bedesmen and women of St Stephen's parish.

Her meticulous foundations are substantial evidence of Joan's participation in the religious conventions of her day. She expressed all the expected concern for the passage of her soul and those of her family through purgatory. Her testament increased her investment in prayers with several obits ranging from 20s. to 60s. at her birthplace, that of her second husband, and at her manors of Manuden and Black Notley and at Saffron Walden. To these she added the prayers of the twelve sisters who looked after the sick at Elsing Spital at a cost of 12s.

Some of her charitable acts have been mentioned: her almschildren – a fostering responsibility not lightly undertaken – and the fact that she had 'regular' bedespeople in her London parish to whom she gave 1d. each every Sunday. She must have been one of the wealthiest parishioners of St Stephen's and have exercised a certain influence there, despite her sex, simply because of her wealth and the very proximity of her house to the church. She could supervise her charity closely, attend her priest's masses, and be certain of respectful consideration from the vicar. She could entertain them both to dinner in her house and enjoy the conversation of a good, honest priest.[106]

She had some eminent priests among her advisers and friends. Richard Nix, bishop of Norwich, acted as her feoffee and shared an interest in the encouragement of education. He was among the 'old school' of clerics, as was Henry Standish, to whom Joan left 40s. to buy apparel which pleased him and 'were yt for my sake'. He was a distinguished Franciscan and another promoter of education.[107] For a woman of Joan's generation and social standing neither of these men was a particularly remarkable acquaintance.[108] Both may have been of great help in securing licences for her chantries. There is nothing to link her

---

[106] Thomas Turpyn was her chantry priest and nothing seems to be known of him. Henry Forthe, vicar 1517-1524, was also vicar of All Saints, Cambridge, and had taught at a grammar school there. The careers of the other vicars do not suggest any interesting connections. Hennessy, *Novum repertorium*, p. 385; Emden, *BRUC*, s.n. Forthe. For the higher standard of education expected from London parish priests at this date, see P. Heath, *English Parish Priests on the Eve of the Reformation* (London, 1969), p. 81. The parish records of St Stephen's suffer from a long gap after 1507 and do not help. The Lollard conventicle in the parish, 1521, presumably escaped Joan's notice, Brigden, *London and the Reformation*, pp. 103-4.

[107] Nix worked with Thomas Bradbury as early as 1493, *CCR, 1485-1509*, no. 665; *DNB*; Emden, *BRUO*, s.n. Nix; C. Crawley, *Trinity Hall, 1350-1975* (Cambridge, 1976), pp. 44-45, 53. Standish, like Driffield, Thomas Bodley's first choice as his chantry priest, was involved in the notorious Hunne case 1512: R. Marius, *Thomas More* (London, 1984), pp. 125-27; Emden, *BRUC*, s.n. Standish; D. Knowles, *The Religious Orders in England*, iii, *The Tudor Age* (Cambridge, 1959), pp. 53-55.

[108] The same can be said of the priors of St John's Clerkenwell and Holy Trinity Aldgate and the abbot of Stratford Langthorne, all in her testament: they were lords or tenants of her lands. See n. 49 above.

with any aspect of the religious controversies of the last twenty years of her life, and it must be concluded, from her age as well as her acquaintance with these men, she too was of the 'old school'. Neither Nix or Standish can have exercised a fraction of the influence and spiritual guidance which, it must be assumed, her brother, John Leche did.

She was well prepared for death. Her burial she left to her executors but only after plenty of verbal direction, for she had 'preserved' £215 with Nicholas Leveson for it and her month mind 'to honour of God,' 12d going to each poor householder of St Stephen's on each occasion. Twenty poor men of the parish were to carry torches and tapers and she carefully specified that their black gowns were to be made up at the executors' expense as well as 'convenient for such poore men to were'. She did not request any avoidance of pomp, but rather, 'I require' the five orders of friars to be present. They were to sing the usual trentalls and further trentalls were to be sung by priests 'destitute of service' in London. No doubt she hoped that the twenty-eight named persons, and the many more unnamed, to whom she left black gowns would turn up, pray for her, and afterwards enjoy a feast at her great house, prepared by Denise. The Mercers' Company would certainly have attended.

Joan's 'piety' and comprehension of God are not knowable – only its worldly outlines are suggested by her activities. She left her soul to God, the Virgin Mary and all the company of heaven. The preamble of her testament said everything that was suitable:

> In the name of Allmyghty god, the holy Trinity, in whom I stedfastly beleve, And by whom, And by the merytte of the dolorous and moost bitter and painfull passion and deth of Iesu Christe, oure Saviour and Redemer, And by our moder holy church . . . trusting to be saved . . .

Joan's last illness took place in her London house during the winter of 1530. She had to attend her, Dr Richard Bartlett, 'famous for his medical knowledge and great experience' (*doctrina et largo medicinae usu insignis*), a past president of the College of Physicians and a future physician to Henry VIII.[109] On 2 March 1530 Denise and her husband were in the house as well as her granddaughter Joan with her husband, Guy Crafford, when Joan's old friend from Saffron Walden, Nicholas Rutland, attended to draw up her will and testament. She made it 'for the helthe of my soule and the profittis of my consanguinitie and frindis', instructing that her debts be paid and any wrongs done by her be righted, 'if proved' before her executors.[110] The indenture of 1526 had prepared the way and the family already knew where the lands were going. It is a clear-headed, admirable document setting down every necessary

---

[109] He attended the duke of Buckingham in 1508, so it is just possible that it was Buckingham's son-in-law, Lord Abergavenny, who recommended him to Joan. Emden, *BRUC*, s.n. Bartlett. He received a black gown from Joan.

[110] PRO, PROB 11/23, ff. 129v-133 (PCC 17 Jankyn). Richard Lany, another notary public was also present.

detail in a positive manner. To perform her testament she specified one year's rent from her house and the proceeds of the sale of her land at West Thurrock.

She died about the end of March, and was buried at the side of Thomas Bradbury in the Lady Chapel of St Stephen Coleman Street.

It has been possible to construct in words a portrait of Joan Bradbury and her family just as informative as Holbein's of the More family. If Joan had commissioned Holbein in 1530, she would have placed herself in the centre, dressed in her best gown furred with foins and marten, her heavy gold collar and girdle of gold and pearl. Her daughter, Denise, her grandchildren, their spouses and children would have sat around her, their places dictated by her. Her dead husbands and brother would have watched from the back of the room, with a few friends still further back. Through windows would be seen the spires of the churches of St Stephen Coleman Street and Saffron Walden, and the walls would be hung with the arms of her husbands, the city of London and the Mercers. It is a family portrait: as a woman Joan was only able to function within the family, but she was clearly comfortable in that role and in control. Within her sphere her achievements were impressive: the girl from Wellingborough became a lady mayoress of London and a benefactress. She appears to have been both generous and competent, with a natural grasp of business and an ability to manage people, which enabled her to accomplish what she set out to do.

In the event, her chantry did not long survive her, and only by 'accident' did a fraction of its many acres remain in the ownership of the Mercers' Company, now known as Lady Bradbury's Estate in Covent Garden. Her name is spoken daily within the Company and the income from her land supports charities, education and some feasting. At Saffron Walden Dame Johanne Bradbury's School continues to flourish as a coeducational day preparatory school.

Bibliography

This bibliography contains only the works used in this volume which relate to London and to the study of women and widows in the middle ages. Further reference may be made to the bibliography in I. Blom, 'The History of Widowhood: A Bibliographical Overview', *Journal of Family History*, 16 (1991).

PRINTED PRIMARY SOURCES

Calendar of Coroners' Rolls of the City of London, 1300-1378, ed. R.R. Sharpe (London, 1913).

Calendar of Early Mayor's Court Rolls Preserved among the Archives of the Corporation of the City of London at Guildhall, A.D. 1298-1307, ed. A.H. Thomas (Cambridge, 1924).

Calendar of Letter Books, Preserved among the Archives of the Corporation of the City of London, 1275-1498, Books A-L, ed. R.R. Sharpe (London 1899-1912).

Calendar of Plea and Memoranda Rolls Preserved among the Archives of the Corporation of the City of London, 1323-1482, 6 vols, ed. A.H. Thomas (vols 1-4) and P.E. Jones (vols 5-6) (Cambridge, 1926-61).

Calendar of Wills Proved and Enrolled in the Court of Husting, London, 1258-1688, 2 vols, ed. R.R. Sharpe (London, 1889-90).

Chambers, R.W., and M. Daunt, ed. *A Book of London English* (Oxford, 1931).

Chew, H.M., and W. Kellaway, ed., *London Assize of Nuisance, 1301-1431*, London Record Society, 10 (London, 1973).

Clode, C.M., *Memorials of the Merchant Taylors' Company* (London, 1875).

Davis, N., ed., *Paston Letters and Papers of the Fifteenth Century*, 2 vols (Oxford, 1971, 1976).

Ekwall, E., ed., *Two Early London Subsidy Rolls* (Lund, 1951).

Fabyan, R., *The New Chronicles of England and France* (London, 1811).

Fitch, M., ed., *Index to Testamentary Records in the Commissary Court of London*, i, *1374-1488* (London, 1969).

—, ed., *Testamentary Records in the Archdeaconry Court of London*, i, *1363-1649*, British Record Society (London, 1979).

Freshfield, E., ed., *Wills, Leases and Memoranda in the Book of Records of the*

Parish of St Christopher le Stocks (London, 1895).

Fry, G.S., ed., *Abstract of Inquisitions Post Mortem relating to the City of London*, 3 vols (London, 1896).

Gairdner, J., ed., *Historical Collections of a London Citizen*, Camden Society, 2nd series, 17 (1876).

Hanham, A., ed., *The Cely Letters, 1472-1488*, Early English Text Society, original series 273 (1975).

J.J. Howard and J. Gough Nichols, ed., *The Visitation of London, 1568*, Harleian Society, 1 (1869).

Kingdon, J.A., ed., *Facsimile of First Volume of MS Archives of the Worshipful Company of Grocers of the City of London, A.D. 1345-1463*, 2 vols (London, 1886).

Kingsford, C.L., ed., *The Stonor Letters and Papers, 1290-1483*, Camden Society, 3rd series, 29, 30 (1919).

Kitching, C.J., ed., *London and Middlesex Chantry Certificate*, London Record Society (London, 1980).

Lyell, L., and F. Watney, ed., *The Acts of Court of the Mercers' Company, 1453-1527* (Cambridge, 1936).

McHardy, A.K., ed., *The Church in London, 1375-92*, London Record Society, 13 (London, 1977).

Nicolas, N.H., and E. Tyrell, ed., *A Chronicle of London, 1089-1483* (London, 1827).

O'Connor, S., ed., *A Calendar of the Cartularies of Adam Fraunceys and John Pyel*, Camden Society, 5th series, ii (1993).

Parsloe, G., ed., *The Wardens' Accounts of the Founders' Company, 1497-1681* (London, 1964).

Riley, H.T., ed., *Munimenta Gildhallae Londoniensis; Liber Albus, Liber Custumarum et Liber Horn, in archivis Gildhallae asservati*, 3 vols, Rolls Series (London, 1859, 1860).

—, ed., *Liber Albus: The White Book of the City of London* (London, 1861).

—, ed., *Memorials of London and London Life* (London, 1868).

Stahlschmidt, J.C.L., 'A London Subsidy temp. Henry IV', *Archaeological Journal*, 44 (1887).

Stow, J., *A Survey of London*, ed. C.L. Kingsford, 2 vols (Oxford, 1911).

Thomas, A.H., and I.D. Thornley, eds., *The Great Chronicle of London* (London, 1938).

Walters, H.B., *London Churches at the Reformation* (London, 1939).

Welch, C., ed., *Register of Freemen of the City of London in the Reigns of Henry VIII and Edward VI*, London and Middlesex Archaeological Society (London, 1908).

SECONDARY SOURCES

Abram, A., 'Women Traders in Medieval London', *Economic Journal*, 26 (1916).

Archer, I., *The Pursuit of Stability: Social Relations in Elizabethan London* (Cambridge, 1991).

Archer, R.E., ' "How Ladies who Live on their Manors Ought to Manage their Households and Estates": Women as Landholders and Administrators in the later Middle Ages', *Woman is a Worthy Wight: Women in English Society, c. 1200-1500*, ed., P.J.P. Goldberg (Gloucester, 1992).

—, and B. Ferme, 'Testamentary Procedure with Special Reference to the Executrix', *Medieval Women in Southern England*, Reading Medieval Studies, 15 (Reading, 1989).

Barron, C.M., 'Richard II's Quarrel with London', *The Reign of Richard II*, ed., C.M. Barron and F.R.H. Du Boulay (London, 1970).

—, 'The Parish Fraternities of Medieval London', *The Church in Pre-Reformation Society: Essays in Honour of F.R.H. Du Boulay*, ed. C.M. Barron and C. Harper-Bill (Woodbridge, 1985).

—, 'The "Golden Age" of Women in Medieval London', *Medieval Women in Southern England*, Reading Medieval Studies, 15 (Reading, 1989).

—, 'The Fourteenth-Century Poll Tax Returns for Worcester', *Midland History*, 14 (1989).

Bassler, J.M., 'The Widow's Tale: A Fresh Look at 1 Timothy 5:3-16', *Journal of Biblical Literature*, 103 (1984).

Beaven, A.B., *The Aldermen of London*, 2 vols (London, 1908, 1913).

Ben-Amos, I.K., 'Women Apprentices in the Trades and Crafts of Early Modern Bristol', *Continuity and Change*, 6 (1991).

Bennett, J.M., *Women in the Medieval English Countryside: Gender and Household in Brigstock before the Plague* (New York and Oxford, 1987).

—, 'Medieval Women, Modern Women: Across the Great Divide', *Culture and History, 1350-1600: Essays on English Communities, Identities and Writing*, ed., D. Aers (London, 1992).

—, E.A. Clarke, J.F. O'Barr, B.A. Vilen and S. Westphal-Wihl, ed., *Working Together in the Middle Ages: Perspectives on Women's Communities*, in *Signs*, 14, (1989). (This has also appeared as a separate book.)

Bird, R., *The Turbulent London of Richard II* (London, 1949).

Bradberry, K., 'The World of Etheldreda Gardiner', *The Ricardian*, 9 (1991).

Brigden, S., *London and the Reformation* (Oxford, 1990).

Brodsky, V., 'Widows in Late Elizabethan London: Remarriage, Economic Opportunity and Family Orientation', *The World We Have Gained: Histories of Population and Social Structure*, ed., L. Bonfield, R.M. Smith and K. Wrightson (Oxford, 1986).

Brown, J.C., and J. Goodman, 'Women and Industry in Florence', *Journal of Economic History*, 40 (1980).

Burgess, C., 'Late Medieval Wills and Pious Conventions: Testamentary Evidence Reconsidered', *Profit, Piety and the Professions in Later Medieval England*, ed., M. Hicks (Gloucester, 1990).

Carlin, M., 'Holy Trinity Minories: Abbey of St Clare, 1293/4-1539', (Centre for Metropolitan History, London, 1987). Typescript available at the

Institute of Historical Research, London.

Carlton, C., *The Court of Orphans* (Leicester, 1974).

Chabot, I., 'Widowhood and Poverty in late Medieval Florence', *Continuity and Change*, 3 (1988).

Charles, L., and L. Duffin, ed., *Women and Work in Pre-Industrial England* (London, 1985).

Clarke, E., 'City Orphans and Custody Laws in Medieval England', *American Journal of Legal History*, 34 (1990).

Clode, C.M., *The Early History of the Guild of Merchant Taylors of the Fraternity of St John, London, with Notices of the Lives of some of its Eminent Members*, 2 vols (London, 1888).

Crawford, A., *A History of the Vintners' Company* (London, 1977).

Crick, E.M., ed., *Marriage and Property* (Aberdeen, 1984).

Crowfoot, E., F. Pritchard and K. Staniland, *Textiles and Clothing, c. 1150-1450: Medieval Finds from Excavations in London* (London, 1992).

Dale, M.K., 'Women in the Textile Industries and Trade of Fifteenth Century England' (unpublished M.A. thesis, University of London, 1928).

—, 'The London Silkwomen of the Fifteenth Century', *Economic History Review*, 1st series, 4 (1933); reprinted in *Working Together in the Middle Ages: Perspectives on Women's Communities*, ed., J.M. Bennett, E.A. Clarke, J.F. O'Barr, B.A. Vilen and S. Westphal-Wihl, *Signs*, 14 (1989).

E. Dixon, 'Craftswomen in the *Livre des Métiers*', *Economic Journal*, 5 (1895).

Dinn, R., 'Baptism, Spiritual Kinship and Popular Religion in Late Medieval Bury St Edmunds', *Bulletin of the John Rylands University Library of Manchester*, 72 (1990).

Duffy E., ' "Holy Maydens, Holy Wyfes": The Cult of Women Saints in the Fifteenth and Sixteenth Centuries', *Women in the Church*, ed., W.J. Sheils and D. Wood (Oxford, 1990).

Ellis, D.S., 'The Merchant's Wife's Tale: Language, Sex and Commerce in Margery Kempe and Chaucer', *Exemplaria*, 2 (1990).

Epstein, S.A., *Wage, Labor and Guilds in Medieval Europe* (Chapel Hill, NC, and London, 1991).

Ferme, B., *see* R.E. Archer.

Fly, H., 'Some Account of an Abbey of Nuns formerly situated in the Street now called the Minories in the County of Middlesex and Liberty of the Tower of London', *Archaeologia*, 15 (1806).

Franklin, P., 'Widows' "Liberation" and Remarriage before the Black Death', *Economic History Review*, 39 (1986).

Goldberg, P.J.P., 'Women in Fifteenth-Century Town Life', *Towns and Townspeople in the Fifteenth Century*, ed., J.A.F. Thomson (Gloucester, 1988).

—, 'Women's Work, Women's Role in the late Medieval North', *Profit, Piety and the Professions in Later Medieval England*, ed., M. Hicks (Gloucester, 1990).

—, 'Marriage, Migration and Servanthood: The York Cause Paper Evidence',

Woman is a Worthy Wight: Women in English Society, c. 1200-1500, ed., P.J.P. Goldberg (Gloucester, 1992).

—, ed., *Woman is a Worthy Wight: Women in English Society, c. 1200-1500* (Gloucester, 1992).

—, '"For Better, for Worse": Marriage and Economic Opportunity for Women in Town and Country', *Woman is a Worthy Wight: Women in English Society, c. 1200-1500*, ed., P.J.P. Goldberg (Gloucester, 1992).

—, *Women, Work and Life Cycle in a Medieval Economy: Women in York and Yorkshire, c. 1300–1520* (Oxford, 1992).

Grant, L., ed., *Medieval Art, Architecture and Archaeology in London*, British Archaeological Association Conference Transactions, 10 (1990).

Gryson, R., *The Ministry of Women in the Early Church* (Collegeville, MN, 1976).

Hampton, W.E., 'The Ladies of the Minories', *The Ricardian*, 4, no. 69 (Sept. 1978).

Hanawalt, B.A., ed., *Women and Work in Preindustrial Europe* (Bloomington, IN, 1986).

—, *The Ties that Bound: Peasant Families in Medieval England* (New York and Oxford, 1986).

—, 'The Widow's Mite: Recovery of Dower in Late Medieval London', *Upon My Husband's Death: Widows in the Literature and History of Medieval Europe*, ed., L. Mirrer (Ann Arbor, MI, 1992).

—, 'Remarriage as an Option for Urban and Rural Widows in Late Medieval England', *Wife and Widow in Medieval England*, ed., S.S. Walker (Ann Arbor, MI, 1993).

Hanham, A., *The Celys and Their World* (Cambridge, 1985).

Harris, B.J., and J.K. McNamara, ed., *Women and the Structure of Society* (Durham, NC, 1984).

Heath, B., *Some Account of the Worshipful Company of Grocers of the City of London* (London, 1869).

Hennessy, G., *Novum repertorium ecclesiasticum parochiale Londinense* (London, 1898).

Herbert, W., *The History of the Twelve Great Livery Companies of London*, 2 vols (London, 1836-7).

Herlihy, D., *Opera Muliebra: Women and Work in Medieval Europe* (New York, 1990).

—, and C. Klapisch-Zuber, *Tuscans and their Families: A Study of the Florentine Catasto of 1427* (New Haven, CT, 1985).

Hollaender, A.E., and W. Kellaway, ed., *Studies in London History Presented to P.E. Jones* (London, 1969).

Howell, M.C., *Women, Production and Patriarchy in Late Medieval Cities* (Chicago and London, 1986).

—, 'Women, the Family Economy, and the Structures of Market Production in Cities of Northern Europe during the Late Middle Ages', *Women and Work in Preindustrial Europe*, ed., B.A. Hanawalt (Bloomington, IN, 1986).

Hutton, D., 'Women in Fourteenth-Century Shrewsbury', *Women and Work in Pre-Industrial England*, ed. L. Charles and L. Duffin (London, 1985).

Jacobsen, G., 'Women's Work and Women's Role: Ideology and Reality in Danish Urban Society, 1300-1550', *Scandinavian Economic History Review*, 31 (1983).

Johnson, A.H., *A History of the Worshipful Company of the Drapers of London*, 5 vols (Oxford, 1914-22).

Keene, D., 'A New Study of London before the Great Fire', *Urban History Yearbook 1984*.

—, *Survey of Medieval Winchester*, Winchester Studies, 2 (Oxford, 1985).

—, *Cheapside before the Great Fire* (London, 1985).

—, 'Shops and Shopping in Medieval London', *Medieval Art, Architecture and Archaeology in London*, ed., L. Grant, British Archaeological Association Conference Transactions, 10 (1990).

—, and V. Harding, *Historical Gazetteer of London before the Great Fire*, i, *Cheapside* (Cambridge, 1987).

Kettle, A.J., ' "My Wife Shall Have It": Marriage and Property in the Wills and Testaments of Later Medieval England', *Marriage and Property* ed., E.M. Crick (Aberdeen, 1984).

Klapisch-Zuber, C., *see* D. Herlihy.

Kowaleski, M., 'Women's Work in a Market Town: Exeter in the Late Fourteenth Century', *Women and Work in Preindustrial Europe* ed., B.A. Hanawalt (Bloomington, IN, 1986).

—, 'The History of Urban Families in England', *Journal of Medieval History*, 14 (1988).

—, and J.M. Bennett, 'Crafts, Guilds and Women in the Middle Ages: Fifty Years after M.K. Dale', *Working Together in the Middle Ages: Perspectives on Women's Communities*, ed., J.M. Bennett, E.A. Clarke, J.F. O'Barr, B.A. Vilen and S. Westphal-Wihl, *Signs*, 14 (1989).

Labarge, M.W., *Women in Medieval Life: A Small Sound of the Trumpet* (London, 1986).

Lacey, K.E., 'Women and Work in Fourteenth and Fifteenth Century London', *Women and Work in Pre-Industrial England* ed., L. Charles and L. Duffin (London, 1985).

—, 'The Production of "Narrow Ware" in Fourteenth and Fifteenth Century England', *Textile History*, 18 (1987).

London County Council, *Survey of London*, xii and xv *The Parish of All Hallows Barking*, parts 1 and 2 (London, 1929, 1934).

Masters, B.R. 'The Mayor's Household before 1600', *Studies in London History presented to P.E. Jones*, ed., A.E. Hollaender and W. Kellaway (London, 1969).

Mathews, W.R., and W.M. Atkins, *A History of St Paul's Cathedral* (London, 1957).

Medieval Women in Southern England, Reading Medieval Studies, 15 (Reading, 1989).

Milburn, T., *The Vintners' Company* (London, 1888).

Miller, H., 'London and Parliament in the Reign of Henry VIII', *Bulletin of the Institute of Historical Research*, 35 (1962).

Milman, H.H., *Annals of St Paul's* (London, 1868).

Mirrer, L., ed., *Upon My Husband's Death: Widows in the Literature and History of Medieval Europe* (Ann Arbor, MI, 1992).

Miskimin, H.A., 'The Legacies of London, 1259-1330', *The Medieval City: Essays in Honour of R.S. Lopez* ed., H.A. Miskimin et al. (New Haven, CT, 1977).

O'Hara, D., 'Ruled by my Friends: Aspects of Marriage in the Diocese of Canterbury, *c.* 1540-1570', *Continuity and Change*, 6 (1991).

Paxton, C., 'The Nunneries of London and its Environs in the Later Middle Ages' (unpublished D.Phil. thesis, University of Oxford, 1992).

Pitt-Rivers, J., 'Honour and Social Status', *Honour and Shame: the Values of Mediterranean Society* ed., J.G. Peristiany (London, 1965).

Phythian-Adams, C., *Desolation of a City: Coventry and the Urban Crisis of the Late Middle Ages* (Cambridge, 1979).

Potash, B., ed., *Widows in African Societies: Choices and Constraints* (Stanford, CA, 1986).

Power, E., *Medieval English Nunneries* (Cambridge, 1922).

—, *Medieval People* (1st edn., London, 1924); new edn., by R. Smith, (Oxford, 1986).

—, *Medieval Women*, ed., M.M. Postan (Cambridge, 1975).

Prior, M., ed., *Women in English Society, 1500-1800* (London, 1985).

Rappaport, S., *Worlds within Worlds: Structures of Life in Sixteenth-Century London* (Cambridge, 1989).

Reddaway, T., and E.M. Walker, *The Early History of the Goldsmiths' Company, 1327-1509* (London, 1975).

Rosenthal, J.T., 'Aristocratic Widows in Fifteenth-Century England', *Women and the Structure of Society*, ed., B.J. Harris and J.K. McNamara (Durham, NC, 1984).

—, 'Other Victims: Peeresses as War Widows, 1450-1500', *History*, 72 (1987).

Roskell, J.S., L. Clark, and C. Rawcliffe, ed., *The History of Parliament: The House of Commons, 1386-1421*, 4 vols (Stroud, 1992).

Rosser, G., *Medieval Westminster* (Oxford, 1989).

Sharpe, R.R., *London and the Kingdom*, 3 vols (London, 1894-95).

—, *see* Printed Primary Sources, *Calendar*.

Sheils, W.J., and D. Wood, ed., *Women in the Church* (Oxford, 1990).

Smith, R.M., ed., *Land, Kinship and Life-Cycle* (Cambridge, 1984).

Sutton, A.F., 'William Shore, Merchant of London and Derby', *Derbyshire Archaeological Journal*, 106 (1986).

Swanson, H., *Medieval Artisans: An Urban Class in Late Medieval England* (Oxford, 1989).

Thrupp, S.L., *The Merchant Class of Medieval London* (Chicago, 1948, reprint Ann Arbor, MI, 1962).

Thurston, B.B., *The Widows: A Women's Ministry in the Early Church* (Minneapolis, MN, 1989).

Todd, B., 'The Remarrying Widow: A Stereotype Reconsidered', *Women in English Society, 1500-1800*, ed., M. Prior (London, 1985).

Tomlinson, E.M., *A History of the Minories, London* (2nd edn., London, 1922).

Uitz, E., *Women in the Medieval Town* (London, 1990).

Veale, E.M., *The English Fur Trade in the Later Middle Ages* (Oxford, 1966).

Walker, S.S., ed., *Wife and Widow in Medieval England* (Ann Arbor, MI, 1993).

Wall, A., 'Elizabethan Precept and Feminine Practice', *History*, 75 (1990).

Ward, J.C., *English Noblewomen in the Later Middle Ages* (London, 1992).

Wensky, M., 'Women's Guilds in Cologne in the Later Middle Ages', *Journal of European Economic History*, 11 (1982).

Wood, M.M., 'Paltry Pedlars or Essential Merchant? Women in the Distributive Trades in Early Modern Nuremberg', *Sixteenth-Century Journal*, 12 (1981).

Wood, R.A., 'A Fourteenth-Century London Owner of *Piers Plowman*', *Medium Aevum*, 53 (1984).

Index

This is a places and names index. Peers are indexed under their titles; bishops under their names. For the majority of entries London should be understood.